MENTAL HEALTH EVALUATIONS IN IMMIGRATION COURT

PSYCHOLOGY AND CRIME

General Editors: Brian Bornstein, University of Nebraska, and Monica Miller, University of Nevada, Reno

Mental Health Evaluations in Immigration Court

A Guide for Mental Health and Legal Professionals

Virginia Barber-Rioja,

Adeyinka M. Akinsulure-Smith, *and*

Sarah Vendzules

NEW YORK UNIVERSITY PRESS

New York

NEW YORK UNIVERSITY PRESS
New York
www.nyupress.org

References to Internet websites (URLs) were accurate at the time of writing. Neither the author nor New York University Press is responsible for URLs that may have expired or changed since the manuscript was prepared.

Library of Congress Cataloging-in-Publication Data
Names: Barber-Rioja, Virginia, author. | Akinṣulurẹ-Smith, Adeyinká Moronkẹ Adeyemisi, author. | Vendzules, Sarah, author.
Title: Mental health evaluations in immigration court : a guide for mental health and legal professionals / Virginia Barber-Rioja, Adeyinka M. Akinsulure-Smith, and Sarah Vendzules.
Description: New York : New York University Press, [2022] | Series: Psychology and crime | Includes bibliographical references and index.
Identifiers: LCCN 2021044598 | ISBN 9781479802630 (hardback) | ISBN 9781479802616 (paperback) | ISBN 9781479802609 (ebook) | ISBN 9781479802623 (ebook other)
Subjects: LCSH: Immigration courts--United States. | Forensic psychology--United States.
Classification: LCC KF4822 .B37 2022 | DDC 342.7308/20269--dc23/eng/20220208
LC record available at https://lccn.loc.gov/2021044598

New York University Press books are printed on acid-free paper, and their binding materials are chosen for strength and durability. We strive to use environmentally responsible suppliers and materials to the greatest extent possible in publishing our books.

Manufactured in the United States of America

10 9 8 7 6 5 4 3 2 1

Also available as an ebook

"A mi padre"

—Virginia

"Mummy, Hawk, Emery, en Reni—Tenki fo di lov"

—Yinka

"To the Bear and the Bosq"

—Sarah

CONTENTS

ABBREVIATIONS

AAO Administrative Appeals Office
ABA American Bar Association
ACES adverse childhood experiences
AG Attorney General [United States]
AOS adjustment of status
APA American Psychological Association
ATDS alternatives to detention
BIA Board of Immigration Appeals
CAIS Clinical Assessment Instruments
CAT Convention Against Torture
CBP Customs and Border Protection
CFI Cultural Formulation Interview
CFI-I CFI-Informant Version
CFR Code of Federal Regulations
COVID-19 referring to coronavirus pandemic
C-PTSD Complex PTSD
DACA Deferred Action for Childhood Arrivals
DESNOS disorders of extreme stress not otherwise specified
DHHS Department of Health and Human Services
DHS Department of Homeland Security
DOJ Department of Justice
DOS Department of State
DSM-5 *Diagnostic and Statistical Manual of Mental Disorders,* 5th edition
DUI driving under the influence
EOIR Executive Office for Immigration Review
FAIS Forensic Assessment Instruments
FMHA forensic mental health assessment
FRIS Forensically Relevant Instruments
FSIQ full scale intelligence quotient
FY fiscal year

GBV gender-based violence

GPS Global Positioning System

HCR-20 Historical-Clinical-Risk Management-20

HHS Department of Health and Human Services

IC immigration court

ICD-11 *International Classification of Diseases,* 11th edition

ICE Immigrations and Customs Enforcement

ID intellectual disability

IHSC ICE Health Service Corps

IJ immigration judge

INA Immigration and Nationality Act

IPV intimate partner violence

IQ intelligence quotient

LGBT lesbian, gay, bisexual, and transgender [also LGBTQ+]

MHPS mental health professionals

NCCHC National Commission on Correctional Health Care

NQRP National Qualified Representative Program

NTA Notice to Appear

OIG Office of Inspector General

ORR Office of Refugee Resettlement

POCI People of Color and Indigenous Individuals

PTSD posttraumatic stress disorder

RNR risk, needs, and responsivity [model]

SAPROF Structured Assessment of Protective Factors for Violence Risk

SIJS Special Immigrant Juvenile Status

STS secondary traumatic stress

T VISA US visa category for victims of trafficking

TPS Temporary Protected Status

U VISA US visa category for victims of crime

USC United States Code

USCIS United States Citizenship and Immigration Services

VAWA Violence Against Women Act

VRAG Violence Risk Appraisal Guide

VRAG-R Violence Risk Appraisal Guide-Revised

VT vicarious trauma

WEIRD Western, Educated, Industrialized, Rich, and Democratic
[populations]

Introduction

Every year since 1990, approximately one million new immigrants have entered the United States . Today, there are over 40 million foreign-born residents in the United States[1], and it is estimated that about 11 million of those residents, roughly 3.3% of the US population, lack proper documentation.[2] This group is composed of immigrants who entered the country with proper documentation but stayed beyond the expiration of their visas, in addition to those who entered the country unlawfully. It is commonly assumed that undocumented immigrants have left their countries by choice. However, many are escaping poverty, violence, persecution, and/or armed conflict. In recent years, the instability in Central America caused by economic crises, gang violence, and organized crime has resulted in an influx of Central American immigrants across the southern Mexico and southern United States borders.[3] Currently, over 50% of undocumented immigrants in the United States migrated from four countries: Mexico, El Salvador, Guatemala, and Honduras. El Salvador and Honduras, which together account for more than 10% of the undocumented population,[4] have two of the highest murder rates of women worldwide, despite not being at war.[5]

Immigrants may take different paths to documented status. Some enter the United States as Lawful Permanent Residents (LPRs, or so-called green card holders) sponsored by family or by employers; others enter on visas that they are later able to convert to a more permanent status; and yet others enter after having won the "diversity visa lottery," as one element of the process has come to be known. Additionally, many immigrants come here as refugees fleeing persecution, and some of them are recognized as such prior to entering.[6] Since 2001, more than 895,000 refugees have entered the United States, mostly after being referred by the United Nations and approved by the State Department. This group is primarily from the Middle East, Asia, and Africa.[7] Most, however, apply for refugee status (i.e., political asylum) at the border or after arriving in the United States; these immigrants are mostly from Central America.

For asylum seekers, migration conditions worsened as immigration policies became more restrictive. With the inauguration of a new US presidential administration in 2017, the use of detention as an immigration enforcement strategy increased exponentially, and immigrants were detained for prolonged periods of time.[8] In addition, under the "zero tolerance" immigration policy enacted in the spring of 2018, nearly all adults entering the country illegally were detained and prosecuted; any accompanying children were placed into shelters or foster care. This policy resulted in more than 3,000 children being separated from their parents; many have yet to be reunited.[9] Furthermore, policies such as "migrant protection protocols" or the "remain in Mexico" framework enacted by Donald Trump's administration (2017–2021) sought to return Central American asylum seekers to Mexico before and between hearings regarding their asylum cases, which resulted in hundreds of asylum applicants being sent back to Mexico to wait out the process under grim conditions. All of these policies were enacted while an increasing number of Central Americans attempted to escape poverty and violence resulting from extreme economic crises and increased gang violence. Even before the Trump administration, however, conditions for asylum seekers and other undocumented migrants who attempted to cross the border were dire. According to the United States Border Patrol, approximately 7,000 people died during their journey between 1998 and 2016.[10] These conditions have remained in place and portend an ominous situation for Joseph Biden's administration (inaugurated in January 2021). For example, news reports indicated that in early 2021 thirteen Mexican citizens were killed after being struck by a truck while crossing the border in an SUV packed with 25 people.[11] Furthermore, in March 2021 the Biden administration encountered more immigrants at the border than during any month since 2001.[12]

In addition to all of these migration challenges, it is easy for any immigrant, including Lawful Permanent Residents, to become deportable. If deportable, these individuals can be placed in "removal proceedings," and many of them will be detained during those proceedings. From 2014 to 2018, there was a 41% increase in the number of removal proceedings initiated in immigration courts (ICs) across the country, to a total of

434,159 in 2018.[13] "Removal" is a technical term used in immigration law. The distinction between "deportation" and "removal" is not one that is relevant for the purposes of this book; as such, we often use the term "deportation" instead of the more technical term. Mental health professionals (MHPs) should keep in mind that "removal" can carry negative connotations and might be a harmful way to refer to the treatment of human beings. Another example is the term "alien," which is used throughout immigration laws and is frequently heard in IC proceedings. When speaking with individuals impacted by the immigration system, MHPs—and immigration lawyers as well—should be mindful of the possible impact of their word choices and not necessarily blindly adopt the terminology of the law simply because it is technically correct.

Parallel to, and sometimes interacting with, the ICs is United States Citizenship and Immigration Services (USCIS). While some types of relief from deportation, such as adjustment of status, can be adjudicated by an immigration judge (IJ) or in front of USCIS, others can be adjudicated only before USCIS. Sometimes this book will refer to the "adjudicator" or "decision maker" rather than the "immigration judge" to recognize that, at times, the person making the decision might be a USCIS employee rather than an IJ.

Unlike in the criminal legal system, the purpose of detention in the immigration system is not to punish or rehabilitate but to prevent noncitizens from absconding and to protect the public. Some forms of detention are mandatory, in that IJs have no authority to review the government's detention decision. Due in part to the Illegal Immigration Reform and Immigration Responsibility Act of 1996, which expanded the categories of immigrants subject to mandatory detention, the number of detained noncitizens has grown since the 1990s, from roughly 85,000 people per year in 1995 to 477,523 in 2012.[14] In 2007, the *New York Times* called immigration detention in the United States the "fastest growing form of incarceration."[15] Individuals in immigration detention are housed in facilities managed by the federal government, in privately run detention centers, or in state and local jails that lease space for this purpose. As of 2014, it was estimated that there were about 34,000 immigration detention beds in approximately 200 facilities across the country. However, more recent reports suggest that the average daily detention population exceeds 40,000.[16]

The trauma, violence, and persecution experienced by many immigrants in their countries of origin, together with migration and postmigration stressors including discrimination or language barriers, make immigrants in the United States more vulnerable to experiencing mental health difficulties.[17] Political instability and increased violence in countries around the globe, paired with the tough immigration policies of the United States, are also expected to increase the rates of mental health and trauma-related symptoms in immigrants and refugees. Although the precise number of individuals with mental illness facing deportation is not known, it is estimated that about 15% of those in deportation proceedings suffer from a serious mental illness,[18] a rate significantly higher than the reported 3–5% in the general population.[19] Since immigration proceedings are civil in nature, immigrants are not guaranteed the same constitutional rights provided to those in criminal court, such as the Sixth Amendment right to assistance of counsel. Therefore, many immigrants proceed through the deportation process without legal representation, raising concerns about whether those immigrants with mental illness or cognitive deficits are able to participate in court proceedings effectively or understand the consequences of deportation.[20]

The extensive histories of trauma experienced by immigrants—combined with the increasingly difficult migration conditions, surging number of immigrants in removal proceedings, and poor mental health care provided to immigrants in detention—all underlie the important role that MHPs and attorneys can play in the IC process. Specifically, psychological evidence is part of many forms of removal relief for which immigrants can apply. Forensic mental health evaluations can be essential in aiding immigration adjudicators to make decisions about removal and detention.[21] For example, persecution-based relief applications (i.e., asylum) are based on fear of persecution and torture and often involve the assessment of psychological symptoms resulting from traumatic experiences or posttraumatic stress disorder (PTSD). Other types of applications can involve the evaluation of the psychological hardships that will be suffered by the immigrant or the immigrant's family if deported or the evaluation of factors such as mental illness, trauma, and substance use that can mitigate the presence of prior criminal conduct. In addition, there are some visas that undocumented immigrants are eligible for if they can prove that they have been victims of a crime or human trafficking while in the United States, which often requires evidence of psychological harm related to these experiences.[22] Finally, mental health experts can conduct evaluations to assist IJs in making decisions about competency for self-representation and about detention based on risk for future violence.

In addition to their role conducting forensic evaluations and expert testimony in ICs, MHPs can also provide additional aid within the immigration system, including short- and long-term services resulting in treatment affidavits for the courts, consultation and psychoeducation about immigrants' mental health to attorneys, and preparation of noncitizens as they navigate the daunting process of undergoing deportation proceedings. Although psychiatrists and psychologists are more commonly involved in playing these roles in ICs, the identifier "mental health professionals/MHPs" is used in this book to incorporate all types of licensed mental health experts, including social workers and mental health counselors. MHPs who conduct psychological evaluations for ICs are typically retained by immigration attorneys, hired directly by the court, or employed by clinics or centers that provide legal and mental health services to refugees or undocumented individuals (e.g., the Center for Human Rights at Weill Cornell Medicine, or the Bellevue Program for Survivors of Torture at Bellevue Hospital Center in New York City).

Immigration attorneys might retain mental health professionals when the application for relief they are pursuing requires psychological evidence (e.g., an asylum application). They might also seek a mental health expert if, in the process of preparing a client for the immigration hearing, the client cannot respond to questions or appropriately engage with the lawyer, effectively raising concerns about the presence of mental health issues. However, many undocumented immigrants do not have legal representation. This lack of representation is significant especially for those in detention. It is estimated that about 70% of detained immigrants do not have legal counsel.[23] Immigrants without representation typically do not know when a mental health evaluation can be useful, and/or they do not have the ability to find or afford one. Without the type of evaluations that can be completed only by MHPs, immigrants are often unable to provide the psychological evidence required for many forms of removal relief applications. Some studies have shown that more than 90% of detained immigrants without legal counsel are unsuccessful in challenging deportation.[24] Fortunately, the numbers of public defenders and private lawyers providing counsel to immigrants have increased in recent years. For example, the New York City Council funded a project in 2014 to provide free legal representation to immigrants in detention who cannot afford a private immigration attorney. In addition, the government recently funded the National Qualified Representative Program (NQRP), which provides free legal representation for detained immigrants who have been found incompetent to represent themselves in their immigration proceedings because of a serious mental illness. Most recently, following the "zero tolerance" immigration policy, the American Bar Association reported in 2018 that large numbers of lawyers responded pro bono (i.e., without compensation) to this "immigration crisis."[25] Although there are no statistics yet available, it is expected that, as the number of immigration attorneys dedicated to this work increases, so will the number of MHPs retained by those lawyers to provide psychological evidence in ICs.

Despite the increased number of lawyers representing undocumented immigrants and the expanded and increased role of MHPs in the IC system, the literature and resources in this area remain very limited. Mental health evaluations conducted for ICs were already described as a type of forensic mental health assessment (FMHA) in an article published in 1995. At that time, the authors stated that "the legal and psychological communities have given little attention to forensic evaluations in immigration cases."[26] Unfortunately, the situation has not changed much since that publication. Only a small number of books and chapters have begun to address this topic.[27] There continues to be a significant need for more theoretical and empirical scholarly work in this area. Recently, the Executive Office for Immigration Review (EOIR) established some guidelines about the required training and expertise of MHPs involved in conducting evaluations with the specific purpose of determining competency to participate in immigration proceedings. However, these guidelines are limited and circumscribed to one type of evaluation. The referral questions and legal issues involved in ICs continue to lack definition and specificity. There remains limited knowledge about the current practices of immigration lawyers and MHPs who work in this context, as well limited empirical evidence of the cross-cultural validity of mental health instruments or specialized forensic tools for use in ICs.[28]

Mental health and legal professionals can make significant contributions to the immigration legal process, but this requires that they understand the immigration law context in which they will practice, in addition to the basic principles of forensic and cross-cultural mental health assessment. The field of FMHAs has barely paid attention to the context of ICs, and similarly the field of cross-cultural mental health assessment has rarely paid attention to the forensic issues that are essential to consider in any court environment.[29] Although answering questions with respect to mental health diagnoses and clinical functioning is part of MHPs' areas of competency, conducting mental health evaluations in ICs requires additional knowledge in the areas of forensic assessment, cross-cultural assessment, assessment of the psychological effects of trauma and torture, and immigration law.[30] Similarly, given the mental health issues faced by immigrants and the frequency with which psychological evidence is part of legal applications for removal relief, immigration attorneys need to understand the mental health issues faced by immigrants and the psycholegal issues involved in removal-relief claims. They also need to collaborate effectively with MHPs.

The purpose of this book is to provide an overview of relevant issues at the intersection of mental health and immigration law. In addition to its contribution to the scholarly literature, it is meant to serve as a resource for MHPs who perform psychological evaluations in ICs and/ or treat immigrants who are undergoing removal proceedings, as well as for immigration lawyers and judges. This is an area that provides great opportunities for research and scholarship, and throughout the book we point out where research gaps currently exist. The diversity of our backgrounds and our collective experiences cover all of the areas of knowledge required to do this type of work. One of the co-authors (Virginia Barber-Rioja) is a forensic psychologist who specializes in forensic psychological assessment and correctional psychology and has performed hundreds of evaluations for a variety of courts, including criminal and immigration courts, with a particular interest in evaluations of Spanish-speaking individuals. The co-second author (Adeyinka M. Akinsulure-Smith) is also a psychologist with expertise in cross-cultural psychology who, along with performing evaluations for a variety of courts, including criminal and immigration courts, also provides clinical services and conducts research related to issues facing forced migrants. The third co-author (Sarah Vendzules) is an immigration attorney who has represented immigrant clients before ICs, USCIS, the Board of Immigration Appeals, and in federal court and has taught at the intersection between immigration and criminal law.

Part I (The Legal Context of Immigration Law) provides an overview of the legal issues relevant to ICs and deportation proceedings. Chapter 1 ("A Brief Overview of the Immigration System and Forensic Mental Health Assessment") offers a primer on the immigration law and IC systems. Chapter 2 ("Detention of Immigrants") provides an overview of immigration detention, a system of incarceration completely separate from the criminal legal system. Chapter 3 ("Forms of Removal Relief and Related Psycholegal Issues") reviews the psycholegal issues relevant to the different forms of relief from deportation available to noncitizens and the related functional abilities that should be the focus of the mental health evaluation.

Part II (Mental Health and Immigration) starts with Chapter 4 ("Roles of Mental Health Professionals"), which reviews the different roles that MHPs can play in the immigration legal system, making a distinction between those who provide treatment to immigrants involved in removal proceedings and who might be called to provide treatment affidavits or to testify as fact witnesses in ICs versus those who provide forensic evaluations to ICs tailored to a specific legal issue and who can be called to testify as expert witnesses. Chapter 5 ("Risk Factors for Mental Health Distress in Immigrants Facing Removal Proceedings") reviews some of the mental health issues commonly experienced by individuals who have migrated and are seeking legal status in the United States while facing the stress related to the threat of deportation. Chapter 6 ("Assessment of Trauma in Immigrants Facing Removal Proceedings") provides recommendations for the assessment of trauma in ICs, which is an important component of most types of evaluations in this context. And chapter 7 ("Vicarious Trauma and Secondary Traumatic Stress in Lawyers and Mental Health Professionals") covers a topic we included based on our experience and those of our colleagues, who frequently report being impacted emotionally by the stories of severe trauma and persecution they hear from their clients.

Finally, Part III (Cultural, Legal, and Forensic Considerations in Immigration Courts" starts with Chapter 8 ("Considerations for Collaboration Between Legal and Mental Health Professionals"), which provides members of both professions with basic ethical obligations as well as a review of some important differences between them and recommendations to optimize collaboration. Chapter 9 ("Cultural Considerations") provides MHPs and, to a certain extent, legal professionals with a review of important issues to consider when working with individuals from different cultures. Chapter 10 ("Forensic Assessment Considerations") offers a review of basic principles of FMHA applied to ICs. Finally, chapter 11 ("Competency to Participate in Immigration Proceedings") and chapter 12 ("Violence Risk Assessment") cover two important areas of forensic assessment in ICs—one related to noncitizens' competency for self-representation, and the other related to the legal question of dangerousness—considered by IJs when making decisions about detention and bonds. We end this volume with a separate section titled "Summary and Future Directions."

It is our sincere hope that this volume motivates and enables students and scholars to push forward with research in the many areas explored here, which will be essential to improve the practice for both mental health and legal professionals in ICs. It will also help MHPs, immigration lawyers, and IJs improve their practices and, hopefully, encourage other clinicians and lawyers to pursue a career in this important area of work and research.

PART I

The Legal Context of Immigration Law

1

A Brief Overview of the Immigration System and Forensic Mental Health Assessment

Immigration law is complicated, frequently changing, and heavily dependent on political decisions by governmental administrations. In addition, unlike the criminal justice system, of which most citizens have a basic idea of its structure and main players, most people know very little, if anything, about the immigration system. This chapter provides an overview of the immigration legal system, covering the foundational information that mental health professionals (MHPs) need to be familiar with before working with immigrants involved in it. This includes the different agencies that form the immigration system, the sources of immigration law, and common immigration scenarios that MHPs are more likely to encounter. Additionally, this chapter covers the different functions that forensic mental health assessments (FMHAs) can play within the immigration system, including how MHPs' specialized knowledge can be useful and, at times, essential to its functioning.

The Immigration System

The "immigration system" discussed in this book consists of four main agencies. First is the Department of Homeland Security (DHS) with its component agencies, which include United States Citizenship and Immigration Services (USCIS), Immigrations and Customs Enforcement (ICE), and Customs and Border Protection (CBP). USCIS is responsible for immigration benefits and processes many kinds of immigration applications. ICE is the enforcement arm: it acts as prosecutor, police, and jailor, initiating proceedings against people who might be deportable, arresting some deportable immigrants, and administering the immigration detention regime.[1] CBP administers the ports of entry into the United States[2] and patrols the border (which actually includes 100 miles from the land border and the coasts, home to over two-thirds of the US population).[3]

Second is the Executive Office or Immigration Review (EOIR, sometimes pronounced "Eeyore"), which is part of the Department of Justice (DOJ). EOIR houses the immigration courts (ICs) and the Board of Immigration Appeals (BIA).[4] ICs are not true courts per se—they are part of an executive branch agency that, in other contexts, acts as prosecutor. Immigration judges (IJs) are more accurately characterized as agency employees and therefore lack the independence of employees of the judicial branch. There are 69 ICs nationwide with approximately 350 IJs.[5] The BIA is the appellate body for the ICs. The board's members, like IJs, are political appointees rather than judges. Because the BIA is not a true court, the head of the DOJ—the United States Attorney General (AG)—can overrule any BIA decision and issue binding opinions that change how the immigration law will be applied nationwide. BIA decisions, including AG opinions, can be overruled by the United States Supreme Court and by circuit courts of appeals (but only in the jurisdiction of that particular circuit). As a result, immigration law can be interpreted differently depending on the geographical area where a particular IC happens to be located (and sometimes the same IC applies the law of different circuits depending on where the immigrant before it is detained).

Third is the Department of State (DOS).[6] The DOS handles applications for visas from abroad, which includes immigrant visas (green cards) and nonimmigrant visas (tourists, students, etc.), runs the embassies and consulates, and handles the visa interviews. Some people who are in the United States applying to change their status will need to physically leave the country to be officially "admitted" under their new status, and they will need to deal with the DOS in order to do so. The DOS also runs the United States Refugee Admissions Program, in cooperation with DHS and the Department of Health and Human Services (DHHS), which decides which people should be allowed to come to the United States as refugees, and it administers the diversity visa lottery, whereby a certain number of randomly selected people from low-immigration countries are allowed to immigrate to the United States each year.[7] These immigration scenarios are not discussed in detail in this book.

Finally, there is the Office of Refugee Resettlement (ORR), which is part of the DHHS.[8] ORR is responsible for the care of unaccompanied minors who arrive at the border. It is also responsible, as its name implies, for helping refugees resettle in the United States.

Sources of Law

The Immigration and Nationality Act (INA) was enacted in 1952 by Congress, and has been amended many times since then. Its provisions are also codified in the United States Code (USC). In IC proceedings, the INA will be cited, whereas in federal court proceedings the same provision of the USC will be cited instead. The two are functionally identical. This book contains citations to both the INA and the USC where possible.

The Code of Federal Regulations (CFR) contains many regulations implementing the provisions of the INA. Regulations are not passed by Congress; they are "promulgated" by the relevant administrative agency (such as DHS) through a rulemaking process. The agency that is charged with implementing the legislation is presumed to have the necessary expertise to fill in any blanks in the legislation and nail down specific details about how it should operate. Agencies are not, however, allowed to elaborate so much on legislation that they change its meaning to something not originally intended by Congress.[9]

Interpretations of immigration law can also be found in agency adjudicative decisions. BIA decisions are largely unpublished and might not be available to the general public or even to immigration attorneys who seek to consult them in their research.[10] IJ decisions are even more difficult to access and are usually available only if an attorney receiving the decision has decided to share it with colleagues. Only the small minority of BIA decisions designated as "published" are binding on the ICs, meaning that there is frequently no precedent decision on point to assist an IJ in the interpretation of a statute or regulation. In the same vein, USCIS, which adjudicates immigration benefit applications, has its own appeals body, the Administrative Appeals Office (AAO). Its decisions are also not considered precedent, but they are likely reflective of the official agency position about the proper interpretation of the statute.

Immigration "law" can also be found in interpretive rules or policy statements put forth by the various agencies.[11] (One example is a parole memorandum, discussed in chapter 2, that was the subject of a lawsuit after DHS started denying parole across the board to asylum seekers.) Immigration law can also consist of agreements entered into by an agency (as with the *Flores* settlement agreement discussed in chapter 2).

Finally, immigration law can be found in court decisions. There is no automatic right to appeal BIA or AAO decisions to the courts. Many matters decided by the agency are not reviewable by the courts because they are considered committed to agency discretion (unless the agency has abused that discretion) or because Congress has specifically deprived the courts of jurisdiction over the matter.[12] And in many cases, even if an issue is reviewable, the court might decline to take the case. Due to a change in the law in 1996, most individual immigration appeals must now be handled by the circuit courts of appeals rather than the district courts.[13] This change curtailed judicial review of agency decision-making, as there are far fewer circuit court judges than district court judges. As a result, fewer immigrants have received their "day in court." Habeas corpus proceedings (despite Congress's best efforts to strip the courts of habeas jurisdiction over immigration matters) and some other matters (e.g., lawsuits such as the *Flores* litigation) are still handled by the district courts. A district court decision is not binding beyond the parties in that particular case, but it might be persuasive to other judges in that jurisdiction and others. For example, if a district court finds, perhaps pursuant to a habeas petition, that a particular crime is not a ground for deportability, that holding will help the immigrant who brought the case but not necessarily anyone else. In contrast, decisions of the circuit courts of appeals are considered binding interpretations of the immigration law for all cases and matters within the circuit. Even district courts, however, can have a good deal of power if a case is brought as a class action. If the court certifies a class and makes an order with respect to that class, its decision can have far-reaching or even nationwide effects. Of course, its ruling is still subject to review by the circuit courts and the Supreme Court.

A "Typical" Immigration Case

There are many different immigration journeys and many different ways in which a noncitizen might interact with any or all of these agencies. This book, however, focuses on the three immigration scenarios that licensed MHPs are most likely to be involved with: (1) People who arrive at the US border seeking asylum and related humanitarian protections; (2) people who are already in the United States but are placed in removal proceedings; and (3) people who are (probably) already in the United States and are applying for a form of immigration status with USCIS. There might be a good deal of overlap among these three scenarios. For example, a person in scenario (3) might be in removal proceedings at the same time that their application with USCIS is pending. And an asylum seeker, if they qualify, will be placed in removal proceedings for their asylum claim to be adjudicated by an IJ. In these proceedings, they might find themselves applying for other forms of relief in addition to asylum, including applications that must be adjudicated by USCIS.

Asylum

Anyone who arrives at a port of entry but is inadmissible due to misrepresentation or due to lacking valid entry documents can be summarily deported,[14] unless they express an intention to apply for asylum or a fear of persecution in their country of origin.[15] Those who express such an intention will be referred for a "credible fear" interview with an asylum officer.[16] The determination to be made by the asylum officer, an employee of USCIS, is both legal and factual: First, do the facts, as the individual states them, potentially make out an asylum claim? Second, is the individual's story credible?[17] During the time that the asylum seeker is undergoing the credible fear interview, they will be detained in CBP custody. If they pass that interview, they will be placed in removal proceedings so that an IJ can adjudicate their asylum claim.[18] They might be detained during these proceedings. If they are detained, it will likely be in the custody of ICE, unless they are considered an "unaccompanied minor," in which case they will be given to the custody of ORR. Individuals who are not eligible for full removal proceedings might still be able to seek asylum or related relief in special "asylum-only" proceedings.[19]

Removal Proceedings

People without proper status (which includes people whose status has expired and those who never had status in the first place), and people who have status but have violated the terms of that status in some way (e.g., a student visa holder accepting work or a lawful permanent resident convicted of a crime), can be deported.[20] Many, but not all,[21] people in the United States have the right to an immigration hearing before being deported, and such hearings must comport with due process.[22]

In removal proceedings, DHS (specifically ICE) is the prosecuting entity. They serve the noncitizen (the "respondent") with a Notice to Appear (NTA) in the IC. The NTA is the charging document that lays out the allegations against the respondent. In the initial hearings, called "Master Calendar Hearings," the IJ takes pleadings about the allegations and decides whether the person is actually deportable as charged. The IJ will also decide whether the person is eligible for any form of relief (e.g., asylum, cancellation of removal, adjustment of status, or voluntary departure). If they are eligible, they will schedule an "Individual Hearing," at which time the relief application will be decided.[23] If the person is detained, and not subject to mandatory detention, the IJ might also schedule a bond hearing to review DHS's detention decision.

Removal proceedings are adversarial in nature. Respondents have the right to present evidence on their own behalf and to cross-examine witnesses.[24] But, because removal proceedings are considered civil proceedings, noncitizens do not share the same rights provided to defendants in criminal court, such as the Sixth Amendment's constitutional right to the assistance of counsel. Further, the protections of the Federal Rules of Evidence (which apply in civil court) do not limit the types of evidence that can be used against them.[25] Instead, the proceedings are governed by principles of "fundamental fairness."[26] Despite the civil nature of removal proceedings, the severe penalties to which noncitizens are subject (deportation, detention) make them, in some ways, more similar to criminal proceedings.[27] Due to the severe consequences and scant procedural protections, removal proceedings have been likened to "death penalty cases in . . . traffic court."[28]

USCIS Adjudications

Many people, both inside the United States and abroad, apply to USCIS for immigration benefits. USCIS processes a staggering 26,000 benefit applications *per day*.[29] Benefits include employment authorization, asylum, naturalization, adjustment of status to lawful permanent resident, various temporary worker visas, and special visas such as the U visa (victims of crime) and T visas (victims of trafficking).

Applications in front of USCIS are sometimes done entirely on the papers, meaning the applicant does not need to physically appear, and sometimes they involve an interview. Adjustment of status usually requires an interview, as does naturalization. USCIS adjudicators are not typically attorneys. They are agency employees trained in the requirements of the particular type of application they adjudicate. They work in various service centers and field offices around the country. Applicants before USCIS bear the burden of proving that they are eligible for the requested benefit and, if USCIS does not feel that the application is sufficient or if they have additional questions, they might request further information of the applicant before adjudicating the application. Applicants for benefits will typically need to get their fingerprints and other biometric information taken as part of the application. Many applications before USCIS carry steep fees, though fee waivers are sometimes available.[30]

The Functions of Forensic Mental Health Assessment within the Immigration System

In general, the purpose of FMHAs in the immigration system is to use psychological evidence to assist the adjudicator (the IJ or USCIS officer) in making decisions regarding immigration legal status (e.g., removal, detention). In particular, FMHAs can serve four major functions within the immigration system: They can provide evidentiary support for a fact or probability that must be found in order for relief to be granted; they can contextualize prior or current behavior in aid of a determination; they can assist a decision maker in assessing the risk posed by an individual; and they can assess the competency of an individual in proceedings. A FMHA can, of course, serve more than one of these functions simultaneously. The MHP and lawyer should be clear about the function that will be served by their report.

Evidentiary Support for a Fact or Probability

Many forms of relief require the applicant to prove that they have suffered some form of harm or that they are likely to suffer harm in the future if not granted relief. FMHAs can help with both of these show-ings. FMHAs can provide powerful evidence to help establish that an applicant suffered harm in the past. The evaluation can show that the individual is still suffering from symptoms related to trauma (e.g., trou-ble sleeping, intrusive thoughts, nightmares, etc.), and can comment on the contributions of the past harm to such symptoms. The MHP cannot necessarily opine on the veracity of the individual's story about what happened to them but can educate the court about psychological factors that might affect recollection of traumatic events and can also comment on malingering or exaggeration of psychological symptoms.

Finally, the FMHA can also help overcome barriers to credibility, as it can provide psychological explanations (e.g., trauma, cognitive deficits) for inconsistencies in the retelling of a story, memory lapses, or poor eye contact, which can be interpreted by the IJ as a lack of credibility or candor.

Contextualization of Prior or Current Behavior

Many forms of relief require an applicant to establish that they have suffered hardship,[31] that they are a person of "good moral character,"[32] or that the balance of the equities (i.e., positive and negative factors) favor them.[33] Additionally, for almost every form of relief, even when the individual meets all the required standards, the adjudicator still retains discretion to deny the application. Immigrant applicants for relief accordingly need to show that they are deserving of an act of grace. This will be harder for applicants with a history of behavior that could make them appear unsympathetic or unworthy. The FMHA can pro-vide context for more problematic behaviors in a way that can help the adjudicator understand why the applicant might have committed them and why they are still worthy of an exercise of discretion in their favor.

An applicant with a criminal history is at a distinct disadvantage in the immigration system. For some, they are presumptively ineligible for many forms of relief; for others, their contacts with the criminal legal system are readily available as reasons for a discretionary denial. An evaluation by a MHP can help an adjudicator understand why the individual might have committed the crime or provide context for the situation the person was experiencing that led them to make the choices they made.

Substance use is another area in which an individual might present problematic behaviors that adjudicators sometimes struggle to understand. The view of substance use disorders as a character flaw is baked in to the immigration law. The myriad misconceptions about substance use circulating through the general public can also be found among judges, attorneys, and USCIS adjudicators. MHPs can play a crucial role in educating these parties about the nature of substance use, helping them understand, for example, that relapse is often a part of the recovery process.

Risk Assessment

FMHAs can also assist the decision maker in assessing the risk posed by the applicant. This is relevant for individuals seeking discretionary release from immigration detention on bond, which requires the IJ to find that the individual does not pose a "danger to the community."[34] It is also relevant for anyone who has to affirmatively prove that it would be in the public interest to allow them to enter or remain in the country.[35] Risk assessment is highly relevant to immigrants seeking to enter the country or adjust their status within the country who have a diagnosed mental illness. An individual becomes inadmissible for having a "physical or mental disorder and behavior associated with the disorder that may pose, or has posed, a threat to the property, safety, or welfare of the alien or others," or for having had such a disorder in the past if the behavior "is likely to recur or to lead to other harmful behavior."[36] Even when risk is not explicitly part of an application for relief, it remains a question lurking in every discretionary application. Adjudicators do not want to grant relief to someone who is going to go on to commit crimes or harm another person. For an immigrant with a criminal history or a history of violence or drug use or serious mental illness or other "negative" behavior, the adjudicator is going to wonder: Is this going to happen again? FMHAs can offer insight into this question.

Competency

The final role played by FMHAs is an evaluation of the competency of a noncitizen respondent in immigration proceedings. Unlike in criminal law, in which an incompetent defendant cannot be prosecuted, immigration proceedings can and do go on when the respondent is not competent to understand or participate. Instead of halting proceedings, IJs are instructed to hold a hearing to assess the mental competency of a potentially incompetent respondent and determine what safeguards might be necessary to proceed with the removal proceedings.[37] FMHAs in service of such a hearing can help the relevant decision makers (the IJ and the government attorney) better understand the individual's history and evaluate their testimony. Additionally, under a new EOIR policy, some detained immigrants who are found incompetent to represent themselves might be eligible for government-appointed counsel.[38] IJs can request FMHAs to assist them in making these competency determinations.

Conclusion

The "immigration system" is a rather amorphous thing, consisting of a number of agencies, adjudicative bodies, and decision makers applying law from a variety of sources and handling different aspects of the immigration decision-making process. Similarly, there is no typical immigration story. Immigrants might interact with multiple agencies and decision makers over the course of a single immigration journey and will consequently need to meet a number of different legal standards in order to gain the ability to live and work in the United States. Many of these legal standards require, or can be greatly helped by, FMHAs. Despite the variety of types of adjudications and standards that need to be met, FMHAs can be said to play four distinct roles within the immigration system. It is important for the MHP who will be performing the FMHA to understand the role (or roles) that the FMHA will play in a particular adjudication. This is something that they should discuss with the attorney (or other party) who has asked them to perform the evaluation.

2

Detention of Immigrants

Immigration detention is civil detention. Unlike criminal detention, it is meant to be preventative rather than punitive. Correspondingly, the procedural safeguards and standards of proof are more lax. Even compared to other forms of civil detention in the United States (the involuntary hospitalization of mentally ill individuals who present an immediate danger to themselves or others and the preventative detention of certain sex offenders), the procedural protections attached to immigration detention are paltry at best. This permissive legal environment, combined with powerful financial incentives that accompany immigration detention (including a law that up until 2017 required a minimum number of people to be detained each day), contribute to immigration detention significantly dwarfing other forms of civil detention in the United States.

Immigration detention dramatically lowers immigrants' chances of success in immigration court. One study found that immigrants representing themselves have a 3% success rate if they are detained but a 13% success rate if they are free. Meanwhile, immigrants represented by counsel have an 18% success rate if they are detained but a 74% success rate if they are free. For both groups, freedom from detention represented more than a fourfold increase in their likelihood of obtaining relief.[1] This chapter provides an overview of immigration detention law, the legality of immigration detention, the current immigration detention regime, abuses in immigration detention, family detention and the detention of minors, mental health care in immigration detention, and the process getting out and reentry from detention.

Immigration Detention Law: Overview

Authority for the civil detention of immigrants comes from the Immigration and Nationality Act (INA) and implementing regulations. The rules that govern a person's detention change as their immigration case moves through different phases. Immigrants can be detained before being put in proceedings,[2] during the pendency of proceedings,[3] and after proceedings are over.[4] Mental health professionals (MHPs) might encounter immigrants detained at any of these stages.

At the border, asylum seekers and other would-be entrants without the requisite visa will generally be detained while Department of Homeland Security (DHS) decides whether they have the right to removal proceedings or whether they can be summarily excluded from the country.[5] If an asylum seeker passes a "credible fear" interview[6] and is placed in removal proceedings, DHS could, in its discretion, continue to detain them or could release them on parole.[7] DHS could also detain any other noncitizen possibly subject to removal, including lawful permanent residents and others who have been in the United States for many years.[8]

Detention can last for months or even years as the case makes its way through the immigration court (IC) and through any Board of Immigration Appeals (BIA) appeals. The average time that an asylum case has been waiting in in immigration court is currently (as of 2021) over 800 days.[9] Detained cases move faster,[10] but here is no data specific to detained asylum cases, and the data that the Executive Office for Immigration Review (EOIR) does keep has a tendency to obscure rather than illuminate.[11] According to Immigration and Customs Enforcement (ICE) detention data from the first four months of FY2021, the average (mean) stay in ICE custody after passing a credible fear interview was 293 days. For FY2020, it was 133.7 days.[12] This data is in line with the opinions of advocates consulted by the authors, who estimated that a detained asylum seeker (before the COVID-19 pandemic) could expect to spend five to six months in detention awaiting an IJ decision and several months longer for a BIA appeal.

Finally, there are a number of immigrants who have a final order of removal from the BIA but who cannot be deported yet for various reasons. For some immigrants, an ongoing legal proceeding (i.e., an appeal to the federal courts) will prevent their removal. If an immigrant chooses to challenge the legality of their removal order in federal court (and assuming they are granted a stay to prevent their removal in the meantime),[13] the review process can easily take years.[14] Other immigrants are stateless, or their country of citizenship is unwilling to accept them.[15] Nominally, the detention of postorder individuals is done to effectuate their removal, but in practice people are often detained even though the chances that they will actually be removed are slim.[16] Detention during this phase can also last for months or years,[17] albeit with some limitations.

Immigration Detention Versus Criminal Pretrial Detention

Detention during the pendency of removal proceedings bears functional resemblance to pretrial criminal detention[18] in that both are used to protect public safety and ensure that the relevant individual will come to court.[19] The two are each other's inverse, however, when it comes to the way detention decisions are made.

In criminal pretrial detention hearings, the state must establish that the individual is a flight risk or a danger. To keep someone in custody without bail, the state bears an even higher burden: it must prove that no amount of bail will protect public safety and prevent the individual's flight. As a result, only 4% of felony pretrial detainees are held without bail.[20] The vast majority, even those charged with very serious crimes, are given the possibility of release whether on bond or some other condition or released on recognizance.[21] Another salient feature of criminal pretrial detention is that the decision to detain is made by the independent judiciary and not by the entity prosecuting the case. The police, of course, make the decision to arrest, but the custody decision is made by a judge. Further, the hearing before the judge must be held within a reasonable period of time (which might vary depending on the jurisdiction but is usually 48–72 hours).[22]

In contrast, in immigration detention hearings the immigrant, not the state, bears the burden of proof. This means that the immigrant must affirmatively prove that they are not a danger to the community or a flight risk in order to secure release.[23] DHS, the prosecuting entity, makes the initial custody decision, and in some cases an immigration judge (IJ) is able to later review that decision. But such review might not take place for weeks or even months, as there is no requirement that it must be completed in any given period of time.[24] For many there will be no review. There are broad categories of immigrants who are subject to mandatory detention, which means that the IJ has no power to order their release on any amount of bond,[25] no matter the strength of the evidence that they are not dangerous or a risk of flight.[26] Even when the IJ does order bond, the decision is automatically stayed if DHS announces their intent to appeal the decision to the BIA.[27]

Statistics on bonds are not readily available due to the way EOIR records (or does not record) data.[28] Nevertheless, a set of data-tracking ICs over the past twenty years reveals that IJs granted bond in fewer than half the cases in which the immigrant was eligible for a bond hearing.[29] The number of immigrants who were subject to mandatory detention and not eligible for a bond hearing was not reported. Another difference between immigration bond and criminal bail is the typical amounts that are set when compared with the seriousness (or lack thereof) of the offense. The INA sets the minimum bond at $1,500, and they are often much higher.[30] The median bond set—the only bond statistic maintained by EOIR—was $8,000 in fiscal year 2019.[31] This is slightly lower than the median criminal bail for felonies in the United States, which is $10,000.[32] (The median felony bond varies great across jurisdictions—in New York, for example, it is only $5,000.)[33] The fact that immigration bonds are so high as to be nearly the same as a felony criminal bond is surprising considering that people in immigration proceedings have been accused of violating only the civil immigration law, not criminal law. It is even more surprising when considering that most immigrants who have criminal records[34] will be disqualified from bond entirely by the mandatory detention statute.

Immigration Detention Versus Other Forms of Civil Detention

Immigration detention also compares unfavorably to other forms of civil detention when it comes to procedural protections. No other civil detention regime puts the burden on the detained individual to prove they merit release. In civil commitment proceedings, the government bears the burden to show, by a preponderance of the evidence, that the person meets the commitment standards.[35] Sex offenders potentially subject to civil commitment at the conclusion of their criminal sentences also benefit from the burden of proof resting with the government to establish that they should be detained.[36] Immigration detention is also the only form of detention in which the person whose liberty is on the line does not have the right to counsel to assist in making their case.[37] The other forms of civil detention—mental health and the preventative detention of sex offenders—both require counsel.

The Legality of Immigration Detention

The courts have repeatedly found immigration detention to be constitutional.[38] They have, however, imposed certain limitations aimed at keeping the detention regime on the right side of the Constitution's requirement that no one be deprived of liberty without due process of law.

Immigrants detained during removal proceedings normally bear the burden of proof in justifying their release, but if removal proceedings are still going on after many months (as they frequently are when the immigrant contests removability or applies for relief), due process might at some point require that DHS justify the need for continued detention.[39] For immigrants who are detained after a final order of removal while DHS attempts (unsuccessfully) to deport them to a country that will not accept them, continued detention on the theory that DHS might eventually be able to accomplish their deportation will become presumptively unreasonable after six months have passed since the removal order became final.[40] Yet, as noted above, the six-month time limit does not apply to those who ask a federal court to review the legality of their removal order.

The Current Immigration Detention Regime

There are approximately 50,000 people in immigration detention on a given day in the United States, and over 500,000 people will be detained over the course of a year.[41] These individuals are held in a combination of DHS facilities, contract facilities run by private for-profit corporations (GeoGroup and CoreCivic, formerly CCA, being notable examples),[42] and state and local jails that have leased bed space, or sometimes entire jails, to ICE.[43] ICE disclosures from fiscal year 2019 list 213 separate facilities where immigration detainees were held. These included 5 DHS facilities (called "service processing centers"), 11 contract detention facilities, 103 state and local jails (13 of which held exclusively ICE detainees), and a Red Roof Inn.[44] State and local jails frequently subcontract to private companies to manage the facility. Approximately 81% of detainees are held in facilities operated by private companies.[45]

A detention bed mandate, in place from 2009–2017, required that a minimum number of people would be detained each day (34,000 at the time it was eliminated).[46] This was a guarantee of revenue to detention facilities. Local quotas, still in existence, have a similar effect: DHS's contracts with detention facilities frequently promise that DHS will pay to house a certain minimum number of people, no matter how many people are actually detained. This incentivizes DHS to make use of the already-purchased bed space.[47] In 2019, there were 46 DHS facilities with such guaranteed minimums, ranging from 40 to 2,400 beds.[48]

Immigration detention centers are located all over the country, but many are found in remote locations.[49] For example, many immigrants to New York City are detained at Buffalo Federal Detention Facility, a DHS facility that is located approximately six hours from New York City in a town (Batavia, New York) of only 15,000 people. DHS has complete autonomy as to when to detain an individual, and nothing prevents them from detaining someone hundreds of miles from their home and family—or even in another state or part of the country where the law is worse for immigrants,[50] where IJs are known to be especially harsh,[51] in remote locations where lawyers are hard to find,[52] or even away from an existing counsel relationship.[53]

The treatment of people in immigration detention is governed, to an extent, by ICE's detention standards. The official Performance-Based National Detention Standards apply in theory to all facilities, but facilities that hold ICE detainees along with other individuals (usually prisoners serving a criminal sentence) are exempted from some of the requirements therein.[54] The separate but similar National Detention Standards for Non-Dedicated Facilities were written for those facilities.[55] Detention standards are incorporated into the contracts that ICE signs with the various facilities, which means that a slightly different version of the standards might apply depending on when the contract was signed.[56] There are also separate standards that govern facilities that detain families with children.[57] None of these standards have been codified into regulations, and they do not have the force of law. As a result, there is no legal mechanism to enforce them.[58]

Abuses in Immigration Detention

Immigration detention has been heavily criticized for a panoply of abuses. These include sexual abuse of detainees,[59] forced sterilization,[60] detainees being fed spoiled food,[61] detainees being forced to work for pennies and therefore subsidize the bottom line of the facility,[62] inadequate health care,[63] and the overuse of solitary confinement for minor disciplinary violations. (See discussion below.)

One notable abuse is the use of *hieleras* (iceboxes) at Customs and Border Protection (CBP) facilities at the border. These facilities are where asylum seekers are held while they undergo a credible fear interview. The temperature in the holding cells for immigrants is kept extremely low, and asylum seekers are frequently stripped of all but a single layer of clothing.[64] In preparation for enduring the *hieleras*, organizations serving immigrants about to surrender themselves to CBP have been known to provide asylum seekers (including small children) with wool socks and thermal underwear because they know it might well be their only source of warmth for several days.[65] A federal court in 2017 made factual findings with respect to conditions at CBP facilities, including the use of freezing-cold temperatures to punish migrants. Notably, the government's own evidence showed it had not fed certain plaintiffs for long periods of time and government attorneys argued in the case that they had no obligation to provide soap, toothbrushes, or other hygiene items.[66]

Another outcome (some might say "abuse") caused by immigration detention is the systematic denial of access to counsel. It can be difficult or impossible to find a lawyer willing and able to travel to a far-flung detention center for meetings and/or court appearances.[67] Though ICE denies that it chooses the location of its detention centers to isolate detainees from counsel, the effect is undeniable.[68] The physical detention environment can also make confidential communication with counsel difficult or impossible. There might be insufficient access to phones or insufficient privacy in meeting rooms or phone booths, meaning that a detainee cannot talk about certain issues (like physical or sexual abuse, sexual orientation or gender identity, or fear of persecution in their native country) without worrying about being overheard by detention center staff or other detainees.[69] These barriers might also affect the MHP–patient relationship.

Immigrant detainees frequently fight back against abusive conditions in detention, including through hunger strikes and other forms of resistance. According to ICE data, hundreds of detainees per year engage in hunger strikes to protest the conditions of their detainment. ICE has retaliated against these hunger-striking detainees with further abuses, including force-feeding, solitary confinement, and threats.[70]

Family Detention and the Detention of Minors

According to the Refugee Convention, signed in 1951 in the wake of World War II,[71] the United States is obligated to accept refugees fleeing persecution who show up at its borders and seek the protection of its laws. It reserves the right, however, to determine who is a "genuine" refugee, that is to say, who meets the legal criteria for asylum, withholding of removal, or relief under the Convention Against Torture. During the period that these determinations are being made, the government has deemed it appropriate to detain many of the applicants, including families with children.

The detention of asylum seekers has been justified on various grounds, most notably to discourage purported abuse of the asylum system. The fear is that people who want to come to the United States for other reasons will say they want to claim asylum, get released, and then fail to show up for their hearings.[72] This fear, however, is belied by data showing that the vast majority of asylum seekers (80–99% by some accountings) do show up to their IC hearings.[73] The high rate of attendance is especially remarkable given EOIR's rampant problems providing notice of court dates to immigrant respondents.[74]

There are very few limitations on DHS's ability to detain adults. The detention of children, however, is governed by the *Flores* settlement agreement.[75] This agreement was the result of a lawsuit filed in the 1980s charging mistreatment of immigrant children in government facilities. In settling the case, the government agreed to provide certain protections for minor children in its care. These protections include the requirement that children be released from detention (to sponsors or to state-licensed child care facilities) as soon as possible and that in the meantime they be held in the "least restrictive" setting possible.[76] The court charged with overseeing the *Flores* settlement ruled in 2015 that the maximum amount of time that children can be held in nonlicensed facilities is 20 days.[77] The settlement agreement is still in effect and has been "partially codified" into the immigration law by the Trafficking Victims Protection Reauthorization Act.[78]

Children who arrive in the United States without a parent or legal guardian are considered "unaccompanied minors" and are given to the custody of the Office of Refugee Resettlement (ORR), which is not part of DHS but rather a part of the Department of Health and Human Services (HHS).[79] The category of unaccompanied minors includes children who come with family members who are not legal guardians (brothers, sisters, aunts, uncles, grandparents, etc.) and children who are separated from their parent(s) by the government.[80] The transfer of control over the children from DHS to ORR happened in 2003, due to pressure from advocates, because DHS was failing in its obligations under *Flores*.[81] ORR's mission, consistent with *Flores*, is to hold these children in the least restrictive environment possible consistent with the best interests of the child and, if possible, to facilitate their release to sponsors.[82]

ORR funds (via a grant process) a network of over 100 facilities nationwide that provide varying levels of care and services to unaccompanied children in ORR custody. In FY2018 these facilities held over 49,000 children over the course of the year and approximately 12,000 at a given time. The facilities consist primarily of shelters but also include (as of 2018) two "transitional foster care" facilities where children placed in foster care receive services during the day, as well as two residential treatment centers providing "therapeutic care and services that can be customized to individual needs through a structured, 24-hour-a-day program" for children with more serious mental health needs. The network also includes nine "staff secure" facilities (where youth movement within the facility is controlled by staff), one of which provides therapeutic care, and two "secure" facilities that operate within existing juvenile detention facilities.[83] In 2018, ORR's network also included two massive "influx" facilities opened during the Trump administration capable of housing thousands of children.[84] Approximately 2,000 children were in these influx facilities in late 2018, when HHS's Office of Inspector General (OIG) performed an inspection. The vast majority of the remaining children were in shelters or transitional foster care, with the residential treatment centers, staff secure, and secure facilities accounting for approximately 200 children out of a total population of 12,000.[85] ORR's capacity has fluctuated significantly: the two large influx facilities closed in 2019, but another influx facility opened in 2021. Meanwhile, ORR has continued to expand the number of facilities in its network.[86] As of February 2021, it had contracts with approximately 200 facilities, with more than 80 added in the previous four years. The number of total beds was 13,200 (though not all were usable due to COVID-19).[87]

Children can be at ORR facilities for much longer than 20 days. In FY2020, the average time a child spent in ORR's custody was 102 days.[88] Most ORR facilities are licensed child care facilities, which means the 20-day limit from Flores does not apply. The Flores settlement also makes an exception for children who have committed a violent crime or "non-petty delinquent act," have threatened violence (to themselves or others), are an escape risk, or are "so disruptive that secure confinement is necessary to ensure the welfare of the minor or others." These children might be held in the more restrictive environment of a secure facility.[89]

Children who are not unaccompanied minors do not go to ORR custody. Instead, they and their families remain in the custody of DHS. There are currently three DHS detention centers that house families: the Berks Family Residential Center in Leesport, Pennsylvania (capacity 96); the Karnes County Residential Center in Karnes City, Texas (capacity 830 and run by the private prison contractor Geo Group); and the South Texas Family Residential Center in Dilley, Texas (capacity 2,400 and run by the private prison contractor CoreCivic—formerly CCA).[90] Berks has been in operation since 2001, and Dilley and Karnes were opened in 2014 in response to the increased number of family units seeking asylum at the southern US border.[91] Berks is the only center of the three that has ever housed entire family units; Dilley and Karnes were designed to house and have only ever housed mothers and children.[92] All three are secure facilities, which means that the detainees do not have free movement around the facility and are not free to leave.

The expansion of family detention under Barack Obama's administration was done with the explicit purpose of deterring people fleeing violence in El Salvador, Guatemala, and Honduras from seeking asylum in the United States.[93] DHS adopted a policy of refusing to set bond for families from these Northern Triangle countries even after they passed their credible fear interviews and of opposing bond requests in ICs.[94] DHS was thwarted in this attempt by lawsuits that challenged the legality of using detention as a deterrent,[95] as well as a court determination that *Flores* applied to children traveling with their families and not just to unaccompanied minors, as the government had argued.[96] After trying unsuccessfully to get Dilley and Karnes licensed as child care facilities, DHS was forced to limit the time that families with children could be detained to 20 days, resulting in the release of many families.[97] Berks had its child care license revoked by the state of Pennsylvania in 2016 but has been allowed to continue to operate while the case was on appeal.[98] An OIG report found that, as of July 2016, the average time families had spent at Dilley and Karnes was only a week. In contrast, the majority of families at Berks (which had just lost its license) had been there for more than six months.[99]

Family Detention and Family Separation under the Trump Administration

The rejected policy of family detention to deter asylum seekers was revived under the Trump administration. DHS again started denying release across the board to asylum seekers who had passed their credible fear interviews, with no consideration of the individual circumstances of the case.[100] To get around *Flores*, the administration (with help of Republican state legislators) again attempted to get the Karnes and Dilley detention centers licensed as child care facilities.[101] The administration also sought to change the law that prevented it from detaining families indefinitely, asking the court to modify the *Flores* agreement[102] and issuing regulations aimed at ending it.[103] These efforts were rejected by the courts.[104]

The Obama administration had released families when forced to comply with *Flores*. The Trump administration, in contrast, announced that it had no choice but to separate the children from their parents.[105] Despite the government's attempts to blame the *Flores* settlement agreement,[106] the separation of families was reported to be a deliberate strategy meant to deter people from trying to seek asylum in the United States.[107] Also as part of its deterrence strategy, the Trump administration instituted a policy of criminally prosecuting every immigrant who tried to cross the border[108] while simultaneously creating conditions that made it impossible to seek asylum the legal way. The administration severely and artificially curtailed the number of people who would be allowed to request asylum the at Border Patrol checkpoints each day. This forced migrants to wait in Mexico for long months in extremely dangerous conditions before they would be allowed to surrender themselves to US authorities.[109] For those who chose to attempt the crossing, the government set up makeshift tent courts along the border and took guilty pleas en masse.[110] Many of the prosecuted immigrants had in fact initially tried to present themselves at a port of entry but were turned away.[111] By charging every parent caught trying to cross with a crime, the Trump administration was able to put the parents into federal criminal custody, separating them from their children.[112] DHS also separated children whose parents had not crossed illegally but rather had presented themselves, as required, at Border Patrol checkpoints. In some cases, DHS claimed that there was insufficient evidence that the children and parents were related,[113] while in others DHS used the fact that the parent had a criminal record as a pretext to claim that the parent was a "danger" to the children, In one documented case a man had his children taken because he was HIV-positive.[114]

Children separated from their parents, whether because of criminal prosecutions or otherwise, are given to ORR custody and their immigration cases are severed from those of their parents, leading to the deportation of many parents without their children.[115] No systems were in place, and no effort was made, to keep track of the parent–child relationship so the family could be subsequently reunited.[116] During this time, ORR greatly expanded its detention capacity, opening two "influx" facilities: Tornillo, a massive 3,800-bed tent city on the border, and Hutto, a 2,300-bed facility run by a for-profit corporation in Florida.[117] Children were held in these facilities for months even though neither of the shelters were licensed.[118] The need for extra detention capacity was caused or exacerbated by new rules that hindered release of children to willing sponsors (usually family members of the children who were already in the United States). ORR signed an agreement allowing DHS to use any information gained during the sponsorship vetting process for enforcement purposes, leading to the arrests of many potential sponsors. It also instituted a fingerprinting requirement for potential sponsors.[119] This made family members afraid to come forward to claim the children. Additionally, in some cases ORR made onerous and seemingly nonsensical demands of potential sponsors before it would agree to release,[120] including rules that operated to hinder the release of children experiencing mental health issues.[121] The rules were justified on the basis of the children's safety, but the effect was to block the release of children from ORR custody. Over the course of a year, the number of children in ORR custody shot up by 97% despite no corresponding increase in the number of unaccompanied minors at the border.[122] During this time, the percentage of children released to sponsors decreased significantly.[123]

The Trump administration's "zero tolerance" policy was short-lived due to a series of court losses,[124] but family separations continued. During the short time the policy was in effect, 2,816 children were separated from their families. However, 1,556 more were separated before zero tolerance and over 1,000 were separated after.[125] As of early 2021, over 500 of the separated children had still not been reunited with their families, and the parents of approximately 300 of them were believed to have been deported.[126]

The same pattern of family separation, unfortunately, repeated itself during the beginning of the COVID-19 pandemic. When a court ordered the release of detained children for their safety, DHS refused to release the parents, effectively forcing the parents to decide whether to keep the children with them or allow them to be released to ORR. This was described by advocates as "family separation 2.0."[127]

The Future of Family Detention and the Detention of Minors

The future of family detention remains unclear. Despite the requirements under *Flores*, some families with children continue to be detained for much longer than 20 days, and DHS has so far been largely unwilling to release parents along with their children. According to reporting from late 2020, before President Joe Biden took office, 68 children at Dilley had been detained for more than 100 days, and 47 children had been detained for more than 300 days.[128] In early 2021, in the first few weeks of the Biden administration, the BBC profiled the child who had spent the longest time in family detention—a nine-year-old girl from El Salvador who chose to remain in detention with her mother rather than be separated from her. She had been in detention at Dilley for over 531 days.[129]

Mental Health Care in Immigration Detention

There are no not exact statistics about the number of people with mental illness in immigration custody. According to a 2010 report by Human Rights Watch and the American Civil Liberties Union, an estimated 15% of detained immigrants have a mental illness. The report also cited DHS data indicating that 2–5% of detained immigrants have a "serious mental illness."[130] This would be approximately 75,000 people annually with mental illness, or 7,500 on a given day at current detention levels. (For people with serious mental illness, this means approximately 10,000 to 25,000 annually or 1,000–2,500 on a given day.) Others have estimated similar numbers,[131] while still others have suggested that the true number might be much higher than either figure.[132]

The provision of mental health care in immigration detention is not specified in the INA or its implementing regulations but instead comes from interpretations of the Constitution and of federal disability law (e.g., the Americans with Disabilities Act and the Rehabilitation Act).[133] Medical care in detention, including mental health care, is overseen by ICE Health Service Corps (IHSC). IHSC employees staff ICE-run detention centers as well as some contract detention centers and oversee the care of ICE detainees in other facilities. In FY2020, the IHSC "administered and managed a health care system that provided direct care to approximately 100,000 detainees housed at 20 designated facilities throughout the nation" and "[o]versaw health care for over 169,000 detainees housed in 148 non-IHSC-staffed facilities[.]"[134] This oversight includes authorizing any treatment at an outside doctor or hospital, the cost of which is reimbursed by DHS.[135]

With respect to mental health care, the ICE detention standards require that there be a mental health staffer on call 24/7 to respond to emergencies, that each detainee receive mental health intake screening no later than 12 hours after arrival, that a comprehensive health assessment be conducted no later than 14 days after entering into ICE custody, that detainees are able to request mental health services on a daily basis, that they receive continuity of care from admission to discharge (including a discharge plan), that they are transferred to an outside facility in a timely manner if required, that they receive prescribed medications as needed, and that they receive mental health care services by appropriately trained and qualified personnel.[136] These standards mimic the National Commission on Correctional Health Care (NCCHC)'s Standards for Mental Health Services in Correctional Facilities.[137] In fact, the ICE standards state that medical facilities within the detention facility shall achieve and maintain current accreditation with the NCCHC and shall maintain compliance with those standards.[138] Despite this, it is not known how many ICE facilities are currently accredited by the NCCHC. The NCCHC's website states that the NCCHC, by its own policy, "does not release such lists [facilities accredited by NCCHC], nor can it respond to inquiries as to whether a given facility is accredited."[139]

ICE has struggled to meet its own standards for mental health care of detainees. It has not been able to hire and retain sufficient qualified staff to provide necessary mental health services, leaving many facilities severely understaffed.[140] The quality of mental health care provided to immigration detainees has been heavily criticized, both by outside advocates and DHS's own inspector general.[141] The problems have likely been exacerbated by ICE's heavy reliance on for-profit facilities to provide care, as well as by ICE's chronic failure to hold its contractors accountable to the detention standards.[142] Some of the problems are also due to the nonrehabilitative nature of detention itself. ORR, for its part, has also struggled to care for children with serious mental health needs, especially those who also exhibit behavior problems: There are limited beds in Residential Treatment Centers, and these centers will not accept children who are aggressive or a flight risk. Only one staff secure facility also provides therapeutic care, and it has only 16 beds.[143] As a result, children with mental health issues might end up in a nontherapeutic facility. At a nontherapeutic staff secure facility in Yolo, California, in 2018, "81 percent of the immigrant children had been detained at the facility due to self-injurious behavior, behavioral problems, or mental health diagnoses. . . . Three of those children were relocated there because they threatened to commit, committed or engaged in 'serious, self-harming behavior.'"[144]

Many individuals with mental illness who have been in the United States for a significant length of time end up subject to mandatory detention because of past contacts with the criminal justice system. Agency guidance that cautioned against the use of detention for people with severe mental illness was rescinded by the Trump administration.[145] Even before Trump, however, the guidance cautioning against detaining people with mental illness made an exception for people subject to mandatory detention because of a criminal record.[146] Because of the use of the criminal justice system to deal with mental illness, many people who have mental illness also have a criminal record. As previously explained, even a very minor criminal record, including a single conviction for marijuana possession, will subject an immigrant to mandatory detention. Once it arrests immigrants, ICE tends to detain those with mental illness at certain facilities, ostensibly because they are better suited to providing mental health services.[147] In many cases, the facilities are located far from where the person lived before being arrested by ICE. This has the unfortunate effect of cutting off individuals with mental illness from visits from family and friends. It also has the effect of isolating them from free legal service providers, which tend to be clustered in major cities.

Immigrant detention facilities have been heavily criticized for their use of solitary confinement, particularly for detainees with mental illness. Solitary is alleged to be the "go-to" tool to deal with people experiencing a mental health crisis, and approximately 40% of detainees in solitary had a mental illness. ICE data reveals that solitary, including extended solitary, is routinely employed: Over a three year period, over 4,000 detainees were kept in solitary beyond the 15 days considered torture by the United Nations; 485 were kept in solitary for 75 days or more.[148] Whistleblowers and investigative journalists have reported on a variety of abuses, including solitary confinement, used to discipline detainees on a hunger strike, to punish detainees who refused to work for $1 a day, to segregate LGBTQ+ detainees allegedly for their safety, and to punish minor offenses such as consensual kissing.[149]

Getting Out of Detention

There are various ways to get out of detention. As noted above, IJs sometimes have the power to order someone released, and DHS usually retains the discretion to release someone if they choose to do so (even when the statute regulations might seem to indicate otherwise, as is the case with the mandatory detention provisions). MHPs can play an important role in helping a person secure release, whether on bond, parole, or otherwise. They can also help advocate for less-restrictive conditions of supervision.

Parole

If applying to DHS for parole (applicable to people considered "arriving" in the United States, including asylum seekers), the standard is whether there are "urgent humanitarian reasons" or a "significant public benefit" for a person to be in the United States. (They must also establish that they are not a security risk or a danger of absconding.)[150] The regulations specify that this might include people for whom "continued detention would not be appropriate" because of a serious medical condition, pregnant women, people who will be witnesses in legal proceedings, and minors who can be released to family members (including also-detained family members). A "serious medical condition" should, arguably, include a mental illness. According to the regulations, parole of these groups "would generally be justified only on a case-by-case basis[.]"[151]

For asylum seekers who have passed a credible fear interview, a 2009 memo provides further guidance, directing DHS officers to interview the asylum seeker within seven days of passing credible fear and to grant parole as long as the person's identity is sufficiently established, they pose neither a flight risk nor a danger to the community, and no additional factors weigh against their release.[152] Flight risk depends in part on family and community ties as well as prior immigration history. DHS officers are directed to consider whether bond or other conditions such as an alternative to detention program can alleviate such a risk.[153] Danger to the community can include evidence of past criminal activity or other activity that gives concern, "including due to serious mental illness," disciplinary infractions in custody, as well as any criminal or detention history "that shows that the alien has harmed or would likely harm himself or herself or others."[154]

Immigration Judge Bond

For those immigrants eligible for a bond hearing before an IJ, the IJ will be asked to determine whether the immigrant is a flight risk or a danger to the community.[155] The burden will be on the individual to prove that they are not a flight risk or danger, except that in some circumstances when detention has become unduly prolonged the burden might flip to the government. Any criminal history will be highly relevant to the danger calculus, as will any other past behavior indicative of potential dangerousness. Because the burden rests with the individual, and it can be difficult to prove lack of dangerousness, individuals are frequently denied bond due to criminal allegations even if they have never been convicted of a crime. For individuals with mental health issues or a history of substance use, the immigration judge might want to understand how their mental health issue or addiction contributed to their criminal history or to any other behavior that could conceivably cause a danger to the community. A mental health diagnosis can cut both ways in this situation: It can help explain a history of behavior, but it can also make the person seem unstable and dangerous to the IJ. For both individuals with mental health issues and those with addiction, the IJ will likely want to see a solid treatment plan in place before they will consider that the individual has met their burden of demonstrating that they are not dangerous and they deserve release.

Department of Homeland Security Discretion

When appealing to DHS's discretion to release or decline to detain an individual outside of the parole context, the standard applicable to bond hearings will be relevant: along with humanitarian considerations, DHS will be primarily interested in knowing if the individual presents a flight risk or a danger to the community. In aid of this, DHS has developed a risk assessment tool to help officers determine whether a particular immigrant presents either of these risks. The full tool is not available to the public, but redacted versions have been obtained via Freedom of Information Act. requests[156] The flight risk tool (or at least the 2013 version of it) focuses on family contacts, residency history, work authorization, legal representation, substance abuse history, school enrollment, property ownership, and "substantial assets." The dangerousness tool focuses on criminal history—both charges and convictions—as well as any disciplinary infractions in prison or detention. Prior DUIs or domestic violence are considered special public safety factors. There appears to be no consideration for the length of time that has passed since the relevant criminal contacts.[157] In 2018, ICE admitted to modifying its risk assessment software so that it would always recommend detention.[158] This practice led to it being sued.[159] Whatever the outcome of the lawsuit, it seems reasonable to predict that ICE will continue to use some form of risk assessment.

If DHS chooses to release someone, they have the option to set a bond and can also release them under various conditions, including participation in an alternative to detention program .

Alternatives to Detention

Programs that address alternatives to detention (ATDs) are designed to ensure that people make their court dates without the need for detention. They have proven extremely effective in securing the attendance of immigrants at their court hearings, at a fraction of the cost of detention. As of 2019, approximately 100,000 immigrants were under supervision by an ATD at any given time. The cost of an ATD is only $4.04 per day on average, and ADTs "have been shown to work with over 95% of individuals to ensure appearance for their final court hearings."[160] These conditions can include in-person office check-ins, telephonic reporting, unannounced home visits, ankle monitors, and even check-in via cell phone with facial recognition technology and GPS location data.[161] ICE officers determine which conditions should be required, but much of the actual supervising is done by a subcontractor, BI Incorporated, which is owned by Geo Group.[162] The only ATD program currently in use by DHS is called the Intensive Supervised Appearance Program.[163] The Family Case Management Program, which was targeted at asylum-seeking families, was ended by the Trump administration (despite a 99% success rate at ensuring compliance with IC dates).[164]

Post–Final Order Custody Review

People with a final order of removal undergo a postorder custody review process. After 90 days have passed, DHS does an initial custody review and might choose to release the immigrant if they can demonstrate that they are not a flight risk or a danger to the community. After six months have passed, DHS will determine whether there is a "significant likelihood" that the immigrant will be deported in the "reasonably foreseeable" future. If they believe that there is not (and assuming the person has been cooperative with DHS's efforts to get the necessary paperwork for their deportation), they will release them from detention unless there are special circumstances such as national security that caution against their release. If DHS believes there is a significant likelihood that the detained immigrant will be deported soon, they will continue to detain them, with periodic reviews every year.[165]

This regulatory scheme arose in response to a United States Supreme Court case holding that indefinite detention with no end in sight violates the Due Process Clause of the Constitution and finding detention for longer than six months to be presumptively unreasonable.[166] People who have been detained for longer than six months after their final order of removal can file a habeas corpus petition in federal court arguing that, despite DHS claims to the contrary, there is no significant likelihood that they will be deported in the reasonably foreseeable future and they should therefore be released. Anyone who DHS is forced to release after a final order of removal will likely be released under an order of supervision that will specify various conditions that they must comply with to avoid re-detention.

Reentry After Detention

Discharge planning is a crucial component of psychiatric treatment in in-patient settings and mental health treatment in correctional settings. The American Psychiatric Association's Psychiatric Services in Jails and Prisons[167] indicates that essential elements of correctional discharge planning include arranging follow-up appointments for inmates with serious mental illness, providing medications and arranging to have prescriptions renewed or reevaluated, and transferring medical records to the referral entity. The detention standards also require the provision of discharge planning to immigration detainees. It is unclear, however, how frequently or consistently this is happening in immigration detention facilities. A case from the US Court of Appeals for the Second Circuit affirmed that ICE, as part of its constitutional duty to provide medical care to those in its custody, is obligated to provide discharge planning for detainees' serious medical needs in order to avoid a lapse in care upon release. The serious medical need that ICE had neglected was mental health care: both plaintiffs had been released from ICE custody without their necessary psychiatric medications and without even a written record of what they were taking. For one of the immigrants involved in this case, the failure to provide him with medications upon release resulted in him becoming severely psychotic and requiring hospitalization.[168]

The provision of comprehensive reentry services to people detained in ICE custody is severely complicated by uncertainty surrounding release dates. When ICE decides to release a detainee, it is not uncommon for ICE to do so with little or no notice. Detainees might find out they are being released only when they are told to pack up their things for departure. Before that moment, they might have been expecting to spend many more months, or possibly years, in detention.[169] A release that happens because of a court victory might be just as sudden. The manner of release also tends to be chaotic: Family or counsel are supposed to be notified that an immigrant is being released, but this frequently does not happen. People detained in far-flung detention centers are not taken back to their homes but rather released at a bus station, sometimes in the middle of the night, and often without proper clothing.[170] If, instead of release, a person's detention ends in deportation, then they are even less likely to get reentry services. There does not appear to be any regular coordination of reentry services between DHS and receiving countries.[171]

Conclusion

MHPs working in ICs can expect to come into contact with patients who have been or who continue to be subject to the immigration detention regime. It is a regime notable for its massive size and the tremendous profits that are made from it, in addition to the complete absence of any meaningful oversight of the conditions in which immigrants are confined. The regime is propped up by laws that give almost complete discretion to ICE to detain an immigrant and that provide little or no protection against unnecessary or unjustified detentions. For those immigrants who are detained and who nevertheless choose to fight their cases, immigration detention can last months or years, and during that time they can expect to be held in an environment akin to that of a jail or prison (and that might, in fact, be a jail or prison) despite the civil nature of the proceedings for which they are detained. Unsurprisingly, detention has dramatic consequences for the ability of detained people to fight their immigration cases: It prevents immigrants from accessing legal resources and evidence they need to prove their cases, it hampers both the attorney–client and the MHP–patient/examinee relationship, and it negatively affects their mental health. MHPs interacting with detained populations should be aware of the possible stressors that their patients might be under due to their detention. MHPs can help detained patients deal with these stressor, and can also, at times, play an important role in helping to secure their release.

3

Forms of Removal Relief and Related Psycholegal Issues

Mental health professionals (MHPs) can play various roles within the immigration system, including as treatment providers, consultants, and forensic evaluators. When the MHP is acting as a forensic evaluator, the goal of the mental health assessment is to assist the adjudicator (e.g., the immigration judge [IJ] or the United States Immigration and Customs Service [USCIS] officer) in making decisions regarding immigration legal status (e.g., removal, detention). Therefore, these evaluations fall under the definition of "forensic mental health assessment" (FMHA).[1] Many legal issues in immigration courts (ICs) include clinical matters (e.g., whether the respondent has an intellectual disability that prevents them from participating in the immigration legal process or whether the mistreatment experienced in the respondent's country of origin has resulted in psychological symptoms of trauma and fear of return). These issues are typically referred to as "forensic mental health concepts," "psycholegal issues," or "functional legal capacities."[2] There is extensive literature with respect to functional capacities involved in certain legal issues in criminal court (e.g., competency, criminal responsibility). However, since FMHAs in ICs have only recently started to be defined, there is limited information with respect to the legal standards and related psycholegal capacities involved in these evaluations. It is essential for attorneys and MHPs to understand the legal issues and related forensic mental health concepts involved in IC proceedings. Although a FMHA might be only one part of the evidence provided to the court, psychological evidence can be crucial to help adjudicators in making removal or detention decisions. The first step, for evaluators, is to understand the legal issues that will be used to frame the evaluation.[3] The legal standards that form the basis for FMHAs in ICs are often complicated and difficult to access without legal training (i.e., the concept of a "a well-founded fear of persecution" is not defined in any statute or regulation but requires jurisdiction-specific research into case law), not to mention how they are constantly changing as new decisions come down or new administrations take power. MHPs do not need to be experts in immigration law. But MHPs conducting FMHAs do need to understand what the attorney they are working with is trying to show, or what the court that has requested their assistance is trying to understand. This chapter explains the legal issues underpinning the major forms of immigration relief and the related forensic mental health concepts/psycholegal issues.

We have chosen to broadly divide the major forms of relief based on the essential legal standard that needs to be established to win each form ("persecution," "victimization," "hardship," "good moral character," and "the balance of the equities"). It might be an imperfect division, and a form of relief might fit into multiple categories at once (e.g., to win relief under the Violence Against Women Act [VAWA], the respondent needs to establish both "victimization" and "good moral character"), but our hope is that it will be useful to illuminate what the immigrant will likely need to prove to qualify for the targeted relief and what will therefore be the likely focus of the FMHA.[4] This discussion is not meant to be a definitive guide to immigration law, but it can be a jumping-off point for conversations with the attorney or court about what they are seeking from a FMHA. It is recommended that the evaluation focus on functional legal capacities as opposed to the ultimate legal question and that the assumptions and definitions used in the evaluation are made clear.[5]

Persecution-Based Relief

Immigrants who fear that they will be harmed or persecuted in their native countries can request political asylum and two related forms of relief: withholding of removal, and relief under the Convention Against Torture (CAT). Asylum, withholding, and CAT all have different requirements, but one characteristic they have in common is that the immigrant applicant will be judged on the *credibility* of their story.

Credibility

When evaluating credibility, IJs are given broad discretion to consider the "totality of the circumstances" and all relevant factors, including "demeanor, candor, responsiveness, inherent plausibility of the account, consistency between the written and oral statements (regardless of when they were made, whether they were under oath, and considering the circumstances under which the statements were made), internal consistency of a statement, consistency of statements with other evidence of record (including the Department of State reports on country conditions), and any inaccuracies or falsehoods in such statements, without regard to whether an inconsistency, inaccuracy or falsehood goes to the heart of an applicant's claim."[6]

IJs are instructed to heavily value consistency when evaluating credibility. They might have a hard time accepting a psychological reason, such as memory difficulties, for inconsistencies in testimony or in a written statement.[7] Similarly, they might be reluctant to overlook inconsistencies in a respondent's testimony that are arguably explained by trauma,[8] either because they are unfamiliar with the effects of trauma on memory or, even if generally familiar with them, unsure how to relate this knowledge to the circumstances of a particular respondent before them.[9]

Credibility determinations based on demeanor are given special deference on appeal because frontline adjudicators are assumed to be better positioned than appellate courts to judge whether the testimony has the "ring of truth."[10] When assessing demeanor, adjudicators might be vulnerable to error if they overestimate their own innate ability to identify deception[11] or base their judgments on factors unsupported by scientific evidence.[12] This can lead to immigrants being found not credible based on, for example, a lack of oral fluidity or a failure to make eye contact.[13]

The "inherent plausibility" of the account is another area in which adjudicators might be vulnerable to error if they evaluate the plausibility of a story of victimization based on what they believe a rational person would do in a given situation[14] and without regard to the effects of trauma, especially cumulative trauma,[15] on an individual's decision-making.

Despite the potential for human error in making credibility determinations,[16] once an adverse credibility determination has been made, it can be extremely difficult to overcome.[17] For this reason, it essential that IJs and other decision makers have access to reliable psychological evidence to assist them in their work.

Asylum

Asylum is available for people who are unable or unwilling to return to their country of origin because of *persecution* or a *well-founded fear of persecution* based on a protected characteristic—race, religion, nationality, membership in a particular social group, or political opinion.[18] Unsurprisingly, a complex body of law has developed around the meaning of these two terms. The term "persecution" is not defined in the INA, but it is generally considered to include threats to a person's life or freedom and other forms of harm or mistreatment.[19] To constitute persecution, the mistreatment must be sufficiently "severe." The severity of the harm depends on the personal characteristics of the individual victim: an action that would cause great harm to one person might not cause the same degree of harm to another.[20] Psychological harm, by itself, can be sufficient to constitute persecution. "Psychological harm" could include the emotional stress caused by seeing members of one's community attacked based on their shared background, the damage to a deeply religious person of being forced to desecrate a religious object, or the emotional harm caused when a perpetrator attacks a victim's family member in order to punish the victim.[21] Because of the victim-dependent nature of the way harm is measured, an asylum claim might rely heavily on evidence of the applicant's psychological and emotional characteristics, including their trauma history.[22] To have a "well-founded fear of persecution," the applicant must show both that they have a subjective fear and that their fear is "objectively reasonable."[23] Having suffered persecution in the past will create a rebuttable presumption of a well-founded fear.[24] If someone has suffered persecution in the past, but does not have a well-founded fear of future persecution for whatever reason, they can still qualify for asylum if they have compelling reasons not to want to return due to the severity of the past persecution or if there is a reasonably probability that they will suffer other serious harm (even if that future harm does not meet the definition of persecution).[25]

Asylum can be sought affirmatively (by an immigrant not currently in removal proceedings) or defensively (by an immigrant in removal proceedings). An affirmative application is adjudicated by USCIS, while a defensive application is adjudicated by the IJ.

Individuals who are stopped at or near the border who wish to seek asylum must first pass a credible fear interview.[26] At this interview, an asylum officer interviews them to determine whether they have a "credible fear" of persecution—that is, whether there is a "significant possibility" that they could establish eligibility for asylum. Asylum officers are instructed to assess both the legal claim and the "credibility" of the applicant.[27] As with IJ decisions, credibility is determined based on factors including the demeanor, candor, or responsiveness of the applicant, the inherent plausibility of the account, and any inconsistencies between the applicant's written and oral statements.[28] Those who pass the credible fear interview are placed in removal proceedings, at which time they will be applying for asylum defensively in front of an IJ (and their credibility and the legal merits of their case will be assessed again).[29] Immigrants could not be detained during these proceedings. Those who fail the credible fear interview are denied the opportunity to apply for asylum and will be subjected to expedited removal.[30]

Asylum is barred by certain criminal convictions, including conviction of a "particularly serious" crime. Many crimes are per se particularly serious, but others will be determined on a case-by-case basis based on the nature of the conviction, the circumstances and underlying facts of the conviction, the type of sentence imposed, and whether the type and circumstances of the crime indicate that the individual will be a danger to the community.[31] Depending on which circuit the particular IC is located in,[32] psychological evidence might come into play in determining whether the individual's crime was particularly serious. For example, despite Board of Immigration Appeals (BIA) cases holding that an IJ cannot consider an applicant's mental health condition at the time of the crime because it does not diminish the "gravity" of the crime, mental health condition can be considered in cases in the Ninth Circuit Court of Appeals.[33]

Immigrants have one year to apply for asylum from their time of arrival in the United States, unless they can show "changed" or "extraordinary circumstances" that would allow them a waiver.[34] In some of these situations, MHPs can be helpful in providing psychological reasons that might explain the delay, such as symptoms of avoidance that are part of trauma-related clinical presentations.[35] Asylum is a discretionary form of relief, which means that, even if an immigrant meets the eligibility criteria, they might need to contextualize or explain any negative factors that could lead the adjudicator to deny their application in discretion.[36] MHPs can also be helpful in this regard.

Withholding of Removal

Withholding of removal requires that the individual demonstrate that their life or freedom would be threatened on account of race, religion, nationality, membership in a particular social group, or political opinion if forced to return to their country of origin.[37] It is similar to asylum, except that the likelihood of harm must be greater—51% (or "more likely than not") as opposed to 10% in asylum,[38] and the severity of the harm must be greater as well: some harms that will constitute persecution for asylum might not be sufficient for withholding.[39] As with asylum, proof that the individual has suffered past persecution will create a rebuttable presumption that their life or freedom would be threatened in the future.[40] Like asylum, withholding of removal is barred by conviction of a particularly serious crime, though the list of crimes that automatically qualify is slightly smaller. Withholding of removal is purely a defensive application, which means it can be granted only in removal proceedings. Removal will be ordered and "withheld," but only to a specified country. Someone who has been granted withholding with regard to one country could still be deported to another country. Individuals granted withholding do not have a path to citizenship, and if they ever leave the United States, their removal order will be considered "executed" and they will not be allowed to return. Unlike asylum, withholding is not a discretionary form of relief. An IJ must grant it if the individual has established that they are eligible.

Convention Against Torture

The Convention Against Torture and Other Cruel, Inhuman, or Degrading Treatment or Punishment, to which the United States is a signatory, prohibits the return of an individual to a place where they are likely to be tortured.[41] A major difference between CAT and asylum/withholding is that the individual, to win CAT relief, does not need to prove that they will be tortured "on account of" one of the five protected grounds (race, religion, etc.). As with withholding, to prevail on a CAT application the individual must prove that it is more likely than not that they would be tortured if forced to return to their country of origin.[42] This is a much higher probability of harm than is required for asylum.

"Torture" for CAT relief is defined in part as "any act by which severe pain or suffering, whether physical or mental, is intentionally inflicted on a person."[43] The regulations specify, rather circularly, that "[t]orture is an extreme form of cruel and inhuman treatment and does not include lesser forms of cruel, inhuman or degrading treatment or punishment that do not amount to torture."[44] The regulations specifically limit the types of mental suffering that can constitute torture:

> [M]ental pain or suffering must be prolonged mental harm caused by or resulting from: (i) The intentional infliction or threatened infliction of severe physical pain or suffering; (ii) The administration or application, or threatened administration or application, of mind altering substances or other procedures calculated to disrupt profoundly the senses or the personality; (iii) The threat of imminent death; or (iv) The threat that another person will imminently be subjected to death, severe physical pain or suffering, or the administration or application of mind altering substances or other procedures calculated to disrupt profoundly the sense or personality.[45]

Acts that have been found to cause mental pain and suffering sufficient to rise to the level of torture include the psychological harm that would be suffered by a parent if their child were subject to harm (e.g., female genital mutilation).[46] The role of a FMHA cannot be overstated here, as it can be essential to establish the severity of the harm that the applicant would suffer.

A FMHA can also be a crucial part of a CAT application when the individual is arguing that they will be tortured as a result of their mental illness. A FMHA can help establish that a mentally ill individual, if untreated (as many will be in countries where mental health care is not available to all), will struggle to conform their behavior to acceptable community standards, making them a target. This can be a CAT claim (and possibly an asylum/withholding claim as well) to countries with widespread negative views of mental illness and a tendency to deal with people with mental illness via the criminal legal system. The treatment of people with mental illness in the jails or prisons of some countries has been found to rise to the level of torture. But the immigrant must prove that they are more likely than not to end up incarcerated due to behavior associated with their mental illness.[47] A country expert can speak to the treatment of people exhibiting symptoms of mental illness, but a FMHA will almost certainly be necessary to establish that the immigrant in question is more likely than not to exhibit such behavior if unable to access treatment.

A CAT application might also involve consideration of the circumstances surrounding a criminal conviction. There are two forms of CAT relief available: withholding and deferral of removal. CAT withholding is not available to everyone: the same bars that apply to withholding of removal apply to CAT withholding, including having been convicted of a particularly serious crime.[48] If someone is not eligible for CAT withholding, CAT deferral is available to them as a backstop.[49] It is a less powerful form of relief, in that it is easier for the government to subsequently revoke it.[50] As with withholding, CAT relief does not prevent an order of removal from being entered. The individual is ordered removed, but that order is withheld or, in the case of CAT deferral, deferred with respect to a particular country.

Immigrants applying for CAT relief are highly likely to be detained. Because many criminal convictions are considered "aggravated felonies" or "particularly serious" crimes under immigration law,[51] CAT deferral will be the only form of relief available to many people in immigration court. Because of the draconian mandatory detention requirements for people with criminal convictions,[52] individuals applying for CAT relief are also much more likely to be held in detention during their removal proceedings. Given how easy it is for mentally ill people to run afoul of the criminal legal system, and considering how, in the United States, prisons and jails are the largest providers of mental health care,[53] a significant number of immigrants with mental illness will find themselves detained and applying for CAT deferral.

Psycholegal Issues Involved in Persecution-Based Relief

Given the high number of individuals seeking refugee status in the United States, evaluations for persecution-based relief are the most common type of FMHA conducted in ICs.[54] The main psycholegal issue involved in these evaluations is "well-founded fear of persecution." As a result, the primary role of a FMHA in this context is to provide psychological evidence of the impact of persecution (e.g., psychological abuse, torture, rape). Psychological evidence of trauma can aid the adjudicator in making decisions about whether it is reasonable to believe that, given the psychological impact of prior traumatic experiences, the asylum seeker would be fearful to re-experience the trauma. It is important to note that, although the evaluator can comment on subjective fear of re-experiencing harm if returned to the native country, the veracity of the event that resulted in the fear is the purview of the adjudicator.[55] In addition, whether the traumatic experience meets the definition of "persecution" or "torture" is also the purview of the legal decision maker. The documented presence of a psychiatric diagnosis, such as posttraumatic stress disorder (PTSD), can strengthen the argument. However, a diagnosis is not needed by law; documentation of trauma-related symptoms and functional impairment might still provide significant support for the claim.

Despite the high frequency with which psychological evaluations are submitted as part of persecution-based relief claims, little is known about how adjudicators use this information or to what extent psychological evidence affects their decisions. However, one study has found that 89% of asylum or withholding claims that included a forensic evaluation from Physicians for Human Rights were granted, compared to the national average of 37.5%, suggesting that FMHAs might contribute to better outcomes in asylum claims.[56] There is also limited information about the current practices employed by MHPs who conduct these evaluations. The Istanbul Protocol provided international guidelines for the evaluation of survivors of human rights abuses.[57] A recent study that compared the efficacy of 20 in-person versus 10 telephonic psychiatric evaluations for asylum seekers created a rubric to assess the quality of the affidavits based off the standards included in the Istanbul Protocol and found that most evaluations included a history of torture or abuse, current psychiatric complaints, diagnoses, and a consideration of malingering.[58] Survey research is needed to have a better understanding of common practices.

Asylum officers are instructed to assess both the legal claim and the credibility of the applicant or whether the fear is "genuine." As a result, the second relevant legal issue is "credibility." Credibility is considered the ultimate legal issue, and a determination of credibility is beyond the scope of the FMHA.[59] However, the FMHA can include information to aid the adjudicator in making credibility decisions. This includes education with respect to how trauma and other psychological conditions can impact memory, how inconsistencies in the account of the traumatic experiences do not necessarily mean that the respondent is not being genuine, and assessing malingering of PTSD symptoms. In addition, one of the factors that the adjudicator considers to make decisions about credibility is the "inherent plausibility" of the account. Psychological evidence of objective fear can also be helpful in aiding the adjudicator in deciding about the inherent plausibility of the account.

Finally, depending on the jurisdiction, clinical information might be helpful in deciding whether the crime that could potentially make the respondent ineligible for asylum is "particularly serious." In these cases, the goal of the FMHA is to provide information as to whether the crime committed was related to symptoms of mental illness. This evaluation requires collecting information about the crime and the circumstances surrounding the crime.

Victimization-Based Relief

Victimization-based relief includes forms of relief or benefits that are based on evidence that the noncitizen has been the victim of certain types of crimes, human trafficking, domestic violence, child abuse, or elder abuse.

U Visa: Victims of Crime

A U visa is a special visa available for crime victims who cooperate with law enforcement.[60] Labeling it a "visa" is slightly misleading because it is frequently requested by people who are already in the country. A U visa will allow an immigrant to enter (or remain lawfully in) the United States for a period of time and, crucially, provides an opportunity to apply for a green card at the end of their time in U status. To be eligible for a U visa, an immigrant must demonstrate that they suffered substantial physical or mental abuse as a result of being the victim of certain serious crimes.[61] "Physical" or "mental abuse" is defined as injury or harm to the victim's physical person or harm to or impairment of the emotional or psychological soundness of the victim.[62] Whether the abuse is substantial depends on a number of factors, including but not limited to:

> The nature of the injury inflicted or suffered; the severity of the perpetrator's conduct; the severity of the harm suffered; the duration of the infliction of the harm; and the extent to which there is permanent or serious harm to the appearance, health, or physical or mental soundness of the victim, including aggravation of pre-existing conditions.[63]

A series of acts might add up to substantial physical or mental abuse even if no single act alone rises to that level.[64] Someone who might not technically be considered the victim under the criminal law, such as a bystander to the crime, can still qualify as long as they suffered direct and proximate harm as a result of the crime.[65] A family member of the crime victim can also qualify as an "indirect victim" in some circumstances, including if the victim was a minor.[66]

Establishing that the abuse suffered was "substantial" is likely to be the most challenging part of a U visa application, especially for a victim who might not have suffered lasting physical harm. Adjudicators can base a decision on their own subjective judgment as to how they imagine a given event would or should affect an individual. This can lead to them underestimating the harm actually suffered by the applicant or failing to grasp the link between the crime and the harm. For example, one U visa applicant was denied for failure to show "substantial" harm when he failed to explicitly tie his PTSD symptoms to the crime. The USCIS adjudicator found that the applicant, who hid in the bathroom while his roommates experienced a home invasion robbery, did not suffer a sufficiently traumatic experience to qualify.[67] In another example, a U visa applicant who was battered by her spouse was denied for failure to establish "substantial" harm:

Though the petitioner describes her nose bleeding from being slapped by the suspect, she does not probatively discuss any permanent or serious harm the incident caused to her appearance, health, or physical or mental soundness. While we do not minimize what the petitioner experienced as a result of being a victim of domestic battery, the overall evidence does not establish that she has suffered resultant substantial physical or mental abuse.[68]

A mental health professional can help in situations like these by providing an objective and clinical assessment of the harm suffered by the immigrant victim.

Violence Against Women Act

Relief under the Violence Against Women Act can take two forms: a self-petition filed with USCIS, or a cancellation of removal application filed in IC. The self-petition is a way for an immigrant who would be eligible for a green card through an abusive family member (spouse, child, or parent) to petition for themselves rather than rely on their abuser to petition for them. VAWA cancellation is a way for that same person to defend themselves against their removal in IC. In either event, the end result is a green card without needing to involve the abusive party. If the abusive party is a spouse, the applicant will have to prove that the marriage was entered into in good faith and not for the purpose of securing an immigration benefit.

To prevail in a VAWA application, the immigrant has to show that they were battered or subject to extreme cruelty by their spouse, child, or parent (this latter if the applicant is a child under 21).[69] "Extreme cruelty" as defined includes but is not limited to:

> [B]eing the victim of any act or threatened act of violence, including any forceful detention, which results or threatens to result in physical or mental injury. Psychological or sexual abuse or exploitation, including rape, molestation, incest (if the victim is a minor), or forced prostitution shall be considered acts of violence. Other abusive actions may also be acts of violence under certain circumstances, including acts that, in and of them-

selves, may not initially appear violent but that are a part of an overall pattern of violence.[70]

VAWA applicants also have to affirmatively show that they have "good moral character," except that children under 14 will be presumed to have good moral character.[71] VAWA applicants who normally would not be able to show good moral character because of certain criminal convictions or other related acts (i.e., prostitution, being a "habitual drunkard") can still show good moral character if they can demonstrate that their crime or act was connected to the abuse.[72] This is based on the understanding that domestic violence victims can be coerced into criminal activity or that extenuating circumstances might exist to explain their actions. The connection between the act and the abuse might not be immediately intuitive for the immigration decision maker (or for the immigration attorney). A mental health evaluation can help establish, for example, how an abuse victim might not have had a gun to her head but would still have been under the coercive control of her abuser[73] or how the abuse that the individual suffered would have contributed to his commission of a crime.[74]

T Visa: Victims of Trafficking

A T visa is available to people who have been trafficked into or within the United States. Like the U visa, it is often requested by people who are already in the United States and allows recipients to eventually gain lawful permanent status. To qualify for a T visa, the immigrant must show that they were subject to a "severe" form of trafficking, which includes both labor trafficking (involuntary servitude, debt bondage, etc.) and sex trafficking. For both, the immigrant must have been induced to participate in sex work or other labor by "force, fraud, or coercion" (except that this is not necessary for sex-trafficking victims under the age of 18).

Coercion, in particular, might be difficult to establish.[75] Different people experience coercion differently, and what might be coercive to one person might not be to another. It is essential that the adjudicator understand, from the point of view of the immigrant, how the trafficker's actions affected them. Adjudicators are at risk of making the wrong decision if they simply place themselves in the position of the immigrant and try to imagine how they would have felt in a similar situation. They could wonder, for example, if a victim who did not take every possible opportunity to flee was truly coerced. Similarly, fraud might be difficult to prove if the adjudicator has a hard time understanding how the immigrant could have believed the lies of the trafficker. A FMHA can help the adjudicator understand the immigrant's educational background, cognitive abilities, life experiences, personal history, cultural context, core beliefs, personality traits, history of trauma, and any other significant factors or vulnerabilities that might have made them more or less susceptible to coercion.

The T visa applicant must also show that they are present in the United States on account of trafficking. They do not need to necessarily show that they were brought to the United States for sex work or forced labor, but they do need to show that their continued presence in the United States is "on account of" the trafficking they suffered or are suffering.[76] For example, an applicant who escaped from trafficking several years earlier might have been too afraid to leave the United States because her traffickers continued to threaten her if she returned to her home country, or she might have remained in the United States to receive services to recover from her victimization. This "on account of" requirement can also be difficult to establish, as it often depends on psychological factors.

A T visa applicant must normally be willing to assist law enforcement in the investigation and prosecution of their traffickers, but there is an exception for a victim who, "due to physical or psychological trauma, is unable to cooperate with a reasonable request for assistance."[77] T visa applicants will also need to show that they would suffer "extreme hardship involving usual and severe harm" if deported.[78]

The T visa has extremely generous waivers to waive almost any ground of inadmissibility, including any prior criminal conviction so long as it was "caused by or incident to the trafficking" and it is in the national interest to grant the waiver.[79] Much as with the VAWA waiver, which requires that a crime or act be "connected to" the abuse, a FMHA can help establish that the ground of inadmissibility was "caused by or incident to" the individual being trafficked.

Psycholegal Issues Involved in Victimization-based Relief

The relevant forensic mental health constructs involved in victimization-based relief are similar to those that are part of personal injury evaluations; that is to say, the assessment of the psychological harm that results from a traumatic event (e.g., being a crime victim for U visa, suffering human trafficking for T visa, or experiencing family violence for VAWA). Whether the level of psychological harm is considered to be "substantial," the form of trafficking considered to be "severe," or the form of abuse considered to be "extreme cruelty," are all questions to be answered by the adjudicator.[80] The literature on personal injury evaluations has broken down the forensic concepts into three different issues that victimization-relief evaluations should also cover:

(a) What are the mental health disorders or symptoms that are present?
(b) What are the functional abilities affected by the trauma?
(c) What is the nature and strength of the connection between the traumatic experience and the psychological harm?[81]

With respect to the first question, PTSD is the most common diagnosis seen in personal injury evaluations. However, the law does not require any specific disorder in the definition of harm for any of the victimization-based applications. In addition, many individuals who are exposed to trauma do not meet the full criteria for PTSD but can still experience significant functional impairment.[82] As a result, a description of symptoms and their impact on functional abilities since the time of the trauma might also be relevant. The main issue is not current functioning but instead how the individual has changed since the traumatic event.[83]

The most complicated aspect of these evaluations relates to the third question, which involves establishing a connection between the harm and the psychological symptoms. There are no tests that are specifically designed or validated to establish this link. This is particularly complicated when considering the high rates of trauma experienced by immigrants. Establishing a post hoc connection between the victimization-based traumatic event and the clinical symptoms or impairment can be complicated. For example, whether the current symptoms are due to the victimization at the base of the claim versus the trauma and persecution experienced in the respondent's native country or migration or acculturation stress can be difficult to elucidate.[84] The case below exemplifies this issue:

> A 25 year-old Mexican female is applying to a U-Visa based on reports that she was sexually abused by her roommate, who is a citizen of the U.S. Specifically, she reported waking up in the middle of the night after she felt someone touching her breasts and vagina. The U.S. citizen was naked and standing next to her bed. After being evaluated, she reported an extensive history of sexual abuse by four different men in Mexico. She reported symptoms of anxiety, depression, and hypervigilance dating back to her childhood and adolescence. These symptoms appeared to have been exacerbated by separation from her family and the recent incident of sexual abuse.

In victimization-based evaluations, evaluators can provide information about the potential contribution of different traumatic experiences and their relative importance to the current presentation.[85] In addition, information should be provided about any possible preexisting conditions that might have been exacerbated by the victimization-based incident and might have increased the degree of harm. For example, the evaluator can provide information about any functional impairment prior to migration, after migration, and between migration and the victimization event. Ultimately, whether the event central to the victimization claim is the legal cause is the purview of the adjudicator.[86]

Hardship-Based Relief

Several forms for relief require that the applicant establish "hardship" to themselves or others if they were deported or denied entry to the country.

Non-LPR Cancellation of Removal

Cancellation of removal for non–Lawful Permanent Residents (LPRs), sometimes called the "ten-year green card," is a way for a person who does not have lawful status, but who has been in the United States for more than ten years, to apply to stay. The most important thing that an applicant needs to demonstrate to win this relief is that a US citizen or LPR spouse, child, or parent would suffer "exceptional and extremely unusual" hardship.[87] This requirement is extremely difficult to meet, and the "ordinary" hardship of losing a parent or being separated from a loved one is explicitly not sufficient.[88] A mental health professional's report can be crucial in establishing the requisite hardship. The report can help show why this particular family member, due to their characteristics and past experiences, is especially vulnerable to the loss of their loved one such that the hardship to them is sufficiently extreme to meet the standard. For example, the immigrant could argue that their child, who has suffered trauma in the past, will suffer hardship far beyond the ordinary if they lose their parent to whom they are extraordinarily bonded.

To qualify for non-LPR cancellation, the applicant must also show that they were a person of "good moral character" during the relevant period.

Extreme Hardship Waivers (212(h); 212(i)) and Unlawful Presence

Immigration law provides for several "waivers," or pardons, that allow someone who is otherwise ineligible for a form of relief to still qualify if they can show that a US citizen or LPR-qualifying relative[89] would suffer "extreme" hardship if they were deported. There are waivers available to pardon certain criminal convictions,[90] or previous misrepresentations on immigration forms,[91] or to overcome immigration peccadillos such as unlawful presence.[92] These waivers depend on the presence of a qualifying relative, but unlike non-LPR cancellation, they require "only" extreme hardship to that relative.

Extreme hardship, while easier to show than "exceptional and extremely unusual" hardship, can still be difficult to prove. The "common consequences" of losing a relative to deportation or having to accompany a deported relative to a new country—family separation, economic detriment, difficulty of adjusting to a new life, lessened education or career opportunities, inferior medical care—will not be sufficient.[93] Psychological evidence can be highly relevant to establishing extreme hardship. Agency guidance provides that, even though economic detriment on its own is not enough, there might be extreme hardship if "the qualifying relative [will] suffer significant emotional and psychological impacts from being the sole caregiver of the child(ren) that exceed the common consequences of being left as a sole parent" or if they will suffer "additional emotional, psychological and/or economic stress" from being unable to provide a safe stable home for children.[94] Relatedly, while harm to the immigrant applicant is not a relevant consideration, the qualifying relative "may suffer . . . psychological trauma due to the potential for harm to the applicant in the country of relocation."[95] Psychological evidence is especially relevant when children are involved because a child cannot be a "qualifying relative" for many waivers, but hardship to a child might still be relevant to the extent that it causes the qualifying relative emotional distress from seeing the child suffer.[96]

A FMHA can be extremely useful because it can help the immigration judge understand how, for example, someone who is not a financial provider still provides important emotional support to their spouse or how the deportation of a beloved family member might cause extreme mental distress (possibly even manifesting in physical symptoms) in the person left behind. Importantly, the evaluation will likely be of the qualifying relative, since it is their distress, not the distress of the immigrant applicant, that is relevant to the analysis.

Violence Against Women Act Fraud Waiver

A VAWA applicant applying for a waiver of any fraud or misrepresentation they engage in during the immigration process must show extreme hardship if they are denied the waiver. Unlike the typical fraud waiver, however, the hardship can be to themselves and need not be to a relative.[97]

T Visa: Victims of Trafficking

In addition to having to show that they were subject to coercion when they were trafficked, a T visa applicant must also show that they would suffer "extreme hardship involving unusual and severe harm" if they were removed from the United States.[98] This hardship requirement is a higher standard than is needed for extreme hardship waivers described above (though probably lower than the "exceptional and extremely unusual" hardship needed for non-LPR cancellation) and cannot be based solely on loss of social or economic opportunities.[99] Relevant factors include both "traditional extreme hardship factors" and psychological factors such as the maturity of the victim, "physical or psychological issues" needing medical or psychological care not reasonably available in the foreign country, the "nature and extent of the physical and psychological consequences of having been a victim of a severe form of trafficking in persons," and the impact of loss of access to the US court system for redress of the harm suffered.[100] T visa recipients who have had the status for several years can apply for a green card. They will have to show the same "extreme hardship involving unusual and severe harm" if denied the green card. They will also have to show good moral character.[101]

Special Immigrant Juvenile Status

Special Immigrant Juvenile Status (SIJS) is a special path to a green card for certain young people. An applicant for SIJS has to show that they were abused, abandoned, or neglected by one or both parents and that it is not in their best interest to be returned to their country of origin.[102] The analysis of the young person's best interest is likely to involve a hardship component (i.e., the hardship they would suffer if they were not allowed to stay in the United States). SIJS is unusual for immigration relief in that it is a state juvenile court judge, not a federal official, who decides whether the young person was abused, abandoned, or neglected and who decides what their best interests would entail. If the state court makes the necessary findings, then—and only then—can the young person apply to the federal government for SIJS.

At the federal level, the young person needs to establish that they are otherwise eligible for a green card (though certain grounds of inadmissibility are waived).[103] As discussed below, there is also a special inadmissibility waiver available for SIJS applicants.[104]

An evaluation by a mental health professional might be useful at the state or federal level or both. At the state level, the FMHA can help to establish that the young person was abused, abandoned, or neglected or that it is not in their best interest to be deported. At the federal level, a

FMHA might be useful to help convince the USCIS adjudicator (or IJ if the young person is applying defensively in IC) to grant the relief.

Other Hardship-Related Relief: Humanitarian Purposes/Family Unity/Public Interest

Other forms of relief, and associated waivers, might have a hardship component. For example, to win an inadmissibility waiver for refugees,[105] or to transition from U nonimmigrant status to Lawful Permanent Resident,[106] or to waive certain grounds of inadmissibility when applying for SIJS,[107] the immigrant needs to show that the grant of relief is justified for humanitarian purposes, or to ensure family unity, or is otherwise in the public interest.[108] The "humanitarian purposes" prong is likely to involve hardship: if a person suffered hardship in the past or would suffer hardship if deported, allowing them to stay would serve a humanitarian purpose. Similarly, it might be in the "public interest" to keep a family from falling into poverty without their main source of income or to keep children from experiencing the negative outcomes (depression, anxiety, slipping grades, etc.) that frequently accompany a parent's deportation.

Psycholegal Issues Involved in Hardship-Based Relief

The concept of hardship is likely one of the most vague within immigration law, especially with respect to psychological parameters.[109] This results in adjudicators having wide discretion about hardship decisions. Unlike other types of FMHA in ICs, hardship evaluations might require the evaluation of the US citizen or Lawful Permanent Resident who would be impacted by the removal of the respondent and not necessarily the respondent facing deportation. The relevant forensic mental health constructs and the focus of the evaluation would depend on the specific family circumstances: Who is the noncitizen facing deportation (e.g., parent, spouse or child)? and Who are the affected US citizens or Lawful Permanent Residents? A common scenario is a situation in which the noncitizen facing deportation has children who have been born in the United States. About five million children who live in the United States have one or more noncitizen immigrant parents; almost 80% of those children are US citizens.[110] In these cases, the psychological evaluation would serve to document the psychological impact of potential parental separation on the US citizen children. After consultation with the attorney, the MHP could explore the potential impact of the children's relocation in the event that the parent is deported and decides to relocate the family (e.g., acculturation difficulties, language and education barriers, potential financial hardship and poverty, exposure to violence, or lack of appropriate mental health or medical treatment). In addition to assessing the effect of parental separation on children, hardship-based evaluations might also include the impact of separation on the spouse. Separation from a spouse can have deleterious psychological effects, particularly if the US citizen or LPR spouse suffers from a mental illness or any disability that might be exacerbated by the separation and for which no appropriate treatment is available if the family were to relocate.[111]

The psychological impact of separation on immigrant families has received more attention in recent years, particularly as the Trump administration enacted more restrictive immigration policies, such as 2017's zero tolerance policy, which resulted in the separation of children from their immigrant parents. However, even before these policies, many children born in the United States have been separated from their immigrant parents by the US immigration system. The Longitudinal Student Adaptation study of 2002 found that 85% of 385 adolescent children of Chinese, Central American, Dominican, Haitian, and Mexican origin reported having been separated from at least one parent during the migration process.[112]

A hardship-based FMHA typically requires interviewing several family members, and it might also require observing family interactions. The following have been identified as important components of these evaluations: assessment of the child's attachment to the noncitizen parent, the child's acculturation to US society, the child's cultural competency in the noncitizen parent's native country, the child's educational competency in the parent's native country's educational system, the child's current psychiatric condition, impact on psychiatric condition if the child were to leave with the parent, and the impact on psychiatric condition if the child stayed in the United States but the parent leaves to the native country.[113]

Although impact on the psychological well-being (e.g., psychological hardship) of the US citizen or LPR family member is the most obvious area in which psychological evidence can be of help, there are other types of hardships for which evidence-based psychological knowledge can aid the adjudicator, such as the impact of financial or educational hardship.[114] A scale developed by Hake and Banks in 2005 lists six major areas of hardship to be explored and that are helpful for the evaluator to consider: (1) medical hardships, (2) psychological hardships, (2) career and educational disruptions, (3) very serious financial hardships, (4) sociocultural hardships, (5) sociocultural hardships upon relocation, and (6) significant risk of physical harm upon relocation due to political or sectarian violence.[115]

It is important to mention that not all separations would necessarily have severe deleterious effects on the family members who stay. For example, in a family with children who have formed strong attachments with other caretakers (e.g., grandparent, aunt, family friend), these attachments can mitigate the psychological harm caused by the separation from one of the parents. Hardship evaluations require a careful analysis of the different relationships, attachments, and resources available to the family. The MHP should be careful not to opine on whether these psychological effects are considered (for example) "extreme" hardship, as this is a legal issue and the purview of the legal decision maker.

Good Moral Character–Based Relief

For some forms of relief, there is a requirement that the applicant show "good moral character" for a defined period of time.

Non-LPR Cancellation, Voluntary Departure, and Naturalization

Good moral character is a requirement for non-LPR cancellation[116] (which also requires a heightened level of hardship, as explained above), certain types of voluntary departure[117] (which allows someone to leave the country without incurring a deportation order), and naturalization[118] (becoming a US citizen).

A showing of good moral character is barred by certain criminal convictions, as well as by a long list of behaviors that include gambling, adultery, engaging in prostitution, being a "habitual drunkard," violating any law relating to controlled substances (except simple possession of a small amount of marijuana), and failure to support dependents. Commission of any "unlawful acts" that adversely reflect on the applicant's character will also bar a finding of good moral character.[119] The individual is allowed to plead "extenuating circumstances" for certain of these bars to showing good moral character—namely, commission of unlawful acts, adultery, and failure to support dependents.[120]

In the absence of the above explicit barriers to showing good moral character, the adjudicator's good moral character determination might resemble the balancing of the equities calculus described below. The adjudicator will simply balance the good with the bad and determine where they believe the applicant falls on the spectrum. Any negative factors might need to be contextualized, explained, or counterbalanced. A FMHA can be useful for this.

Psycholegal Issues Involved in Good Moral Character Relief

The concept of good moral character (beyond the statutory bars) has not been well defined in immigration law[121] and therefore is open to significant subjectivity and interpretation, both by the MHP and the legal decision maker. Given the close relationship in immigration law between good moral character and certain crimes or behaviors, the goal of the FMHA in these evaluations is to contextualize those behaviors. There is no research on current practices employed by MHPs who conduct good moral character evaluations; neither are there any guidelines for practice. However, the psycholegal issue involved is similar to assessment of culpability or mitigation evaluations conducted in criminal court for sentencing purposes.[122] This process primarily involves reviewing any situational factors that might have contributed to the commission of those crimes or negative behaviors—in other words, providing information about how and why the behavior took place.[123] These evaluations typically cover the following factors as potential contributors or explanations for negative behaviors: adverse childhood experiences (including history of abuse or neglect), developmental immaturity, peer pressure, coercion, trauma-related reactions, limited or lack of formal education, symptoms of neurodevelopmental, neurocognitive, or any other types of psychiatric disorders, history of brain injury, intoxication, or situational stressors (e.g., homelessness, financial stressors). The goal of the evaluation is to provide a clinical formulation that contextualizes the negative behavior to illustrate that the criminal behavior was more the result of external factors and less of free will. This information can aid the decision maker in understanding any factors that might have undermined the immigrant's controls when the crimes were committed.[124]

In addition to understanding the offense, understanding the offender[125] is also important in good moral character evaluations. This involves a description of the immigrant's life. This can point to mitigating factors, such as a history of suffering due to extreme traumatic experiences, family losses, or any other adversities, as well as to underlying positive personality characteristics such as generosity or empathy. For this purpose, it is useful to consider involvement with religious organizations, history of employment, relationships with family, social or community networks, and volunteer work.[126] Like all FMHAs, good moral character evaluations can significantly benefit from third-party interviews and collateral information. In addition, psychological testing can be helpful to identify positive personality characteristics and rule out what are considered negative ones (e.g., antisocial personality, narcissism). It is important to remember that the role of the MHP in these evaluations is to provide explanatory formulations and to avoid moral statements about whether any of the mitigating factors should meet the legal standard.[127]

Equities-Based Relief

Some forms of relief that do not require persecution, victimization, hardship, or good moral character still rely ultimately on a discretionary balancing of the equities. In addition, most forms of relief except CAT and withholding have a second discretionary step when the adjudicator decides whether the immigrant should be granted the relief as an exercise of administrative grace.

Adjudicators exercising discretion are instructed to balance the "negative factors evidencing an alien's undesirability as a permanent resident" with the "social and humane considerations present on his or her behalf to determine whether relief appears in the best interest of this country."[128] There are few limits to what an adjudicator can consider when exercising their discretion to grant or deny relief. BIA and USCIS guidance provides a nonexhaustive list of appropriate factors for consideration, including history of employment, "public safety" or national security concerns, "moral depravity or criminal tendencies" as reflected by a criminal record, and any other "indicators of an applicant or beneficiary's character."[129] These negative factors should be balanced with positive factors including family ties and closeness of family relationships, history of employment and paying taxes, "respect for law and order, good character, and intent to hold family responsibilities," and the immigrant's "value and service to the community." Hardship to the immigrant or the immigrant's family if the relief is denied can also be considered.[130]

Substance use could be used as a negative discretionary factor, which might be surprising to those accustomed to viewing addiction as a disease, but the concept of substance use as a character flaw is reflected in the Immigration and Nationality Act itself[131] and is deeply integrated into the practice of immigration law.[132] Immigration adjudicators might receive little or no training on substance use disorders, and there is no case law to guide them as to whether substance use should factor into discretionary decisions as a negative factor or as mitigating one. As a result, adjudicators could default to their own understanding of addiction when deciding whether to grant discretionary relief.[133] An adjudicator could view substance use as indicative of "criminal tendencies," or of poor character, or of a public safety concern.

Similarly, a history of mental illness–related or trauma-related contact with law enforcement could be seen as indicative of "criminal tendencies" or of a public safety concern. A U visa recipient trying to get a permanent green card will need to show that their continued presence in the United States is "justified on humanitarian grounds, to ensure family unity, or is in the public interest"[134] and that any "adverse factors" are balanced by positive equities.[135] In practice, this can require an applicant with any record of law enforcement involvement to affirmatively prove they do not pose a danger to the public safety.[136] A mental health evaluation can be relevant to help contextualize and explain the circumstances that led to the law enforcement contact and might also be useful to help the adjudicator predict (as best as anyone is able to tell the future) whether the person can be expected to have similar problems in the future. A balancing of the equities is also considered in cancellation of removal, adjustment of status, Temporary Protected Status (TPS), and Deferred Action for Childhood Arrivals (DACA).

Cancellation and 212(c)

Cancellation of removal for LPRs is a way for those with certain criminal convictions to apply to be allowed to stay in the country.[137] The applicant's criminal history is the obvious negative factor, and there might be others as well. These must be balanced by positive equities. Section 212(c) relief is essentially the same and is in fact the predecessor to cancellation of removal that was eliminated from the immigration law and replaced by cancellation. It remains available for certain very old convictions.[138]

Adjustment of Status

Adjustment of status (AOS) is an application for a green card. Contrary to what the general public tends to believe, there is no way for most people who would like to immigrate to the United States to do so. To be eligible for a green card, an immigrant must normally have a family connection or be requested by an employer.[139] While the majority of AOS applications involve people coming from abroad, AOS can also be used as relief in immigration court by someone who has the requisite family connection to be immediately eligible for a green card.[140] AOS can even be used by someone who already got a green card but became deportable, as long as they are still admissible and immediately eligible for a green card again.[141] USCIS adjudicates the first part of an AOS application—the establishment of the necessary relationship (i.e., parent/child, bona fide marriage)—and normally adjudicates the second step (eligibility to adjust) as well, except that, if the immigrant is in removal proceedings at the time of the application, the second step will fall to the IJ.

AOS, with certain limited exceptions,[142] is discretionary, which means that even if the immigrant is eligible they can still be denied in discretion. Despite this, AOS was traditionally a relatively straightforward application that did not require extensive intervention to convince adjudicators to grant it. Long-standing BIA case law, and corresponding USCIS guidance, provided that AOS should generally be granted if the applicant was eligible. Only when "compelling negative factors" were present would the applicant be required to demonstrate countervailing positive equities. That guidance was amended, however, in 2020 to remove any reference to the presumption in favor of granting AOS.[143] (Note, however, that the underlying case law has not changed.)[144] Another Trump administration action, the proposed public charge rule announced in 2019, would add further barriers to AOS requiring increased intervention by mental health professionals. The proposed rule would make anyone inadmissible who is at risk of becoming dependent on public benefits, including anyone with a medical condition that is likely to require extensive treatment or institutionalization or that will interfere with the person's ability to provide for themselves, unless they have private health insurance or the means to pay for their own treatment. Immigrants would need a FMHA to establish that they are not likely to require extensive treatment or institutionalization for a mental illness.[145]

Temporary Protected Status and Deferred Action for Childhood Arrivals

TPS and DACA are humanitarian programs to provide status for people already in the United States. IJs (who have the authority to adjudicate TPS applications for immigrants in removal proceedings) are permitted to deny TPS applications according to their discretion, even if the applicant is eligible.[146] The discretionary factors to be considered include the usual factors that should be considered in discretionary applications plus additional factors relevant to TPS, including the individual's safety if they were deported. Adverse factors, including criminal history, must be offset by "significant additional equities." The ultimate question remains whether granting TPS would be in the best interest of the United States.[147] Similarly, a DACA application might be denied at the IJ's discretion even for an eligible applicant.[148]

Psycholegal Issues Involved in Equities Based Relief

The psycholegal issues involved in equities-based relief are similar to those for good moral character. When immigration adjudicators make decisions based on a balancing of the equities, they consider positive and negative factors similar to how judges in criminal court consider mitigating and aggravating circumstances when making sentencing decisions. However, unlike in criminal court, where mental illness and substance use histories tend to be seen as mitigating factors, in IC they can be seen as indicative of "criminal tendencies" and as a public safety issue. In these cases, the role of the MHP is to educate the court about these disorders in general and about their specific clinical manifestation for the immigrant in particular. With respect to substance use, it is helpful for the MHP to educate the court on the nature and course of substance use disorders and their biological and psychological underpinnings.

Other Areas in Which Psycholegal Issues Are Present

Although these are not forms of relief per se, the following are areas within immigration law where psychological evidence can also be helpful.

Bond

While bond is not a form of relief, bond determinations present multiple issues for which a FMHA might be relevant and helpful in assisting the IJ in their decision-making. When deciding whether to grant bond, an IJ must decide if the applicant is a flight risk or a danger to the community.[149] The evaluation of dangerousness to the community might rely heavily on a FMHA, especially if the individual has a history of behavior that has been influenced by their mental illness or drug use. The main psycholegal issue, therefore, is likely to be risk of violence. It should be noted, however, that danger to the community can also include things such as danger to property or the danger posed generally by the drug trade, so the FMHA might not be limited solely to the question of violence. The issue of dangerousness is extensively covered in chapter 12.

The evaluation of flight risk, too, might rely on a FMHA, as the IJ will consider the relative strength of the underlying application (i.e., asylum, cancellation, etc.) when deciding whether the individual is likely to return to court. The immigrant might have to establish that they have a strong case for relief in order to be granted bond. Accordingly, the IJ's bond decision might incorporate any of the considerations discussed above, including good moral character, hardship, persecution, and the like.

Overcoming a Deadline

Immigration law contains many hard-and-fast deadlines. There is a strict one-year deadline for filing an asylum application that can be overcome only in extraordinary circumstances. Immigrants attempting to reopen their removal proceedings are also subject to strict deadlines, and if they miss them they will be barred from reopening even if the issues they raise are clearly meritorious. As with the asylum one-year bar, these filing deadlines can be overcome if the immigrant can show that their mental health prevented them from complying with the deadline.[150] In these cases, a FMHA can provide an evaluation of any psychiatric disorders, cognitive or intellectual impairment, or trauma-related symptoms that might have interfered with the immigrant's ability to meet the deadline (e.g., side effects from psychiatric medications, memory impairment resulting from trauma or stress, active psychiatric symptoms such as depression, psychosis, and anxiety, or lack of appropriate treatment).

Competency

Competency to participate in immigration court proceedings is also relevant to the discussion when psycholegal issues are present. Competency is discussed in detail in chapter 11.

Conclusion

Many forms of relief or other determinations that need to be made in ICs or administrative relief adjudications have a psycholegal component.

Generally, a FMHA will be called upon to help establish at least one of five things: persecution (past or future), victimization, hardship (to the immigrant or others), good moral character, and whether the balance of the equities favor a grant of relief. In addition, a FMHA might be relied upon to establish risk of flight or danger to the community in the context of bond, extraordinary circumstances in the context of a missed deadline, or(as will be discussed in chapter 11) competency to participate in immigration court proceedings. More than one of these issues might be present in a single case or even in a single application for relief. We recommend that MHPs conducting FMHAs at the behest of an immigration attorney work closely with the attorney to understand and clarify the legal issue(s) that will be implicated by the evaluation. For attorneys, we recommend that they spend time thinking through the psycholegal issues present in their case and that they communicate those issues clearly to the MHP.

PART II

Mental Health and Immigration

4

Roles of Mental Health Professionals

Just as the general public often has little understanding of the many roles that mental health professionals (MHPs) can play in the legal system, immigration attorneys often have a limited understanding of how MHPs can assist them and their immigrant clients in deportation proceedings. By the same token, MHPs often do not fully grasp the differences between immigration courts (ICs) and the federal/state criminal and civil courts, or even recognize that ICs are a separate entity. With unprecedented numbers of people seeking asylum and immigrants facing deportation,[1] it is critical that MHPs not only understand the unique nature of ICs but also be cognizant of the significant contributions they can offer immigrants, immigration attorneys, and IC officials to increase the quality of decision-making in deportation proceedings.[2]

The importance of such contributions by MHPs to ICs is underscored by the fact that a number of adjunctive bodies and foreign refugee boards (e.g., Australian and Canadian refugee boards) have accepted that mental health issues, such as psychological trauma, might compromise both the ability of immigrants to provide testimony and their perceived credibility. In recognition of such challenges, the US Department of Homeland Security now makes available resources on posttraumatic stress disorder (PTSD) and cross-cultural interview techniques as part of its adjudicators training.[3]

Even though clinical graduate programs offer basic and advanced training in therapeutic techniques and service provision, most MHPs are not prepared to work within the immigration legal system. Yet, depending on their experience and expertise, licensed MHPs' involvement in immigration proceedings can provide a range of invaluable services in ICs that extend beyond traditional psychotherapy to immigrants. Such services can include conducting forensic evaluations, testifying as a witness in ICs, and serving as a consultant to attorneys and/or immigration officials.[4] This chapter reviews the different roles that MHPs can play in ICs and provides some practice recommendations for MHPs and immigration attorneys.

The Roles

When working with a client in any clinical setting, it is always important to recognize that the MHP's role will vary depending on *who* the client is.[5] The same is true when working within the IC setting. In this context, the client might be the immigrant, their attorney(s), or the immigration adjudicator(s). Having a clear sense of who the client is will guide the type of role and relationship the MHP will develop with that immigrant. For example, in traditional clinical assessment, the client is the individual being evaluated. However, when the MHP is retained by the immigration attorney to conduct an evaluation in IC, the client is the immigration attorney.

Given the myriad of roles that MHPs can play in an IC, it is critical that they have a clear sense of what each role entails.[6] Clarifying why the individual has been sent to see the MHP (the referral question) can help determine the MHP's role and inform next steps. MHPs might receive referrals from sources as diverse as members of the immigrant community, immigration attorneys, and even immigration judges (IJs). They can and do provide services in a variety of settings, including through one of the nine State Department–approved "voluntary organizations" paid to settle refugees in the United States (including Church World Service, Ethiopian Community Development Council, Hebrew Immigrant Aid Society, International Rescue Committee), through local community-based organizations, or through the National Consortium of Torture Treatment Programs.[7] They could also offer their services to ICs as part of their private practice or their work with nongovernmental organizations, with academic medical centers offering services,[8] or at the request of an immigration attorney.[9] Regardless of the setting in which the MHP works, or who requests the service, there are two main distinctions with respect to roles: therapist versus forensic evaluator, and fact witness versus expert witness.

Therapist

Traditionally, MHPs in this role seek to improve emotional functioning and promote healing in order to enhance the individual's quality of life.[10] In working with immigrants who have had traumatic experiences, the hope is that by operating within a trauma-informed framework to develop and build a trusting relationship, the MHP will assist the individual in attaining emotional stabilization, support the integration of their traumatic experiences, and support them as they seek to heal and rebuild satisfying interpersonal connections within their new cultural setting.[11]

MHPs who are trained in trauma-informed practices work with great sensitivity to carefully assist their clients to unpack the traumatic experiences that brought them to seek their services in a careful and thoughtful manner. Unfortunately, due to the vagaries of the immigration process, this measured therapeutic process can be negatively affected by ICs when the immigrant is forced "to disclose experiences and give information at a pace that is seriously out of alignment" with therapy.[12] For example, sometimes a MHP must put aside fundamentals of good therapeutic care (such a building a therapeutic alliance or creating a secure space) to focus on the immediate anxiety associated with a sudden date at IC.[13] Thus, what is most convenient for the IC might be favored over best practices for the emotional well-being of the client. Furthermore, during a court hearing, the client might be forced to recount the details of their traumatic experiences. Such pressure can be detrimental to the therapeutic process, as it forces an abrupt disclosure of traumatic material at a time and place that is not in the client's best interests.

Not only are IC dates and hearings assigned according to the whims of IC, they can be abruptly changed for a host of reasons, such as prevailing political agendas,[14] an IJ's illness or retirement, a government attorney's request for more information, an unnotarized document, a pandemic or other natural event,[15] or even due to the assignment of the wrong language interpreter at an asylum hearing (e.g., when a *Creole* language interpreter is assigned instead of a *Krio* language interpreter for a Sierra Leonean asylum seeker; Creole is the lingua franca of Haiti, while Krio is the lingua franca of Sierra Leone). In fact, it is also a common practice to double-book court dates for major hearings such that two people are scheduled to have their hearing at the same time before the same judge. When both parties show up, there is not enough time to complete both hearings on the scheduled day.[16] Sadly, in such situations, one will get bumped—possibly for a year or more.

Understandably, such unpredictability can create an inordinate amount of stress for the immigrant, and accordingly this influences the therapeutic relationship and process. During such circumstances, the therapist must demonstrate compassionate flexibility—the ability to temporarily put aside whatever treatment plan was in place in order to focus on preparing the client for their court date, or console and support the distressed individual whose court date has been arbitrarily pushed into the distant future, creating sometimes six months to several years of waiting.[17] In this role, the MHP must also have the skills to offer healthy and supportive coping strategies for immigrants who become overwhelmed with reoccurrences of intrusive memories or depressive symptoms because of the unexpected delay or their anxiety at having to testify in IC.[18]

For some MHPs, the therapist role can extend to providing education and anticipatory guidance to the applicant about the legal process (e.g., What exactly is IC? What might happen in IC? Who might be present in IC?) or psychoeducation about potential reactions (e.g., "you might experience an increase in debilitating psychological symptoms such as increased nightmares or depression or intrusive memories as your hearing date draws closer"). For many, the prospect of going to IC is terrifying and is compounded by the very real possibility of deportation. Being asked to provide detailed information about some or all of the most horrifying or shameful events in their lives, in front of strangers, can be overwhelming.[19] In other cases, the therapist can take on an additional "accompanier role," in which they simply escort their client to IC and attend the hearing with the individual. In this capacity, the MHP provides a supportive and calming presence for their anxious client immediately before, during, and after the court hearing.[20]

Forensic Evaluator

In contrast to the therapeutic role, in which the MHP relies on information from the client, is supportive and empathetic, and seeks to develop a strong therapeutic alliance while cultivating a relationship that can last over an extended time period, all in an effort to benefit the psychological well-being of their client, the main role of the forensic evaluator is to provide objective and neutral opinions that will benefit the court. In taking on this role, the MHP looks beyond the information obtained from the immigrant and incorporates information obtained from collateral sources. In addition, the relationship is brief and focused, typically based on one or two sessions. Most important, unlike the therapeutic or purely clinical role, in the forensic role the MHP's stance aspires to be neutral, more emotionally distanced and objective, and the basis of the relationship is evaluative and not therapeutic.[21] In fact, the forensic evaluator should avoid nurturing the immigrant's perception that their role is a "helping" one.[22] While the MHP who takes on a therapeutic role might be viewed as a "patient advocate" and possibly biased in favor of their client, the role of a forensic evaluator aspires to be objective.[23] In IC, the forensic evaluator is expected to conduct an independent clinical assessment and write a psychological report with information determined by the legal issue (e.g., the impact of the reported experiences on the individual's current mental health functioning, or the individual's competency to participate in immigration proceedings). The information provided by the forensic evaluator might lead to a decision that will not benefit the immigrant and could, in fact, harm them (e.g., deportation). Although a MHP could be motivated by social justice reasons in their desire to serve as forensic evaluator, it is important to remember that the purpose of this role is not client's advocacy but rather to educate the court so that immigration officials can make decisions regarding removal proceedings. The credibility of MHPs can be seriously jeopardized if IJs believe that advocacy for removal relief is the main motivation of the evaluator. To avoid this type of bias, the forensic evaluator has to engage in a process of scientific testing and report data and opinions that result from the principles of forensic mental health assessments, which are further explained in chapter 10. Ideally, the information provided to the IC will be research-based, although in some situations information based on theoretical constructs or "educated intuition" is also permissible.[24]

MHPs working in this role should be aware of the concept of forensic alliance, which refers to MHPs' tendency to lean their opinions toward the side retaining their services.[25] Forensic alliance could lead experts to be biased toward the side of the immigration attorney or the immigrant even in ways that are outside conscious awareness. There is no research on forensic alliance in ICs, but MHPs should become familiar with the research available on this concept in criminal court and the steps they can take to minimize its impact on their final opinions.

Witness

Mental health professionals who provide treatment and assessment can be called to testify in ICs. In ICs, as in other court settings, witnesses can fall into one of two categories: fact witness or expert witness. MHPs must be aware that there are significant differences between expert witnesses and "lay witnesses" or "witnesses of fact."

Fact Witness

The therapist role can give way to becoming a fact witness, a role that involves more direct interaction with the IC. As a fact witness, the MHP can write affidavits and/or testify in an IC in support of their client's immigration claim. Although in this capacity the MHP can testify only about specific comments or events that they personally witnessed or heard during therapy,[26] in assuming the role of a fact witness, the MHP can offer vital information that can serve to educate IC officials about the impact of the applicant's experiences on their psychological functioning. Drawing from data gathered from their clinical interactions, the MHP can provide a written mental health assessment in the form of an affidavit or declaration (a written statement confirmed by oath or affirmation) that can be used in IC.[27] Primarily, an affidavit or declaration for the IC written by a MHP in the therapist role should focus on mental health issues. This legal document and the MHP's testimony can serve as powerful corroborating evidence of past experiences and psychological scars by outlining the immigrant's presentation (their symptoms) at the start of treatment, their diagnosis, and their therapeutic progress.[28] Based on their therapeutic encounters, the MHP can bolster the credibility of the applicant's narrative ("she reported on this date that x happened") or potentially help the court evaluate the risk the individual might pose to people ("she is making significant progress in treatment as evidenced by *xyz*").

A MHP who is a therapist and then becomes a fact witness does not need to have any special qualifications to testify in IC other than the credentials that allow them to provide psychotherapy according to the jurisdiction within which they practice. There has been some dispute in the field about this practice, as some professionals have argued that, when MHPs assume what might be viewed as a forensic role for clients they are treating (thus taking on multiple relationships), they might adversely affect the therapeutic relationship and might also appear biased to the IC.[29] In order to uphold the therapeutic alliance, it is crucial to maintain transparency; the MHP must carefully review and explain what they are doing to their client and have their consent at all the stages, particularly as this can be an incredibly stressful and at times even a destabilizing experience for the immigrant.

Expert Witness

When MHPs conduct a forensic evaluation for an IC, they can testify and provide information to the court based on the opinions and conclusions included in their report. In this role, the MHP will be testifying as an expert witness. There are no rules of evidence specific to IC, although the court is guided by the principles that underlay the Federal Rules of Evidence. However, testimony that might be excluded from federal court could be allowed in IC, because IJs have broad discretion with respect to admissibility of expert testimony. If the IJ believes the expert to be insufficiently qualified, they might exclude the testimony or might accord it minimal weight.[30] Forensic evaluators should be familiar with the Federal Rules of Evidence as they apply to testimony in federal courts and endeavor to meet their requirements. Specifically, Rule 702 regulates "Testimony by Expert Witness":

> A witness who is qualified as an expert by knowledge, skill, experience, training, or education may testify in the form of an opinion or otherwise if:
> (a) the expert's scientific, technical, or other specialized knowledge will help the trier of fact to understand the evidence or to determine a fact in issue;

(b) the testimony is based on sufficient facts or data;

(c) the testimony is the product of reliable principles and methods; and

(d) the expert has reliably applied the principles and methods to the facts of the case.[31]

By agreeing to testify as an expert witness, the expectation is that the forensic evaluator is committed to providing a truthful, objective, and unbiased report to the IC.[32] Unlike the fact witness, whose role is limited to testifying about specific comments or events they personally witnessed during therapy, a MHP serving as an expert witness can offer professional opinions related to the psycholegal issue as well as facts.[33] Their primary task is to assist immigration officials in making legal decisions; this typically includes providing information about psycholegal issues (competency, hardship) related to the referral question. Their testimony can also be used in more nontraditional ways that are purely informative and advise legal personnel about a range of behavioral health issues, including the potential impact of deportation.[34]

In order for a MHP to be considered an expert, they need to have "specialized knowledge" beyond that of the trier of fact.[35] In general, in the context of ICs, specialized knowledge to be an expert witness requires expertise in forensic and multicultural assessment and some general knowledge about immigration law. Other important skills include diagnostic assessment, psychological testing, and expertise in the evaluation of psychological reactions to trauma.[36]

Whether a MHP can be considered an expert in court varies by state. Baker and colleagues argue that "social workers and mental health specialists can provide crucial testimony regarding an asylum applicant's past persecution or fear of future persecution, as well as explanations for behavior caused by trauma that a judge or asylum officer could misunderstand (such as inconsistences or gaps in the applicant's time line)."[37] Clinical and counseling psychologists, as well as psychiatrists, are typically considered expert witnesses. Licensed clinical social workers can be deemed experts in criminal and family courts, although they are sometimes not allowed to offer opinions about diagnoses or some psycholegal issues such as competency. Regardless of the type of degree, it is of utmost importance for MHPs to ensure that they have engaged in the type of training and experience that provides them with the "specialized knowledge" to provide useful information to the trier of fact. This is particularly important in an IC, a setting in which it is rare to have an opposing expert; the IJ is relying on a single expert's opinion.[38]

Support to Immigration Attorneys

Although traditionally the role of the MHP in ICs has primarily focused on either treatment or assessment of immigrants, there are other ways in which the MHP can provide support to immigration attorneys and IC officials as well. MHPs can use their knowledge of mental health and clinical skills to teach immigration attorneys effective strategies and safe methods for obtaining trauma narratives and/or history from immigrants without retraumatizing them.[39] Providing immigration attorneys with in-depth psychoeducation, such as how to identify symptoms that are associated with PTSD and depression, or why it might be difficult for an applicant to provide detailed information about their traumatic narrative on demand, can reduce the pressure placed on immigrants and can increase empathy from their attorneys. MHPs can also educate immigration attorneys about their own possible psychological reactions to listening to their clients' trauma histories. Increasingly, researchers have acknowledged the emotional impact of working with forced immigrant populations, particularly those who have experienced extensive traumas. A number of studies have documented the effect of secondary traumatic stress and vicarious trauma—repeatedly listening to traumatic stories—on service providers.[40] Data about the impact of working with traumatized immigrant populations on immigration attorneys is limited.[41] However, secondary trauma has been reported in attorneys working with victims of domestic violence and abuse[42] and other traumatized clients,[43] as well as in immigration judges.[44] Drawing on their expertise and training, MHPs can work with immigration attorneys to develop training that can provide information and support to enhance immigration attorneys' capacity to cope effectively with secondary traumatic stress and vicarious trauma.[45]

Recommendations for Mental Health and Legal Professionals

Whatever role a MHP takes on in IC—therapist, forensic evaluator, witness, or consultant—there are a number of best practices in which they ought to engage.

For Therapists:

- Maintain communication, transparency, and the therapeutic alliance. Discuss the possibility and meaning of being a fact witness with the client as early as possible in the treatment. Explore the client's understanding of what a fact witness is and does, how the client feels about the therapist writing a report on their experiences, what will and will not be included in the report, whether the client can change their mind and decide this course of action is not what they want, and what it might be like to for the client to have their therapist discuss their treatment in court, in front of people they have never met before.
- If asked to write an affidavit for the IC, review the written report with the client, explain what it includes, and get their perspective. How do they understand what has been written about them? This activity can allow for further psychoeducation about mental health and their progress in treatment.
- Anticipate various scenarios with the client about the actual court hearing. If you are a fact witness, will the client be allowed to sit in the courtroom while you testify and are cross-examined? What might that be like for them? How might this impact the therapeutic relationship? What if the IJ asks them to wait outside? Will you be allowed to be present for their testimony, or will you have to wait outside? These decisions are made by the particular IJ—they are out of your and the client's control.

For Forensic Evaluators:

- No matter how the client was referred to you, always take time to inform them of the purpose of the evaluation and obtain written consent.[46]
- Focus the evaluation on the psycholegal issues and keep out information that is not relevant to the referral question.
- Take care to conduct the evaluation in a manner that is not intimidating

or comes across as an interrogation. This is particularly important for clients who have experienced trauma at the hands of authority figures.

- Demonstrate cultural sensitivity by using culturally valid instruments[47] and interpreters as needed.[48]
- Become familiar with the principles of a forensic mental health assessment as they apply to ICs (see chapter 10).

For Immigration Attorneys Working with MHPs

- View the MHP as a member of your client's team no matter what role they will play. This approach can work only to your client's benefit.
- Develop and maintain clear and ongoing communication.
- Communicate early and often (e.g., do not wait until the last minute to request an affidavit).
- Whether working with a MHP with extensive experience and knowledge of IC or one who is a novice, it is always a good investment to take some time to prepare them to testify. Have they done so before? What was their experience? Is the MHP expected to testify in person, or can they do so telephonically?
- Review the questions you plan to ask them prior to the actual hearing.
- Be sure to clarify the psycholegal issue that the MHP's evaluation needs to address.

Finally, no matter what the licensed MHP's discipline is—counseling, psychiatry, psychology, or social work—it is their responsibility to review and make sure they fully understand all related specialty guidelines and ethical codes of conduct in their respective fields. Specifically, the National Association of Forensic Counselors has maintained guidelines of Ethical Standards and Code of Conduct,[49] and the American Academy of Psychiatry and the Law also provides Ethical Guidelines for the Practice of Forensic Psychiatry.[50] Psychologists providing services in IC should become familiar with the American Psychological Association (APA)'s Specialty Guidelines for Forensic Psychology,[51] the APA's Guidelines on Multicultural Education, Training, Practice, and Organizational Change for Psychologists,[52] and the APA's Guidelines for Providers of Psychological Services to Ethnic, Linguistic, and Culturally Diverse Populations.[53] Finally, in the field of Social Work, the National

Organization of Forensic Social Workers also maintains a Code of Ethics for its members.[54]

Conclusion

MHPs can and do provide critical services within the immigration legal system. Key tasks for MHPs in this setting can include providing treatment to immigrants undergoing removal proceedings and becoming a fact witness as a result; being asked to conduct a forensic psychological evaluation and to testify as an expert witness; providing support to immigrants as they endure what can be an overwhelming process; and providing support and psychoeducation to the immigration attorneys and the adjudicators. No matter which role the MHP takes on in the IC, they must be aware of the different responsibilities involved and the ethical codes that guide their particular mental health discipline. MHPs must recognize that many of these roles fall outside the traditional realm of psychotherapy. For those providing services in IC, each of these roles compels the MHP to move out of the confines of traditional treatment, pushes them out of their offices, and requires them to provide critical services beyond the 50-minute hour.[55]

5

Risk Factors for Mental Health Distress in Immigrants Facing Removal Proceedings

The impact of the migratory experience and immigration status on the mental health of immigrant populations has been well documented in the psychological literature.[1] While many immigrants exhibit extraordinary resilience in the face of daunting hardships (such as the loss of family, country, culture, language, and multiple other changes), clinicians and researchers have reported high levels of psychological distress including anxiety, depression, posttraumatic stress disorder (PTSD), adjustment disorder, somatization, psychosis, substance use, and suicidal disorders among immigrants who were forced to leave their home countries as a result of events that threatened their lives, health, livelihood, and freedom, especially among those who, due to these events, were unable to implement practical and systematic plans prior to their departure.[2]

Other immigrants might have experienced stressors/trauma in the immigration process in other ways. At times, immigrants arrive independently. Other times, they have been separated from a parent for years while the parent worked in the United States to earn enough money to bring them to this country. And still others times, immigrants might have been smuggled in by traffickers or brought by spouses who became abusive toward them.[3] It is important for mental health professionals (MHPs) to recognize that for many immigrants, no matter what type of immigration relief the individual is seeking from the immigration court (IC), the prospect of facing IC proceedings can serve to further compromise their already distressed psychological well-being. This additional and often chronic stressor can add to the immigrant's ongoing challenges by negatively impacting their emotional and behavioral functioning and ultimately their presentation in IC.

While it is critical that MHPs are cognizant of the roles they can play in ICs (e.g., therapist versus forensic evaluator), regardless of the role, both MHPs and lawyers working with immigrants in ICs must have the knowledge and skills to recognize and address the mental health issues that this population tends to experience, as well as the resulting emotional distress and behaviors that can influence the immigrant's ability to provide a coherent and plausible narrative in court. Given the centrality of the immigrant's credibility to the outcomes in ICs, such recognition is important; often those who report the most difficulties might be seen as the least credible.[4] While it is not the place of immigration attorneys to provide mental health services, the ability to recognize emotional distress in their immigrant clients through collaboration with MHPs can help their clients gain access to appropriate resources or services to diminish the impact of such distress on the outcome of their IC case.

For many immigrants facing deportation proceedings, the period between submitting their documents requesting a change in status and receiving a decision from an IC can vary from a few months to several years.[5] During this extremely stressful and uncertain period, many are terrified of being deported. The chronic stress experienced during this period is further compounded by the reality that many immigrants who find themselves in such circumstances often feel as if they are living in limbo, as they are unable to make any plans for the future. For immigrants, this is a particularly vulnerable time during which their mental health is extremely fragile. For those requesting asylum, the protracted wait can be detrimental to their mental health.[6]

In addition to the high prevalence of mental health symptoms,[7] other factors including language or limited financial and social resources[8] can create further barriers for this population. Furthermore, attorneys and MHPs must appreciate that testifying in IC often compels the immigrant to disclose deeply personal and often distressing information about their past. For many, attempts to revisit such memories can and will create an overwhelming sense of shame and heighten their PTSD symptoms, leaving them reluctant or unable to disclose their experiences as they struggle to manage such negative emotions. Psychological factors including shame, reduced concentration, and distrust, as well as a multitude of physical problems, can influence the immigrant's ability to remember and discuss their experiences and histories. Emotional and somatic difficulties can interfere with their ability to provide a clear and coherent narrative about what happened to them. Such problems are further complicated by sociocultural factors that can also impede the recall of experiences that are viewed as shameful. This chapter covers different immigrant groups who are particularly vulnerable to experiencing psychological distress during the IC process.

Populations at Risk for Additional Emotional Distress in Immigration Court

All immigrants can experience psychological distress during the IC process as a result of their prior adverse experiences, stressful migration experiences, stressors related to adjusting to a new culture, undocumented status, and the stress inherent to all court proceedings. However, certain groups of immigrants are likely to be at increased risk given their particular trauma histories. These include survivors of sexual violence, those discriminated due to sexual orientation and gender identity, victims of intimate partner violence (IPV), immigrants in detention, children and adolescents, and immigrants who have been separated from their families.

Survivors of Sexual Violence

Emotional and somatic difficulties can interfere with the ability of many immigrants to provide a clear and coherent narrative about what happened to them. Such problems are further complicated by sociocultural factors that can also impede the recall of traumatic experiences that are viewed as shameful. A number of studies have documented reports of shame, difficulty with disclosure, high levels of dissociation, and PTSD among survivors of sexual violence who were asked to evaluate their experiences of disclosure to a state immigration official.[9] Like other traumatized immigrants, the experiences of survivors of sexual violence are further exacerbated by the disorientation that comes from being an immigrant in a new country (culture shock), limited language skills in that new setting, lack of access to resources, and uncertain legal status. The struggle to disclose experiences of sexual violence has also been documented in survivors of human trafficking[10] and female genital mutilation/cutting.[11]

It is important for MHPs and attorneys to recognize that while there is increased awareness of the prevalence of sexual violence against females, the experiences of male survivors of sexual violence are too often ignored or underestimated, as males are much less likely than females to disclose sexual assaults.[12] While there is limited information of male survivors of sexual violence, available research points to the fact that males experience many of the same barriers regarding disclosure of sexual violence as females, including stigma and shame. However, these barriers are further compounded by confusion and ignorance around their own sexual identity, guilt, fear that their masculinity is compromised, and resulting isolation.[13] All of these factors lead to a heightened sense of emotional distress, making it less likely for this population to come forward willingly about their experiences.

Sexual Orientation and Gender Identity

Global statistics demonstrate elevated levels of violence targeting individuals based on sexual orientation and/or gender identity.[14] The exact figures of lesbian, gay, bisexual, and transgender (LGBT) persons forced into migration around the world and seeking refuge in the United States is hard to come by for a variety of reasons, including persecution by their own families and communities. Understandably, due to the extensive homophobia and transphobia they have experienced, many do not self-identify as LGBT.[15] As underscored by Shidlo and Ahola, this population reports "a history of multiple traumatic events across their lifespan, including verbal, emotional, physical, and sexual abuse and assault, harassment, shunning, spitting, discrimination in housing and employment, destruction of property, blackmail, forced prostitution, forced heterosexual marriage, 'corrective rape' and coerced sexual orientation conversion interventions."[16] Unlike other persecuted immigrant populations, LGBT persons typically have endured such persecution directly from immediate family and community members starting from early childhood and extending into their adult lives.[17] Furthermore, in contrast to other forced migrant populations who are able to rely on their immigrant communities in the new country while awaiting the IC's decision, LGBT immigrants who left their countries due to persecution often self-isolate from their cultural communities due to their fear of being further persecuted because of their LGBT identities, or, if they do seek support from the community, that they are in danger of being ostracized there.[18]

Although empirical data on the mental health of LGBT forced migrants is limited,[19] existing evidence suggests that this population often experiences persecution-related psychological distress. Mental health problems noted include recurrent depression, anxiety disorders, PTSD, social isolation, somatization, substance use, and traumatic brain injury.[20]

It is important for MHPs and immigration attorneys to recognize that LGBT forced immigrants, due to their histories of persecution, might experience not only fear and shame disclosing their sexual orientation or gender identity but also special difficulty providing detailed information about the traumatic experiences they endured as a result of it. Thus, providers must adjust their expectations and understand that this population faces numerous stressors due to their LGBT identity, which might prevent them from accessing and utilizing services.[21] Furthermore, bearing in mind the diversity of experiences, MHPs must also understand that there is no global LGBT experience or way of presenting. This understanding is critical as MHPs might be asked to explain this to an immigration judge who expects a certain type of coming-out narrative.[22]

Finally, it is important to acknowledge that there are immigrants for whom the discourse focused on lesbian, gay, bisexual, and trans identities is confining. Emerging queer migration scholarship draws attention to the oppressive immigration system and how it negatively impacts the queer population. The system does not acknowledge their voices, as the discourse reinforces Western colonial and heteronormative assumptions.[23] This evolving scholarship highlights the fact that many refugees/asylum seekers who define themselves as nonheterosexual and nonbinary are forced to define themselves as LGBT members,[24] as if these are the only identities one possesses, and thus must adhere to this identity if they want to seek asylum and fit into Western society.[25] If they refuse to be identified as such, the legitimacy of their claims is questioned.[26] As Murray argues, these difficulties "create substantial challenges and anxieties for anyone placed into this process."[27] Such restraints can have a detrimental impact on the immigrant, leaving them reluctant and/or feeling unsafe to discuss their experiences of persecution regarding sexuality or gender identities in IC.

Victims of Intimate Partner Violence

Although the prevalence and incidence of intimate partner violence is a significant ongoing problem for many women and men in the United States, disclosing abuse to authorities and/or seeking help is a much more difficult hurdle for the immigrant population. The impact of IPV on mental health among the immigrant population includes higher rates of depression, PTSD, suicidal ideation, and low self-esteem compared to the nonimmigrant population with IPV experiences.[28] In addition to mental health issues, the complex dynamics of IPV among the immigrant population might also lead to extreme disturbance in one's sense of safety as well as a mistrust of the legal and welfare systems. While it is well documented that diversity within immigrant groups, such as cultural difference[29] and socioeconomic status,[30] might play a significant role in not opening up about experiences of IPV, uncertainty regarding their current immigration status and isolation significantly contribute to keep them from seeking help or leaving the abusive relationship.[31] Particularly, the very notion of going to IC can be overwhelming and create further emotional distress for immigrants seeking relief through the Violence Against Women Act. Many studies have documented the harsh realities of immigrant spouses of citizens or permanent residents who experience IPV.[32] The lack of knowledge of their legal rights, vulnerabilities associated with being undocumented, limited access to social and financial resources, language barriers, lack of social support, increased isolation, and loneliness might all adversely affect their mental health outcomes, combined with the uncertainty and fear about what will happen to their immigration status and reputation in their community if they disclose the experiences of abuse.[33] Having already sustained emotional, physical, sexual, or financial anguish as a result of their IPV experiences, such individuals often have limited alternatives to residing with their abusers because they have been intimidated and as a result are too afraid to report their experiences to authorities.[34] This fear of immigration authorities is exacerbated by abusive spouses who use the power of their own immigration status to keep their immigrant partner in a subordinate position, leaving the survivor terrified of the IC process. Therefore, understanding the particular and complex needs of each individual's situation and providing the necessary help and resources to them, including a safe, cultural- and gender-responsive approach and environment, is of paramount importance for MHPs and immigrant attorneys who work with this population.

Immigrants in Detention

With the number of forcibly displaced people around the world continuing to rise (by the end of 2019, it was at an all-time high of 79.5 million),[35] several high-income countries, such as Australia, Canada, United Kingdom, and the United States, adopted tougher measures including imprisoning a higher number of immigrants while the decision about their immigration status was processed.[36]

These actions have been implemented as an effort to discourage immigrants from entering these countries. Despite the repeated findings in the literature demonstrating high levels of mental health distress— anxiety, depression, PTSD, suicidal ideation, and behavioral difficulties experienced by adults, adolescents, and children held in immigration detention[37]—the practice of detaining immigrants in detention centers, operated like prisons and often located in remote and rural areas, remains in place.[38] In the United States there are approximately 50,000 people in immigration detention on a given day, and more than 500,000 people will be detained over the course of a year.[39]

This confinement in prison-like settings can serve to further amplify previous traumatic experiences, creating additional health risk.[40] The majority of detainees do not receive legal representation (due to limited pro bono services), and those who are represented experience challenges communicating with their attorneys.[41] Specifically, LGBT immigrants in detention, often at risk for increased violence from both detention staff and other detainees, are also at risk of being placed in solitary confinement for their "own protection."[42] All of these issues are compounded by the fact that mental health services in migrant detention are "extremely rare,"[43] leaving many retraumatized by their detention experiences.

Children and Adolescents

By the end of 2019, there were an estimated 79.5 million forced migrants seeking asylum in high-income countries; of those, 40% (estimated at

30–34 million) were children below 18 years of age.[44] Undocumented children and youth experience similar mental health conditions to those reported in adults, including mood and anxiety disorders;[45] they also struggle with additional stressors—including fear of deportation of themselves or their parents, anger, social isolation, and lack of a sense of belonging—all factors that are detrimental to their social development, educational achievement, economic well-being, and mobility.[46]

Between 2010 and 2019, approximately 400,000 unaccompanied and separated children applied for asylum in 117 industrialized countries.[47] For such children with traumatic histories who might themselves end up in detention, mental health issues are often exacerbated. Despite a paucity of information, available studies have noted that this population is especially susceptible to the impact of trauma, displacement, and loss, with high rates of emotional distress that persist even after resettlement.[48] Needless to say, such critical factors impact vulnerability and will influence the young person's ability to present themselves in IC.

Family Separation

Under the Trump administration an increased number of families were separated at the border. However, family separation is not a new experience for immigrants. Immigrant children are often separated before they migrate, at the border, and in the United States when family members are deported. Despite how common this experience is, there is limited empirical literature on the impact of family separation in immigrant children or children of immigrants. A study published in 2017 examined the mental health (including symptoms of PTSD and psychological distress) of 91 US--born Latinx children following parental detention and deportation. This study used validated measures administered to the children, the parents, clinicians, and teachers. Results found that rates of PTSD symptoms, depression, anxiety, and internalizing and externalizing problems were significantly higher in the group of children with at least one parent facing deportation compared to children whose parents were permanent residents and not facing removal.[49] Another study published in 2020 found that immigration-related separation had a significant impact in the parent–child relationship of Latinx immigrant youth.[50] The authors note that research has consistently shown that a positive and consistent relationship with an adult caregiver represents a crucial protective factor against a number of negative outcomes. Another study published in 2021 found that externalizing behaviors (i.e., behaviors that create difficulties in the child's external world, such as rule-breaking or aggressive behaviors) in West African immigrant children were strongest in parent–child dyads that experienced more than one year of separation.[51] In a paper published in 2020, Wylonis and Billick presented 12 studies in which forensic psychiatric evaluations supported the immigrant parents of US citizen children's petition for permanent residence based on hardship. In this study, the authors pointed to parent–child attachment, the child's educational status, language proficiencies, acculturation to US culture, and psychiatric distress caused by the potential deportation as the factors most helpful in describing the harmful effects on the child to the threatened deportation of the parent.[52]

Though there are few studies that have specifically explored the harmful psychological effects of separation on children of deported immigrants, there is extensive research on the cumulative impact of adverse childhood experiences (ACEs). The Centers for Disease Control and Prevention's Kaiser Permanente ACE study found that there was a correlation between the number of ACEs and a number of negative mental health outcomes including depression, anxiety, substance use, and suicide attempts.[53] Parental separation is typically just one of many ACEs of children of undocumented immigrants. These children have increased rates of poverty, mental health issues, and low educational attainment.[54] Parental separation can have a cumulative effect over other ACEs in children of immigrants. The Society for Research in Child Development published a "Statement of Evidence" in 2018 in response to the "zero tolerance" policy that provides a summary of research on the harmful effects of family separation.[55] This can be a helpful resource for evaluators conducting hardship-based evaluations.

Attitudes Toward Undocumented Immigrants

Finally, in reflecting on mental health issues faced by undocumented immigrants, MHPs and immigration attorneys should understand that, beyond the special populations outlined above, additional factors related to attitudes toward immigrants can further compromise the emotional well-being of immigrants who are facing IC. These factors revolve around the ongoing shifts in attitudes toward undocumented immigrants shaped by a rise in xenophobia, which is fostered by certain political climates and creates a hostile environment for this population. Such hostilities are manifested in dramatic changes in rules and regulations toward immigrant populations. For example, in recent years, there has been a significant drop in the number of forced migrants allowed to enter the United States.[56] Such nationalistic attitudes have led to unprecedented major transformations in US immigration policy and practice, creating over 1 million removal cases[57] and leaving the already "overburdened and under-resourced" ICs[58] further compromised. Such dramatic changes serve to add to emotional distress to immigrants who are now forced to endure resultant lengthy waits for IC dates and a recent significant hike in immigration application fees.[59] Given the reality that many already struggle with high unemployment and that there are very limited pro bono services available,[60] the process of submitting the paperwork to IC and finding adequate representation becomes an additional mental health stressor. Considering that asylum seekers who have legal representation are three times as likely to be granted asylum,[61] the lack of counsel is a huge stressor, as obviously the many who cannot afford competent expertise in IC are less likely to succeed.

Conclusion

It is clear that immigrants' experiences in the United States and navigating IC might heighten the impact of previous trauma, creating additional mental health risk and thereby influencing the immigrants' ability to constructively assist in their own case. Although all immigrants are likely to experience some degree of psychological distress during immigration proceedings, some might be more vulnerable than others based on their trauma histories. Specifically, immigrants who have been victims of sexual assault or IPV, those who have been tortured or persecuted because of their LGBT status, those in detention, children and adolescents and immigrants who have been separated from their family might all be at significantly high risk of experiencing mental health difficulties. Despite this, immigrants facing IC rarely seek advice from mental health experts. In addition, since it is not within their areas of expertise, attorneys might underestimate the effect of psychological distress on the immigrant's ability to recount their story. A strong collaborative relationship between the attorney and the MHP in which they provide information about the process to the immigrant can serve to allay anxieties that might decrease emotional distress. In addition, MHPs can also provide education to the attorney and immigration adjudicators about the impact of these often overlooked factors on the behavior and presentation of the immigrant in IC.

6

Assessment of Trauma in Immigrants Facing Removal Proceedings

Psychological evidence of trauma can be an important component of many different types of forensic mental health assessments (FMHAs) in immigration court (IC) (e.g., victimization-based relief, persecution-based relief, competency, hardship). Although the recommendations included in this chapter were developed in the context of assessing trauma in asylum seekers, they are applicable to immigrants applying for other forms of relief as long as their trauma history is relevant to the type of relief they are seeking.

A licensed mental health professional (MHP) can take on a variety of roles within the IC setting. While it is essential that MHPs and attorneys recognize the distinctions among these roles, it is even more important that all parties concerned (including the immigrant) understand the difference between assessing trauma in order to provide therapeutic services (a clinical evaluation) and assessing trauma for an immigrant facing removal proceedings (a forensic evaluation). In the role of the forensic evaluator, the goal of the assessment is to provide information that is neutral and objective, even if it does not benefit the immigrant.[1]

Documentation of psychological symptoms and functioning as the result of traumatic experiences represents key supporting evidence in many forms of removal relief in IC; as a result, the need for training and expertise on the assessment of trauma-related presentations for MHPs working in this capacity cannot be overstated. This chapter highlights relevant issues for consideration when documenting and evaluating psychological trauma in immigrants. Although the focus of the evaluation will vary based on the referral question and legal issue, trauma evaluations in IC often benefit from looking beyond direct traumatic experiences. These evaluations typically require a full review of changes in the individual's level of functioning as a result of trauma, comorbidity factors, past and current stressors, risk and protective factors, and barriers that can influence well-being and functioning—all while including individual strengths and recognizing the influence of developmental and cultural factors.

The Assessment Process

In many ways, the assessment process itself is similar to the typical FMHA conducted in criminal court. Typically, the sessions are organized as follows: a preparatory phase, the initial meeting (during which the MHP and the immigrant first meet and the assessment begins), subsequent meetings (these evaluations typically require several meetings), and the final session. The MHP must be flexible and bear in mind that the assessment process relies on several elements and might need to take place over one very long session rather than the ideal of several shorter sessions.

Preparation

In this preparatory phase, communication is typically limited to interactions between the attorney and the MHP. During this first phase, there are several important tasks to be accomplished. The primary one is for the MHP to acquire a clear understanding of the reason for the referral. Understanding why they have been asked to conduct the evaluation and the expectations of the attorney in question are key factors in helping the MHP to determine whether they indeed have the qualifications to conduct such an evaluation. MHPs are responsible for ensuring that the activities that are required to answer the referral question (e.g., clinical interviewing, diagnosing, psychological testing) are within their scope of practice based on their discipline and license and to identify any activities that might be defined by law as being beyond the boundaries of practice in accordance with their profession's standards. In general, expertise in the cross-cultural assessment of trauma is an area of competency necessary to conduct these types of evaluations.

The MHP must clarify and explain their role as a forensic evaluator to the attorney, as not all immigration attorneys have experience working with mental health experts. The MHP should seek to develop a respectful and transparent relationship with the attorney. Additional key tasks include determining whether an interpreter will be needed, who will be responsible for providing the interpreter, and how the work with the interpreter will be facilitated.

During this preparatory phase, the MHP and the attorney will determine the location in which the evaluation will take place. Whether it will be held in the MHP's office or the attorney's. Ideally it should take place in a secure and confidential location in which the immigrant can feel comfortable. Having said this, in certain instances this might not be feasible. For immigrants held in detention (a far from ideal setting) there might be no choice but for the MHP to go to the facility to conduct the evaluation. Depending on the facility in which the immigrant is being held, additional coordination with the detention facility will be required. Such coordination is typically the attorney's responsibility.

The COVID-19 pandemic dictated a shift to telehealth with contact sessions conducted via telephone[2] or video via secure online platforms[3] to ensure safety for all parties concerned. Many MHPs are now using telephone and secure online platforms to conduct evaluations. Although more research is needed to explore the effectiveness of telehealth FMHAs, some studies have found that "[t]elemental health is effective for diagnosis and assessment across many populations (adult, child, geriatric, and ethnic) and for disorders in many settings (emergency, home health) and appears to be comparable to in-person care."[4]

In situations when the only viable option is to conduct the evaluation via an online platform, the MHP must ensure that the client has access to the necessary technology and a secure space. Additionally, the benefits and risks of videoconferencing, including but not limited to patient confidentiality, which differ from in-person sessions, must be part of that initial discussion. Again, as with in-person evaluations for detained immigrants, videoconferencing will require additional coordination, as there might be limits on the amount of time allowed per session, and scheduling will depend on the vagaries of the particular facility. If the MHP believes that the conditions of the location (e.g., noise distractions, frequent interruptions) might have impacted the immigrant's presentation and clinical opinions, this must be acknowledged in the final report.

The First and Subsequent Sessions

No matter what location is finally selected for the evaluation, and even though the evaluation is not a therapeutic session, building rapport that leads to trust in order to create a sense of security is critical.[5] Transparency and clarity are also critical, and during the first evaluation session and beyond, the MHP must share important information with the immigrant: Who the MHP is, what their role is, what the interview will entail, who will have access to the information, and so on. Beyond outlining all the steps involved, in an effort to build rapport and reduce retraumatization, the MHP can acknowledge the awkwardness of the task at hand (divulging difficult information to a stranger) and anticipate possible feelings of guilt or shame that might arise when discussing personal, embarrassing, stressful, and traumatic experiences.

As in the preparatory meeting with the attorney, during the first session with the immigrant, it is also helpful to explore their own expectations of the outcome of the evaluation while reviewing and allaying concerns regarding confidentiality. When working within the confines of a detention setting, MHPs should acknowledge the challenge of conducting an evaluation in that setting. If conducting such an evaluation via telephone or a secure online platform, MHPs should enquire about the immigrant's location during the course of the interview(s) and use clinical judgment to determine privacy and security. If the determination is made that the location is neither private nor secure, the evaluation should be terminated.

Should the assessment require several sessions, after the first one the MHP must conduct a check-in at the start of each subsequent meeting. Such a check-in should include a review of the purpose of the session (i.e., the assessment), a reminder of the MHP's role, an inquiry into any thoughts or questions that might have come up in the interim, a reminder of when the previous session ended, and the plan for the current session. Each session should close with a summary of what was accomplished and a plan for the next one (if there is to be one).

Finally, when conducting an assessment of trauma for the IC, it is important for the MHP to recognize that they walk a tightrope. In order to gather the necessary data to write the report, the MHP must conduct the interview while managing the countless emotions the immigrant could be experiencing. Furthermore, they must understand that while recounting the events of trauma can be extremely stressful and potentially retraumatizing for the immigrant, it can also be very distressing for the MHPs themselves.

The Clinical Interview

The clinical interview for the assessment of trauma typically focuses on gathering data that might support a diagnosis of posttraumatic stress disorder (PTSD) or other trauma-related disorders. The first step is the assessment of trauma exposure, including peritraumatic factors (e.g., severity, intensity, frequency and duration, proximity to the traumatic stressor). The MHP should also assess factors documented to increase the risk of PTSD, such as pretrauma factors (e.g., gender, prior trauma exposure, history of adverse childhood experiences, prior psychiatric difficulties) and posttrauma factors (e.g., availability and levels of social support, exposure to ongoing stressful life events, exposure to new trauma).

The assessment of PTSD includes identifying symptoms consistent with the American Psychiatric Association's *Diagnostic and Statistical Manual of Mental Disorders*, 5th edition (*DSM-5*),[6] including intrusion symptoms (criterion B), avoidance symptoms (criterion C), negative alterations in cognition and mood symptoms (criterion D), and alterations in arousal and reactivity symptoms (criterion E). Furthermore, the evaluation should include an assessment of the duration of the symptoms and chronology (the *DSM-5* requires that the symptom duration be of at least one month—criterion F), and an assessment of related clinical distress or functional impairment (criterion G). This latest criterion requires that the clinical distress and impairment be associated with the trauma-related symptoms. This can be quite challenging when evaluating immigrants, as they are likely to experience co-occurring psychopathology that could also cause clinical distress (e.g., anxiety or depression) and are also likely to have experienced several traumatic events.

Although "classic" PTSD is typically the focus of these evaluations, given the multifaceted traumatic experiences of many immigrants in IC, we recommend that MHPs consider the role of Complex PTSD (C-PTSD) when evaluating immigrants. For immigrants who have often endured extensive, prolonged, and repeated interpersonal trauma (such as torture, armed conflict, sexual violence, and physical assault) over time, the evaluating MHP must recognize that the current *DSM-5* criteria for PTSD might not adequately capture the individual's full range of experiences, traumatic symptoms, and disorders. C-PTSD[7] and disorders of extreme stress not otherwise specified (DESNOS)[8] are classifications that have been posited to highlight the experiences of such traumas.

Although there is substantial debate within the scientific community as to whether C-PTSD constitutes a clinical entity separate from PTSD, and although neither C-PTSD nor DESNOS are formally recognized as a separate disorder in the *DSM-5*,[9] the diagnosis of C-PTSD has been included in the World Health Organization's *International Classification of Disease and Related Health Problems*, 11th edition.[10] This diagnosis defines the qualifying event as "exposure to a severe traumatic event of an extreme and prolonged nature and for which escape is difficult or impossible, such as captivity or torture." In addition to the classic symptoms of PTSD (e.g., re-experiencing, avoidance, and alterations in arousal), this disorder includes "disturbances in self-organization," which include affective dysregulation, negative self-concept, and disturbed relationships. While there is limited research regarding C-PTSD in forced migrants,[11] a pilot study noted extensive C-PTSD symptoms among asylum seekers,[12] and another study found that C-PTSD was more common (36.1%) than PTSD (25.2%) in a sample of Syrian refugees.[13]

It is also important to remember that immigration law does not require a diagnosis of PTSD even in persecution-based relief applications,[14] as well as that individuals exposed to trauma often do not meet full *DSM-5* diagnostic criteria for PTSD but experience trauma-related symptoms ("subthreshold PTSD") that can result in substantial functional impairment.[15] Description of these symptoms and how they affect functional-related abilities might be more relevant than a diagnostic label. It is also important to note that the opposite is also true: not all individuals who experience even severe forms of trauma present with any trauma-related symptoms. Finally, though clinical interviews for the assessment of trauma typically focus on individual deficits, MHPs should also explore personal resources or resilience that the asylum seeker might have used to survive traumas encountered and that might have been protective against PTSD.

Assessment Measures

When evaluating PTSD in forensic contexts, the MHP should approach this task by conducting a multimethod assessment. While a standard, structured, or unstructured detailed clinical interview would help determine many of these factors, psychometric measures can be included in the interview to supplement and complement the findings of the assessment. Providing more objective data from psychological assessment instruments is always desirable in forensic assessments, and the assessment of trauma is best accomplished by using several valid and reliable instruments. However, it is critical for MHPs to understand that, while there are several relevant psychometric measures of trauma, most have only been validated with Western, Educated, Industrialized, Rich, and Democratic (WEIRD) samples, raising the question of whether they can be applied to non-Western populations.[16] Given that the majority of those in ICs are from non-Western cultures and English is not their first language, these measures might not do their experiences justice. Furthermore, additional factors might render the findings of standardized instruments less useful, including the respondent's educational level and reading capacity. Finally, for many immigrants, especially those experiencing C-PTSD, such instruments often do not reflect the developmental aspect of trauma, deficits in affect/self-regulation, identity disturbance, dysfunctional behavior, or patterns of revictimization.[17] In sum, the challenges of using psychometric instruments in IC can be so great that evaluators assessing trauma in this context are often forced to rely on a thorough clinical interview and collateral sources of information.[18] In this situation, the evaluator might want to consider the *cultural formulation interview*,[19] as it represents a more structured way of considering culture when conducting clinical interviews. When using assessment measures, the MHP could consider using trauma exposure measures, which focus on the trauma history and provide a detailed history of exposure to traumatic events, in combination with symptom measures, which assess the symptoms that result from the trauma exposure.[20] There are two types of PTSD-related measures: clinician-administered measures and self-report measures. Clinician-administered measures are preferred for the assessment of trauma-related presentations because they have several advantages over self-report measures, including an opportunity to clarify more complex symptoms, distinguish between overlapping symptoms, and engage in differential diagnosis from co-occurring disorders.[21] The following tables include some commonly used instruments (trauma exposure, clinician-administered, and self-reported) that have been used specifically with immigrant populations, both adults and children. In addition to PTSD measures, there are a number of self-report measures used for the assessment of general personality functioning and psychopathology that include scales to assess for trauma-related symptoms and PTSD.

Cross-Cultural Assessment of Trauma

Even though there is evidence that PTSD is a disorder that applies cross-culturally, there are significant variations in the clinical expression of symptoms.[22] Therefore, MHPs should always consider cross-cultural variations of trauma and think critically about how those variations might shape the experiencing of PTSD when assessing trauma across cultural groups. To effectively assess trauma cross-culturally, it is necessary to consider the diversity of traumatic exposure (the types of trauma, the extent of cumulative trauma, ongoing vulnerabilities); how an individual's experience and expression of trauma might differ across different cultural groups (the presence of cultural syndrome in facilitating the emergence and continuation of PTSD); the impact and continuum of social and cultural stressors and sociopolitical contexts on trauma survivors; and any protective factors that might help to alleviate symptoms and alter the

TABLE 6.1. Trauma assessment measures validated for use with immigrants

Source	Name of tool	Description	Format	Some of the populations with which these instruments have been studied
Craig et al. 2008	PTSD Screening and Diagnostic Scale (PSDS)	Developed to measure the presence of PTSD as defined by the *DSM-IV* diagnostic criteria.	38-item self-report	Bosnian refugees
Davey et al. 2014	Impact of Events Scale–Revised (IES-R)	An instrument that is used to measure PTSD symptoms and assesses current subjective distress for any major live event. It is not used for a diagnostic measure.	22-item self-report	Middle Eastern refugees in Australia
Dietrich et al. 2018	Short Screening Scale for Posttraumatic Stress Disorder (SSS-PSD)	SSS-PSD is a tool developed to assess one-month prevalence rate for indications of PTSD and severity of hyperarousal and avoidance.	7-item self-report	Adult refugees in Germany (predominantly Syrian)
Dietrich et al. 2019	Essen Trauma Inventory (ETI)	Developed to assess the severity of traumatization and PTSD that is consistent with the criteria in *DSM-IV*.	46-item self-report**	Syrian and Iraqi refugees in Germany
Filone and DeMatteo 2017*	Trauma Symptom Inventory-2 (TSI-2)	An instrument for assessing a variety of trauma and stress-related symptoms. It is a revised version of the original TSI and can be used as a useful tool to frame empathic interventions based on client's traumatic experiences (Briere 1995).	136-item self-report	Immigrant population with trauma histories
Foa et al. 1993; Kaltenbach et al. 2018	PTSD Symptom Scale—Interview Version [PSS-I]	An instrument for assessing PTSD symptoms; makes a diagnostic judgment based on *DSM-IV* criteria, including severity and frequency of the symptoms	17-item semistructured clinical interview	Children and adult refugees in Germany (predominantly Syrian and Afghan refugees)
Foa et al. 1995; Norris and Aroian 2008	Posttraumatic Stress Diagnostic Scale (PDS)	Developed to measure for assessing PTSD that is consistent with the *DSM-IV*. It is primarily used to measure the severity of PTSD symptoms related to a single identified traumatic event.	49-item self-report	Immigrant populations (Arab)
Hinton et al 2006	Clinician-Administered PTSD Scale (CAPS)	CAPS is a structured interview for measuring core and related symptoms of PTSD. It measures the frequency and intensity of each of the 17 *DSM-IV*–based PTSD symptoms.	17-item semistructured clinical Interview	Cambodian refugees
Hollifield et al. 2006	Comprehensive Trauma Inventory-104 (CTI-104)	Developed to measure a wide range of traumatic war-related events and how much impact the event had in refugee communities. The instrument is consistent with *DSM-IV*.	104-item self-report	Refugee populations (Kurdish and Vietnamese)
Hollifield et al. 2009	New Mexico Refugee Symptom Checklist-121 (NMRSCL-121)	Developed to assess physical (somatic) and emotional (psychological) symptoms in traumatized non-Western populations.	121-item self-report/clinician-administered	Vietnamese and Kurdish refugee populations

Citation	Instrument	Description	Format	Population
Hollifield et al. 2013*	Refugee Health Screener-15 (RHS-15)	Developed to screen symptoms of anxiety, depression, and PTSD in refugee populations. It is not used for a diagnostic measure but to guide people who need care into treatment.	15-item self-report/clinician administered via interpreters	Refugee population
Ibrahim et al. 2018	Posttraumatic Stress Disorder Checklist for DSM-5 (PCL-5)	A screening instrument to measure PTSD as well as symptom severity and making provisional PTSD diagnosis (*DSM-5*).	20-item self-report	Asylum seekers and immigrant populations in refugee camps in Kurdistan region of Iraq
Kissane et al. 2014	Structured Interview for Disorders of Extreme Stress (SIDES)	An instrument used to measure a broad range of symptoms related to complex posttraumatic stress symptoms (and DESNOS) as well as symptom severity across refugee and immigrant populations.	45-item semistructured interview (6 subscales)	Immigrant population with extreme, complex, and chronic trauma histories
Kubany et al. 2000; Craig et al. 2008	Traumatic Life Events Questionnaire (TLEQ)	An instrument for assessing various frequencies and severity of traumatic experiences in adulthood (assesses occurrence of 23 events).	23-item self-report	Bosnian refugees
Mollica et al. 1987	Hopkins Symptom Checklist-25 (HSCL-25)	Developed to screen symptoms of anxiety and depression in clinical refugee samples. It is not used for a diagnostic measure. Simple in its language and appropriate for all levels of educational attainment.	25-item self-report	Refugee population
Mollica et al. 1992	Harvard Trauma Questionnaire (HTQ)	HTQ is a widely used culturally sensitive assessment tool that measures a variety of trauma events and PTSD symptoms based on *DSM-III-R*.	Most versions are based on four general sections,** self-report/ clinician-administered	Refugee population
Nose et al. 2020	The Life Events Checklist (LEC)	Developed to measure potentially traumatic events in respondent's lifetime.	16-item self-report	Male asylum seekers and refugees in Italy
Weine et al. 1995	The Communal Traumatic Experiences Inventory (CTEI)	Developed to measure traumatic events experienced by the survivor of communal trauma and was specifically designed for Bosnian refugees of ethnic cleansing.	36-item clinician-administered questionnaire	Bosnian refugees
Weiss and Marmar 1997; Matheson et al. 200	Impact of Event Scale (IES)	IES-R is developed to sensitively and specifically assess trauma symptoms and measure as an index of PTSD symptoms (not as diagnostic instrument).	22-item self-report	(Muslim) Somali refugees
Vallieres et al. 2018	International Trauma Questionnaire (ITQ)	ITQ is used to measure the ICD-11 diagnoses of PTSD and CPTSD in a humanitarian context.	25-item clinician-administered**	Syrian refugee population in Lebanon

* To determine whether the instrument is appropriate for use with larger immigrant and non-Western populations, further validation studies are needed.

** Number and content of items may vary across versions.

TABLE 6.2. Trauma assessment measures validated for use with immigrant children

Source	Name of tool	Description	Format	Some of the populations with which these instruments have been studied
Bean et al. 2007	Hopkins Symptom Checklist-37A	HSCL-37A is a modified version of HSCL-25. It assesses symptoms of internalizing (anxiety, depression) and externalizing problems that are associated with reactions to trauma in refugee adolescents.	37-item self-report	Culturally diverse refugee adolescents in Netherlands and Belgium
Bean et al. 2006	Reaction of Adolescents to Traumatic Stress questionnaire (RATS)	Developed to assess posttraumatic stress reactions in refugee adolescents. The instrument is consistent with the *DSM-IV*.	22-item self-report questionnaire (3 subscales)	Culturally diverse refugee adolescents in Netherlands and Belgium
Ellis et al. 2006	UCLA Posttraumatic Stress Disorder Index	An instrument used to assess PTSD in children and adolescents.	22-item self-report/verbally administered	Somali refugee adolescents in New England
Ahmad et al. 2000	The Posttraumatic Stress Symptoms in Children (PTSS-C)	Developed to diagnose PTSD that is consistent with *DSM-IV*, as well as to assess posttraumatic stress symptoms not specific for PTSD and the severity of posttraumatic stress symptoms both for children from West-oriented and Middle East cultural background.	30-item semi structured clinician administered interview	Refugee youth: Iraqi Kurdistan refugee camp, Kurdistanian refugee children in Sweden, and Swedish children
Hall et al. 2014*	Child PTSD Symptom Scale Interview Format (CPSS-I)	An instrument to diagnosis PTSD and assess symptom severity in children who have experienced a traumatic event (adopted to Somali community).	52-item questionnaires administered as an interview (culturally responsive)	Somali refugee children and adolescents in refugee camps in Ethiopia
Dyregrov et al. 1996; Sack et al. 1997	The Impact of Event Scale (IES)	An instrument used to assess posttraumatic stress reactions in children.	15-item questionnaire self-report	Children exposed to warfare in Croatia and Bosnia and Herzegovina; Cambodian refugee youth in United States
Hall et al. 2014*	The Achenbach Child Behavior Checklist (CBCL)/Youth Self Report (YSR)	An instrument used to measure internalizing symptoms (emotional distress) and externalizing symptoms (maladaptive behavior).	112-item questionnaires administered as an interview	Somali refugee children and adolescents in refugee camps in Ethiopia

* To determine whether the instrument is appropriate for use with larger immigrant and non-Western populations, further validation studies are needed.

duration of PTSD.[23] In addition, MHPs working with traumatized individuals from diverse cultural groups should be aware of two main threats to content validity in PTSD assessment measures: overinclusion and underinclusion.[24] "Overinclusion" refers to the reliance on specific items to describe PTSD that are not necessarily applicable to various cultures. For example, while avoidance/numbing symptoms are commonly experienced in Western societies, multiple studies have shown that these items "may present less consistently across cultural settings."[25] "Underinclusion" refers to items that are missing from the criteria but that represent prominent features of trauma response in other cultures. For example, somatic symptoms (e.g., bodily heat, neck soreness, or sudden shortness of breath) and particular dissociative experiences are prominent aspects of PTSD in some specific cultural and diverse settings.[26] In the same vein, it is important to be flexible and inclusive when considering certain criteria so as to cover a wide range of trauma symptoms when working with diverse cultural groups (e.g., inquire about the details of any reported recurrent distressing dreams rather than simply focusing on the precise content).[27] It is also important to consider the concept of "racial trauma" and how this might impact the individual's clinical presentation when assessing trauma cross-culturally. "Racial trauma" has been defined as a form of race-based stress experienced by People of Color and Indigenous Individuals (POCI), who react to real or perceived experiences of racial discrimination, such as threats of harm and injury, humiliation, or shaming events. Racial trauma involves individual and collective injuries due to exposure and re-exposure to race-based stress, and it can result in clinical reactions similar to PTSD.[28] Although most research on racial trauma has been conducted in POCI citizens and not immigrants, immigrants might be subjected to similar experiences of race-based stress.

Factors That Can Influence the Assessment Process

From the start, MHPs conducting trauma assessments must bear in mind a range of factors that might influence their conclusions. In addition to the barriers described above, other factors can influence final conclusions and need to be taken into consideration, as they can influence the type and amount of information the immigrant is willing to share, as well as their presentation when describing their traumatic experience(s).

Time Element

Both attorneys and the MHPs conducting trauma assessments for ICs should set aside ample time for each session (although the length of time available for each session might be out of both the MHP's and the client's control depending on whether or not the individual is incarcerated). MHPs must understand that depending on where the individual is physically located during the scheduled evaluations—incarcerated or within the community—there might be variable time during and between sessions. Finally, both the attorney and the MHP must factor in adequate time between completing the evaluation and writing the final report. Depending on the details and extent of the immigrant's trauma history, preparing a report can take a considerable amount of time.

Credibility and Malingering

Given what is at risk for the immigrant who is facing deportation proceedings, the MHP working within the IC setting, as in any FMHA, must assess the immigrant's credibility and consider the possibility of symptom exaggeration, feigning, or underreporting while taking into consideration the individual's cultural realities. However, before forming conclusions about symptom validity, MHPs must consider additional factors present in immigrants that might be contributing to difficulties recounting traumatic experiences and that could be misinterpreted as malingering or minimization. These include a lack of trust in the MHP conducting the evaluation, problems associated with trauma (e.g., hyperarousal, impaired memory, denial, numbing), fear of putting significant others at risk by disclosing information, or having been blindfolded, drugged, or having lost consciousness during their traumatic experience.

Gender

MHPs must recognize the impact of gender-based violence (GBV), especially sexual violence, on asylum seekers they might evaluate. As we have seen, many who have experienced sexual violence could be reluctant to disclose their experience because of the shame and stigmatization associated with it.[29] In addition, male survivors of sexual violence tend to be particularly reluctant to discuss such traumatic experiences.[30]

When possible, if an immigrant has a preference for an expert of a particular gender, this request should be respected and accommodated, especially if a desire for same-sex interviewing is expressed. In working with survivors of GBV, the MHP should weigh cultural and individual factors to determine the most appropriate interviewing strategy.

Setting

When conducting psychological evaluations of immigrants in detention, it is also important for MHPs to bear in mind that the conditions of detention and its remote location have been found to aggravate psychological symptoms of distress.[31] Furthermore, the lack of a sense of confidentiality and security in such settings might make the immigrant reluctant to engage in the assessment process.

Conclusion

The scope of an evaluation conducted to document psychological evidence of trauma depends on the referral question and psycholegal issue being addressed. In general, in order to fully document an immigrant's traumatic experience and their psychological functioning for IC, it is imperative that the MHPs review all aspects of the individual's functioning. The MHP must conduct a thorough multimethod assessment that not only captures the individual's traumatic experiences but also incorporates their life history, changes in functioning, and any and all current "self-relating difficulties, such as affect dysregulation, relational disturbance (including abandonment concerns and interpersonal sensitivity), identity problems, cognitive distortion, somatization, and avoidance responses such as dissociation, substance abuse, and self-injurious behavior."[32] As a result of the variability in individual experiences and circumstances, the degree of physical and psychological signs, symptoms, or consequences, each immigrant's history and experiences are unique. This variability will be demonstrated in the manner in which immigrants present themselves during the interview, how they recount their experiences, and the amount and detail with which they are able to recall information and recount events of their trauma. It is the responsibility of the MHP who agrees to take on this role to fully capture and document this lived experience.

7

Vicarious Trauma and Secondary Traumatic Stress in Lawyers and Mental Health Professionals

Many professionals accustomed to working with individuals navigating the complex immigration legal system can appreciate the distressing conditions (e.g., violence, poverty, human rights abuses, economic distress) that led their clients to flee their homelands in search of safety. These professionals also understand the strenuous migratory journeys undertaken and recognize the additional burdens encountered by their clients as they face a complicated system that seeks to bar them from entering or remaining in the United States. What is often overlooked or underestimated by mental health professionals (MHPs), attorneys, and others working in immigration courts (ICs) is the strain that working with this population can place on the providers themselves.

In this chapter, we discuss the physical, behavioral, psychological, and spiritual toll that working with this population within the IC setting can have on MHPs, immigration attorneys, and others, including law clerks, translators, immigration judges (IJs), United States Citizenship and Immigration Services adjudicators, asylum officers, and Immigration and Customs Enforcement attorneys. (Even though not all members of this group provide services to clients in the traditional sense, we refer here to the group of affected individuals collectively as "service providers," with the understanding that anyone who encounters trauma narratives is at risk, but those who have the most direct contact with clients are likely to be the most impacted.) We highlight the challenges faced along with the risk factors for these service providers. The chapter concludes with best practices for all professionals working with this population at the personal, professional, and organizational levels to promote resilience and reduce this occupational hazard.

The Impact of Traumatic Narratives on Service Providers

Whether serving as a MHP or as a legal professional in ICs, an integral component of this work is interaction with the particulars of many cases of traumatic stress. Repeatedly bearing witness to the suffering of others by listening to graphic descriptions or looking at the visual after-effects of events stemming from armed conflict, human rights abuses, sexual violence, or torture can have a deleterious impact on providers' wellbeing. This "cost of caring" among those who "listen to client's trauma stories of fear, pain, and suffering" means they can often feel these same emotions secondarily,[1] which can leave them susceptible to vicarious trauma (VT) and secondary traumatic stress (STS). While these two concepts are widely used—often interchangeably, as the literature makes clear—there are differences between them.[2]

"Vicarious trauma" is used to describe the negative shift that can occur in helping professionals' core belief systems and cognitive schemas about self, others, and the world as a result of empathically engaging with the traumatic experiences of their clients.[3] It has been argued that such changes in the cognitive schemas of helping professionals lead to disruptions in feelings of safety, trust, esteem, intimacy, and sense of control.[4] Even though VT can be viewed as a normal reaction to the repeated experience of engagement with traumatic material, it might have serious consequences, including declining professional performance and impaired personal wellbeing.[5] "Secondary traumatic stress" refers to emotional and behavioral reactions that trauma caregivers could experience as a result of exposure to their clients' traumatic materials while helping or wanting to help them.[6] Caregivers could experience STS, and over time this might lead to the changes in outlook that characterize VT.

While VT and STS share common triggers and the terms have been used interchangeably, clinicians and researchers have highlighted distinct differences. Unlike the gradual changes in the providers' cognitive schemas due to cumulative exposure to the traumatic experiences of their clients brought about by VT, professionals faced with STS experience more observable and sudden-onset reactions that are almost identical to the symptoms seen in posttraumatic stress disorder (PTSD) (e.g., anxiety, avoidance, hyperarousal, sleep disturbances). Just as primary trauma victims could develop PTSD after a direct experience to trauma, being repeatedly exposed to a client's traumatic narratives might lead to a "secondary trauma" in service providers.[7] Because both VT and STS can be experienced concurrently and are very similar; for the remainder of this chapter, "STS" will be used to capture this occupational hazard—the experiences of professionals who work with trauma survivors.

Traumatic Narratives and Service Providers Working Within the Context of the Immigration Court

The detrimental effects on MHPs of working with traumatized populations have been well documented in the psychological literature.[8] The price of such work has been found to impact not only the psychological well-being of professionals serving traumatized individuals but also the organizations in which they work, as evidenced by high turnover rates and organizational dysfunction,[9] ultimately further compromising the already fragile mental health of clients.

While those working in the mental health field have become increasingly aware of the cost of caring, the legal field has been much slower to acknowledge and even slower to respond to this challenge.[10] Despite this delay, there has been a growing recognition that legal professionals working with traumatized clients are not immune to the impacts of STS.[11] However, this recognition has been mostly confined to those practicing family law,[12] working with victims of domestic violence,[13] and within the criminal, family and juvenile courts.[14]

This limitation is particularly jarring as professionals practicing in the field of immigration law—attorneys, adjudicators, and others—are often repeatedly exposed to immigrant trauma.[15] Whether these professionals are working with asylum seekers, with victims of domestic violence, torture, and human rights abuses, or with unaccompanied children, traumatic experiences are often the basis for the individual's presence in the immigration system. Trauma is pervasive throughout the immigration process. Despite this reality, there have been only three studies exploring the impact of STS on legal professionals working in the immigration system. Two focused on asylum lawyers. One, examining 57 immigration attorneys, found hours spent each week on asylum cases to be associated with symptoms of secondary trauma. The other, examining 70 immigration attorneys, reported similar findings.[16] The third studied the experiences of 96 IJs. The findings of the third study concluded that IJs, with their huge caseloads adjudicating traumatic narratives, suffer from extensive traumatic stress.[17] Each of these studies highlighted the potentially detrimental impacts of working with traumatized immigrant populations on these professionals during the course of their careers.

Overall, the findings of these studies are consistent with what has been noted among MHPs working with traumatized populations: repeated exposure to traumatic materials leads to problematic symptoms affecting the helping professional negatively (e.g., distressing emotions, intrusive imagery and thoughts, poor concentration, numbing or avoidance, somatic complaints, physiological arousal, addiction or compulsive behaviors, and impairment of daily functioning) within and outside the work context and influences their functioning in personal, social, professional, and organizational roles.[18] The issue is compounded by the complexity of immigration law, its high level of uncertainty, large caseloads, the backlog of cases, and the limited availability of resources. All of these conspire to overwhelm immigration service providers.[19] Bearing this reality in mind, it is imperative that MHPs, immigration attorneys, and other impacted personnel, as well as the organizations in which they provide services, recognize the effects of STS and take active steps to mitigate its impact.

Risk Factors for Developing Secondary Traumatic Stress

Researchers have identified some critical variables that influence the likelihood of STS, such as trauma history, poor emotional wellness, younger professionals who are newer to the field, gender (females), limited availability of social support, low education and low socioeconomic status, and coping styles.[20] Most licensed MHPs are guided by a code of ethics, which includes the importance and need for self-care as an ethical obligation; that is, that they owe the same duties to self as to others. Yet, despite self-care being included in all major ethics codes for MHPs, it is striking that many MHPs continue to provide services despite their personal and ongoing distress. A survey of 658 psychologists noted that among the reported barriers to self-care were lack of time, denial of issues, shame, and lack of motivation.[21] Some authors have described a "chronic lack of selfcare"[22] among MHPs.

A similar issue also plagues those in the legal profession who work with trauma survivors yet appear unable to acknowledge and address their own struggles.[23] The issue for attorneys is compounded by the fact that they are not formerly trained to work with emotions and as a result their reactions might range from denial of the impact of work-related emotions to overidentification with such experiences.

In order to provide effective services to clients (or, in the case of adjudicators, to ensure high quality and unbiased decision-making), it is the responsibility of MHPs, legal professionals, and everyone working within the immigration system not only to acknowledge STS but also to address it through intervention and prevention at the personal, professional, and organizational levels.

Recommendations for Intervening and Preventing Secondary Traumatic Stress

The first step to addressing STS among professionals working in the ICs is to acknowledge the extensive distress that repeatedly being exposed to traumatic narratives can evoke. In order to be truly beneficial, however, changes must be instituted and integrated at three levels: the personal, the professional, and the agency/organizational, with the recognition that these levels interact and influence each other.

Personal Level

Many attempts to address STS focus on individual efforts by service providers to reduce their personal experience of STS. Often they attempt to incorporate better stress management strategies, healthier self-care strategies, and enhanced time management skills.[24] While self-care can be viewed as an ethical mandate and such interventions can contribute to the reduction of STS, addressing STS at only this level can be inadequate and places the burden of intervention and prevention entirely on the practitioner. It is important that the organizations these providers work for recognize the traumatizing impact of this work and also take responsibility to ensure that self-care is a priority within the organizational setting.

Professional Level

In reviewing the literature, it is striking that neither graduate mental health programs nor legal programs provide uniform education about STS, despite the reality that many of the students and trainees in both fields will and do encounter STS via interactions with their clients. Given that age/lack of experience is a noted risk factor for STS,[25] this is an important issue. Training programs should offer education and resources about STS early on. In addition, once professionals are already working with this population, time should be set aside routinely for both attorneys and MHPs to review and discuss their reactions to their cases and their interactions with the IC system.

As professional identities evolve and solidify, it is important that professional associations offer continuing education training in order to provide instruction about STS and highlight the professional ethical responsibility of self-care. Additional efforts to address STS at the professional level can also come through professional peer support networks.[26]

Agency/Organizational Level

While acknowledging the detrimental nature of STS is a good starting point, simply relying on service providers to address STS at the personal and professional levels places the onus of the burden on the individual and can leave the professional feeling that they are at fault. It is critical that the agencies/organizations through which these professionals provide services also take responsibility for and make a commitment to addressing STS.[27] By demonstrating a commitment to change at the level of leadership through actions that filter throughout the organizational structure, institutions working with immigrants can support the providers who work for them and promote resilience in their staffs. There is also a need for the development of innovative approaches such as the Joyful Heart Foundation Retreat,[28] a holistic healing arts retreat found to effectively improve well-being and support resilience among counselors, advocates, and lawyers serving trauma survivors.

To promote resilience, work environments should encourage flexibility and creativity, promote continuing education, and provide an atmosphere in which professionals can freely share their reactions to cases without fear of being judged or viewed as incompetent. A range of suggestions for both MHPs and legal professionals have been made. These include: (a) providing information and education about STS via in-service training;[29] (b) providing supervision that includes reflecting on the impact of the case on both MHPs and attorneys;[30] (c) providing peer support (access to a network of experienced professionals to turn to for guidance for both trainees and permanent staff),[31] (d) providing self-care activities within the organization;[32] (e) diversifying caseloads; and (f) providing personal development opportunities, increased autonomy, and a culture in which STS is recognized and addressed.[33] At the agency/organizational level, addressing STS as a team can also help to reduce the isolative effects of STS and build group cohesion and positive peer relations.[34]

Finally, in order to mitigate the impact of STS, MHPs with expertise in the field can play a key role via consultations.[35] Such consultations can occur in the form of facilitating support groups[36] or providing in-house training[37] to mental health and legal practitioners and the agencies/organizations they work for.

Conclusion

Ongoing exposure to narratives of trauma and torture can have profound psychological effects on MHPs, immigration lawyers, IJs, and other service providers. While there are a number of studies focused on the impact of STS on MHPs, there are only a few that have examined the experiences of those who work with immigrants.[38] As we have seen, even fewer have focused on legal professionals working in this field.[39] Though there are some best practices, which should be followed to attempt to alleviate the impact of STS, it is clear that further research is needed to fully appreciate the impacts and identify the most appropriate interventions to promote resilience.

PART III

Cultural, Legal, and Forensic Considerations in
Immigration Court

8

Special Considerations for Collaboration Between Lawyers and Mental Health Professionals

SCENARIO 1: An attorney seeks an evaluation of a client to support an application for withholding of removal from a country with a history of jailing and persecuting the mentally ill. The attorney is hoping for a diagnosis that will impress the immigration judge with how ill the client is to support the claim. The mental health professional is not able to make that type of diagnosis given the constraints of the information available to her and the setting in which she is forced to conduct the interview. The attorney would also like the mental health professional to say that client's substance use disorder is "cured" or "in remission." However, this is not consistent with the course of the illness for that specific person.

SCENARIO 2: A mental health professional is working with an asylum applicant who has several children. The mental health professional learns from the parent that she is currently abusing her youngest child. The attorney is distressed to learn that the mental health professional intends to report this information to child protective services.

SCENARIO 3: A mental health professional writes a report in support of an immigrant's application for relief. Some of the information disclosed by the client turns out to be inconsistent with the client's written statement that has been submitted to the court. The attorney asks the mental health professional to delete the inconsistent information from her report.

The scenarios above illustrate some common areas of conflict between immigration attorneys and licensed mental health professionals (MHPs). Attorneys and MHPs are subject to different ethical and professional standards, and their goals might also differ and at times even oppose each other. This can create tension and conflict, which can ultimately affect the success of the attorney's representation of a client. This chapter reviews the different goals and ethical obligations of attorneys and MHPs, as well as common points of potential misunderstanding and conflict, and provides recommendations for an effective collaboration between them.

Immigration Attorneys' Ethical Obligations

Attorneys have a well-defined code of ethical rules to which they must adhere or risk losing their license to practice law. These obligations can be found in the model rules and the commentary on those rules put forward by the American Bar Association,[1] which have been generally adopted, albeit sometimes with modifications or carve-outs, by most (but not all) state bar associations.[2] Local rules add an additional layer: The Executive Office of Immigration Review has issued rules for attorneys who practice before it,[3] and these rules are also applicable to practice before the Department of Homeland Security, which includes United States Citizenship and Immigration Services (USCIS) and Customs and Border Protection.[4]

Attorneys are expected to be zealous advocates and make as compelling a case as possible for their clients. At the same time, however, they have competing ethical obligations of honesty and fair dealing. They must constantly walk a line between advancing their clients' interests and staying on the right side of the ethical rules.

Duties of Loyalty and Confidentiality

Attorneys owe duties of loyalty and confidentiality to their clients. As advocates, they are expected to do what is necessary to win a case, within the bounds of professional discretion, the law, and the ethical rules.[5] This duty of loyalty is perhaps the most central to legal ethics and the practice of law.[6] Complementary to this duty, attorneys are expected to keep client confidences. With limited exceptions, they are not ethically permitted to disclose any information related to the representation of a client.[7] This means that any information that attorneys learn in the course of representing a client, whether it comes from the client or from another party, is confidential.[8] Confidentiality should not be confused with attorney-client privilege. "Confidentiality" refers broadly to the attorney's ethical obligation not to expose client information. "Attorney-client privilege" is a rule that prevents attorneys from being compelled (i.e., by a court) to testify about or disclose certain client information. Attorneys can be *ethically* bound not to disclose a piece of information, but if there is no privilege, then they are still *legally* bound to disclose it if ordered to do so.

The duties of loyalty and confidentiality are subject to some important exceptions. Attorneys are permitted to disclose client information (1) if they think it is necessary to prevent reasonably certain death or serious bodily harm[9] or (2) if they learn that the client has used or plans to use them in furtherance of crime or fraud that is reasonably certain to result in substantial injury to the financial interests or property of another.[10] Even then, the rule is permissive rather than mandatory.[11] As discussed in the next section, however, attorneys are also affirmatively bound by a duty of candor that at times requires them to break their duties of loyalty and confidentiality.

Duty of Candor

Attorneys are considered officers of the court and have a duty of candor to any tribunal before which they practice.[12] They must not submit false information; neither may they allow false information to stand uncorrected.[13] This rule takes precedence over the aforementioned duties of loyalty and confidentiality.[14] "Tribunal" is probably defined broadly enough to include immigration courts (ICs) or an administrative agency such as USCIS.[15]

Typically, if an attorney learns *before* filing an application information that makes the client ineligible for the benefit sought, the attorney can avoid the need to disclose client confidences by simply declining to file the application. But, if the attorney learns after the fact that their side has already submitted a false representation to the tribunal, they might not be able to avoid disclosing the client's confidential information. The ethical rules require that they take remedial measures to correct the falsehood.[16] In some instances, merely withdrawing the offending application or withdrawing from the representation might be sufficient, but in others it might be necessary to affirmatively correct the misrepresentation by disclosing confidential information.[17]

The American Bar Association (ABA) Model Rules and the federal regulations differ, in an important way, about whether an attorney is responsible for information that they do not know for certain is false. According to the Model Rules (and therefore most state rules), "[t]he prohibition against offering false evidence only applies if the lawyer *knows* that the evidence is false." Under this rule, a lawyer who reasonably believes the evidence is false can still present it to the court, because "a lawyer should resolve doubts about the veracity of testimony or other evidence in favor of the client." The Rules caution, however, that the lawyer's knowledge of falsity can be inferred from the circumstances and does not have to be confessed to. The lawyer cannot, therefore, "ignore an obvious falsehood."[18] In contrast, the federal regulations governing practice before ICs and the USCIS provide that an attorney violates the duty of candor when they present information in "reckless disregard" of its falsity.[19]

Attorneys also have a more limited obligation not to lie to third parties in the context of their representation.[20] They are not supposed to lie by omission either, except that there is considerable ambiguity as to when an omission becomes a lie, especially considering the competing obligation to advocate zealously for a client and not unnecessarily disclose client information.[21]

Generally No Duty to Report Crime or Abuse

Attorneys are not obligated to turn in their clients if they confess to a crime committed in the past or lay out their plans to commit a crime in the future. In fact, to do so could violate confidentiality rules and cause the attorney to lose their license. As explained above, attorneys are allowed to disclose a crime when necessary to prevent reasonably certain death or serious bodily harm or when the client has used the attorney to further the crime.[22] But, if a client tells the attorney that they plan to commit a crime that does not involve death or serious bodily harm, the attorney may *not* disclose it unless the client has involved them in some way.[23] The public good is considered to be greater served by allowing people to speak freely with their attorney—ABA Rule 1.6 Comment 2 states: "The client is thereby encouraged to seek legal assistance and to communicate fully and frankly with the lawyer even as to embarrassing or legally damaging subject matter. The lawyer needs this information to represent the client effectively and, if necessary, to advise the client to refrain from wrongful conduct"—so long as that attorney does not cross the line into advising the client on how to commit a crime.[24]

In keeping with attorneys' duty of loyalty and confidentiality to their clients, attorneys are not mandatory reporters. They do not need to make a report to the relevant authorities if their client discloses that they have harmed their children. They *might* report only if they believe that they must do so to prevent reasonably certain death or serious bodily harm to the child. If the harm discussed is retrospective, not prospective (i.e., the client disclosed past events rather than plans to commit the harm in the future), the harm is not likely to be considered "reasonably certain."

An attorney might run into trouble, however, if they are representing two clients whose interests become adverse to one another. It is common for an attorney in asylum cases to represent a whole family on the theory that their interests are aligned (if the parent gets asylum, so do the children as derivatives of that application). But an abused child might be eligible for one of several different forms of immigration status *because of* the abuse inflicted on them by a parent. In this instance, the child client's interest is no longer aligned with the adult client's interest and the attorney cannot ethically continue to represent both parties.

Duty to Respect Client Autonomy

Attorneys are obligated to follow a client's wishes as to the goals of representation, but while they are expected to "consult" with the client as to how to achieve those goals, they are not necessarily required to always defer to clients about strategic decisions.[25] An example would be a client directing a lawyer to make an argument that the lawyer believes will harm the case. If the client is unhappy with the lawyer's representation, they can presumably find new counsel.[26] Things get slightly more tricky, however, when counsel is assigned and the client has no other option. What would be an acceptable assertion of authority by a retained attorney may be an abuse of power by an assigned one. Things get even more tricky when the client has "diminished capacity," which in the context of the ABA model rules is defined as when "capacity to make adequately considered decisions in connection with a representation is diminished, whether because of minority, mental impairment or for some other reason."[27]

When representing a client with diminished capacity, an attorney must, "as far as reasonably possible, maintain a normal client-lawyer relationship." This means that the lawyer is obligated to respect the client's autonomy and follow their direction in which objectives to pursue and, to an extent, how to pursue them, rather than taking a more paternalistic approach and doing what the attorney thinks would be in the client's best interest.[28] The attorney is allowed to act more paternalistically only if the client is at risk of "substantial harm," and even then the attorney is instructed to take the least intrusive protective action possible.[29]

This ethical rule sets up a potential conflict with the Board of Immigration Appeals (BIA)'s view that attorneys will be able to step in and make decisions for mentally ill clients who lack competency, and this will be a sufficient safeguard to ensure that the proceedings comport with due process.[30] As an example of how this might play out, a client tells their attorney that they wish to be deported rather than remain in detention any longer. "Substantial harm" presumably includes deportation,[31] but deportation might not be a "substantial harm" to every client in every circumstance. In this particular scenario, the attorney fears that the client might be underestimating the danger that awaits them in their home country—a place where they have no family and where they have not lived since childhood. What should the attorney do? The ABA approach would be more likely to allow the client to dictate the goals of the representation, while the BIA would seem to anticipate a more protective approach.[32]

Mental Health Professionals' Ethical Obligations

All mental health organizations provide a set of ethical standards or guidelines for their practice. In this chapter, we discuss those that regulate the practice of psychology. However, each MHP should follow their own professional organization's ethics rules.

The American Psychological Association (APA)'s *Ethical Principles of Psychologists and Code of Conduct*[33] (hereinafter referred to as the "Ethics Code") includes a Preamble, five General Principles (Beneficence and Nonmaleficence, Fidelity and Responsibility, Integrity, Justice, Respect for People's Rights, and Dignity), and specific Ethical Standards. The Preamble and General Principles are considered aspirational goals and are not themselves enforceable rules. However, the Ethical Standards set forth enforceable rules for conduct as psychologists. Of note, the Ethics Code is binding on psychologists who are members of the APA, those practicing in states that have adopted the Ethics Code into their administrative code, and those who work in organizations that have also adopted the Code.[34] Some of the Ethical Standards are reviewed in the next section as they apply to MHPs who work in ICs.

Ethical Standards

The APA's Ethical Standards establish that "psychologists provide services . . . within the boundaries of their competency based on their education, training, supervised experience, consultation, study, or professional experience" (2.01.a). This principle emphasizes the need for MHPs in ICs to develop expertise in the areas of forensic mental health assessments, cross-cultural psychology, and immigration law before agreeing to accept referrals in this setting. In addition, the Ethical Standards establish that "psychologists refrain from entering into multiple relationships" (3.05.a). For example, MHPs should refrain from being retained as an expert witness involving an immigrant they have treated. In section 3.07, the Ethical Standards explain that when psychologists are providing services at the request of a third party, they need to clarify at the outset the type of services they will be providing (e.g., treatment versus forensic assessment versus consultation) and who is the client (e.g., immigrant versus attorney).

When MHPs provide forensic assessments in ICs, they are directed by the Ethical Standards to obtain informed consent in a language that is "reasonably understandable" to that person (3.10.a) and to inform the individual of the limits of confidentiality and the purpose and nature of the activity (3.10.d). Chapters 9 and 10 in this volume provide information about notification and informed consent in ICs.

Notably, the Ethical Standards require psychologists to use assessment instruments that are valid and reliable in the population tested. This can be challenging in ICs when most psychological testing available has been normed with populations that differ from those of the immigrants. However, the standards direct psychologists to describe the limitations of their opinions when the methods used have not established their reliability or validity with the immigrant population evaluated (9.02.b).

Specialty Guidelines for Forensic Psychology

In addition to the Ethics Code, the APA has published a set of aspirational guidelines (*Specialty Guidelines for Forensic Psychology*, 2013)[35] to assist psychologists who provide services in legal settings. The guidelines cover the following areas: Responsibilities; Competency; Diligence; Relationships; Fees; Informed Consent, Notification and Assent; Conflicts in Practice; Privacy, Confidentiality, and Privilege; Methods and Procedures; Assessment; and Professional and Other Public Communications. Psychologists working in ICs should be knowledgeable of all of these principles. Although these guidelines are aspirational, MHPs are strongly encouraged to consider them when evaluating immigrants in IC.

Conflicts Between Immigration Attorneys and Mental Health Professionals

Tensions between psychology and law have been described extensively in the literature.[36] The generation of knowledge and decision-making standards are approached differently by these disciplines. Even though courts have been employing licensed MHPs as experts for decades, there remain a number of obstacles to this collaboration, some of which are at the most basic level, arising out of conflicts between the values of both disciplines.[37] Examples of conflicts include psychology's empirical epistemology versus law's authoritarian epistemology; the experimental methodology in psychology versus the adversarial process in law; psychology's probabilistic and tentative conclusions versus law's emphasis on certainty; and psychology's academic and abstract orientation versus law's reactive orientation.[38] These different sets of values and approaches, paired with the different ethical standards that guide both disciplines, can create tensions between MHPs and attorneys as they try to work together in ICs. When these tensions are not resolved, they can interfere with the eventual disposition of the case. As a result, it is important for both MHPs and attorneys to be educated about these potential conflicts ahead of time. The next sections describe some areas of conflict specific to the IC context drawn from our practice and the experiences of our professional colleagues.

Mandatory Reporter Versus Often Cannot Report

Depending on the jurisdiction in which the MHP is practicing, there are laws that govern their responsibility with respect to reporting clients if child abuse is suspected. For example, in the state of New York, MHPs are deemed mandatory reporters if, in their professional role, they are presented with a reasonable cause to suspect child abuse;[39] similar laws exist nationwide.

In contrast, as explained above, attorneys are bound by the duty of confidentiality to their clients and often *cannot* ethically report that their client has abused a child. Consider the example where an attorney is aware that a client has abused their children. Assuming that the attorney is not otherwise ethically bound to report that information, it would also not be ethical for the attorney to cause or allow that information to be communicated to someone who is a mandatory reporter. Remember that attorneys owe a duty to advance their clients' interests, and they also are obligated to inform clients of the potential legal implications of their actions. It would not be ethical for the attorney to knowingly send a client into a situation in which the attorney knows they will make disclosures that will likely result in their arrest or other negative consequence. However, the attorney is also not permitted to advise a client on how to successfully commit a crime. So the attorney must walk a fine line between advising the client of consequences of disclosing certain information to a mandatory reporter (permitted) and affirmatively advising the client to lie or withhold information (potentially not permitted).[40] This knowledge is important for MHPs, as they should know that reporting to the immigrant's lawyer does not relieve them of their obligation to report abuse. Instead, they should be educated about the appropriate contacts to report suspected abuse if this information arises in the context of an evaluation being conducted for an IC. Ideally, however, MHPs should not report suspected abuse without letting the referring attorney know that they are planning to do so or have done so. The attorney will need to know this information, as it has the potential to seriously impact the client's immigration case.

Simplicity Versus Nuance

The key to understanding many of the points of conflict discussed herein is the fact that attorneys, when acting as storytellers, value simplicity. There is a common perception of attorneys as being adept at handling complexity and nuance: to even enter the legal profession, prospective law-school applicants have to pass a test of their reasoning skills that contains questions such as "X is true if Y except in the case of Z but only when not W."[41] Once the person is licensed, much of the work of being a lawyer involves the application of messy facts to ambiguous law. But this is only half of the picture.

To be successful in litigation, an attorney must be able to take a complex situation and distill it into a simple narrative. Attorneys face decision makers who are vaguely interested at best or actively disinterested or hostile at worst. They need to catch the attention of that decision maker—and keep it. In addition, they need to make the decision maker care enough about the case that they are motivated to help the client. This is especially true when the client bears the burden of proof or persuasion, as is the case in most immigration adjudications.

First and foremost, attorneys must be storytellers. In service of their craft, they employ metaphor and analogy, pithy anecdotes, even catchy turns of phrase (if it rhymes, even better).[42] This is famously true of attorneys who practice before juries but is equally true of those who practice before judges and administrative agencies. The goal is to tell a compelling story and win the case. Complications and qualifications are not compelling. While nuanced thinking must go into the crafting of a narrative, there might not be much room for nuance in the final product—the filing that will go to the decision maker.

Partiality Versus Impartiality

MHPs, unlike attorneys, do not have the same inherent tension built into their professional rules between loyalty and honesty. MHPs working as expert witnesses could feel a desire to help a client better their situation, but their obligation is to be as impartial as possible. As noted earlier, the APA's *Specialty Guidelines for Forensic Psychology* state that "psychologists strive for accuracy, impartiality, fairness, and independence . . . strive to be unbiased and impartial . . . (1.02)."[43] This principle is similar for other MHPs in their roles as expert witnesses in court. This significant difference between the goals of MHPs and attorneys can manifest in several conflictual situations. The most obvious one occurs when attorneys push MHPs to form conclusions or opinions that are not fully supported by the data. In a more subtle way, this conflict manifests in disagreements about what goes into the report. Once the MHP has submitted the report to the attorney, it is not unusual for the attorney to want to edit the report. There are many reasons why this might happen. Sometimes it might be due to typos or facts that have been misstated (e.g., dates). Other times it is because the attorney has concerns that information in the report might be harmful to the legal case that the attorney is trying to make or otherwise paint the client in a negative light.[44] Attorneys could also have trouble understanding some parts of the report that include too much jargon. It is important to remember that the attorney is trying to put the strongest possible spin on a situation without spinning off into outright lying, and the attorney could perceive that the report does not support this position. This question—"to edit or not to edit"—has not been specifically addressed by the APA *Guidelines*.

To answer this question, it is important for the MHP to understand that an immigration case can be tanked by a tiny detail. For example, a statement that the client supported himself by sex work can potentially implicate the prostitution ground of inadmissibility. Information about drug use can trigger additional grounds of inadmissibility, many of which are not possible to waive. Information about suicidal ideation or a history of suicide attempts can trigger inadmissibility under the "mental disease or defect" ground. Even a seemingly innocuous statement about being forced to cook for a rebel army might rise to the "material support" to terrorism ground. Additionally, asylum applicants in particular are judged harshly for any inconsistencies, however minor, in their story, and they might be found incredible based on something in the MHP's report that conflicts with their testimony or written statement. Some facts can be disclosed proactively and not harm, or even help, an immigration case. Others, once the attorney knows them, can prevent the attorney from being able to ethically proceed with filing the application on behalf of the client. Still others, while not necessarily material to the case, nevertheless paint the client in a negative light or unnecessarily complicate the story the attorney is attempting to tell about the case and the client. Because immigration law is so situation-dependent, and because of the harsh consequences that can be triggered by the disclosure of certain information, an attorney could ask for certain details in a report to be removed or modified.

It is not acceptable for the MHP to make edits to the report that would exclude or change opinions or information that is relevant to support those opinions. However, most MHPs agree that it is permissible to edit the report if the attorney points to errors, jargon that can be explained in lay terms, typos, or otherwise inappropriate information that is not relevant to the referral question (e.g., incriminating statements, details about prior crimes that are not relevant to the psycholegal issue, and so on).[45] Given the specific impact that errors in little details can have in IC, MHPs are encouraged to think about the purpose of including historical details (e.g., dates, timelines) in the report, particularly with immigrants who, due to trauma or other psychological reasons, could have recollection difficulties. In addition, many of these issues can be avoided by having a conversation prior to the initiation of the evaluation if and/or when the MHP and attorney agree on the referral question. The more concrete this conversation is, the less opportunity for disagreement about what information is relevant versus irrelevant in the report. If edits are made to the report, a copy of the first version should be retained, as well as any revised versions produced prior to the final copy.[46] Ultimately, attorneys have to be aware that, even knowing the possible immigration consequences for the client, the MHP must use their expert clinical judgment as to the contents of the final report, and there might be details that the MHP simply cannot omit from the report. In that case, it will be up to the attorney to make a strategic and ethical decision about whether they can use the report, even with the damaging detail, or whether they must discard it (or even whether they must now change their strategy of the case to avoid running afoul of the duty of candor).[47]

"Unbelievable" or "Unsympathetic" Stories: To Edit or Not to Edit, Revisited

Attorneys and courts might have a hard time understanding and accepting a client's story if it does not conform to how they think a person would or should react in a given situation. An attorney could, in drafting the client's statement, change it so much that (while the facts are all true) it becomes almost unrecognizable to the client. The attorney could do this with the best of intentions, hoping to craft a narrative that the court will find compelling and believable, but in doing so they can harm the client by trying to make them fit into a box that that they believe the law requires. For example, an attorney could encourage a client who needs to show she was coerced into participating in sex work to refrain from mentioning other times when she engaged in sex work voluntarily. This can be harmful because it can imply to her that the attorney thinks her story is not "good enough" or that she is at fault for her abuse. It can also harm the case if the client comes to feel she cannot speak freely about what really happened to her and is unable to testify compellingly. It can be even more harmful if this "bad" fact later comes out.

The moment when an attorney is thinking about asking a MHP to take a "bad fact" out of a report should be a moment for the attorney to pause and reflect: Is this really a bad fact? Or do I just think so because there are things I don't understand? While the requirements of immigration law dictate that clients must fit in certain "boxes" to be eligible for relief ("victim"/"abused"/"coerced"/"persecuted"/other), these boxes might not be as fixed as the attorney might assume. MHPs can be invaluable allies to attorneys in this situation. Their expertise can help deepen and broaden the attorney's understanding of human behavior and help to push the court into a broader understanding as well. Attorneys ought not automatically run away from what they think are "bad facts." Instead, they should endeavor to think more expansively about what is "believable" or "sympathetic" and strive to tell the client's story in a way that is compelling but also stays true to its heart.

Other Conflicts Related to Psychoeducation

Other conflicts between MHPs and attorneys arise from a simple lack of knowledge about psychological issues, which in part results from the many myths and misunderstandings about mental health held by the general public. Below are some examples.

DIAGNOSIS

When requesting a mental health evaluation, attorneys might be hoping for a diagnosis, especially one that is particularly severe or likely to impress the immigration decision maker (e.g., posttraumatic stress disorder in an asylum case). A diagnosis of a mental health disorder might help the attorney explain (perhaps in an oversimplified way) a client's behavior or allow a client to fit into a category of people who merit relief. Attorneys might have a limited understanding of what goes into forming a diagnosis or that diagnoses are fluid and not static concepts. Attorneys also might not be aware that most diagnoses require, in addition to a set of symptoms, either clinically significant distress or impairment in functioning. To deal with this situation, the MHP should understand why the attorney is seeking what they are seeking: the attorney might think that a diagnosis can mean the difference between life and death for a client pursuing a fear-based claim. At the same time, the attorney should understand that the MHP is bound to the principles of objectivity and impartiality. This situation might present an opportunity to educate the attorney or the court about the diagnostic process. For example, describing functional legal capacities and how they relate to the specific psycholegal issue does not necessarily require a diagnosis.

SUBSTANCE USE

The topic of substance use is typically one about which attorneys and decision makers hold many misunderstandings. A history of substance use can be seen as a sign of poor "moral character" and can be significantly prejudicial for an immigration case. In addition, the immigration judge (IJ) could be expecting to see a certain "recovery" narrative from a respondent who has had past experiences with drug or alcohol use. For example, the IJ might want to see a statement that the client/patient has been "cured" of their substance use disorder. To conform with this narrative, the attorney might hope to tell a simple story of addiction and recovery, though the client's actual substance use history might be more complicated. This is an area in which MHPs can be very useful in educating the legal actors involved.

DANGEROUSNESS AND TREATMENT

The relationship between mental illness and violence is one that is often inflated by the general public. A court considering releasing a detained individual or granting them immigration relief will be concerned about public safety. In ICs, this is particularly the case when the immigrant has a mental illness, especially if they have a history of contact with law enforcement. This presents an opportunity for the MHP to educate the attorney and the IJ about this relationship in general and how it applies to the specific situation of the immigrant in particular. Furthermore, in these situations, it is not uncommon for the IJ to want to see a treatment plan that conforms to a certain idea of what treatment should look like (e.g., inpatient treatment, detoxification, residential rehabilitation) and that involves a much higher level of supervision than needed given the clinical presentation. Their grant of relief might be conditional on this treatment, and so the attorney might push the MHP to make certain recommendations, which could lead the MHP to feel pressured to conform that plan to the court's expectations, even if it is not clinically necessary. This is also a good opportunity to educate the court about the most appropriate treatment plan given the clinical needs (e.g., civil commitment laws). Sometimes, a range of treatment plans might be appropriate. When this is the case, the MHP should discuss this with the attorney before making a decision and could incorporate the attorney's feedback about treatment options that might optimize the chances of release.

MALINGERING

Malingering refers to the immigrant's genuineness with respect to reported psychological symptoms. With the final goal of avoiding deportation, immigrants could be motivated to exaggerate or feign psychological symptoms. This can become an area of conflict when the MHP informs the attorney that the client is malingering. Attorneys could try to question this finding based on the inconsistency with their own observations of the client or could ask the MHP to remove that finding from the report. The attorney could also not understand that MHPs might be unable to form conclusions about the immigrant's diagnoses or symptoms if the immigrant is found to be exaggerating or malingering.

Recommendations

Best practices for attorney-expert collaboration have been described in asylum cases (see *Expert Witnesses in U.S. Asylum Cases: A Handbook*).[48] Although these recommendations apply specifically to asylum cases, many are applicable to all types of evaluations in IC, and it is useful to become familiar with these recommendations. In addition, the Catholic Legal Immigration Network's recently published *Practice Advisory Representing Noncitizens with Mental Illness* is also useful, including helpful recommendations for lawyers to effectively work with MHPs.[49] These include ascertaining whether the MHP has the necessary expertise to competently assess the client; explaining the scope and focus of the forensic evaluation to the MHP; discussing the use of an interpreter in advance; inquiring about the psychological testing that will take place and the language in which it will be given; proactively explaining the details of testimony and relevant dates and deadlines; and discussing, in advance, the framing and editing of the evaluation (i.e., will the MHP be comfortable framing the evaluation in a way that assists with adjudication of the immigration case? How comfortable are they making edits after receiving the practitioner's feedback?).[50]

Conclusion

ICs and MHPs do different things and operate under different rules even when they share the same client and even when they might both desire the same outcome for that individual. Understanding each other's ethical obligations and why each party is doing what they are doing might help combat frustration on both sides. And, for MHPs, understanding how attorneys and institutional decision makers think might expose areas in which the MHP can educate the attorney, the client, or the court. In this way, MHPs can play an important role by helping clients be better informed, helping attorneys become more effective advocates, and helping judges and adjudicators make better decisions.

9

Cultural Considerations

(WITH THE COLLABORATION OF MARIA APARCERO-SUERO)

More than 276 languages are spoken in immigration court (IC) proceedings.[1] This means that, in practically all situations, mental health professionals (MHPs) who work in ICs will be evaluating someone who is vastly different from themselves in most domains including race, language, culture, ethnicity, religious beliefs, and socioeconomic status. In addition, immigrants are significantly diverse in terms of country of origin, migration history, trauma experiences, reasons for migration, levels of acculturation, gender identity, and sexual orientation. Mental health professional organizations have established that cultural competency is a key component of clinical practice.[2] Being culturally competent is even more critical when conducting forensic mental health assessments (FMHAs) in ICs, as many immigrants have left their countries because of trauma or persecution that they experienced precisely due to their cultural identities (e.g., gender, sexual orientation).

The field of multicultural mental health assessment is vast and cannot be covered in one chapter. With that in mind, this chapter summarizes important principles involved in the practice of cross-cultural FMHAs in ICs. The chapter starts by explaining important concepts and terminology and providing a short review of the multicultural approach to clinical practice. It then covers the application of this multicultural approach specifically to FMHAs. Finally, the chapter covers special considerations when using interpreters and performing psychological testing. Of note, although the chapter generally refers to MHPs, many of these principles are also relevant to immigration attorneys who are similarly tasked with representing clients from diverse cultural backgrounds.

Definitions

There is some confusion surrounding the definition of key concepts such as *race, ethnicity, minority, culture,* and *acculturation.* Understanding the meanings of these terms is particularly important in ICs, as examiners typically evaluate the psychological impact resulting from abuse and discrimination due to the immigrant's belonging to these categories. "Race" has been subject to different definitions. Traditionally, it has been used to refer to an individual's biological group in which people share physical characteristics. However, this definition has been controversial and currently is mostly rejected; some scholars have noted that biological racial categories have more within-group than between-group variation.[3] The American Psychological Association (APA) defines "race" as "a category to which others assign individuals on the basis of physical characteristics, such as skin color or hair type, and the generalizations and stereotypes made as a result." The concept of race is relevant because it supports racism and discrimination, which can exacerbate psychiatric conditions and affect diagnostic assessment.[4]

Because of controversies surrounding that term, some have proposed the use of the term "ethnicity" instead, which is more clearly based on a range of shared values, customs, and language. The APA defines "ethnicity" as "the acceptance of the group mores and practices of one's culture of origin and the concomitant sense of belonging."[5] Ethnicity is rooted in shared history, language, religion, geography, and other factors, which distinguish one group from others.[6] According to these definitions, individuals can have multiple ethnic identities. In addition, individuals of different races might share the same ethnicity and vice versa.

The definition of "minority" has also been debated. In the United States, "racial/ethnic minority" is typically defined as referring to membership in a non-White cultural group (e.g., African American, Asian American, Hispanic/Latinx). However, this definition is limited because it is purely based on a numerical concept and ignores the power asymmetries between different groups.[7] A better definition of "minority" includes members of a racial/ethnic group that are different from others (typically the majority) and that occupy a subordinate position.[8] This definition is especially relevant in the context of evaluations for ICs because many individuals have left their countries of origin due to discrimination and violence based on their minority status.

Finally, "culture" is a broader term in concept defined as "a constellation of practices, symbols, values, and ideals that are constructed and shared by a community, transmitted from one generation to the next, constantly renegotiated and subject to change, and operating at the individual and society level."[9] Culture is influenced by, among other things, factors such as language, caretaking practices, media, education, religion, and spiritual traditions, as well as historical, economic, ecological, and political forces.[10] "Acculturation" refers to the adoption of culture by individuals living in a new society and includes aspects such as the level of assimilation within the new society, familiarity with the new cultural norms, or fluency of the language spoken in the new country.[11]

A Multicultural Approach

MHPs who conduct evaluations for ICs will encounter individuals with a vast range of *multiculturalism*. In this context, the term "multicultural" incorporates contextual factors of intersectionality, including race and ethnicity, and aspects of identity related to culture, gender, age, sexual orientation, gender identity, disability, socioeconomic status, religion, spirituality, or immigration status, among others.[12] The concept of *intersectionality* incorporates an ecological model that acknowledges the different systems affecting immigrants, including immediate family, friends, teachers, and others with direct influence over the individual (i.e., *microsystem*); the different social entities found in the microsystem that impact the individual's life such as home, school, and community (*mesosystem*); sociopolitical factors such as laws, immigration policies, and government (*exosystem*); the cultural context (*macrosystem*); and the passage of time and the historical context in which the individual exists (*chronosystem*).[13]

A multicultural approach requires *cultural competency*, which has been defined in mental health settings as a process through which the evaluator understands the importance of culture and cross-cultural relations, is vigilant to the dynamics that result from cultural differences, and adapts services to meet the unique needs of the individual's cultural identity.[14]

Demonstrating cultural competence goes beyond developing a theoretical understanding of how culture can affect an individual's behavior, cognition, emotion, and overall identity. It requires *awareness*, which involves ongoing self-reflection about one's worldview and cultural identity; *attitude*, which involves sensitivity, respect, empathy, and awareness about the other person's cultural context; *knowledge* about how cultural, geographical, and sociopolitical forces influence behaviors; and *skills* to effectively communicate in multicultural situations.[15] It would be naïve to believe that any one person can have a full understanding of all different cultures. However, that is not what is required of the culturally competent clinician; instead, what is required is an ongoing process of learning about others' cultures through repeated exposure and about the limitations of one's expertise.[16] As stated by Evans and Hass, "cultural competence" requires "brutal self-questioning to develop self-reflecting skills around personal biases and privilege."[17]

Although the importance of using a cultural lens is inarguable, it is also essential to consider individual differences and avoid overrelying on the immigrant's culture while underconsidering the impacts of the examiner's own culture in the evaluation. Evaluators must recognize that they also bring their own culture to the table. The APA's *Ethical Principles of Psychologists and Code of Conduct* states that psychologists must recognize the impact of their own cultural identity on their values and assumptions when evaluating individuals from different cultural backgrounds.[18] Related to this is the concept of *cultural (mis)attribution bias*, or "the tendency to see racial/ethnic minorities as members of a group and cultural beings whose traits and behaviors are shaped by cultural processes, but less by psychological processes, and, second, to perceive Whites (e.g., European Americans) as individual actors whose traits and behaviors are shaped by psychological processes, but determined less by cultural influences."[19] By overemphasizing the role of culture in others and underemphasizing it in oneself, the evaluator can deny the immigrant's individuality while ignoring that the evaluator is also a cultural being with *values*, *ideologies*, and *biases* that shape how they perceive the other.[20] Although this concept needs further investigation, it seems important for MHPs to balance consideration of the immigrant's cultural and individual factors with their own cultural values and how they shape their perception of the immigrant.

Developing cultural competency requires practice and self-reflection. The following are some recommendations for MHPs who aspire to develop the cultural competency necessary to work in the context of ICs, plus a list of relevant organizational guidelines:

(a) Attend didactic activities on the subject of cultural competency and multicultural practice of psychology/psychiatry/counseling/social work, such as completing workshops or reading materials on the subject, including professional guidelines.[21]

(b) Access literature that focuses on characteristics of the immigrants' cultures. If possible, reach out to a cultural consultant who is familiar with the immigrant's culture.

(c) Develop skills through practice, supervision, and consultation. Cultural competency is not accomplished through a single workshop or course.[22]

(d) Approach the evaluation with active curiosity about the examinee's culture, going beyond the typical clinical interview to include questions that explore how multiculturalism has shaped the examinee's identity, while also considering individual factors.

(e) Incorporate, if available, collateral information such as interviews with family, friends, or members of the same culture/community.

(f) Engage in an ongoing critical evaluation of one's own culture and its impacts on one's own values, beliefs, and biases.

The Multicultural Forensic Evaluation Process

Generally, mental health evaluations are conducted with the purpose of evaluating different clinical domains (cognitive/intellectual/emotional/behavioral) to generate a formulation and a treatment plan targeted at improving one or more areas of functioning. However, the purpose of FMHAs is to assess specific areas of functioning as they relate to a specific legal question.[23] Therefore, FMHAs are more targeted and specific than other, more exploratory mental health evaluations conducted for treatment purposes. Depending on the forensic referral question (competency/persecution/hardship), the MHP will select different assessment methods, for example, structured versus unstructured clinical interview, psychodiagnostic interview, mental status exam, self-report measures, psychometric testing, and the like. Regardless of the methods used to form forensic opinions, the forensic evaluation process in ICs needs to be "culturally valid," which refers to whether the assessment tools and the procedures used to complete a clinical evaluation are sensitive to the examinee's cultural identity.[24] Cultural validity is essential because it facilitates the development of rapport, which is important to gathering information, and minimizes the probability of forming inaccurate conclusions due to cultural ignorance or biases, which is particularly important in forensic settings. Incorrect diagnoses or forensic formulations due to a lack of cultural sensitivity can have serious consequences for the immigrant's legal status. The following are cultural considerations as they apply to the different aspects of FMHAs in ICs, from background research on the immigrant's cultural background prior to the face-to-face meeting to final diagnostic considerations.

Background Research on Culture

The first step before initiating the evaluation involves gathering information about the immigrant's culture.[25] A culturally responsive assessment calls for some degree of familiarity with the immigrant's culture prior to the interview. The more information about the immigrant's cultural background, the more accurate the outcome of the evaluation is likely to be. When searching for information about the immigrant's culture, it is important to trust the source of information and conduct a critical review of the sources available. For example, some information can be easily available through Wikipedia, but more reliable information is likely to be obtained from official government websites or independent agencies, such as Amnesty International or Human Rights Watch. More in-depth information might require consultation with someone who is very familiar with the immigrant or refugee's country/society of origin. Immigration attorneys sometimes hire so-called country experts who offer evidence about specific conditions in the country. MHPs can also consult with country experts to learn about the examinee's culture. In addition, community service agencies that serve that particular cultural group can also be utilized. These agencies typically exist in areas with a high concentration of immigrants from a specific region. The cultural consultant can also be another MHP with extensive experience working with a particular cultural group. For example, the state of Washington certifies clinicians as an "Ethnic Minority Mental Health Specialist" after the following requirements have been met: the individual has established competency with one specific cultural group and has demonstrated support from the specific community, or has accumulated a minimum of 100 hours of training specialized on ethnic minority issues.[26]

Although there is no published guidance on what information is most important to obtain prior to the interview, the following are some suggestions. First, the MHP should know the primary language spoken by the examinee. If the evaluator speaks the language of the examinee, the evaluator should assess the immigrant's level of fluency and whether there are regional dialects that might be relevant if an interpreter is needed. Second, the evaluator should be familiar with the religious/ spiritual traditions of the examinee, as well as cultural concepts of distress defined by the American Psychiatric Association's *Diagnostic and Statistical Manual of Mental Disorders*, 5th edition (*DSM-5*) as "ways that cultural groups experience, understand, and communicate suffering, behavior problems, or troubling thoughts and emotions."[27] There are three types of cultural concepts of distress:

- Cultural syndromes of distress: "[C]lusters of symptoms and attributions that tend to co-occur among individuals in specific cultural groups, communities, or contexts and that are recognized locally as coherent patterns of experience."[28]
- Cultural idioms of distress: "[W]ays of expressing distress that may not involve specific symptoms or syndromes, but that provide collective, shared ways of experiencing, and talking about personal and social concerns."[29] (For example, the concept of "nerves" in some Hispanic groups, or the term "depression," which may be used to describe a syndrome such as major depressive disorder or as an idiom of distress: "I feel depressed.")
- Cultural explanations of distress: "[L]abels, attributions, or features of an explanatory model that indicate culturally recognized meaning or etiology for symptoms, illness, or distress."[30]

Part of understanding cultural concepts of distress also involves understanding patterns of emotional expression and self-disclosure.[31] Some cultural groups will consider some topics taboo, such as alcohol or substance use, thoughts of suicide, or psychiatric medications.

While some of these topics cannot be avoided during the evaluation, understanding these patterns can help the MHP frame questions in a culturally sensitive manner.[32] The examiner should also become familiar with gender roles, which can impact the interview itself. For example, some cultures might restrict interactions between a man and woman who are not married to each other. Furthermore, issues of social class or class-bound values are also important. Specifically, the concept of *cultural mistrust* has been used to describe general suspiciousness that helps individuals who have been discriminated against cope with issues of racial injustice.[33] A lack of understanding about this concept can lead evaluators to misinterpret this cultural mistrust as a lack of cooperation or even as forms of psychopathology such as paranoid beliefs.

Finally, it is important to have knowledge about the examinee's level of acculturation. Knowing how long the individual has been living in the new country prior to the interview can be beneficial. Information about the country of origin can become almost irrelevant if the individual is fully acculturated to the new culture. Information on the extent to which the individual has acculturated or assimilated to the new culture will most effectively be gathered during the interview itself.

Informed Consent and Notification

This section highlights the importance of being aware of potential cultural factors that can affect informed consent in ICs. The informed consent process is deeply rooted in Western concepts of autonomy and self-determination.[34] However, in many non-Western cultures, autonomy is not prioritized and is in fact discouraged. Some authors have warned against standard applications of informed consent, as these can be perceived as "alienating and dehumanizing" by individuals unfamiliar with Western standards.[35] Despite these concerns, MHPs have a clear mandate and ethical obligation to obtain informed consent, and any deviations from traditional standards should be done with caution. However, sensitivity to these issues should help evaluators approach this process in culturally sensitive ways.[36] For example, the APA's Ethics Code states that "psychologists obtain appropriate informed consent to therapy or related procedures, using language that is reasonably understandable to participants."[37] When verbal consent is used, it is important to ensure understanding by, for example, asking the immigrant to repeat the information back in their own words. As previously noted, the immigrant's understanding of the verbal consent should be documented in the report. The use of written documents is recommended, as they can help increase the examinee's understanding of the process. Therefore, written informed consent forms should always be translated into the immigrant's native language. If written informed consent is provided, the form should be signed by the immigrant, thereby indicating that they have read, understood, and agreed to the conditions of the informed consent.[38]

The Clinical Interview

The clinical interview is an essential part of all mental health evaluations. However, there are significant differences between clinical interviews conducted for forensic purposes versus other clinical purposes. As we have seen, in the latter, the goals of the interview typically include initiating a therapeutic relationship, collecting information for diagnostic purposes, or making a treatment plan.[39] In the forensic context, the goal is to collect information relevant to the forensic referral question and thus to the psycholegal issue. The clinical forensic interview resembles investigative interviewing, as it involves direct questioning and often confrontations regarding information that is found to be inconsistent.[40] The clinical interview approach and whether the MHP decides to use structured versus unstructured interviews will depend on the referral question and the legal issues. However, regardless of the approach, all clinical interviews conducted for ICs require a cultural approach. Without a cultural context, the opinions formed based on the information collected can unintentionally result in over- or underdiagnosing or pathologizing the examinee.

During the clinical interview, the information needs to be collected in a culturally sensitive or culturally humble manner. *Cultural humility* has been described as requiring the following three skills: being other-oriented, understanding that immigrants are experts on their own cultural experience, and approaching them from a position of respect and curiosity.[41] Being culturally humble can be challenging in a forensic context in which the MHP occupies the place of the expert whose final opinion can have a profound impact on the immigrant's life. MHPs need to find the balance between creating a space of curiosity where the immigrant feels heard and welcome while gathering the information necessary to answer the forensic referral question, even when that entails confronting the immigrant about inconsistencies or not-credible reports.

Developing rapport in the context of immigration evaluations, as in any other forensic context, can be complicated because the immigrant could feel coerced or obligated by their lawyer or the judge to undergo the examination, even if they prefer not to share information. Speaking the language of the examinee—not only linguistically but also culturally—facilitates the alliance.[42] A clinical interview conducted within a cultural framework can help build trust and rapport and assist the MHP in obtaining more accurate information.

Several cross-cultural assessment models have been proposed. For example, in 2008 Hays proposed using a clinical interview that explores 10 domains, which he referred to by its acronym—ADDRESSING: Age and generational influences, Developmental disability, Disability acquired later, Religion, Ethnicity, Socio-economic status, Sexual orientation, Indigenous heritage, National origin, and Gender.[43] However, the Cultural Formulation Interview (CFI) of the *DSM-5*[44] is currently considered the primary framework for conducting a culturally competent interview and diagnosing culturally diverse individuals. This interview provides a framework for clinicians to access information about cultural factors that might affect an individual's mental health issues.

The CFI is a product of the 2007–2013 DSM revision process, and it is composed of three types of semistructured interviews that offer guidelines on how to conduct the assessment. It was created through a literature review on clinically based cultural assessments, a field trial with 321 patients, and expert consensus. The three components include a 16-item questionnaire, the CFI-Informant Version to obtain information from caregivers, and 12 supplemental modules that expand on these assessments, including a supplemental module on immigrants and refugees.[45] This module (Module 11) can be particularly helpful for MHPs working in ICs because it covers important factors that might influence these groups' clinical status, including premigration difficulties.[46]

The CFI assessment covers the following five dimensions:

- *Cultural identity of the individual*: The CFI assesses the individual's cultural identity with a series of open-ended questions. The responses to these questions are then integrated into the cultural formulation. Assessing the immigrant's cultural identity is fundamental because it influences his/her behavior, cognitions, and interpersonal relationships. It also influences how the individual experiences and manifests mental health problems.[47]
- *Cultural conceptualization of distress*: Culture can influence the meaning that individuals attribute to symptoms of mental illness or emotional distress and also to the way in which those symptoms are expressed. It also informs the levels of self-awareness into mental illness and the likelihood that someone will seek help.[48] For example, Tibetans do not have language for depression, and in Buddhist cultures, adversity and feelings of sadness are supposed to be treated with acceptance, making it less likely for this group to seek psychological help.
- *Psychosocial stressors and cultural features of vulnerability and resilience*: This dimension goes against the more "rational" Western approach to understanding mental illness and diagnosis, which ignores the cultural context. Considering the cultural and social contexts (e.g., migration stress, the stress of facing deportation or family separation) is essential when understanding clinical distress, symptom expression, and functional impairment. The CFI assesses the social environment and the role of religion, family, and other social networks (e.g., friends, neighbors, coworkers) in providing emotional, instrumental, and informal support. It also considers the individual's cultural reference group when assessing clinical functioning.[49]
- *Cultural features of the relationship between the individual and the clinician*: As previously noted, the evaluator needs to be aware of their own cultural identity and how it affects the interpretation of the information being obtained. The differences in culture, language, and social status between the immigrant and the MHP might affect the development of rapport, cause difficulties in communication due to language difficulties, and thereby affect the final diagnoses and opinions.[50]
- *Overall cultural assessment*: After gathering all of the information through the CFI, the forensically relevant results are summarized into the forensic formulation and diagnoses within the cultural framework.[51]

The CFI is a promising tool that represents an effort to provide a more structured way of conducting culturally informed interviews. Growing research suggests that it is useful for rapport and building trust, eliciting information, and enhancing clinicians' understanding of the examinee's illness. However, comparative efficacy research is needed to examine the specific contribution of the CFI when compared to traditional mental health assessments.[52] In addition, more research exploring its utility in forensic contexts is required.

Mental Status Exam and Behavioral Observations

An important component of all clinical interviews is the mental status exam or a section describing behavioral observations. This section aims to describe the individual's verbal and nonverbal behavior, emotions, and thoughts. Some MHPs use standardized questions, whereas others include a more informal evaluation of the examinee's current clinical functioning.[53] It is important to consider the examinee's cultural context in order to avoid misinterpreting these observations and either over- or underpathologizing the examinee.[54] Although all domains of the mental status exam are vulnerable to cultural influences, attitude, emotions, and level of insight are particularly so.[55]

Attitude is the examinee's level of cooperation and engagement with the examiner. There are many reasons why individuals can decide not to cooperate or answer some questions, such as when the information could be used in ways that might hurt them. There might also be motivations to minimize or exaggerate clinical presentations for some specific outcome. There are also reasons related to culture that might lead the immigrant to decide not to disclose certain information. For example, individuals from certain cultures could believe that some information about themselves will negatively reflect on their families and therefore decide not to share that information. This is common in societies that are more collectivistic than individualistic, such as Asian and Hispanic societies.[56] Finally, the concept of cultural mistrust, previously mentioned, might explain why some individuals who have experienced racism and discrimination could simply not trust the examiner.[57]

Emotional expression/affect, another important component of the mental status exam, can also be influenced by culture. The assessment of affect is relevant for the diagnoses of many clinical entities, including depression, posttraumatic stress disorder (PTSD), anxiety, schizophrenia, or psychopathy. Cultures differ, however, with respect to how much they value emotional expression versus emotional restraint, and some cultures might emphasize the avoidance of certain feelings that are considered detrimental, such as anger or frustration.[58] In addition, some cultures determine to whom emotions can be shown. Culture might determine, for example, whether a male can cry in front of a female MHP or even another male. For cultures that value emotional restraint or consider the expression of emotions damaging, the lack of emotional expression during the interview can be misinterpreted by examiners as callousness, "flat affect," or coldness if culture is not taken into consideration.[59]

Insight/self-awareness into one's mental health issues or actions is assessed during the mental status exam primarily because it is typically used as a prognostic sign by clinicians. For example, lack of self-awareness is considered a risk factor for violent behavior in some risk assessment instruments and related to a decreased chance of treatment adherence. Some cultures, however, might consider psychiatric symptoms to have their origins in spiritual or physical factors. Other cultures might not even have a language for certain psychiatric disorders or symptoms. It is important to avoid misinterpreting these beliefs as a lack of insight related to a poor predictor of treatment response.[60]

Diagnostic Considerations

Mental health evaluations in most clinical contexts require that the evaluator establish whether the examinee meets diagnostic criteria for a psychiatric disorder included in a recognized diagnostic manual such as the American Psychiatric Association's *DSM* or the World Health Organization's *International Classification of Disease and Related Health Problems*, 11th edition (*ICD-11*). In forensic contexts, in contrast, the evaluation is focused on psycholegal abilities, and therefore a diagnostic label might not be needed. In fact, a narrative description of the individual's cognitive, emotional, or behavioral functioning is often more helpful than a diagnostic label.[61] In the context of ICs, a formal diagnosis is not necessarily required to describe the psycholegal abilities. For example, for asylum evaluations, establishing that the immigrant meets the criteria for PTSD might help support the presence of psychological sequelae related to trauma, which might in turn help support the immigrant's experience of "well-founded fear of persecution." But individuals often experience trauma-related symptoms as a result of persecution or torture that do not meet the classic *DSM-5* definition of PTSD. Describing the symptoms and how they relate to functional impairment can be sufficient. In other situations, the law has more clearly defined the expectations.

In the context of ICs, it is particularly important to carefully consider whether to include a diagnostic label. This is because there is limited research on the cross-cultural validity of many of the labels in Western diagnostic classification systems such as the *DSM-5* or *ICD-11*. Some authors have stated that these manuals are ethnocentric and rely on a narrow understanding of culture[62] and that the use of traditional systems of psychiatric classification can make an "ethnic dividing line" between those seen as the "other" culture and those who are not.[63]

The CFI is a step in the right direction with respect to considering culture when deciding on diagnostic labels. It is a tool to enhance clinical understanding of cultural factors affecting psychopathology, but it should not be used as the only basis for making a clinical diagnosis. Further, the CFI is relegated to section III of the *DSM* and separated from section II, which includes all diagnostic categories. Section II focuses on symptom presentation only, and it is mostly decontextualized from culture. In fact, there is rarely information on how culture is to be accounted for in relation to specific disorder criteria.[64] Some exceptions include major depressive episodes, in which the DSM warns that "clinicians should recognize that . . . in many cultures somatic symptoms are very likely to constitute the presenting complaint,"[65] or the notation under "Antisocial Personality Disorder," which states that this diagnosis is correlated with a low socioeconomic status.[66]

Despite the relative lack of attention paid to culture by traditional psychiatric classification systems, it is well established that culture can impact symptom presentation and should be taken into consideration when diagnosing all disorders within the *DSM*. The phenomenon of cultural variability of psychopathology has been referred to as "pathoplasticity" and defined as the "diversity in clinical presentation" (e.g., symptoms, course, prognosis) across cultural groups.[67] The definition of "schizophrenia," for example, might vary from one culture to another, including the content or severity of symptoms. Some studies have found a better prognosis for individuals with schizophrenia in underdeveloped versus developed countries, which has been attributed to sociocultural factors.[68] The prevalence of different diagnoses also varies across cultures.[69] Cultural factors can also influence symptom expression. For example, "*ataque de nervios*" has been described as a way of expressing anxiety disorders in Latin America.[70] Other threats to cultural validity previously mentioned include the evaluator's bias in clinical judgment related to his/her prejudice or unintentional ignorance about the immigrant's culture, language differences, and inappropriate use of clinical and personality tests.[71]

If the MHP decides that assigning a diagnostic label is required given the referral question, the following precautions are recommended. First, only diagnoses that are relevant to understanding the psycholegal questions should be included.[72] Second, all the information gathered about the immigrant's culture ought to be considered when determining the presence or absence of any of the symptoms listed under the diagnostic criteria, including expressions of clinical distress and functional impairment. Third, the evaluator should acknowledge any limitations related to the lack of cultural validity of any of the methods and procedures used to arrive at a certain diagnostic level.

The Use of Interpreters

Given the variety of languages and dialects spoken by immigrants in the United States, MHPs working in ICs will inevitably have to use interpreters. If the English fluency of the immigrant is in question and the evaluator is not fully fluent in the immigrant's language, it is recommended that an interpreter who can engage in a neutral verbatim, or word-by-word, translation be used.[73]

Avoiding phone interpretation is recommended, and ideally the interpreter should be certified by a court or any other certifying body and have experience interpreting during mental health evaluations. However, for some rare languages, it might be difficult to find a certified interpreter. If this is the case, it is important not to select anyone who has any connection to the immigrant (e.g., family member or attorney) to avoid any real or perceived conflicts.[74] Another important consideration involves whether to select an interpreter who, in addition to sharing the language with the immigrant, also shares the culture. In general, it is preferred that the interpreter be from the same country as the immigrant and even from the same region, so that the interpreter can provide another source of information about the immigrant's culture and increase the immigrant's comfort during the interview.[75] This can be particularly important when working with less-common languages, such as Tibetan or Fulani. However, it can also be discomforting, specifically regarding issues of confidentiality, if the immigrant fears that the information reported can make it back to their shared community. In addition, a shared cultural background can also be activating for the interpreter, particularly if they have experienced similar traumatic experiences.[76] A conversation about these issues must take place prior to the interview both with the immigrant and the interpreter.

During the preinterview meeting with the interpreter, the MHP should explain the purpose of the evaluation, the confidentiality rules, and the process of a mental health evaluation. The interpreter should also be asked to avoid any back-and-forth with the immigrant that does not involve the evaluator. If the interpreter is new to mental health evaluations, the MHP should provide an explanation of some concepts, as this will help facilitate translation during the interview (e.g., trauma, hallucinations, suicidality, etc.).[77]

Before beginning the evaluation, the MHP should introduce the immigrant and the interpreter to each other and clarify to the immigrant the role of the interpreter, including the fact that this person will not be making any decisions about the evaluation or the legal case and is bounded by confidentiality rules.[78] To avoid any potential awkwardness, the MHP should also explain that they will maintain eye contact with the immigrant during the evaluation and ignore the interpreter.[79] During the interview, the MHP should gently interrupt and redirect the interpreter if errors are being made, such as engaging in a back-and-forth with the immigrant without translating or providing interpretations of what the immigrant meant instead of translating simultaneously.[80] During the evaluation, it is also important to remember to speak slowly and use dialogue in smaller segments.[81] If the evaluation involves several meetings, it is recommended that the same interpreter be used.

Psychological Testing

An important decision to be made by MHPs conducting FMHAs in ICs is whether psychological testing instruments can add valuable information to what can be gathered through the clinical interview and collateral sources. Psychological testing can provide important and more objective data to support the expert's opinion. However, there are several challenges to using psychological testing in ICs. First, most psychological tests have been developed for a specific purpose, in a specific cultural and linguistic context, and for use with a specific group of people. Usually they have been developed for, and validated in, individuals from majority-cultural backgrounds who are native English speakers, raising concerns about their use with culturally and linguistically diverse individuals. The validity of tests' cut-off scores and standardized norms rest on how closely the examinee resembles the group of people that formed the normative group. Most studies use Western, Educated, Industrialized, Rich, and Democratic (WEIRD) samples, which limits the generalizability of their findings to racially, ethnically, culturally, and linguistically diverse samples.[82] Moreover, the low level of acculturation of recent immigrants or other individuals evaluated in IC makes the use of mainstream society testing norms even less appropriate.[83] Second, the linguistic diversity of immigrants involved in IC often requires the use of interpreters, which further limits the possibility of using psychological testing. Third, many immigrants in IC have low levels or lack formal education, which rules out the possibility of using certain testing instruments. In sum, the challenges of using psychometric instruments in ICs can be such that the risks and obstacles of using testing might outweigh the potential benefits. However, to make this decision, MHPs need to understand how cultural factors impact the validity and utility of psychological tests for use with individuals from diverse backgrounds. The utility of psychological measures across diverse groups (i.e., cultural or cross-cultural validity) needs to be evaluated rather than assumed.

There are two main approaches, known as "etic" and "emic," to test development or translation and adaptation of existing measures into different languages, nationalities, and cultures.[84] The *etic approach* assumes that psychological constructs are universal and extrapolates measures developed in one cultural group to be used in a different group by translating them into another language (i.e., translation and back-translation methodology). Alternatively, the *emic approach* recognizes and attempts to understand the impact of culturally specific experiences, norms, values, and beliefs on psychological constructs. The etic approach might increase the risk of cultural bias in psychological testing because it assumes measurement equivalence and ignores possible unique experiences and cultural factors that lead to group differences in response style, psychological constructs, and test validity.[85] Unfortunately, a systematic review of the first 96 issues of the *Journal of Cross-Cultural Psychology* found that most studies (93%) used an "imposed etic" on their methodologies.[86] Cross-cultural biases that reflect imposed etic might come from cultural differences in psychological constructs (i.e., construct biases), noncomparable groups (sample biases), and cultural differences in test administration and formats (instrument and administration biases).[87] Cross-cultural researchers promote integrating the emic and etic approaches (i.e., culture-specific adjustments to assessment methods) into psychological research and assessment, considering both cross-culturally relevant and culturally specific constructs.[88] The Chinese Personality Assessment Inventory (CPAI) is an example of the use of a combined etic/emic approach to develop a culturally sensitive instrument.[89]

Once the instrument has been translated and adapted, it must be studied to establish its reliability and validity (i.e., convergent, discriminant, and construct validity) for use with each targeted culturally diverse population.[90] The development of new norms for the translated tests using demographically representative samples might be necessary for an accurate interpretation of the assessment data.[91] The lack of comparability between the new intended population and the original normative sample in terms of traditional values, backgrounds, culture, and language abilities might hinder any meaningful conclusions. However, the appropriateness of existing norms also depends on the examinee's level of acculturation or assimilation to mainstream society. When individuals from another culture demonstrate high levels of acculturation to the mainstream US society, the use of original normative data might be appropriate.[92]

Before using a psychological assessment instrument, MHPs must consider the empirical support for the cross-cultural and clinical validity of measures used with respect to an immigrant's group membership. Although some instruments are available in more than one language, their validity with non-WEIRD populations might be limited or unknown given the paucity in cross-cultural research examining measurement equivalence and psychometrics. When the examinee's background differs from those in the normative sample, MHPs must acknowledge the limitations of their assessment related to the lack of cultural validity of the instrument used and the impact on test interpretation.[93] MHPs must also refrain from translating measures or test instruments at the moment of the evaluation.[94]

Most psychological assessment instruments typically used in forensic settings have been translated into languages other than English, but the extent to which those translated versions have been systematically evaluated differs. Below we provide an overview of the cross-cultural research on psychological tests that are typically used in criminal court contexts and that might be appropriate for use with culturally diverse populations in ICs. We review personality inventories (the Minnesota Multiphasic Personality Inventory [MMPI][95] and the Personality Assessment Inventory [PAI][96]), cognitive assessment instruments (Weschler Adult Intelligence Scale—Fourth Edition [WAIS-IV][97] and the Bateria IV Woodcock-Muñoz[98]), and malingering/symptom validity instruments. Multiscale inventories can inform diagnosis, personality style, and response bias, while cognitive tests can shed light on examinees' ability to understand their legal rights and charges against them, as well as on neurological impairment secondary to trauma. The selection of any of these tests should be based on the referral question, and as stated previously, not all FMHAs in ICs require the use of psychological testing. In addition, and depending on the state licensing requirements, these tests are typically to be used and interpreted only by psychologists.

Personality Assessment

In the next sections, we review the cross-cultural utility of instruments commonly used to assess personality and psychopathology.

Minnesota Multiphasic Personality Inventory

The Minnesota Multiphasic Personality Inventory-2 (MMPI-2)[99] and the Minnesota Multiphasic Personality Inventory-2 Restructured Form

(MMPI-2-RF)[100] are the most widely translated and internationally used personality and psychopathology inventories. They assess for a wide range of psychopathology and personality traits in addition to response styles (e.g., inconsistency and potential minimization or exaggeration of symptoms). The MMPI-2 and MMPI-2-RF are intended for use with adults who have at least an eighth-grade reading level to ensure understanding of the item content. An adolescent version (14–18 years old), the MMPI-A, is also available.[101] The MMPI-2 and MMPI-2-RF have been translated into 24 and 12 languages and dialects, respectively.[102] For example, three different Spanish translations are available: (a) Spanish for the United States, (b) Spanish for Mexico and Central America, and (c) Spanish for Spain. MHPs must select the most appropriate translation and norms based on the examinee's background. Importantly, the MMPI-2 and MMPI-2-RF have been adapted to multiple cultures using the etic approach, and therefore the examination of the psychometric properties of the translated versions of these instruments is necessary to account for potential cultural biases.

Despite these instruments having been translated into dozens of languages, there has been a dearth of empirical work conducted on the cross-cultural validity of their translated versions, especially on the validity scales.[103] Existing evidence has found variability in the effectiveness of the validity scales to identify dishonest responding within and across translated versions of the MMPI-2 and MMPI-2-RF; therefore, it is unclear whether the validity scales on translated versions of these instruments are as useful as on the English-language instruments.[104] Also, research on the translated versions tends to be less methodologically sound (e.g., simulation studies with nonclinical control groups) compared to research on the English-language instruments, which affects the generalizability of their findings.[105]

Research conducted in the United States using the English-language MMPI-2 and MMPI-2-RF has found significant but small differences between racial/ethnic minorities and European American individuals (or normative sample), with minorities producing higher scores on the validity and clinical scales.[106] Similarly, differences in scores were found between a sample of Mexican and Puerto Rican adults who completed the Spanish version of the MMPI-2 and the US normative sample. Although significant, the differences were small in size.[107] Given the small differences observed, they are unlikely to impact interpretive conclusions; therefore, the use of the MMPI-2 and MMPI-2-RF with highly acculturated, culturally diverse individuals in the United States might provide valid and clinically useful profiles. When individuals retain their native cultural values (i.e., low acculturation), MHPs need to integrate cultural considerations into the clinical interpretation.

Besides the US norms, normative data are available for other countries such as Spain, Argentina, Mexico, and China, among others. MHPs might need to contact local test publishers to obtain the test administration and interpretation materials. Of note, when evaluating the appropriateness of normative data, MHPs should focus on other characteristics besides language. For instance, they must be aware of the cultural and clinical heterogeneity among Spanish-speaking populations and consider how individual differences (e.g., subculture, national origin, level of education, etc.) might impact test scores and their interpretation. In other words, empirical evidence is informative the more similar the examinee is to the normative sample. However, even when local norms for the translated versions of the MMPI-2 and MMPI-2-RF are available, these instruments do not assess non-Western, culturally specific and relevant personality and psychological constructs.

Recently, the MMPI-3 has been published in both English and Spanish, and both language versions include their independent US normative data.[108] The English-language normative sample is representative of the US population in terms of race/ethnicity, age, and education, increasing the utility of the MMPI-3 across diverse groups. The Spanish-language normative data was also collected in the United States and included individuals from different ancestral origins (e.g., South America, Mexico, Central America, Europe, Caribbean Islands, etc.) who were also diverse in terms of age and level of education. The development process and validity research conducted for the Spanish-language MMPI-3 found significant differences between the Spanish and English normative samples, which justified the need for Spanish-language norms. Thus, the availability of Spanish norms increases the utility of the MMPI-3 with Hispanic/Latinx individuals in the United States; however, a potential limitation to the cross-cultural validity of the MMPI-3 Spanish norms is that information about acculturation or number of years in the United States was not collected. Previous research has shown that culturally diverse individuals' level of acculturation to mainstream society affected their MMPI scores;[109] future research should examine the utility of the Spanish-language MMPI-3 with low-acculturated Spanish-speaking individuals. The MMPI-3 is not yet available in any other languages.

Personality Assessment Inventory

The PAI is also a multiscale, self-report measure of personality and psychopathology that contains several scales to assess response styles. There are adult and adolescent versions of the PAI, both of which require at least a fourth-grade reading level to understand item content. The original (English) version of the PAI has been translated into multiple languages, including European Spanish, Canadian French, Chinese, German, Greek, Italian, Korean, and Vietnamese. Most translated versions of the PAI use primarily an etic approach to test development (i.e., a standard translation and back-translation methodology). An exception is the CPAI, which adopted a combined emic/etic approach and included a set of culturally specific traits present in collectivist, Chinese-speaking countries. For example, in Chinese culture, individuals with mental health problems tend to focus on somatic rather than mood-related symptoms because it destigmatizes psychiatric illness; therefore, the CPAI better captures somatic presentations of psychological conditions as well as other significant values, facets, and traits of personality common in the Chinese culture.[110] The CPAI manual also includes Chinese normative data. The CPAI has been used in Hong Kong, mainland China, Singapore, Taiwan, and certain regions of Malaysia. In addition to culturally relevant psychological constructs, the CPAI also includes personality constructs commonly found in English-language or Western psychological tests, maximizing its utility with Chinese individuals living in Western countries.

The psychometric properties of the Spanish translation of the PAI are among the most researched. They have been examined across various Spanish-speaking countries and with Spanish-speaking individuals in the United States. It is important to note that the original Spanish-language PAI[111] uses the same US norms as the English-language PAI, although today standardized data is available from several Spanish-speaking countries such as Spain,[112] Chile,[113] and Mexico,[114] based on adaptations of the PAI conducted in those countries. Research conducted in the United States has found significant differences on validity and clinical scale scores between Hispanic individuals and the US normative sample.[115] The differences in clinical scale scores were small, but researchers recommended caution when interpreting the positive and negative impression management scales with Hispanic individuals, especially in clinical samples.[116] International research outside the United States has also found mean differences across Spanish-speaking countries.[117] Overall, evidence supports the cross-cultural validity of the PAI with Spanish-speaking populations. Although significant differences between groups have been observed, they are unlikely to impact interpretative conclusions given their small effect size, as long as MHPs select the most appropriate norms. Depending on the examinee's cultural background and acculturation level, MHPs need to decide whether the original or other adapted Spanish version of the PAI is indicated.

And finally, validation and standardized data for other translated versions of the PAI are available in peer-reviewed articles. However, the extent of the cross-cultural research with people from different cultural backgrounds is limited. In short, evidence supports the cross-cultural applicability of the PAI, but the differences observed between US normative data and country-specific data in clinical and validity scale scores underscore the need to use culturally relevant (local) norms. As addressed above in the context of the MMPI-2/RF, MHPs should focus on individual characteristics beyond language to select the most appropriate norms and note that the translated versions of the PAI, except for the CPAI, do not assess non-Western, culturally specific psychological constructs.

Cognitive Assessment

The level of familiarity with test stimuli and testing procedure, the nature and degree of formal education, and cultural values are important to consider when evaluating the cross-cultural validity of cognitive assessments. For example, some cultures (e.g., US culture) prioritize processing speed, while others (non-Western cultures and some European countries) emphasize the depth of processing and avoiding mistakes.[118] Similarly, in Mayan culture (Mexico) and other collectivistic cultures, it is normative to collaborate rather than work independently.[119] In Asian cultures, being dialectical in thinking is more common than in European countries.[120] These cultural differences can impact the validity of cognitive test score interpretations with culturally diverse individuals. Sometimes to reduce the potential impact of cultural factors on verbal cognitive measures, MHPs decide to use nonverbal cognitive measures. The cultural differences just mentioned, however, can also impact the validity of these measures.

Wechsler Adult Intelligence Scale—Fourth Edition

The WAIS-IV is the most widely used intelligence test in the United States. It is a comprehensive test of cognitive abilities that assesses verbal comprehension, perceptual reasoning, working memory, and processing speed. It also provides a general estimate of cognitive functioning (i.e., the full scale intelligence quotient, or FSIQ). The WAIS-IV can be administered to individuals 16 years old or older and takes 60–90 minutes to complete. The Wechsler Intelligence Scale for Children—Fifth Edition (WISC-V) is the equivalent of the WAIS-IV for individuals between the ages of 6 and 16. The WAIS-IV has been adapted and standardized in many countries, including Spain, Mexico, Colombia, Chile, Canada, Australia, New Zealand, England, and most European countries. The Escala de Inteligencia de Wechsler para adulto—Tercera Edition (EIWA-III) is the Spanish-language adaptation of the WAIS-III suitable for individuals in/from Puerto Rico. Nonetheless, MHPs should be cautious when using the EIWA-III due to the limited published data, limitations in the standardization study, and insufficient information about age groups provided in the technical manual.[121]

For examinees who have recently immigrated to the United States, the adapted tests available in their first language might be more appropriate due to the cross-cultural differences observed in test scores across normative groups. MHPs should be aware of the imposed etic in the adapted versions of the WAIS and critically evaluate how familiarity with the test stimuli, testing procedure, opportunity for formal education, and assumptions about knowledge, values, and communication impact the cross-cultural validity of the test. Furthermore, comparing test scores across different sociocultural, ethnic, and racial groups should be avoided given the differences across norms. MHPs should refer to the literature when interpreting test scores and reporting conclusions regarding the examinee's current cognitive functioning. The suggested cut-off scores for average, borderline, or impaired functioning might not be equivalent across cultures/normative groups.[122]

Bateria IV Woodcock-Muñoz

Another commonly used cognitive test with Spanish-speaking individuals in the United States is the Bateria IV Woodcock-Muñoz, the Spanish version of the Woodcock-Johnson test—Fourth Edition (WJ-IV).[123] It can be administered to individuals between the ages of five and 95. The English-language WJ-IV tests and manuals were translated and adapted for use with primarily monolingual Spanish-speaking individuals in the United States. A group of professionals from several Spanish-speaking countries translated and adapted the test items to increase its utility across Spanish-speaking individuals. The calibration data for new items was based on a sample of 601 native Spanish speakers in the United States, most of whom were of Mexican origin or nativity. The Bateria IV data was equated to the WJ-IV norms, allowing for the direct comparison of an individual's score in each version and making this test especially suited to evaluate bilingual individuals in the US psychoeducation context.

Compared to the WAIS-IV, the Bateria IV focuses more on general intelligence and academic achievement. The Bateria IV consists of two assessment instruments: Test of Cognitive Abilities and Test of Achievement. The former includes 14 subtests that assess general intellectual ability, cognitive abilities, and aspects of executive functioning; the latter includes 13 subtests that assess oral language ability, reading, mathematics, writing, phonological awareness, and academic knowledge. The Bateria IV also allows calculating the comparative language index, which combines information from the WJ-IV and Bateria IV language clusters to provide information about the examinee's dominant language and proficiency level in each language compared to their same age- or grade-level peers.

An important limitation of the Bateria IV for use in ICs is that the cross-cultural validity with Spanish-speaking individuals outside of the

United States or individuals with low acculturation to US mainstream society is largely unknown. Of note, the Bateria III normative sample did include individuals in the United States and several Spanish-speaking countries (from larger to smaller sample size: Mexico, Costa Rica, Panama, Argentina, Colombia, Puerto Rico, and Spain); however, with the release of the Bateria IV, this instrument will likely be discontinued. Until more research on the cross-cultural validity of the Bateria IV is available, MHPs should consider other cognitive measures, acknowledge the nature and sources of potential biases, and state the limitations of their conclusions.

Tests of Nonverbal Intelligence.

Evaluators in IC can also consider language-free tests, which might be appropriate when evaluating individuals of limited language ability. For example, the Test of Nonverbal Intelligence—Fourth Edition (TONI-4)[124] assesses fluent reasoning and estimates global cognitive ability. However, it is important to remember that even tests of nonverbal intelligence are not devoid of cultural influences.

Malingering/Response Style

Some of the psychological tests commonly used in forensic psychological evaluations, such as the MMPI and PAI, contain embedded validity scales to assess response style, including symptom minimization or exaggeration and feigning. In addition, other measures have been specifically developed to assess for symptom exaggeration, feigning, or insufficient effort. These measures can be administered as part of a (neuro)psychological assessment battery. These measures can be divided into two domains of response bias: the assessment of feigned psychological/psychiatric symptoms and the assessment of feigned cognitive deficits. The assessment of exaggerated or feigned symptoms tends to rely on self-report, while the detection of insufficient effort or feigned cognitive impairments relies on performance-based measures. The validity of these instruments is context-specific (i.e., validated for a specific disorder and population). For example, a particular instrument might be valid for detecting feigned psychotic symptoms or mild head injury–related symptoms but less so for detecting feigned mood symptoms or intellectual disability (ID), respectively. In determining which instrument is more appropriate, MHPs need to consider the type of symptoms being evaluated, the context in which that evaluation is being conducted, and the examinee's background. The most popular instruments to identify feigned psychiatric symptoms include the Structured Interview of Reported Symptoms-2 (SIRS-2),[125] the Structured Inventory of Malingered Symptomatology (SIMS),[126] and the Miller Forensic Assessment of Symptoms Test (M-FAST).[127] The most popular performance-based detection measures to identify insufficient effort or exaggerated cognitive deficits/ID are the Test of Memory Malingering (TOMM),[128] the Dot Counting Test (DCT),[129] the Word Memory Test (WMT),[130] and the Rey 15-Item Test (FIT).[131]

Many of the available feigning measures have been widely researched and normed in North America using samples formed mostly from White, English-speaking individuals. Although these measures have been translated into different languages, there is a dearth of research examining their utility when used with diverse individuals. Additionally, most of these measures lack culturally specific normative data for the targeted populations, relying on the US norms for interpretation of the test scores, which limits their generalizability for use with diverse populations. We now review the existing evidence regarding the use of these measures with linguistically, ethically, and culturally diverse populations.

Structured Interview of Reported Symptoms-2

The SIRS-2 is a 172-item structured clinical interview that includes multiple methods to detect overreporting of psychopathology: rare symptoms, symptom combinations, improbable or absurd symptoms, blatant symptoms, subtle symptoms, selectivity of symptoms, severity of symptoms, and reported versus observed symptoms. The SIRS-2 also includes supplemental scales that examine inconsistent responding and exaggeration of cognitive symptoms and virtues. The English version of the SIRS-2 has demonstrated strong interrater reliability, validity, and classification accuracy. The SIRS-2 has been translated into Spanish[132] and Chinese (Mandarin)[133] using the standard translation and back-translation methodology. The Spanish translation of the SIRS-2 has demonstrated equivalent psychometric properties to the English-language version of the SIRS-2 in two samples of monolingual and bilingual Spanish-speaking outpatients in the United States. The Chinese translation of the SIRS-2 has demonstrated excellent specificity; however, variability in sensitivity rates was found across study designs.[134] Clinical evidence has suggested that the use of the Improbable Failure (supplemental) scale, designed to screen for feigned cognitive deficits, might not be culturally appropriate with individuals with low levels of acculturation, low educational attainment, or those educated outside of the United States. Existing evidence on the translated versions of the SIRS-2 is promising, but additional research examining their psychometric properties with individuals in the United States and abroad is needed.

Structured Inventory of Malingered Symptomatology

The SIMS is a 75-item, true-or-false self-report screening instrument for exaggerated or feigned psychiatric or neurological symptoms. It includes detection strategies that focus on rare, illogical, or atypical symptoms, as well as general simple knowledge. The normative data (i.e., cut-off scores) are based on predominantly healthy, White, female undergraduate students in the United States. The SIMS has been translated into European Spanish, Dutch, and German using the translation and back-translation method. Compared to English, German, and Spanish nonclinical controls, Dutch nonclinical controls had significantly lower mean scores in the SIMS.[135] Despite those differences, all translations of the SIMS have demonstrated comparable psychometric properties to the English-language version of the SIMS and utility in identifying potential feigners.[136]

Miller Forensic Assessment of Symptoms Test

The M-FAST is a 25-item structured interview designed to screen for overreported or feigned psychiatric symptoms in forensic settings. It includes multiple detection strategies including reported versus observed symptoms, extreme symptomatology, rare combinations, unusual hallucinations, negative image, and suggestibility. Research supports the use of the M-FAST as a screening tool for exaggerated psychopathology. However, the literature is limited regarding the utility of the M-FAST to identify feigned depressive and anxiety symptoms, and its use to screen for feigned cognitive symptoms is not indicated.[137]

Regarding the cross-cultural validity of the M-FAST, a study conducted in the United States with a racially/ethnically diverse sample of incarcerated Caucasian, African American, and Hispanic males found that the English-language version of the M-FAST performed similarly across groups.[138] Furthermore, the M-FAST has been translated into Spanish using a multistep translation and back-translation method; however, only one study conducted in the United States with bilingual, Hispanic, male inmates has examined its utility and psychometric properties.[139] This study found that the Spanish version of the M-FAST performed similarly to the English M-FAST when using a slightly different cut-off score. Importantly, level of acculturation did not significantly impact the M-FAST score. There is a need for more research on the Spanish M-FAST using a clinical comparison sample and samples of monolingual Spanish speakers in the United States and abroad.

The M-FAST has also been translated into French, Farsi, Korean, and Turkish. Overall, these translated versions of the M-FAST have demonstrated relatively good classification accuracy, with the M-FAST demonstrating the lowest sensitivity and specificity rates when used with a sample of predominantly French-speaking African immigrants in the United States.[140] This evidence suggests that the risk of false positives (i.e., misclassifying an individual with genuine symptoms as feigning) might be higher when using the M-FAST with culturally, linguistically, or/and ethnically diverse individuals different from the normative sample (i.e., English-speaking, North American individuals). Nevertheless, given that the M-FAST is intended as a screening measure, the somewhat lower specificity rates should not necessarily lead to severe psycholegal implications, because a classification of potential malingering by the M-FAST always warrants a thorough feigning assessment with additional testing.

Test of Memory Malingering

The TOMM was designed to discriminate between genuine memory impairments and insufficient effort via a recognition test. Research has shown that even honest patients with genuine psychological and neurological impairments performed better than chance. A meta-analysis of 21 studies conducted with English-speaking, North American samples found adequate mean sensitivity and high mean specificity.[141]

The TOMM has been translated into Spanish, German, and French. Of note, the European Spanish version of the TOMM includes its own normative data.[142] In general, the translated versions of the TOMM have demonstrated good specificity rates but show considerable variability in sensitivity rate. The lowest sensitivity rates were found when used with a sample of predominantly French-speaking African immigrants in the United States instructed to feign PTSD symptoms.[143] The studies conducted in Germany and Latin American countries did not report sensitivity rates, so it is unclear how effective the TOMM is in identifying insufficient effort or feigned memory deficits in these populations.

Furthermore, cross-cultural differences that influence test performance have been found across studies examining the use of the TOMM with Spanish-speaking individuals in the United States, Spain, and Latin American countries. For example, there is variability in false-positive rates (i.e., specificity) across Spanish-speaking populations, with the highest false-positive rate being found in a sample of responders from Paraguay (25%),[144] while the false-positive rates in other countries are very low. Additionally, low levels of acculturation, education, and country development (i.e., gross national income per capita) have been associated with poorer performance on the TOMM among Hispanic genuine performers.[145] Contrarily, no effect of education on TOMM scores has been found among non-Hispanic, English-speaking, North American samples. Therefore, when evaluating Hispanic individuals, MHPs should consider regional differences, level of education, and exposure to US culture (for individuals in the United States) to determine the appropriateness of using the TOMM.

Other Performance-Based Measures of Feigning

The Dot Counting Test (DCT), Word Memory Test (WMT), and Rey 15-Item Test (FIT) were also designed to identify suboptimal effort in cognitive tasks and feigned cognitive deficits. When used with English-speaking individuals, research has shown that these instruments run the risk of misclassifying individuals (i.e., lower classification accuracy) with a high false-positive rate, especially among individuals with genuine impairments.[146] Although these instruments have been translated into other languages, their cross-cultural validity research is very limited. Besides the English-language, North American norms (i.e., cut-off scores), there are no other normative data available to interpret culturally and linguistically diverse individuals' performance on these tests. Overall, existing cross-cultural research has found that the DCT, WMT, and FIT demonstrated lower sensitivity and higher false-positive rates among non–English-speaking populations.[147] Furthermore, research has suggested that performance on the DCT and FIT might be affected by levels of acculturation and education.[148] Therefore, MHPs should not rely on these instruments when conducting forensic psychological evaluations for ICs.

To conclude the examination of these instruments, the assessment of feigning is critical to an accurate interpretation of test scores. It should be part of any mental health evaluation, especially those conducted in forensic settings in which psychological evaluation findings can impact legal outcomes. It is recommended that MHPs rely on multiple indicators of noncredible responding, including more than one validity measure and information obtained from an interview, clinical observations, medical and legal records, and collateral informants. As defined in the *DSM-5*, MHPs can determine that an individual is malingering only when there is evidence of intentional feigning or symptom exaggeration in addition to secondary gain motivations. Furthermore, the validity of feigning instruments depends on the type of symptoms being evaluated and the examinee's background. Unfortunately, the literature on the cross-cultural validity of feigning instruments and on the impact of culture and demographic characteristics on validity indicators is limited.[149] Although the existing evidence is promising and encouraging, more research is needed to support the use of these instruments with linguistically, ethnically, and culturally diverse individuals within the United States and abroad. Particularly, the prevalence and assessment of response bias in ICs is an area that has not yet been investigated. Thus, it is essential that MHPs stay informed of advances in cross-cultural feigning assessment to choose appropriately validated instruments within the examinee's specific culture and cut-off scores to accurately classify individuals as genuine or probable feigners. Special attention should be paid to the examinee's levels of acculturation and educational attainment to determine the appropriateness of the test and available normative data. When the examinee's background does not resemble the normative group, cautionary statements should be included about the interpretation of the test scores and how the examinee's background (e.g., culture) might have impacted their performance. Test results should be supported with a comprehensive clinical interview and collateral information in order to minimize the potential for erroneous conclusions.

Conclusion

Given the cultural variability of individuals involved in the IC system, it is essential for MHPs who conduct evaluations in this context to do so with cultural competency. This expertise is developed though academic and didactic trainings, practice, and self-reflection. MHPs need to take a multicultural approach throughout the entire FMHA process (i.e., preparation for the interview, informed consent, clinical evaluation, mental status exam, diagnostic considerations, final opinions, and selection of interpreters if indicated). MHPs also need to consider how cultural factors might impact the validity and utility of psychological tests they may want to use as part of their evaluations with immigrants. There are many gaps in knowledge that call for further research to guide MHPs when conducing FMHAs with culturally diverse individuals in ICs. Specifically, practice guidelines for the cross-cultural assessment of trauma and torture are needed, as is research on the validity of the Cultural Formulation Interview in forensic settings. Furthermore, research needs to explore the way in which culture and acculturation impact the reliability and validity of existing psychological testing and also needs to develop assessment instruments that are property normed and validated specifically with immigrants involved in the IC system.

10

Forensic Assessment Considerations

The purpose of mental health evaluations conducted in the context of immigration law is to assist the trier of fact (e.g., the immigration judge [IJ] or United States Citizenship and Immigration Services [USCIS] adjudicator) in making decisions regarding the immigrant's legal status or detention status. To the extent that these evaluations are performed with the goal of assisting the legal decision maker, they fall under the definition of forensic mental health assessments (FMHAs).[1] It is important to note that the inclusion of the term "mental health" in FMHAs does not restrict these evaluations to determining the presence or absence of mental illness. In fact, many FMHAs involve the evaluation of psychological phenomena or behavioral predispositions that are relevant to the legal question and do not involve psychopathology. For example, this would be the case in IC when providing information about the legal issue of the "good moral character" of the immigrant. The term "psychological" more accurately captures the broad range of dimensions evaluated; however, "mental health" is preferred to avoid the appearance that FMHAs are restricted to being performed by psychologists, since FMHAs represent an activity practiced by other disciplines, including psychiatry and social work.[2]

Possessing the mental health education and training necessary to be a psychiatrist, psychologist, social worker, or mental health counselor is not by itself sufficient to conduct FMHAs for ICs. Further specialized training in forensic and cross-cultural assessment is needed. This chapter identifies the main differences between mental health assessments in forensic versus other clinical contexts, reviews some of the most important principles that guide best practice standards of FMHAs as they apply specifically to the IC context, and covers the issue of credibility and malingering in IC cases.

Clinical Versus Forensic Mental Health Assessments

Probably the most important difference between therapeutic/clinical and forensic evaluations relates to the referral question and thus the purpose of the evaluation. Most mental health evaluations are conducted with a therapeutic purpose (e.g., therapy) or with the purpose of making treatment determinations (psychiatric emergency room, diagnostic, or intake evaluations). The purpose of the FMHA, in contrast, is to assist the legal decision maker or the attorney. FMHAs are a type of mental health evaluation conducted to assess a person's clinical functioning (e.g., capacities, abilities, or behavioral tendencies) only as it relates to a specific legal question.[3] Therefore, unlike in other clinical settings, the focus is on functional legal capacities and not necessarily on diagnostic labels. If a diagnosis is offered, the relationship between the diagnosis and the functional capacity needs to be explained. For example, in a competency evaluation, the examiner will need to make a connection between the symptoms of schizophrenia and the immigrant's competency to participate in immigration proceedings. This requires knowledge of immigration law and experience in translating immigration law's definitions of "human abilities" and "conditions" into concepts that are amenable to clinical investigation.[4] In addition, whereas in a clinical evaluation the mental health professional (MHP) can decide to include as much information as possible in the report, as we have seen, in FMHAs; information that is not relevant to the referral question should not be included.[5] The decision about what is and is not relevant would depend on the legal issue facing the IJ. However, for some legal issues that have been extensively described in the forensic mental health literature (e.g., competency), which information might be relevant is more clearly defined than for others (e.g., asylum).

Another important distinction between these two types of evaluations is the type of psychological assessment techniques used. In the therapeutic/clinical context, the evaluator uses Clinical Assessment Instruments (CAIs) developed with the purpose of assessing, diagnosing, and developing treatment plans. For example, general psychological tests can provide information about the immigrant's cognitive, clinical, or personality functioning, which can be helpful if assessing an area of functioning that is relevant to the referral question (e.g., trauma related symptoms for asylum referrals). However, these instruments were not developed to specifically assess constructs that are of legal relevance. In the forensic context, in addition to CAIs including psychological test data, the evaluator can use Forensically Relevant Instruments (FRIs), which were developed in the same way as CAIs but provide information about an area of functioning that has particular relevance in the forensic context, such as malingering. Finally, the forensic evaluator can use Forensic Assessment Instruments (FAIs), which are tools developed specifically to assess legal constructs (e.g., instruments to assess competency to stand trial).[6] FAIs are ideal in the forensic context, but there are none developed specifically with the purpose of assessing legal constructs that are relevant to immigration law. This is a new and needed area of research. In fact, there are significant challenges even to using CAIs due to the cultural, linguistic, educational, and socioeconomic diversity of immigrants and the lack of appropriate test norms and validation studies. Due to these limitations, and specifically in the area of asylum evaluations, the internationally recognized guidelines for evaluating survivors of torture published by the Istanbul Protocol established the clinical interview as the standard for assessment methodology.[7] Whenever possible, MHPs in ICs should use FRIs, and when using CAIs such as psychological tests, the results should be explicitly connected to the relevant legal constructs.

Principles of Forensic Mental Health Assessment Applied to Immigration Court

Establishing a set of principles for any specific area of clinical practice is important because it informs training, promotes theory and research in that area of practice, and improves the quality of practice. Based on a review of the literature in the areas of law, science, ethics, and practice, a broad set of 29 foundational principles of FMHAs were initially described by Heilbrun in 2001 and later revised in 2009. They are specific to FMHA preparation, data collection and interpretation, written communication, and testimony.[8] This integration describes the foundational aspects of the field of FMHAs for the courts, lawyers, and MHPs.[9] Although these principles apply to all FMHAs, most of the literature has

focused on their application to criminal and civil contexts. The following are a subset of FMHA principles applied to the IC system.[10]

Preparation

One of the key principles of forensic mental health assessments applied
to IC is preparation.

RELEVANT FORENSIC ISSUES

Identifying the relevant psycholegal or forensic issues[11] in immigration
law can be more challenging than in other areas such as criminal law
because the psycholegal issues have not been as well defined by law or
discussed in the forensic mental health literature. The only exception is
competency: the Executive Office of Immigration Review (EOIR) has
recently defined the functional capacities to be assessed by MHPs when
evaluating competency evaluations. As an example of a less well defined
psycholegal issue, in an asylum case a possible legal issue is whether
the respondent experiences "well-founded fear of persecution." The psycholegal issue involves an assessment of the psychological impact of the
traumatic event caused by the persecution, sometimes with the aim of
helping the adjudicator determine the credibility (or lack thereof) of the
applicant's testimony, sometimes with the aim of establishing whether
the harm was sufficiently severe to qualify as persecution.

ACCEPT REFERRALS ONLY WITHIN AREA OF EXPERTISE

MHPs should accept referrals only within their area of expertise.[12]
Expertise to conduct FMHAs in IC requires more than being a licensed
MHP. It requires expertise in FMHA, cross-cultural assessment, and the
psychological impact of trauma. It is important to ensure that MHPs
have the appropriate training and experience before becoming involved
in these evaluations. In IC, although immigration lawyers are generally
the ones retaining MHPs, it is the IJ who makes decisions about the
admissibility of expert testimony.

The MHP does not need to be an expert in immigration law, as the
immigration attorney can be an important source of information about
the specifics of the case. It is highly advisable, however, to have a basic
knowledge of immigration law in order to understand the context in

which the FMHA will be used. In addition, MHPs conducting evaluations in IC for the first time are advised to seek supervision or consultation from other experienced MHPs.

DECLINE THE REFERRAL WHEN IMPARTIALITY IS UNLIKELY

MHPs should decline the referral when impartiality is unlikely.[13] The role of the MHP is to provide a detailed, accurate, unbiased, and impartial report in order to assist the IJ in making the most appropriate decision.[14] This requires an aspiration to be objective. MHPs can lose the important influence they can have as experts when they appear to be advocating for the immigrant rather than providing an objective opinion.[15] This does not mean that the evaluator might not be affected by the stories heard during evaluations with immigrants. As we have seen, immigrants will often share terrible stories of trauma, torture, and persecution. The MHP should be attuned to the psychological impacts that these evaluations are causing. However, it is important that MHPs do not see themselves as advocating for any single outcome (e.g., removal versus remaining in the country legally). If after honest self-reflection the MHP believes that this will not be possible, the referral should be declined.

As discussed earlier, forensic evaluators should be familiar with the concept of forensic alliance, which refers to experts' tendency to lean their opinions toward the side retaining their services.[16] Although there is no research regarding how this applies to IC, there is no reason to believe that it would be any different. Evaluators should become familiar with the literature about this concept and take steps to minimize its impact on their opinions.

CLARIFY THE EVALUATOR'S ROLE WITH THE ATTORNEY

It is also important to clarify the evaluator's role with the attorney.[17] In the context of IC, it is not uncommon for MHPs to be retained by immigration attorneys who have never worked with a mental health expert before. As noted in chapter 4, clarifying the role of the MHP (e.g., as an evaluator, consultant, or treatment provider) is crucial. It is also important to clarify the referral question. Some experienced attorneys have a clear sense of the question being asked of the MHP (e.g., competency to proceed, psychological impact of trauma). Others might believe that identifying mental health issues broadly will be somehow helpful with the case. In the latter situation, the MHP can work with the attorney to narrow down the referral question. In addition, the MHP and the attorney need to agree on whether the MHP will be writing a report or speaking to the attorney about their conclusions before writing a report. Some attorneys will ask MHPs not to write a report if the conclusions are not favorable to the case.

CLARIFY FINANCIAL ARRANGEMENTS

Clarifying financial arrangements is another aspect.[18] For MHPs who work in torture clinics or human rights organizations, FMHAs are often part of their salaried employment. Other MHPs might be paid by the immigration attorneys. It is important to establish the fee beforehand and to clarify that the payment, whatever the amount, is not contingent on the expert's opinion. If the MHP is charging an hourly fee, it is important to make clear what activities are chargeable (e.g., clinical interview, review of records, report-writing, testimony, conversations with the lawyer, etc.), as well as how many hours the MHP expects to spend on the report. In ICs, it is also common for MHPs to charge a flat rate regardless of the amount of time required for the full evaluation or to do this work pro bono. Although it is possible to maintain neutrality and objectivity no matter the arrangement, the MHP should explore their motivation for doing the evaluation (particularly if doing the work pro bono) and be prepared to answer questions about this during testimony. Finally, immigrants without legal representation could offer to pay the MHP directly. This arrangement is generally discouraged. As Evans and Hass have noted, without an attorney involved the MHP has no way of making sure that the report will end up being used for the purpose it was intended.[19]

Data Collection and Interpretation

The following sections address important issues related to data collection and interpretation.

USE MULTIPLE SOURCES OF INFORMATION

MHPs should use multiple sources of information.[20] Any individual could offer information that is inaccurate or biased because of cognitive impairment, memory, or concentration difficulties resulting from trauma or migration stress, or because of a conscious attempt to distort information due to an external incentive (e.g., avoiding deportation). To increase the objectivity and reliability of opinions, it is important for the MHP to consider, in addition to the clinical interview, multiple sources of collateral information. FMHAs typically involve four types of sources of information: third-party interviews, collateral sources of information, interviews with the examinee, and test/assessment data.[21] By the time the MHP meets with the immigrant, the lawyer has likely already collected a declaration. In addition, medical or educational records as well as third-party interviews with family members, friends, or treatment providers can be very helpful. However, in IC it is not uncommon for MHPs to be unable to access any, or only a limited amount of, collateral information. If this is the case, this should be considered a limitation of the final conclusions and acknowledged in the report and testimony.

USE RELEVANCE AND RELIABILITY AS GUIDES FOR SEEKING INFORMATION

The MHP should use relevance and reliability as guides for seeking information.[22] The MHP's goal is to identify and collect information relevant to the hypothesis to be tested, ensure that the data used to form opinions is relevant and reliable, consolidate the data, and form an opinion about the referral question based on the data.[23] This can be particularly challenging when MHPs use psychological testing given the limited cross-cultural validity of psychological tests.

PROVIDE APPROPRIATE NOTIFICATION OF PURPOSE AND LIMITS OF CONFIDENTIALITY

MHPs should provide appropriate notification of purpose and limits of confidentiality.[24] The informed consent process is particularly important in FMHAs because the evaluation is ordered by a third party (typically the immigration attorney and, on occasion, the judge). Informed consent includes three basic components: knowledge, voluntariness, and legal capacity.[25] In ICs, this means that the respondent needs to be knowledgeable about the purpose and nature of the evaluation (i.e., to inform the immigration removal case), to make the decision in the absence of any coercion or duress, and to do so in the absence of acute symptoms of psychopathology or cognitive deficits that might impair their ability to understand the nature and purpose of the evaluation.

In criminal proceedings, depending on the legal referral question, informed consent might not be required to proceed with the evaluation (i.e., competency evaluations). This has not been thoroughly discussed in ICs. Therefore MHPs should always consult with the attorney, if there is one, before proceeding with the evaluation if a lack of consent or capacity is suspected. Even in this situation, MHPs should attempt to seek the immigrant's assent to gain cooperation. In addition, immigrants must be informed of the limits of confidentiality and the fact that the information they provide will be shared with the immigration attorney and potentially the Department of Homeland Security (DHS) and the IJ. However, other than sharing the information with legal players as indicated, MHPs need to abide by a strict level of confidentiality, particularly if the immigrant is a victim of a crime and there is a risk that the perpetrator could locate the victim (e.g., cases of human trafficking or labor criminal activity).[26] Depending on the case, it might also be important to discuss with the immigrant the ways in which sharing their story might have an emotional impact and to have a plan should severe psychological symptoms arise (e.g., re-experiencing, depression, suicidality).

It is recommended that several components be covered during the notification and informed consent process in IC.[27] (In addition, the final report should contain a notification section, which documents how the information was provided and the immigrant's response to that explanation.) Below we identify nine individual but related components:

- Who has requested the evaluation (e.g., in the context of IC it is typically the immigration attorney, but it can also be the government [DHS], attorney or the judge)?
- What is the role of the examiner (including whether being paid and by whom)?
- What is the purpose and nature of the examination (e.g., to assist the court with the disposition of the immigration legal case)?
- What are the limits of confidentiality (e.g., that the information shared could be discussed with the immigration attorney and included in a

written report to be shared with the immigration attorney and potentially with other legal parties)?

- Information about the voluntary or involuntary nature of the participation (including potential consequences of refusing to participate).
- Information about who will receive copies of the report (e.g., the immigration attorney who can then decide to share it with other legal players).
- Clarification that the evaluation is not being conducted for treatment purposes.
- Information about whether the immigrant will have access to the report or whether the examiner will provide any feedback about the results of the evaluation.
- A warning about the possible psychological impact of sharing details about the immigrant's trauma history.[28]

USE IDEOGRAPHIC AND NOMOTHETIC EVIDENCE

MHPs should use ideographic and nomothetic evidence.[29] One of the most valuable ways to approach the FMHA is by integrating two types of evidence: ideographic and nomothetic. Ideographic data focuses on information specific to the individual and the unique circumstances of the case, and it compares characteristics of the specific situation in question with the individual's characteristics at other times. For example, in an asylum evaluation, the MHP can compare the individual's level of functioning pre- and postexposure to the traumatic event. "Nomothetic data" refers to comparing the individual with a group that shares characteristics with the individual. In general, it refers to norm-based instruments. When conducting evaluations of individuals in IC, access to nomothetic data can be difficult given the limited number of tests normed with individuals who share the same cultural background as the immigrant being evaluated. As a result, it is more common to rely on ideographic data. However, as evaluators develop experience and accumulate a number of evaluations with individuals of a particular culture, they might be able to make some comparisons when appropriate. If normed-based tests are available, the combination of information unique to the individual and their circumstances and a reference group is preferred.[30]

USE SCIENTIFIC REASONING IN ASSESSING CAUSAL CONNECTIONS BETWEEN CLINICAL CONDITIONS AND FUNCTIONAL ABILITIES AND DESCRIBE LIMITS TO THE FINDINGS

Be sure to use scientific reasoning in assessing causal connections between clinical conditions and functional abilities and describe limits to the findings.[31] Forming conclusions in a FMHA is a process of hypothesis testing. For example, the MHP could obtain information during the clinical interview that then is verified or unverified through psychological testing or collateral sources of information. The final opinions or findings are formed through consideration of all sources of available information and through the acknowledgement of any limitations that those sources of information might have.[32] For example, if the MHP has used a testing instrument with cultural limitations with respect to the normative sample, this needs to be recognized. The MHP needs to be prepared to explain the conclusions despite any of the existing limitations.

THE ULTIMATE LEGAL QUESTION

There is significant debate as to how directly forensic evaluators should answer the ultimate legal question.[33] Examples of the ultimate legal question in IC would include whether the respondent is competent or whether they meet criteria for asylum relief. Some authors believe that when judges and attorneys expect MHPs to comment on the ultimate legal issue it is appropriate to do so, whereas others have noted that evaluators should restrict their opinions to the functional legal capacities and stay away from opining about the ultimate legal question, which might incorporate not only psychological or clinical data but also moral, political, and community values.[34] Given that FMHAs in ICs have only recently begun to be defined, and given the rapidly changing nature of immigration law, MHPs likely ought to refrain from directly answering the ultimate legal question. In fact, although restricted to the area of competency, the EOIR appears to instruct MHPs in this direction by stating that the role of the MHP is "to provide information to the court about the mental health of the respondent so the court can make an informed decision about the respondent's competency."[35] Similarly, in the context of other legal issues such as asylum, it is the IJ, not the MHP, who is charged with making the ultimate decision on relief. To avoid the appearance of advocating for the respondent, and the IJ's resulting lack of trust, the MHP should comment on whether the respondent shows signs or symptoms of psychological trauma but should not comment on the ultimate issue of asylum relief.

DESCRIBE FINDINGS AND LIMITS TO THOSE FINDINGS

MHPs should describe their findings and any limits to those findings.[36] If the MHP arrives at conclusions through a thorough consideration of the data, including multiple sources of information, and acknowledges any existing limitations, it is unlikely that the opinions will change unless significant new information comes to light. In addition, the MHP should consider alternative explanations for the findings.[37] For example, in an asylum case, the MHP should consider any other events or reasons that might explain the trauma-related symptoms in addition to the claims of rape or torture that are reportedly related to the fear of persecution.

Written Communication

Written communication plays an important role. In ICs, full forensic reports are not always required. Sometimes affidavits or declarations are instead provided to the court. Both affidavits (sworn and witnessed by an official such as a notary public) and declarations under penalty of perjury are acceptable forms of evidence in ICs.[38] Typically, when the MHP is involved in a forensic role as an expert witness, a full report is required. There are several principles that apply to writing forensic reports, which we describe in the following sections.

ATTRIBUTE INFORMATION TO SOURCES

When documenting the evaluation in the report, all information included should be attributed to a specific source or sources.[39] This practice is also recommended by the "Specialty Guidelines for Forensic Psychology" published by the American Psychological Association (APA).[40] Being able to attribute all information included in the report to a specific source allows the IJ or attorney to understand where the information is coming from; it also adds credibility to the conclusions. For example, in a report about asylum, the MHP should identify whether specific information about a specific symptom (e.g., hypervigilance) originates from testing data, self-report, observation by the examiner, or observation by the attorney or a third-party source.

USE PLAIN LANGUAGE AND AVOID TECHNICAL JARGON

In their reports, MHPs should use plain language and avoid technical jargon.[41] Unlike other clinical reports, which are written for fellow clinicians, FMHAs are written for an audience that typically does not have any clinical or mental health training (e.g., judges, lawyers). This is particularly the case in ICs, as MHPs have only recently started to be used as experts in immigration proceedings. As a result, MHPs should try to avoid including any technical language that is not accessible to the layperson.

WRITE THE REPORT IN SECTIONS

The report should be organized into logical sections.[42] When the courts require a full forensic report, there is no one single format that is used, and MHPs have autonomy to decide how to format the report and what information to include. It is important, however, to remember that a written report represents the best opportunity for MHPs to share their thought process and communicate professionalism.

While the Federal Rules of Evidence do not necessarily apply in ICs, they are still instructive as to best practices and should be followed as much as possible to increase the report's credibility. Federal Rule of Civil Procedure 26.2(a) requires that written reports include the following:

- A complete statement of all opinions to be expressed and the basis and reasons for therefor;
- The data and other information considered by the witness in forming the opinions;
- Any exhibits to be used as summary of support for the opinions;
- The qualifications of the witness, including a list of all publications authored by the witness within the preceding ten years;
- The compensation to be paid for the study and testimony; and
- A listing of any other cases in which the witness as testified as an expert at trial or by deposition within the preceding four years.[43]

As an example of deviation from the Federal Rules, IJs generally do not require a list of publications or other cases in which the expert has testified to be included in the report. Nevertheless, these are often included in the curriculum vitae provided to the court. Meanwhile, the EOIR has provided guidance on the components of a report, but only as it applies to competency for removal evaluations. Experts should therefore make an effort to ascertain the requirements of the specific jurisdiction and judge so that they know what will be expected of their report.[44] If retained by an immigration attorney, it is helpful to discuss the format of the report beforehand.

Apart from the requirements of the court, there are several elements that have been considered by FMHA scholars as important for inclusion in forensic reports.[45] These include:

- Referral Question
- Notification/Informed consent
- Sources of Information
- Background Information
- Behavioral Observations and Mental Status
- Psychological and Medical Testing
- Psycholegal Opinions

Two areas that are worth elaborating further: Whether a diagnostic section should be included, and whether test scores should be included. Reports have traditionally included a diagnostic section under which diagnoses following the APA's *Diagnostic and Statistical Manual of Mental Disorders* (DSM) are listed. In FMHAs, delineation of the functional legal capacities is more relevant than the diagnoses. Particularly given the questionable cross-cultural validity of some of the diagnoses in the DSM, in some IC cases it might be more appropriate not to include a separate heading for diagnoses in reports. A description of the symptoms and clinical presentation and how they relate to the psycholegal issue might be more helpful. Similarly, when using psychological testing, some psychologists include testing scores in their reports, while others describe the test results without including specific scores. Given the limitations of using psychological testing cross-culturally, it is advisable to explain general results without including specific scores. In addition, particularly in ICs, test scores rarely speak directly to the ultimate legal issue, and they could be considered jargon that most laypersons would not understand without context. When deciding on whether to include test scores, MHPs should consider the referral question, whether the scores are needed to communicate the relevant findings, and the audience.[46] They might also consider consulting the attorney. The attorney, as a layperson and someone likely familiar with the IJ who will be reading the report, can offer an opinion as to how the test scores will be understood and received.

Some forensic reports include an executive summary on the first page. This is typically no longer than one paragraph that summarizes clinical and psycholegal opinions. Including an executive summary runs the risk of having the IJ or the lawyers skip the rest of the report; however, if the report is long and complex, having the main conclusions at the beginning might be helpful.[47]

Finally, an important consideration when writing forensic reports is to distinguish between "observations, inferences, and conclusions" as stated in the "Specialty Guidelines for Forensic Psychology."[48] This has also been referred to by Grisso as distinguishing between facts, inferences, and opinions.[49] Facts or observations are pieces of data that can be verified. For example, it is a *fact* that the respondent was arrested right after crossing the border and detained for three months. An *inference* would be that the three months in detention caused anxiety and fear. A *conclusion* or *opinion* in this situation would be that the anxiety and fear experienced during detention exacerbated existing trauma-related symptoms. It is important for inferences and opinions to be linked to facts. Typically, this is accomplished by organizing reports in sections as outlined above, including the facts organized under "Background Information" or "History" and the inferences and opinions under the "Opinions" or "Conclusions" section. The MHP could also decide to provide an inference and opinion in a sentence preceded by or followed by the facts.[50] Using the example above:

Ms. Ruiz was arrested a day after crossing the border and placed in detention by ICE for three months. She reported that she experienced anxiety and fear, which likely triggered the return of nightmares related to her experience of being sexually assaulted. This finding supports the idea that Ms. Ruiz's months in detention retriggered/ exacerbated preexisting symptoms of PTSD related to the rape that she experienced in Guatemala.

Testimony

MHPs in ICs are often called on to testify and be cross-examined by the Immigration and Customs Enforcement attorney. The following principles apply to forensic testimony.

BASE TESTIMONY ON THE RESULTS OF PROPERLY PERFORMED FMHA

Testimony should be based on the results of a properly performed FMHA.[51] Testimony provided in court should be based on the facts, inferences, and opinions delineated in the report. No new opinions should come up during testimony that have not already been included in the report, unless new facts come to light during testimony that cause the expert to change opinions. Testifying on the information included in the report allows for lawyers to prepare effectively for direct and cross-examination and for the IJ to also ask questions accordingly.[52]

TESTIFY EFFECTIVELY

Be effective when providing testimony.[53] This principle encompasses both *substance* and *style* of testimony. The "substance" element is related to the FMHA principles described above. The "style" element relates to how the expert presents, speaks, and behaves, all of which can affect credibility. A series of books have been written about testimony in FMHA.[54] It is important to note that these have not been written with ICs in mind and that much of the literature on effective expert testimony takes into consideration opinions of jurors. Court hearings in IC do not include juries, and therefore some of the findings might not fully apply. However, there is no reason to believe that many of the principles identified by the literature as important for effective expert testimony in criminal court would also apply to ICs. Prior to the COVID-19 pandemic, one difference between ICs and other courts was that IJs would often allow testimony by experts telephonically. This became common practice in criminal courts due to the pandemic. Little has been written about providing effective telephonic testimony. Regardless, there are some components of effective testimony that have been described, which should apply to all courts whether in person or via telephone or videoconference. These principles were developed after a review of more than 100 studies, which identified aspects of effective expert testimony.[55]

- *Credibility*: Expert witnesses who are considered credible are confident (self-assured, well spoken, poised, relaxed), likeable (kind, friendly, respectful), trustworthy (truthful, honest, reliable), and knowledgeable (logical, informed, educated, scientific).[56]
- *Clarity*: Experts who communicate in a clear, comprehensive manner and who avoid jargon tend to be more persuasive.
- *Clinical knowledge*: Research has found that jurors and judges prefer experts who focus on clinical versus scientific knowledge. For example, information about symptoms of mental illness was found to be preferred over statistics or information about diagnostic reliability.
- *Certainty*: Witnesses who express a higher level of confidence in their opinions are found to be more effective. Tentativeness or unwillingness to draw conclusions are seen as less desirable.

Finally, whether testimony is taking place in person or telephonically/through videoconference, it is very important to prepare. If the expert is retained by the immigrant's attorney, it is recommended that the MHP and the attorney schedule some sessions to prepare for testimony. This would include both the MHP educating the immigration attorney about the findings in the report and the most important points or conclusions more strongly supported by the facts, as well as pointing to the weaknesses and anticipating questions that often come up during cross-examination. Ultimately, it is important for MHPs to remember that their job is not to "win the case" or to advocate for the immigrant but to provide detailed, accurate, objective information to assist the adjudicator in making the most informed and appropriate decision.[57]

Assessing Credibility and Malingering

Credibility is a concept that is at the core of many immigration evaluations.[58] For example, a psycholegal issue in an initial asylum screening involves "well-founded fear of persecution," which is defined as a "significant possibility" that the respondent can establish in a hearing before an IJ that they have been persecuted or have a well-founded fear of persecution if returned to the country of origin.[59] At this stage, asylum seekers and refugees will likely not have any physical or other type of evidence of the persecution suffered, other than their own testimony. Therefore, the perceived credibility of testimony can be key in these types of interviews. When IJs make decisions about credibility, issues such as inconsistent accounts, vagueness, and implausible information might be weighted heavily, particularly in cases where there is limited collateral information and the case relies primarily on the respondent's account.[60] Even small inconsistencies that are not material to the facts of the case can result in an overall finding of lack of credibility.[61] Adjudicators must consider the totality of the circumstances when making determinations about credibility,[62] but the legal definitions of "credibility" do not take into consideration psychological factors such as how the trauma experienced might impact their ability to provide believable testimony. The courts appear to rely on the idea that the truth does not change and that individuals must be able to recount experiences in detail.[63] In fact, some studies have found that 40–77% of asylum claims that have been denied include credibility as a reason.[64]

MHPs can be very helpful in assisting the adjudicator when making decisions about credibility. In fact, in situations in which no corroborating information is available, the report and testimony provided by the expert might carry the most weight when the adjudicator is making decisions about credibility.[65] MHPs can educate the court with respect to how providing inconsistent information with respect to biographical accounts, dates, sequences of events, and the like is actually quite common, particularly when individuals are remembering information about traumatic events.[66] They can also provide information learned from the research on witness evidence, which has shown that in general people recall more details that are central to an event when that event has high levels of emotional impact and that their recall of central details is often at the expense of the recall of peripheral details.[67] Individual factors often present in refugees, such as trauma, depression, sleep difficulties, or malnutrition, can also affect memory retrieval.[68] This has been empirically examined in two different studies. One study conducted in

England with 27 Kosovan and 12 Bosnian refugees found that discrepancies in repeated descriptions of one traumatic and one nontraumatic event were quite common. Furthermore, this study found that for participants with high levels of posttraumatic stress disorder (PTSD), the number of discrepancies increased with the length of time between interviews, particularly around details peripheral to the account. These results question the assumption that inconsistency of recall means poor credibility of accounts.[69] Another study conducted with a group of 28 individuals who had been granted asylum found no significant differences between genuine reports and reports by those asked to exaggerate. It also found that both groups presented with high levels of discrepancies.[70] Furthermore, studies have found that involuntary memories of traumatic experiences take place spontaneously, whereas voluntary memories of the facts involved in the traumatic experience are more difficult to be retrieved.[71] In addition to trauma, other psychological conditions can interfere with the respondent's proper ability to recall and retell information. These include cognitive or intellectual deficits, acute psychopathology, symptoms of anxiety or depression, stress, and/or low levels of formal education. While MHPs can explore whether any of these factors can explain inconsistencies in reporting, ultimately they should not comment directly on the overall credibility of the respondent's report, as this is the purview of the legal adjudicator.

It is important to mention that it is not uncommon for immigrants to reveal factual information during the mental health evaluation that they have not previously shared with their attorneys or written in their affidavits. This does not necessarily mean that the respondent is being deceptive, but the MHP needs to understand the reasons for this. If there are any gaps, they can assess whether this is due to deficits in psychological or cognitive functioning or due to deception.[72] When MHPs engage in careful exploration, it is common to find psychologically plausible explanations for the reported inconsistencies.[73] When the MHPs cannot clinically explain these inconsistencies, they should speak with the attorney, as the attorney could then decide that a report is not beneficial for the respondent.[74]

While credibility is a legal concept, *malingering* is a clinical concept. "Malingering" is defined by the APA as the "intentional production of false or grossly exaggerated physical or psychological symptoms, motivated by external incentives such as avoiding military duty, avoiding work, obtaining financial compensation, evading criminal prosecution, or obtaining drugs."[75] Avoiding deportation is the presumed possible external incentive in immigration evaluations. It is important to distinguish malingering from *factitious disorder*. Factitious presentations are also characterized by feigning, but the incentive is internal, with the individual's apparent aim being "to assume the sick role."[76] It is estimated that malingering occurs in 15–17% of forensic criminal cases[77] and in about 20–30% of personal injury civil litigation cases,[78] which typically involve the assessment of PTSD. There is not enough research to estimate the prevalence of malingering in immigration evaluations. However, ICs represent a medico-legal context, and avoiding removal can be a strong incentive for malingering. As a result, just as in any other forensic context, MHPs should always consider the possibility of malingering and should include this consideration in their reports. Although credibility and malingering are two different concepts, ruling out malingering can also assist IJs in making determinations about credibility. The absence of malingering can be used by the attorney to support the fact that the overall report of the respondent is credible; similarly, if the MHP concludes that the respondent is malingering, that calls into question the respondent's overall credibility.[79]

Particularly relevant to mental health evaluations in IC is the assessment of PTSD symptom exaggeration or overreporting. For example, in asylum evaluations, the presence of trauma-related symptoms or PTSD can be the only evidence of persecution, which is the basis for the claim. However, the identification of malingered PTSD symptoms (either through falsification or exaggeration) is one of the most challenging tasks for MHPs,[80] particularly when evaluating cross-culturally. This is in part because of the heterogeneity of the disorder; it has been calculated that PTSD comprises as many as 636,120 combinations of symptoms.[81] In addition, there is no single tool that has been extensively validated as the go-to instrument for the assessment of malingered PTSD, and systematic methods to distinguish genuine versus exaggerated or feigned cases of PTSD are still being developed.[82] In addition, some studies have found that individuals who have experienced childhood abuse or veterans with PTSD can endorse trauma-related symptoms that can be misinterpreted as symptom exaggeration in psychological testing.[83] This might also be the case with asylum seekers or refugees who have experienced prolonged torture that is more consistent with clinical presentations that have been referred to as "Complex PTSD." This diagnosis is not included in the APA's *DSM-5* and has only recently been included in the World Health Organization's *International Statistical Classification of Disease and Related Health Problems*, which defines "traumatic experience" as "exposure to a stressor typically of an extreme or prolonged nature and from which escape is difficult or impossible."[84] Clinicians who are not familiar with this clinical presentation could confuse symptoms that have not traditionally been associated with PTSD, such as affective dysregulation, with feigning or exaggeration. Furthermore, cultural and linguistic differences add to the challenges of distinguishing bona fide versus feigned symptoms of trauma, since trauma can have clinical manifestations that vary across cultures.

Despite all of these challenges, MHPs can still provide helpful information to ICs about malingering. A multiprong approach is necessary for all malingering evaluations, and this is particularly true in the context of ICs given the challenges previously mentioned. In this type of evaluation, an awareness of an external incentive is combined with a clinical evaluation, collateral information, and testing data.[85] The following steps have been recommended for the detection of malingered PTSD: reviewing of collateral information and relevant records, conducting the evaluation, considering misattributed PTSD, considering malingered or factitious PTSD, and considering performing psychological testing.[86] In ICs, collateral information is often limited. Sometimes the only records available are the legal records provided, which can include the respondent's declaration. Nevertheless, the MHP should consider conducting third-party interviews with family members, friends, or treatment providers when available or reviewing records including legal documents, medical, school, or vocational records.

During the clinical interview, it is recommended that open-ended questions be first asked with respect to the history of trauma and resulting symptoms. Starting with structured interviews or self-report questionnaires from the beginning could suggest symptoms to the respondent that they might then readily endorse.[87] Spontaneously reporting symptoms that are highly consistent with bona fide PTSD can provide support for the diagnosis. More details can be elicited through further questions that follow the diagnostic criteria or through structured interviews or self-administered questionnaires. In addition to behavioral observations, there are several factors to consider when conducting the clinical interview. Intrusion symptoms such as dreams and flashbacks, as well as hypervigilance and exaggerated startle responses, are often perceived by the layperson as the hallmark of PTSD and therefore are more likely to be feigned. As a result, it is helpful to be able to validate the presence of these symptoms through consistency in reporting and collateral information.[88] Avoidance symptoms are less likely to be known by the layperson as being part of PTSD and are therefore less likely to be feigned. If feigned, the layperson is more likely to understand avoidance literally (e.g., avoiding movies that remind them of the event) and not the more subtle symbolic associations (e.g., avoiding a place due to a smell that triggers memories).[89] Symptoms of negative cognitions and mood, particularly those seen in complex PTSD presentations such as affective dysregulation, are also less known and therefore less likely to be feigned. It is also important to remember that malingering does not preclude the possibility of genuine psychopathology. Immigrants who have experienced traumatic experiences that have resulted in bona fide symptoms could also decide to exaggerate or make up symptoms, either because of a desire to avoid deportation.

Evaluators must also consider other forms of psychopathology that might explain the symptom presentation. These include substance use, major depressive disorder, and personality disorders. Once other etiologies have been ruled out, then feigning can be considered. It is important to remember that feigning is the deliberate fabrication or gross exaggeration of psychological or physical symptoms without any assumption about its goals. Malingering can be concluded only if there is a clear external incentive.[90] Several approaches have been recommended for the identification of feigning in general, particularly when psychological testing is not available. Some of these include identifying symptoms that are rarely endorsed by individuals with PTSD or that are improbable or absurd, endorsing symptoms indiscriminately, endorsing symptoms that do not typically occur simultaneously, or reporting an excessive severity in symptom presentation.[91]

Psychological testing is highly recommended when assessing malingering and can provide crucial, objective information. However, as we have seen, many of the available feigning measures have been normed in North America, using samples of White, English-speaking individuals. Although some of these measures have been translated to other languages, their cross-cultural validity has not yet been fully demonstrated. MHPs working in ICs must engage in a risk/benefit analysis when making determinations about whether to use psychological tests for feigning. If tests are used, some recommendations from the research in the area of personal injury evaluations might be helpful to the immigration context. Specifically, research has suggested increased accuracy when multiple measures are used, specifically both Symptom Validity Tests (SVTs) and Performance Validity Tests (PVTs). SVTs evaluate malingering through self-report measures, whereas PVTs, also referred to as "effort-based" tests, evaluate symptom presentation based on the examinee's performance on neurocognitive tasks. Both types of tests use a variety of detection methods such as identifying uncommon presentations compared to a genuinely impaired normative group, or identifying atypical combinations or unusual severity of symptoms. The Trauma Symptom Inventory-2 (TSI-2)[92] presents as a promising instrument to be used in ICs. It is a psychometric instrument used to evaluate trauma-related symptoms and contains symptom validity scales. The validity of the overreporting scale (ART) of the TSI-2 to detect feigning of PTSD was examined in a sample of West African asylum seekers. The authors found only a 40% rate of sensitivity among those instructed to feign and a 10% rate of false positives among those with high levels of PTSD.[93] Meanwhile, another study that examined the TSI-2 among immigrants with histories of trauma found that the same scale likely functions similarly in the standardization sample compared with the immigrant sample.[94] Further research will clarify the utility of this scale and other instruments in the IC system.

Conclusion

MHPs can make significant contributions to the immigration legal process by offering specialized knowledge that can assist immigration adjudicators in making better-informed decisions about noncitizens' immigrant legal status. This requires MHPs to develop knowledge and expertise on the principles that guide the practice of FMHAs, as well as immigration lawyers to understand basic forensic evaluation procedures. Although there is extensive literature about the principles of FMHAs applied to criminal and other civil procedures, very little has been written about their application to the IC system. This chapter has provided a summary of some important FMHA principles and how they apply to evaluations conducted to aid adjudicators in IC. However, a review of this chapter is not enough to prepare clinicians with no prior forensic training to conduct forensic evaluations in immigration proceedings; additional reading and training are needed.

Although some of the issues raised in IC proceedings are similar to those encountered in criminal or other civil proceedings, psycholegal issues in IC tend to be more vague and lack the type of extensive literature that has guided other types of forensic evaluations (e.g., competency in criminal court, criminal responsibility in criminal court, or mental injury in civil court). In addition, there are several factors that further complicate FMHAs in ICs, including the lack of FAIs developed to address immigration law issues, the limited knowledge about common practices in forensic evaluations in IC, and, most important, the vast cultural variability in immigrants' identities and backgrounds. These evaluations often have to be conducted in a language other than English, with individuals who have little knowledge of the US legal and immigration systems, and with limited sources of collateral information (e.g., records from the noncitizens' countries of origins or access to third-party interviews), which make it difficult to corroborate much of their reported experiences. Finally, there is a very limited number of psychological assessment instruments that have been property normed and validated in the populations being evaluated in IC. Despite all of this, the expertise that MHPs have to offer to ICs far outweighs all of these complications. However, forensic evaluators and lawyers have to use some caution. First, MHPs should not answer to the ultimate legal issue in ICs. Second, MHPs should acknowledge the limitations of their opinions and make it clear when some of the opinions or conclusions carry uncertainty; lawyers and adjudicators need to accept the probabilistic nature of some clinical opinions.[95] Third, immigration lawyers and adjudicators should examine the foundations of the clinical opinions offered by MHPs.[96] Finally, MHPs should not provide professional opinions outside their areas of expertise.

11

Competency to Participate in Immigration Proceedings

The question of whether a criminal defendant is competent to participate in the criminal process is the most common type of forensic mental health assessment (FMHA) conducted in criminal court.[1] However, whether immigrants are competent to participate in immigration court (IC) proceedings is a question that has only recently been asked of mental health professionals (MHPs). The concept of competency to participate in criminal proceedings originated in English common law and can be traced back to the seventeenth century as a reaction to defendants who, instead of entering the required guilty plea, would stand "mute." The court would then be required to determine whether the defendant stood mute "of malice" or "by visitation of God." The former would be subjected to torture, whereas the latter, also referred to as "lunatic," were spared from the process.[2] American courts also recognized the concept of competency early on. For example, in 1835, the man who attempted to assassinate President Andrew Jackson was found incompetent to stand trial. This was based on a recognition that it is not enough for defendants to be physically present during the trial process; they also need to be mentally present so that the rights guaranteed under the Sixth Amendment (e.g., to effective counsel, to confront accusers, and to present evidence) can be preserved.[3] The competency standard exists to protect not only defendants' rights but also the dignity and reliability of the process and thereby society's interests.[4]

As we have seen, because immigration proceedings are civil rather than criminal in nature, many of the protections accorded to criminal defendants (including the right to counsel) are not guaranteed for respondents facing removal. In actual practice, however, many aspects of removal proceedings are more similar to criminal than other civil proceedings.[5] As with criminal proceedings, removal proceedings are David versus Goliath, with individuals expected to defend themselves while a government lawyer plays a prosecutorial role.[6] Furthermore, as with criminal sentences, deportation and detention decisions can result in an individual being deprived of their liberty and can have other serious consequences for immigrants' lives and livelihoods as well. The United States Supreme Court, in holding that immigration consequences are so important that criminal defense attorneys must advise their clients of them, acknowledged the extent to which the criminal and immigration systems have become entwined.[7] Scholars have argued that this recognition of deportation as more than a mere "collateral" consequence potentially requires that respondents in removal proceedings be accorded some of the same rights as criminal defendants.[8]

As has been noted, a number of undocumented immigrants who are detained during removal proceedings suffer from serious mental illness such as schizophrenia or other psychotic disorders, bipolar disorders, and posttraumatic stress disorder. Immigration detention facilities often provide inadequate screening for, assessment of, and treatment of mental illness, likely exacerbating the acuity of psychopathology. Even individuals who have already been found incompetent to stand trial in criminal matters might be transferred to immigration detention at the conclusion of criminal proceedings instead of to hospitals for competency restoration.[9] In fact, it is not unusual for detained immigrants to have been found incompetent to stand trial in criminal courts several times in the past. Without proper protections, all of these factors can lead to immigrants with mental illness being deported without understanding the removal process, their legal status, or the consequences of deportation.[10]

It is only recently that ICs have begun to consider the issue of competency and to incorporate any safeguards in removal proceedings for immigrants suffering from mental illness. Evaluations of competency are becoming more common in IC, increasing the need for MHPs to perform these evaluations. Competency evaluations in IC are similar to those conducted in criminal court, but they are also different in significant ways.[11] Most important, because immigrants facing removal proceedings do not have the right to counsel, the question of competency is necessarily different: someone might be competent to participate meaningfully in their own case with the help of counsel and still be incompetent to perform the functions necessary to represent themself. This chapter reviews the legal standards for competency in criminal court and the relevant case law and policy and clinical guidance with respect to this issue in IC.

Legal Standards and Procedures for Competency in Criminal Court

In this country, the criminal standard for competency was established in *Dusky v. United States* (1960), when the Supreme Court held that the test for competency must be whether the defendant "has sufficient present ability to consult with his lawyer with a reasonable degree of rational understanding—and whether he has a rational as well as factual understanding of the proceedings against him."[12] In *Drope v. Missouri* (1975), the Supreme Court elaborated on the standard to include the idea that the defendant must be able to "assist in preparing his defense."[13] The *Dusky/Drope* standard is applied federally, and all states have adopted some version of it.[14] The competency issue can be brought up at different points in the process, and the terms "adjudicative competency" or "competency to proceed" are preferred to "competency to stand trial" (CST), as they more accurately reflect the different types of competencies that are relevant to the criminal process (e.g., to plea, to represent oneself, to waive rights, to be sentenced).[15]

In criminal court, the issue of competency can be raised by any officer of the court (judge, defense attorney, or prosecutor) if there is a bona fine doubt about the defendant's competency. The threshold is typically low, and most times the courts order a competency evaluation once the issue has been raised. In most jurisdictions, two MHPs (licensed psychologist or psychiatrist) are then called on to conduct the assessment and write a report, after which a hearing is scheduled to adjudicate the issue. In more than 90% of the cases, the opinions of the evaluators are not disputed and the courts follow the recommendations of the MHPs.[16] For defendants found incompetent, the criminal process is postponed until competency has been restored through mental health treatment and psychoeducation or, in some jurisdictions, until a determination is made that the defendant is not likely to ever regain competency.[17] In some jurisdictions, for defendants charged with misdemeanors who are found incompetent, the charges are dropped and they might be civilly committed to mental health treatment.

Legal Standards and Procedures for Competency in Immigration Court

In later sections, this chapter addresses standards for competency under the "nationwide" policy for detained and unrepresented individuals. First, however, the chapter looks at legal standards and procedures for competency in immigration court.

Background

Several cases, in both IC and federal civil court, have shaped the policy relating to competency. We discuss these in the sections immediately below.

MATTER OF M-A-M- (2011)

The decision In re M-A-M-[18] represented the first time that the Board of Immigration Appeals (BIA) provided any guidance on competency and removal proceedings in approximately 50 years.[19] In this case, the respondent was a citizen of Jamaica who was admitted to the United States as a lawful permanent resident at the age of 10. Based on his prior convictions, which included drug possession and sale, the Department of Homeland Security (DHS) charged him as deportable. At his first hearing before the immigration judge (IJ), the respondent, who had trouble providing his name and date of birth, shared that he had been diagnosed with schizophrenia and required medication. At the second hearing, he indicated that he had a history of mental illness and that he was not receiving treatment in the detention facility. He continued to make similar statements at subsequent hearings. At the final hearing, when the IJ asked whether he could proceed, he indicated that he would do the best he could. The IJ did not make an explicit finding regarding competency, and the respondent appealed with the assistance of an attorney.[20] The legal issues presented by this case included: When should IJs make competency determinations? What factors should IJs consider?

What procedures should they employ to make those determinations? What safeguards should IJs prescribe to ensure that proceedings are sufficiently fair when competency is not established?[21] The BIA held that, if "indicia of incompetency" are present, the IJ must make further inquiry to determine whether a respondent is competent. The standard for competency put forth in *M-A-M-* is very similar to the *Dusky* standard (which, notably, assumes that the defendant will have counsel—a benefit that is not a given in immigration court):

> The test for determining whether an alien is competent to participate in immigration proceedings is whether he or she has a *rational and factual understanding* of the nature and object of the proceedings, *can consult with an attorney* or representative if there is one, and has a *reasonable opportunity to examine and present evidence and cross-examine witnesses.*[22]

M-A-M- notes that a "mental competency evaluation" is one tool available to IJs to assist them in their competency determinations. The opinion implies that DHS might arrange for such an evaluation if the IJ requests it but is otherwise silent on how such evaluations should be provided or funded.[23]

If the IJ finds that the respondent lacks sufficient competency to proceed, the IJ will evaluate appropriate safeguards.[24] The *M-A-M-* opinion included some examples of safeguards, including identifying a friend, family member, or guardian to assist the respondent in front of the court; waiving the respondent's appearance; allowing the hearing to be closed to the public; refusing to accept an unrepresented respondent's admission that they are appropriate for removal; or facilitating "medical treatment in an effort to restore competence."[25] Later opinions added further possible safeguards including requirements about how the Notice to Appear should be served,[26] as well as the suggestion to give individuals with mental illness the benefit of the doubt by assuming they believe their story to be true even if it seems unbelievable.[27] Another possible safeguard listed in *M-A-M-* is the appointment of counsel. The opinion also contemplates that IJs might, at their discretion, move to administratively close the case if concerns about competency remain despite the courts' efforts to implement appropriate safeguards.[28] The United States Attorney General, however, foreclosed this option in 2018 by issuing a precedent opinion holding that IJs lack the authority to administratively close cases, even if the respondent is incompetent, and the Executive Office of Immigration Review (EOIR) subsequently issued regulations to cement the change.[29]

Because of its overreliance on IJ discretion, the *M-A-M-* framework has failed to fully protect the rights of detained immigrants with mental illness. IJs, who are not MHPs and who are not required to have any training in mental health, are the final arbiters of competency[30] and have been given, at every stage of the process, little guidance and much leeway. Though the BIA suggests some "indicia of incompetency" that might trigger a competency inquiry, it is ultimately up to the IJ to determine whether an inquiry is necessary.[31] If they decide to conduct an inquiry, IJs might seek an evaluation of the respondent[32] or might choose to proceed on their own without the benefit of expert assistance.[33] If the IJ finds the respondent incompetent, it is the IJ who gets to determine what safeguards might be sufficient to make the hearing "fair."[34] While IJs must articulate the rationale for their decisions,[35] they will be overruled only if their findings are "clearly erroneous."[36] Finally, unlike in criminal law, nothing prohibits the IC from proceeding against a person who is so incompetent that they cannot understand the nature of the proceedings against them or participate in their own defense. Immigrants who meet this standard can still be deported so long as safeguards (which might not even rise to the level of appointed counsel) are employed.

THE *FRANCO* CLASS ACTION LAWSUIT

The 2013 class action *Franco-Gonzalez v. Holder* is another landmark case.[37] Jose Antonio Franco-Gonzalez was a Mexican immigrant who had been found incompetent to stand trial in 2005 due to a diagnosis of mental retardation with an IQ estimated to be between 35 and 55, which is significantly below the average IQ of 100. As a result, he could not identify his age or remember his phone number. Despite this, he was not appointed an attorney for his immigration proceedings and was incarcerated in an Immigration and Customs Enforcement (ICE) facility for four years while awaiting removal. Immigrant rights and civil rights organizations brought a class action lawsuit on behalf of Franco-Gonzalez and hundreds of other detained immigrants who had been diagnosed with severe psychiatric disorders, many of whom had been found incompetent to stand trial in criminal court proceedings.[38] After years of litigation, the judge issued in 2013 an order requiring immigration courts in Arizona, California, and Washington to provide a "qualified representative" to detained immigrants with mental illness.[39]

THE "NATIONWIDE" POLICY

Simultaneously, the Department of Justice (DOJ) and DHS announced a "nationwide policy" for respondents with serious mental illness who are *both unrepresented and detained*.[40] Under the policy, as in *M-A-M-*, IJs are instructed to evaluate competency if there is evidence that the respondent might suffer from a mental illness that could render them incompetent to proceed. The standard for competency, however, is different from *M-A-M-*, as explained more fully below, because it asks specifically about competency to represent one's self rather than merely participate in the proceedings and cooperate with counsel if there is any. Further guidance is also provided to IJs about what "indicia of incompetency" might entail. Another significant difference is the option (but not the requirement) for IJs to request independently conducted and government-funded FMHAs to assist with their competency determinations. The initial announcement of the policy also mentioned the possibility of bond hearings after six months of detention, but there is nothing in the subsequent detailed guidance issued by EOIR about such hearings.[41]

If a respondent is found incompetent, a "qualified representative," who might be an attorney or an accredited representative,[42] will be appointed.[43] To meet the demand for counsel, DOJ/EOIR funded the National Qualified Representative Program (NQRP).[44] The NQRP, which is a network of providers organized and overseen by the Vera Institute of Justice, has been given the difficult task of representing people with mental disabilities, some of which are quite severe. They operate using a model of "zealous, person-centered . . . representation" in which attorneys must routinely make ethical decisions that consider both the client's expressed needs and goals, as well as the necessity of protective action when the client's capacity is severely limited.[45] Clients are represented by a team that includes attorneys or accredited representatives and MHPs. A significant part of the NQRP's work on behalf of clients includes reentry planning, which is important for release requests (to assure the IJ or ICE that the individual will not be a danger), to support claims for discretionary relief, and to ensure the client's own safety and their ability to continue to access treatment. The NQRP is able to provide representation to every detained immigrant identified under the nationwide policy.[46]

The effects of the policy change have not been as widely felt as might be hoped. As its name implies, the policy was supposed to be operational nationwide by 2013, but that goal has not been met. In 2015, it was operational in only a handful of locations.[47] As of 2021, significant progress had been made, and the policy had been "activated" in approximately 27 ICs out of a total of 69,[48] with providers serving courts in 24 of the 31 states that have ICs.[49] Even in jurisdictions where the policy has been activated, however, there is no publicly available data on how often DHS actually alerted IJs to mentally ill detained immigrants, how many IJs ordered a FMHA, and how many people were found incompetent as a result.[50] It can be assumed that some immigrants who are incompetent to represent themselves are still being forced to proceed without an attorney. The NQRP, which provides counsel for anyone appointed to act as a qualified representative in both *Franco* and nationwide policy states, has provided representation for 2,099 people in the eight years the policy has been in operation[51]—approximately 250 people per year. The number of detainees each year who are in need of these services is likely far higher given an annual detainee population of 500,000, approximately 15–30% of whom are estimated to have a mental illness and 2–5% of whom are estimated to have a "serious" mental illness.[52]

Hopefully the policy (and the NQRP) will continue to expand until it has achieved nationwide coverage.[53] Even then, however, further steps might be necessary to ensure that immigrants with mental illness truly receive adequate protections.[54] The jurisdictions covered by the *Franco* court order demonstrate some concrete differences from the rest of the country that point toward best (or at least better) practices. In the *Franco* states, unlike in the rest of the country, there is no presumption of competency, and IJs are instructed to proceed as if the respondent is incompetent if the evidence is insufficient, so long as there is "reasonable cause to believe that the [respondent] is suffering from a mental disorder that may impair his or her ability to represent him- or herself."[55]

Additionally, Franco sets out detailed procedures and timelines for the screenings that are supposed to be conducted by ICE and for the sharing of any information collected with the court,[56] as well as procedures for third parties to notify ICE that someone might be suffering from a mental illness.[57] Under the nationwide policy, ICE detention facilities are subject to less rigorous, and less binding, screening requirements.[58] Most important, perhaps, the *Franco* court has appointed a monitor to ensure that its order is actually being implemented.[59] In non-*Franco* states, there is no monitor and no equivalent mechanism to track or enforce compliance with the policy.

Standards for Competency under the "Nationwide" Policy for Detained and Unrepresented Individuals

The competency standards for immigration covered by the "nationwide" policy are laid out in a document titled "Phase I of the Plan to Enhanced Procedural Protections to Unrepresented Detained Respondents with Mental Disorders"[60] (hereinafter referred to as the "Phase I Guidelines"—as of 2021 there has been no "Phase II"). This document makes clear that it is not intended to "negate or alter" the obligations of the EOIR under *Franco v. Holder*. It also states that, as per *M-A-M-*, the respondent is presumed to be competent for self-representation but that this presumption is rebutted if an IJ finds, by a preponderance of the evidence, that the respondent is unable to perform the necessary functions (listed below) as a result of a mental disorder. It also provides a legal standard for competency, guidelines to judges on how to determine if a respondent is competent to appear pro se (i.e., self-represent without assistance of counsel), a system of referral for a mental health examination, a list of qualifications for the examining professional, and procedural protections and safeguards that IJs can consider for noncompetent respondents. Overall, the Phase I Guidelines do a better job than *M-A-M-* of providing guidance for what might constitute indicia of competency.

COMPETENCY TO REPRESENT ONESELF

The Phase I Guidelines instruct IJs to use the following when determining if a respondent is competent for self-representation:

A respondent is competent to appear pro se (self-represent) in a removal or custody redetermination proceeding if they have a:

1. rational and factual understanding of:
   a. the nature and object of the proceeding;
   b. the privilege of representation, including but not limited to, the ability to consult with a representative if one is present;
   c. the right to present, examine, and object to evidence;
   d. the right to cross-examine witnesses; and
   e. the right to appeal
2. reasonable ability to:
   a. make decisions about asserting and waiving rights;
   b. respond to the allegations and charges in the proceeding; and
   c. present information and respond to questions relevant to eligibility for relief.[61]

The Phase I Guidelines explicitly state that the inability to perform any of the functions previously listed have to be linked to "mental disorder," which includes intellectual disability and is defined as "a significant impairment of the cognitive, emotional, or behavioral functioning of a person that substantially interferes with the ability to meet the ordinary demands of living."[62]

PROCEDURAL ISSUES

The guidelines offer IJs three stages to screen for and decide issues of competency:

1. *Detecting indicia*: IJs are instructed to be vigilant and attentive for indicia of mental disorder and related incompetency throughout all stages of the proceedings. The indicia might come from any reliable sources, including family members, friends, legal, social or health care service or providers, as well as from observed behaviors or records. Phase I includes some examples of indicia, such as a history of outpatient or inpatient psychiatric treatment, self-injurious behavior or suicide attempts, limited academic achievement, poor memory, attention, or concentration, disorganized, paranoid, or grandiose thinking, hallucinations, poor intellectual

functioning, or lack of responsiveness in court. If there is "bona fide doubt," then the IJ is instructed to move to the next stage.

2. *Conducting a judicial inquiry*: The IJ is instructed to explain to the respondent the purpose and the process for conducting the judicial inquiry and to ask a series of questions to make a decision about competency. The Phase I Guidelines provide IJs with a sample advisal and suggested questions. After the judicial inquiry, the IJ can make one of three determinations: (a) that there is reasonable cause to believe that respondent is competent; (b) that the respondent is incompetent by a preponderance of the evidence; or (c) that the evidence is not sufficient to rebut the presumption of competence but the IJ has "reasonable cause" to believe that the respondent has a mental disorder. In this case, the IJ should move to stage 3.

3. *Conducting a competency review*: The IJ will conduct an evidentiary hearing to determine whether the presumption of competency has been rebutted. At this stage the judge will consider whether to refer the respondent for a mental health examination.[63]

MENTAL HEALTH EXAMINATION

If the IJ cannot make a determination about the respondent's competency, they are instructed to complete a mental health examination referral form that provides the MHP with any available information about the nature and object of the proceedings (e.g., allegations and charges, potential forms of relief, anticipated complexity of the issues), as well as with any information that caused the judge to question the competency of the respondent. Any collateral records should also be attached to the referral.[64]

The Phase I Guidelines also set out required qualifications for the MHPs, which include, at a minimum, a license to practice psychology or medicine; specialized training in psychiatry, clinical psychology, or counseling; completion of EOIR-approved training in conducting mental health examinations of respondents in immigration proceedings; and the ability to document successful completion of approved continuing education in forensic assessment (minimum 100 hours). In addition, the Phase I Guidelines offer other relevant considerations, such as experience conducting competency examinations and familiarity with the respondent's language and culture.[65] Finally, the EOIR's approved training includes the following components: an introduction to immigration law and procedure; determinations of competency in immigration proceedings; the process of conducting mental health evaluations for immigration court; report-writing; ethics and professional consideration; working with an interpreter; and cultural competency.

Psycholegal Abilities

The EOIR's guidelines identify the main psycholegal issue related to competency to participate pro se (without representation by counsel) as "whether the respondent has present ability to represent him- or herself"[66] (in contrast with the criminal standard of whether the person is capable to participate with the assistance of counsel) and direct MHPs to assess the following:

a) Respondent's rational and factual understanding of:
    1. The nature and object of the proceedings, including its adversarial nature;
    2. The allegations and charge(s);
    3. Possible outcomes of the proceedings; and
    4. Roles of participants in the proceedings.
b) Respondent's sufficient ability to:
    1. The privilege of representation, including but not limited to, the ability to consult with a representative if one is present;
    2. The right to present, examine, and object to evidence;
    3. The right to cross-examine witnesses; and
    4. The right to appeal.
c) Respondent's ability to:
    1. Make decisions about asserting and waiving rights;
    2. Respond to the allegations and charges in the proceeding; and
    3. Present information and respond to questions relevant to eligibility for relief.
d) Any other factors the mental health professional deems relevant to the respondent's competence to represent him- or herself.[67]

The literature on competency in criminal proceedings has identified five psycholegal abilities: understanding (rational understanding); appreciation (factual understanding); reasoning; decision making; and consulting and assisting.[68] Although they have been researched in criminal proceedings, they are described below with some suggestions as to how these might apply to the IC context.

UNDERSTANDING

"Understanding" in the criminal context refers to factual understanding involving general, legally relevant knowledge (not necessarily applied to the individual's particular case). In IC, this would mean the respondent's understanding of immigration proceedings in general.[69]

APPRECIATION

"Appreciation" in the criminal context refers to rational understanding; it involves the application of the factual information to the specific case of the respondent in a way that is reality-based. Put simply, it is the ability to comprehend information about the specific charges. In IC, this would translate into the immigrants' ability to understand how the immigration proceedings specifically affect them. Incorporating the information in the EOIR's guidelines, "rational and factual" understanding involve consideration of the following information:

- The roles of participants within the legal process, including the immigration attorney (as being on the respondent's side), the IJ (as making the final decision about removal), and the ICE attorney (as playing a prosecutorial role, that is, finding information to support removal), and a guardian or qualified representative if there is one.
- The nature and object of the proceeding, including its adversarial nature (e.g., the process by which the respondent ended up in IC or ICE detention, the process and purpose of the immigration court hearings, or the fact that the ICE attorney would collect information to support removal). Given the fact that immigrants facing deportation do not have the right to legal representation, it becomes particularly important that they have a clear understanding of the IC system.[70]
- The allegations and charge(s). The respondent needs to understand why they are being prosecuted for removal—for example, whether the respondent became involved in IC due to undocumented status or a prior felony conviction. While the reason for prosecution is typically clear to defen-

dants in criminal court, in IC the reason for prosecution can be due to an arrest that took place decades ago and about which the respondent might not even remember the details.

- Possible outcome of the proceedings. For example, this can refer to the difference between involuntary and voluntary removal in that the former prevents the respondent from returning to the United States for a period of 10 years. In addition, deportation can have serious consequences for the life and personal well-being of the respondent and their family. The MHP needs to explore if the respondent understands all of the possible implications of removal to the country of origin.
- The right to present, examine, and object to evidence (e.g., testimony from family or community members attesting to good moral character).
- The right to cross-examine witnesses and the right to appeal.
- The privilege of representation and the ability to consult with a lawyer or representative if there is one. It is important for the respondent to under-stand that the chances of avoiding deportation increase if the respondent obtains legal representation and all of the advocacy resources available (e.g., pro bono representation, a guardian, or qualified representative).[71]

REASONING

"Reasoning" in the criminal context refers to the capacity to weigh rele-vant information and arrive at coherent and communicable decisions. In IC, the respondent must be able to engage in appropriate reality-based reasoning and to communicate information in a way that is not dis-torted by psychopathology. The outcome of the decision is not relevant; instead the examiner needs to focus on the process used to arrive at that decision. For example, sometimes respondents can opt for voluntary deportation. Even though this decision might seem to be the wrong one to the MHP or the respondent's representative, as long as the decision is rationally made, this choice in and of itself should not be considered a sign of incompetency.

DECISIONAL CAPACITY

"Decisional capacity" refers to the individual's decision-making capac-ity as it applies to their specific context or legal situation.[72] Specific to this psycholegal issue, the guidelines state that respondents need to be able to "make decisions about asserting and waiving rights, respond to the allegations and charges in the proceedings, . . . present information, and respond to questions relevant to eligibility for relief."[73] If the respondent does not have legal representation, the MHP needs to explore their understanding of the relevant evidence required to support relief (e.g., psychological evidence of trauma/persecution) and select relevant witnesses. The MHP also must explore how the respondent intents to present their case to the judge and make decisions about their rights.[74]

CONSULTING AND ASSISTING

"Consulting and assisting," the last psycholegal ability discussed here, has been described by the literature in the context of criminal law as the ability of the defendant to consult with counsel and assist in their own defense. In the context of immigration law, the respondent might not be assigned an attorney but instead a guardian at the respondent's request. Therefore, MHPs need to explore the respondent's ability to make decisions about who should represent them and the pros and cons of different choices. If the respondent already has representation, it is always helpful and recommended to observe the interaction between the respondent and the attorney, guardian, or other legal representative in order to explore whether the respondent is able to understand the information, learn new information, and overall communicate effectively.

The EOIR guidelines direct the MHP to consider any other factors that might be relevant. An important factor to be considered under this section is the respondent's ability to comport themselves during court proceedings. This might be particularly relevant in IC. It is relatively common for immigrants to be required to discuss their histories of trauma in court, as this might be the most relevant evidence of persecution and therefore for relief. However, reliving the trauma might cause significant distress for some respondents, to the point of them not being able to withstand the overwhelming anxiety in court. Even if the respondent has other functional abilities intact, such as a factual and rational understanding of the proceedings, this factor could arguably render them incompetent to proceed.

Clinical Issues and Competency

There is essentially no research identifying the clinical or demographic variables that make some respondents more likely to be found incompetent to participate in immigration court. However, some of the research in the criminal context can serve as guidance. The most robust finding is that psychotic symptoms are the most likely to interfere with defendants' ability to proceed with trial. In a meta-analysis published in 2011, the authors found that defendants diagnosed with a psychotic disorder were eight times more likely to be found incompetent to stand trial. This study also found that unemployed defendants and those with prior histories of psychiatric hospitalizations were twice as likely to be found incompetent.[75] Although the first finding (e.g., psychotic disorders as a risk factor for incompetency) would probably apply to competency in IC, the other two variables are more complicated. Immigrants might have histories of unemployment due to their undocumented status and not an inability to be engaged in employment. In addition, they might have not been hospitalized due to insurance issues, or their hospitalization might have taken place in their countries of origin. For reasons explained below, it is also likely that education deficits play a more significant role in IC.

Practical Considerations for Mental Health Professionals

In addition to the psycholegal abilities and clinical/demographic variables discussed above, there are several practical considerations that MHPs should be aware of. We discuss several in the sections below.

Cultural Considerations

There are several differences between competency evaluations in criminal court versus IC that have implications for the practice of MHPs. As we have seen, cultural considerations are essential during evaluations in IC in general, particularly in competency evaluations. Research on CST has found that attorneys, when presented with case vignettes that varied only with respect to whether the defendant was English- or Spanish-speaking, were more likely to rate the Spanish-speaking as

less mentally ill and were also less likely to refer them for CST evaluations, indicating that attorney decisions were influenced by language.[76]
Although the specific reason for this effect is not known, cross-cultural
bias is a possible explanation. If this is the case, cross-cultural bias might
also translate to lawyers and IJs in IC, which could result in underi-
dentification of respondents with mental illness and competency issues.
Furthermore, just as in criminal proceedings, the presence of a mental illness is considered a prerequisite in competency evaluations in
IC, which means that the MHP has to demonstrate that the relevant
functional/psycholegal abilities previously mentioned are impaired as
a result of a "mental disorder" (including intellectual disability). Similar to definitions in criminal court, the Phase I Guidelines define this
as "significant impairment in the cognitive, emotional or behavioral
functioning of a person that substantially interferes with the ability to
meet the ordinary demands of living."[77] Applying this definition to the
IC context can be complicated given the different ways in which culture can affect manifestation of illness. In addition, it is not unusual
for immigrants to have very low levels of formal education or not have
attended school at all. This can significantly interfere with their ability
to learn new information and understand the complexities of immigration law. Furthermore, many immigrants are unfamiliar with the legal
(both criminal and immigration) system in the United States. Many
immigrants come from rural areas and worked the fields, and their lack
of formal education did not interfere with the "ordinary demands of
life," but it might significantly interfere with their ability to represent
themselves. Whether this can be considered a "mental disorder" for the
purposes of competency findings in IC is an open question. The role of
the MHP in this situation is to clearly delineate the deficits in the functional abilities related to competency and to explain what reasons are
contributing to this (including cognitive and intellectual deficits related
to limited formal education). Whether this can result in a finding of
incompetency is up to the legal decision maker.

Related to the above is the fact that immigration law and the IC system are intricate and rapidly changing. In addition, respondents can be
from countries with an inquisitorial criminal justice system; they might
lack general understanding not only of IC but also of its adversarial nature. In fact, in our experience, very few immigrants have factual knowl-

edge of the role of the ICE attorney. To be able to assess the respondent's factual understanding or ability to learn new information, the MHP must have at least a foundational knowledge of immigration law and IC proceedings, as well as some understanding of the judicial system in the immigrant's country of origin. Furthermore, the concept of sufficient factual understanding might vary depending on who is representing the respondent, given that IC allows for "qualified representatives" who do not need to be attorneys.[78]

Self-Representation

Since immigrants facing removal proceedings do not have the constitutional right to assistance of counsel, competency evaluations in IC mostly involve the question of whether the respondent is competent to appear pro se, that is, to represent themselves without the benefit of counsel. The Supreme Court first considered the issue of whether a different standard should apply in criminal court for CST versus pleading guilty or waiving counsel (self-representation) in *Godinez v. Moran* (1993).[79] In this case, the court decided against using different standards and indicated that the *Dusky* standard was to be considered regardless of the specific type of competency. However, the Supreme Court revisited this issue of competency for self-representation in *Indiana v. Edwards* (2008).[80] In this case, the court decided that a defendant who had been found competent to stand trial could nevertheless be denied the right for self-representation, which acknowledged that competency to proceed pro se requires a higher standard (or requires a higher level of competency) than does competency to stand trial. However, it did not comment on how this should be determined.

In IC, both *M-A-M-* and the Phase I Guidelines have delineated tests for determining competency, with the *M-A-M-* standard generally applicable to both pro se and represented individuals and the Phase I Guidelines applicable to unrepresented detained individuals.

Given the complexities of the immigration process, it can be argued that competency for self-representation in IC could require an even higher standard than in criminal court. Some authors have stated that respondents in IC must be "more" competent to represent themselves than criminal defendants. In part, this is because the burden of proof in seeking relief in IC, unlike in criminal court, resides with the respondent, and therefore they have to affirmatively prove the case, which requires more active participation.[81]

In addition, in order to assess competency for self-representation, the examiner needs to know what is being asked of the respondent. Evaluations need to be specific to the legal course of action being applied. For example, a respondent with cognitive impairment may not be competent to provide testimony about their history of persecution in an asylum; however, the same respondent may be competent in a different case that relies on documentary evidence and does not require them to testify.[82] Finally, evaluations should take into consideration the presence of any assistance that the unrepresented respondent can count on—for example, the presence of a guardian or other support person who will be able to help them.

Furthermore, in jurisdictions such as the state of New York, where all detained immigrants have legal representation, MHPs are often retained by immigration attorneys and not the courts, and therefore none of the procedural steps in the Phase I Guidelines take place. It is unclear whether the examiner should follow the Phase I Guidelines in these situations. Although they echo the *Dusky/Drope* standard, the guidelines are meant to be used to evaluate competency to proceed pro se. Since both *M-A-M-* and the guidelines follow the *Dusky* standard, it is likely that MHPs should use the *Dusky/Drope* standard but apply it to the specific components of IC and add the functional ability of assisting counsel. In addition, although the Phase I Guidelines were developed to assess competency for self-representation, many of the principles can be useful even if the respondent has representation.

Competency Assessment Instruments

Several FAIs have been developed to evaluate competency in criminal court. The three that have been researched and used the most are likely the McArthur Competency Assessment Tool-Criminal Adjudication (Mc-CAT-CA),[83] which uses standardized administration and produces scores that can be compared with a normative group of defendants; the Fitness Interview Test-Revised (FIT-R),[84] which provides a semistructured interview guide for assessing the relevant psycholegal abilities; and the Evaluation of Competency to Stand Trial-Revised (ECT-R),[85] which contains both structured and semistructured interview components, also produces scores, and allows for assessment of specific competencies, such as competency for self-representation. Although these instruments assess the functional legal abilities that are also relevant in IC (e.g., understanding, reasoning, and appreciation), they are not fully applicable to the immigration context, as they were developed, tested, and validated in criminal court contexts. In addition, the research validating these instruments in culturally diverse groups is limited.

When evaluating detained respondents for competency to proceed pro se, the Phase I Guidelines state that MHPs should "use structured and standardized assessment tools and methods whenever possible." However, they do not provide any suggestions for what types of instruments to consider. Although using structured and standardized assessment tools is always desirable, the reality is that no forensic assessment tools have been appropriately validated for use in IC. However, although not published, an instrument for evaluating competency for removal proceedings has been developed. This instrument starts with a traditional biopsychosocial assessment, followed by a mental status examination and behavioral observation sections. The competency section follows a model similar to the FIT in that it includes questions relevant to the psycholegal abilities required in immigration court but leaves room for the clinical judgment of the examiner.[86] This instrument has been used in some deportation proceedings after being approved by judges and attorneys for the respondent and the government.[87]

Competency Restoration

The Phase I Guidelines do not provide detailed information about what happens once a respondent is found not competent to proceed pro se, other than offering the safeguard of providing a qualified representative, which does not necessarily mean an attorney. Similarly, someone incompetent under the *M-A-M-* standard does not necessarily get even the safeguard of counsel (though the identification of pro bono counsel is one of the safeguards that IJs can consider). Unlike in criminal proceedings, in IC, after an individual has been found incompetent, the case is not automatically suspended or terminated.[88] Also unlike in criminal proceedings, there is no formal process to provide respondents with mental illness treatment to "restore" competency. Although treatment is included as a possible safeguard in both *M-A-M-* and the Phase I Guidelines, there is no mention of the mechanisms through which this would take place, and it is unclear how it might actually be implemented. The detention facility could be requested to offer treatment and medications to the respondent; however, there is no guarantee that this request would be followed or that the treatment would be of adequate quality. In addition, the respondent could refuse to take medications or participate in treatment, even if offered. If this is the case, civil commitment might be indicated, but neither IJs nor DHS are authorized to initiate civil commitment.[89] The IJ could also decide to release the respondent on bond and mandate treatment in the community for the purposes of restoration as a condition of the release as long as the respondent is not subject to mandatory detention (as many respondents with mental illness unfortunately are due to the criminalization of the symptoms of mental illness). If the respondent is subject to mandatory detention, ICE might conceivably be prevailed on to allow release under similar conditions (though this has been highly unlikely in recent years).

Once the respondent is in treatment, competency should be reassessed on a regular basis to determine when the respondent is be ready to proceed. An important question is what happens if the respondent is not restorable—for example, if competency is related to a severe intellectual disability that is not likely to change with treatment. For criminal proceedings, the Supreme Court in *Jackson v. Indiana* (1972) stated that defendants found incompetent could not be "held more than the reasonable period of time necessary to determine whether there is a substantial probability that he will attain the capacity in the foreseeable future."[90] Although the court did not comment on a specific time frame or time limit, many states have adopted limits on the maximum time a defendant who has been found incompetent can be held; moreover, if it is determined that the defendant is unlikely to regain competency, the commitment based on incompetency must be terminated.[91] Since no similar legislation or regulation is available for immigration proceedings, the length of time a respondent can be detained for the purpose of restoration is at the discretion of the IJ,[92] although the constitutional limitations as to how long someone can be detained for removal proceedings might conceivably be applicable in this situation.

Other Considerations

The Phase I Guidelines provide some additional information that is relevant to MHPs. They make it clear that "the role of the mental health professional is to identify and describe for the court any cognitive, emotional, or behavioral impairments the respondent has and their effects, if any, on the respondent's ability to perform the functions required to be competent to represent him- or herself."[93] This suggests that the MHP is not to comment on the ultimate legal issue of competency. In fact, the Phase I Guidelines further state that the purpose of the mental health examination "is to provide information to the court about the mental health of the respondent so the court can make an informed decision about the respondent's competency."[94] This is also generally true of other psycholegal issues in immigration court—the IJ is the ultimate arbiter of eligibility, and the MHP, to preserve credibility with the court, should generally refrain from opining on the ultimate legal question.

The guidelines also state that there is no requirement to obtain informed consent from the respondent for the evaluation, although the respondent must be notified of "the purpose of the evaluation, the procedure to be utilized, the lack of privilege and confidentiality . . . the possible uses of the examination report, [and] how information obtained . . . may be shared."[95] As is the case in criminal proceedings, the MHP is also directed to write a report based on all available information, even if the respondent refuses to participate.

The Phase I Guidelines include the following as necessary components of competency reports:

- [I]dentify the specific matters referred for the evaluation;
- list any evaluation procedures, techniques, and tests used in the examination;
- list all sources of information considered by the mental health professional;
- describe all aspects of the respondent's social, educational, vocational, medical, and mental health histories, and other factors as necessary;

- describe the respondents presentation and behavior during the evaluation (including reports of exhibition of signs or symptoms of mental disorder) and response style;
- provide opinions on each issue referred for evaluation and identify any issues about which the mental health professional could not give an opinion;
- provide a factual basis for any opinions offered on the report; and
- identify the mental disorder that is the case of the incompetency (if indicated).[96]

Conclusion

Although there is no question that some progress has been made to improve protections for mentally ill respondents facing deportation, more needs to be done. Deportation has very significant consequences for immigrants and their families, and as a result the same reasons that prevent the government from taking to trial incompetent defendants should likewise prevent removal of incompetent respondents.[97] The decision in *M-A-M-* represented the first time that the courts put forth a standard for competency in IC, and the EOIR guidelines provided additional and very important guidance for IJs and MHPs. However, many questions remain unanswered. First, the Phase I Guidelines have yet to be implemented nationwide, and therefore the mandated training for MHPs has not expanded across all jurisdictions. This means that in many places around the country there is still no process for IJs to retain MHPs to conduct these evaluations. As the guidelines extend to other states and ICs, MHPs are expected to become more involved in these evaluations. Second, the Phase I Guidelines apply only to situations in which the respondent is unrepresented and the competency evaluation is ordered by the IJ. In situations in which the respondent is represented, the less-protective standard established by the court in *M-A-M-* still applies. Third, there remains uncertainty about what options are available to an IJ when a respondent is found to be incompetent, both in terms of treatment and possible administrative closure or termination of removal proceedings. Finally, since competency in removal proceedings is such a new type of FMHA, there is a significant need for research in this area to study clinical, demographic, and cultural variables that might make some respondents more likely to be found incompetent than others and to develop FAIs that are culturally sensitive and can be used to assess competency in IC.

12

Violence Risk Assessment

Whether someone is at risk for violence is an important question that arises in many legal contexts (e.g., criminal, civil, juvenile, family decisions). For example, risk of future violence or recidivism is an important factor when considering civil commitment, sentencing decisions, imposition of the death penalty, juvenile transfers into adult court, and release of individuals who have committed a sex offense under sexually violent predator laws.[1] Although there is essentially no literature from the mental health field with respect to the issue of risk assessment in the context of immigration court (IC), risk for future violence is also an important consideration in this context. First, when immigrants seek discretionary release from immigration detention on bond, immigration judges (IJs) have to consider flight risk and, in addition, whether the individual poses a "danger to the community."[2] Second, risk assessments are also relevant for individuals who have a mental illness and are seeking to enter the United States, adjust their status to Lawful Permanent Resident, or apply for various other forms of relief. Under current immigration law, an individual becomes inadmissible (and ineligible for the change of status or relief) for having a "physical or mental disorder and behavior associated with the disorder that may pose, or has posed, a threat to the property, safety, or welfare of the alien or others."[3] Third and finally, even when dangerousness is not explicitly part of the application for relief, for discretionary claims the question of dangerousness is often a consideration for adjudicators.

In all of these contexts, legal decision makers often rely on the expert opinions of mental health professionals (MHPs), who need to have the necessary level of training and expertise to engage in this process. The costs of making errors in risk assessment evaluations can be significant. In the context of ICs, the results of a risk assessment can determine someone's ability to stay in the country versus being deported and whether an immigrant will wait in detention while undergoing removal proceedings. IJs do not wish to grant relief or release from detention to individuals who might end up engaging in violence or criminal behavior in the community. As a result, it is important to perform these evaluations according to the highest standards of clinical practice.[4] This chapter provides an overview of the foundations, important concepts, and main risk assessment instruments, as well as special considerations in the cross-cultural assessment of risk.

Dangerousness Versus Risk

Within a few decades, the scholarship on risk assessment has grown significantly and the role of violence risk assessment has expanded rapidly within the practice of mental health. Significant progress has been made with respect to the tools available to assess risk for violence and recidivism.[5] The concept of *dangerousness* was introduced into civil commitment statutes in *Lessard v. Smith* (1972),[6] and the critical role of dangerousness in civil commitment proceedings was later reinforced by *O'Connor v. Donaldson* (1975), in which the United States Supreme Court stated that the mere fact of being mentally ill alone could not justify the state's decision to involuntarily commit a nondangerous individual indefinitely.[7] In the landmark case *Baxtrom v. Herold* (1966),[8] Baxtron, who had remained in the same prison under the custody of the New York Department of Mental Health beyond the expiration of his sentence, was finally released after the Supreme Court found that he had been denied equal protection. At the time, evaluations of dangerousness were being performed by psychiatrists and psychologists without following any specific structure or tool and based solely on clinical judgment or instinct. *Baxtrom* established that inmates whose sentences were expiring also had the right to civil commitment procedures and a judicial determination that they were "dangerously mentally ill."[9] In addition, as a result of this decision, hundreds of other individuals who were mentally ill were released to the community. Researchers found very low rates of violence and recidivism after release, highlighting the poor reliability of the opinions of psychiatrists about dangerousness, as well as the less-than-expected correlation between mental illness and violence.

Risk assessment is one of the areas of the law that most often relies on experts' opinions from MHPs.[10] However, MHPs did not always agree on the usefulness of expert testimony on this issue. In *Barefoot v. Estelle* (1982),[11] the Supreme Court underscored the disagreement between the clinical and legal communities with respect to the admissibility of clinical opinions on dangerousness. Barefoot had been sentenced to death in Texas, and two psychiatrists were hired by the prosecution to form opinions in response to hypothetical questions about the defendant's risk. In this case, the American Psychiatric Association submitted an amicus brief stating that testimony based on hypothetical questions should be prohibited and asking for restriction of psychiatric testimony about dangerousness based on research indicating that experts' predictions of violence resulting from unstructured clinical methods were unreliable. The Court rejected the argument that psychiatrists were not competent to form opinions about risk for future violence with an acceptable degree of reliability and refused to exclude the testimony of the psychiatrists.[12] Decisions after this case have surprisingly posed no issues with the admissibility of expert testimony based on unstructured clinical methods, despite mounting evidence of the unreliability of this approach. For example, in *Kansas v. Hendricks* (1997),[13] the Supreme Court approved of indefinite civil commitment of individuals convicted of sex offenses who are found "dangerous" due to mental illness, without specifying the procedures to be used to assess dangerousness.

Because courts continued to ask MHPs to provide expert testimony on risk assessment, and acknowledging the unreliability of unstructured clinical procedures to predict dangerousness, scholars and clinicians began to focus on risk factors that were empirically related to violent behavior. Although the term "dangerousness" continues to be used in legal language, since the 1990s there has been a transition in academic and clinical settings from "dangerousness" to "risk."[14] The concept of dangerousness does not have much clinical utility, as it tends to be treated as a dichotomy in legal contexts: a person is either dangerous or not dangerous. However, the concept of risk allows clinicians to focus on levels of risk, which fall within a continuum of probability. Using the concept of risk increases specificity and decreases the chances that clinicians will rely on personal values when forming opinions.[15] To make the legal concept of dangerousness applicable to clinical practice, dangerousness has been broken down into three components: (1) *risk factors* (i.e., variables that research has found to be associated with the probability that aggression will occur), (2) *harm* (the amount and type of aggression being predicted), and (3) *risk level* (the probability that harm will occur). As a result, all violence risk assessments should be able to answered three questions: Risk of what outcome? How high is the risk? And what risk variables contribute to the risk?[16]

Contemporary approaches to risk assessment were also influenced by Andrews and Bonta in the 1990s when they provided an approach to evaluating and rehabilitating offenders through the risk, needs, and responsivity (RNR) model.[17] This theory was created as a model of recidivism (including violent and nonviolent offenses) risk assessment and prevention.[18] The *risk principle* states that those who are more likely to engage in crime in the future should receive the most intense forms of intervention and supervision; the *needs principle* states that the intervention should address the deficits or needs (referred to as criminogenic needs) associated with the probability of reoffending; and the *responsivity principle* refers to using intervention modalities that are most likely to elicit a positive response in the individual.

At this time, and after decades of research, it is clear that, when the focus is on risk factors, structured and validated approaches to violence risk assessment can accomplish on average moderate levels of accuracy, whereas unstructured clinical approaches do not show an ability to predict violence. In addition, general recidivism can be significantly reduced by approaches that follow the RNR model.[19]

Relevant Concepts in Risk Assessment

There are several relevant concepts in risk assessment.

Prediction Versus Management

Evidenced-based risk assessment and management is defined as

> the process of gathering information about people in a way that is consistent with and guided by the best available scientific and professional knowledge to understand their potential for engaging in violence and/or recidivism in the future and to determine what should be done to prevent them from doing so.[20]

This definition involves both *prediction* and *management*. The main goal of prediction is to determine the likelihood of violence in the future. The main goal of management is to determine strategies to reduce the risk of these events.[21] When the primary goal is prediction, *static risk factors* (e.g., mostly unchangeable through intervention) are most relevant (including age, gender, history of antisocial behaviors, and history of violence). When the primary goal is management, *dynamic factors* (e.g., mostly vulnerable to change through intervention) are most relevant including impulsivity, acute psychiatric symptoms, violent thoughts, treatment adherence, and self-awareness).[22]

Whether the MHP is going to focus primarily on prediction versus management would depend on the psycholegal question. For example, in evaluations in the context of sexual violent predator laws, the question to be answered is mainly the likelihood that the individual will engage in sexual violence if released.[23] However, when individuals are released to the community through alternatives to incarceration (i.e., diversion programs) or under postrelease supervision, the goal is both prediction and management.[24] In the context of IC, it is not uncommon for IJs to go beyond the question of dangerousness and ask the MHP to make treatment recommendations or ask for community management strategies that might mitigate the risk in the event that the respondent was released on bond. Although prediction and management can be seen as two separate processes, the MHP's opinions regarding risk prediction often vary based on the future living conditions of the immigrant and the social support or treatment available. Conversely, the MHP's recommendations about community management will often depend on the immigrant's level of risk.[25]

Dynamic and Static Risk Factors

Static risk factors are more relevant when the main goal is *prediction*, whereas dynamic risk factors are more relevant when the main goal is *management/prevention*. In the context of IC, in which both prediction and management are often relevant, both types of risk factors are important for consideration. Causal dynamic risk factors have been defined as those that (1) "precede and increase the likelihood of violence," (2) "change spontaneously or through intervention," and (3) "predict changes in the likelihood of violence when altered."[26] The term "risk status" has been used to describe the combination of static risk factors, whereas "risk state" describes the combination of static and dynamic risk factors. To mitigate risk or prevent the possibility of violence, MHPs establish the risk status but focus on interventions that change the individual's risk state.[27]

It is now well established that contextual variables significantly influence risk for violence and recidivism, and thus risk assessment instruments have incorporated situational risk factors.[28] Situational risk factors are important when considering immigrants' reentry back into the community from detention. In addition to individual characteristics, risk assessment needs to consider the contexts to which individuals are being discharged.[29] IJs tend to base decisions about dangerousness solely on immigrants' prior behaviors—for example, whether the individual has been convicted of a violent offense in the past. However, historical risk factors are only one of many other types of factors that need to be considered. The McArthur Violence Risk Assessment study,[30] a large-scale, multisite study that examined the risk of violence in the community for those discharged from inpatient psychiatric facilities, listed four types of violence risk factors: historical, dispositional, contextual, and clinical.[31] *Historical risk factors* are those that belong to someone's past; *dispositional risk factors* include the individual's predispositions, tendencies or traits; *contextual risk factors* incorporate the past and present situations in which violence took place and is likely to take place (e.g., social support, stress, weapon availability); and *clinical risk factors* include symptoms of mental disorder, substance use, and clinical functioning.[32]

Approaches to Risk Assessment

There are two main and well-supported approaches to risk assessment depending on how the available information is selected, weighed, and combined before reaching a final opinion. These are *professional judgment* and *actuarial decision-making*.[33] Before covering these two types of risk assessment, it is important to mention a third, not empirically supported, approach: *unstructured clinical judgment*.

Unstructured Clinical Judgment

This risk assessment approach is based solely on the clinical judgment of the MHP, who decides what sources of information to use and how to combine, weigh, or prioritize them. The MHP evaluator uses their judgment unaided by any additional tools.[34] Research over the past 60-plus years has demonstrated that this informal approach is subjective and therefore lacks interrater reliability (agreement between examiners) and has low accuracy.[35] In addition, this approach lacks transparency about the process that was followed to arrive at a conclusion.[36] Although there is no data on risk assessment practices in IC, it has been our observation that this is the most common approach used by MHPs in IC. This is typically the case when the risk assessment is being conducted by a MHP with clinical but not forensic training. In fact, a study that examined the risk assessment practices of community psychiatrists found that 96% reported using clinical judgment only.[37] MHPs in ICs are discouraged from using this approach, as it is not adequate or useful to assess risk; it is also problematic from ethical and legal perspectives.[38] This is not to suggest that risk assessment should be devoid of clinical judgment, and in fact clinical judgment is necessary through the process of FMHA risk assessment. This judgment, however, needs to be structured by focusing on risk and protective factors empirically found to be relevant for violent risk.[39]

Actuarial Risk Assessment

This method falls within the other extreme of the spectrum when compared to unstructured clinical judgment. It is based on mathematically derived formulas to arrive at a probability. Factors that distinguish individuals who engage in violence and those who do not are selected, weighted, and combined according to an algorithm to provide an estimate of the probability that an individual will engage in future violence.[40] The items that form actuarial tools have been empirically selected based on the strength of their association with violence in a given sample.[41] This approach provides an estimate of the likelihood of future violence over a specific period.[42] The advantage of this approach is that it has empirical support and high interrater reliability. Unlike unstructured clinical judgment, this approach is characterized by transparency in that reviewers or adjudicators can understand the process and the risk factors considered to form opinions. Yet the actuarial approach has several problems that make it less desirable in the context of the IC system. Since the risk factors are derived from specific samples (e.g., derivation samples), they might not generalize or perform as optimally when they are applied to groups of people who differ demographically or culturally from those in the derivation samples. Some meta-analytic studies have supported this phenomenon, known as *shrinkage of predictive validity*, for several actuarial risk assessment instruments. These instruments experienced a decrease in validity when used in new samples versus the derivation samples.[43] In addition, actuarial instruments have been criticized for not considering the context or unique characteristics of the individual.[44] There might be risk factors that are relevant for the particular situation of the immigrant but that were excluded from the actuarial formula. To address this issue, some actuarial risk assessment approaches have incorporated the possibility of a "professional override" to allow professionals to use their clinical judgment to modify risk classification.[45] However, this approach is recommended only in rare situations and is vulnerable to evaluators' biases. Furthermore, actuarial risk assessment is primarily based on historical/static risk, which precludes the ability to assess risk change over time and to inform violence prevention interventions.[46] Finally, some actuarial risk assessment tools for recidivism (e.g., the Correctional Offender Management Profiling for Alternative Sanctions, or COMPAS) have been criticized for being racially biased and for not being transparent about how the information is being weighted.[47]

Structured Professional Judgment

The structured professional judgment (SPJ) approach includes risk factors that are not necessarily obtained from a particular data set but that the literature has found to have an empirical or theorized relationship with violence. Once the items or risk factors are selected, they are operationalized so that their presence can be reliably coded.[48] Evaluators use a variety of sources of information (e.g., clinical interview, review of records, third-party interviews), after which they rate the presence and relevance of the risk factors. Unlike actuarial risk assessment, SPJ approaches do not include scoring of instruments. The final opinion is based on clinical judgment that is structured by addressing the items included in the tool. The language used to communicate the final determination involves opinions about low, moderate, or high risk for violence or reoffending. The proposed treatment and supervision plan, as well as the environment of the individual, are taken into consideration when forming the final risk judgment.[49] Greater interrated reliability is obtained with SPJ procedures compared to unstructured clinical judgment approaches because all examiners using the SPJ method pay attention to the same items. Since the focus of the SPJ approach is not only prevention but also management, SPJ instruments include static and dynamic risk factors. In addition, the SPJ approach allows for consideration of individual risk factors that might apply to one case in particular, even if not included in the tool's list of risk factors. Given the variability in terms of demographic, cultural, and clinical variables of immigrants, as well as the emphasis on considering management interventions when released, this approach is recommended in ICs.

Violence Risk Assessment Tools

Several actuarial risk assessment and SPJ tools have been published for the assessment of different types of violence (e.g., general violence, sexual violence, intimate partner violence) both for juveniles and adults. There has been a significant debate in the literature with respect to the superiority of actuarial versus SPJ approaches to risk assessment. A review of the empirical evaluation of both approaches and instruments is beyond the scope of this chapter. However, information can be found in several sources,[50] and three instruments to predict violence and recidivism in adults are briefly described below.

Violence Risk Appraisal Guide

The Violence Risk Appraisal Guide (VRAG)[51] is an actuarial measure that includes 12 items to predict violent recidivism within 7–10 years postrelease. The total scores range from -26 to +38 and result in 9 probability bins from lowest to highest chance of violent reoffending. A revised version was later developed (VRAG-R) in a similar way (using a sample of 1,261 male offenders who were later released). This revision extended the length of the follow up period to up to 49 years.[52] The VRAG-R includes the following 12 items:

1. Lived with both parents until age 16
2. Elementary school maladjustment
3. History of drug or alcohol problems
4. Marital status
5. Nonviolent criminal history
6. Failure on conditional release
7. Age at index offense
8. Violent criminal history
9. Number of prior admissions
10. Conduct disorder
11. Sex offending history
12. Antisociality

Historical-Clinical-Risk Management-20 Version 3

The Historical-Clinical-Risk Management-20 (HCR-20)[53] was first published in 1995 and is a risk assessment tool within the SPJ approach that is used to assess the risk of future violence in adult offenders with a history of violence and/or mental illness, personality disorders, and substance use disorders. The developers of this instrument sought to create an evidence-based instrument based on a conceptualization of risk assessment that was preventive rather than predictive, based not only on research but also on consultation with front-line clinicians, included a list of operationally defined risk factors, and resulted in a final risk judgment that did not result from numerically adding the risk factors but instead was based on clinical judgment.[54] The empirical literature has consistently demonstrated the utility of the HCR-20 as a good predictor of violence in a number of different samples (e.g., psychiatric, forensic, correctional). It has been translated into several languages and is the world's most commonly used violence risk assessment tool.[55]

The HCR-20 includes 10 static risk factors and 10 dynamic risk factors. The *static* or *historical risk factors* pertain to the events experienced by the individual in the past, including psychosocial adjustment and history of violence. The dynamic risk factors are divided between five *clinical risk factors* reflecting the person's current and recent functioning plus the five *risk management items* that incorporate the examiner's opinion on the feasibility of the treatment/supervision plans available for the individual.

The following is a list of the risk factors included in the HCR-20 (version Three):[56]

Historical Scale (History of Problems With . . .)
- H1. Violence
- H2. Other Antisocial Behaviors
- H3. Relationships Employment
- H4. Employment
- H5. Substance Use
- H6. Major Mental Disorder
- H7. Personality Disorder
- H8. Traumatic Experiences
- H9. Violent Attitudes
- H10. Treatment or Supervision Response

Clinical Scale (Recent Problems With . . .)
- C1. Insight
- C2. Violent Ideation or Intent
- C3. Symptoms of Major Mental Disorder
- C4. Instability
- C5. Treatment or Supervision Response

Risk Management Scale (Future Problems With . . .)
- R1. Professional Services and Plans
- R2. Living Situation
- R3. Personal Support
- R4. Treatment or Supervision Response
- R5. Stress or Coping

Based on information collected through clinical interview and collateral sources, the evaluator considers the presence and relevance of the risk factors and the availability of management plans and comes up with a final risk judgment for future risk. This final judgment is made based on three levels: *Low* or *Routine*, which indicates that the person is not in need of any special intervention to manage violence; *Moderate* or *Elevated*, which indicates that the person requires some special intervention to manage violence; and *High* or *Urgent*, which indicates that there is an urgent need to develop a risk management strategy.[57]

It is important to note that some instruments have been developed that focus specifically on protective factors. For example, the Structured Assessment of Protective Factors for Violence Risk (or SAPROF) follows the SPJ approach and is intended to be used in conjunction to the HCR-20, although it can also be used together with actuarial tools. This instrument provides an overall judgment of the level of protection in the specific assessment context.[58]

Level of Service/Case Management Inventory

The Level of Service/Case Management Inventory (LS/CMI)[59] is an instrument developed to assess the risk and needs factors of late adolescents and adult individuals with a history of criminal behavior and is intended to be used by MHPs and security staff (e.g., corrections or parole officers). It shares features of both SPJ and actuarial methods. The development of this instrument was based on extensive research examining the correlates of offending in male and female Canadian samples. It is used as both a prediction and management tool to aid professionals in the treatment, planning, and management of offenders.[60]

The LS/CMI includes 43 items that fall into the following categories:

- Criminal History
- Education/Employment
- Family/Marital
- Leisure/Recreation
- Companions
- Alcohol/Drug Problem
- Procriminal Attitude/Orientation
- Antisocial Pattern

This instrument structures the clinical assessment of the individual's risk for violence and recidivism, identifies targets for treatment, and quantifies the likelihood for clinical recidivism, allowing evaluators to make decisions about levels of supervision.[61]

Finally, it is important to mention that instruments that assess for the personality construct of psychopathy, specifically the Psychopathy Checklist-Revised (PCL-R),[62] although not developed as a risk assessment instrument per se, have been used as an indicator of future violence and recidivism. However, there is significant debate within the field as to whether this instrument should be used as a sole indicator of future violence or whether it adds incremental validity over and above other instruments or risk factors.[63] Furthermore, although the concept of psychopathy appears to be valid cross-culturally, more research is needed to establish the validity of instruments such as the PCL in certain cultures, particularly those typically involved in IC proceedings. As a result, evaluators should use caution when using psychopathy measures as risk assessment tools in IC. We recommend against using the PCL as a sole indicator of risk in IC.

Mental Illness and Violence

As is the case with the general public, legal decision makers often hold misconceptions about the relationship between violence and mental illness. This is particularly important in the context of IC, as a finding that a respondent has a mental illness can automatically be linked to dangerousness and result in prolonged detention or removal. Although a full review of the relationship between violence and mental illness is not within the scope of this book, the following is a brief review of what is known about this relationship.

There is extensive literature with respect to the relationship between violence and mental illness. The vast majority of individuals with a mental illness do not engage in violence, and the majority of violence perpetrated in society cannot be attributed to mental illness (only about 3–5%).[64] Therefore, the relationship between mental illness and violence can be said to be modest. It is higher for those with additional risk factors, such as alcohol and other substance use; histories of involuntary commitment to inpatient psychiatric hospitals; histories of being victimized; histories of being exposed to trauma; lack of adherence to medication or treatment; or antisocial personality traits, among others.[65]

However, it is worth mentioning that there is a significantly high correlation between mental illness and suicide, with some studies finding that about 90% of individuals who commit suicide have a history of some combination of depression, other mental disorder, or substance use.[66] In addition, individuals with mental illness are more likely to be victims of violence compared to the general population and more likely to be victims of violence than perpetrators of violence.[67]

Despite these findings and the conclusion that the correlation between mental illness and violence is not strong enough to justify many policies implemented against people with mental illness—and certainly not to justify incarceration solely based on mental illness—it is important to note that mental illness is not irrelevant to violence risk.[68] Specifically, some symptoms of mental illness are more relevant than others. For example, a meta-analysis found that psychotic symptoms (e.g., hallucinations, delusions, disorganized thoughts) are associated with violence.[69] In addition, other factors also affect whether a person with mental illness presents a risk of violence, such as self-awareness into their symptoms, adherence to treatment, or response to treatment. Therefore, for some immigrants the presence of mental illness might be completely irrelevant to violence risk, whereas for others it might be associated. MHPs need to gather information about how mental illness manifests for a particular individual; the different types of symptoms; whether prior violence has been directly associated with those symptoms; the individual's self-awareness into their mental illness; and their history of treatment response or adherence. In addition, even for individuals for whom specific symptoms of mental illness might have been associated with violence in the past, clinical symptoms are considered a dynamic risk factor that are, for most people, vulnerable to change and mitigation through appropriate interventions. Access to adequate community treatment following a discharge from hospitalization, for example, has been found by research to reduce subsequent violent acts.[70] MHPs in ICs need to be prepared to provide education to the IJ on these issues.

Cross-Cultural Considerations of Risk Assessment

The literature on the validation of risk assessment instruments is extensive. However, validation samples have been composed mostly of White participants. Despite the fact that risk assessment instruments have generally been found to be able to predict future violence and recidivism in non-White individuals, there is considerable concern with respect to the presence of disparities in prediction accuracy cross-culturally.[71] Although to our knowledge there is no data on the validity of risk assessment instruments specifically within immigrant groups in removal proceedings in the United States, some studies have found that non-White offenders tend to receive either higher or lower scores compared to White offenders.[72] These concerns have led the Canadian courts (see *Ewert v. Canada* [2015])[73] to strongly caution against the use of several actuarial risk assessment instruments with Aboriginal inmates. When using risk tools that have primarily been validated with White individuals in North America, over- or underestimation of risk is possible when using those instruments in other groups, such as immigrants who come from remote areas in Central America or sub-Saharan Africa. This is likely due to three factors: (1) omission of risk factors that might be relevant for the immigrant group, (2) inclusion of risk factors that are more relevant for White individuals but not as relevant for immigrants, and (3) risk factors that manifest differently cross-culturally.[74]

The concerns with respect to the cross-cultural validity of risk assessment instruments are different for actuarial versus SPJ approaches. For actuarial tools, the concern is primarily the fact that the norms are sample-specific, and the more the individual being evaluated deviates from the derivation sample, the higher the concern with respect to generalizability. SPJ instruments include items that have been identified by the empirical literature as being associated with violence, but this research also took place mostly in the context of Western culture. However, SPJ tools allow evaluators the opportunity to incorporate culture-specific factors into the final opinions. This requires specific training on cross-cultural assessment to prevent cultural biases from jeopardizing the accuracy of final conclusions.[75] Some risk assessment tools, such as the LS/CMI within the RNR model, consider culture under the responsibility principle as something to be taken into account when considering the individual's learning style. However, the model does not provide specific information about any structured way of considering culture; most important, this need is considered only during postrisk decision-making, which relegates culture to the back end of the process.[76] It is clear that the cross-cultural applications of risk assessment instruments require further research. Specifically, authors have pointed to two areas that require further exploration: the interrater reliability of risk assessment tools cross-culturally, and the possibility of rater cultural bias.[77] It is also important to remember that a risk assessment is conducted in the context of a clinical interview and evaluation. As a result, the assessor needs to approach the process with cultural competency. This can serve to increase the accuracy of the risk assessment's final opinion.

Practical Considerations for Risk Assessments in Immigration Court

When immigration lawyers approach MHPs to request a violence risk assessment, the referral question tends to be broad and to lack specificity. It is crucial for the MHP to obtain further information about the purpose for the risk assessment. For example, when the respondent is seeking discretionary release from immigration detention on bond, the IJ is required to find that the respondent does not pose a "danger to the community." In this case, and particularly if the respondent has a history of arrests or convictions for violent offenses, a comprehensive violence risk assessment might be needed. However, if the respondent does not have a violent history, but does have a mental illness and is seeking to adjust their status, an evaluation of how mental illness manifests for that person in particular, whether it has ever been associated with violent behavior, and a general education about the connection between mental illness and violence might suffice. Narrowing down the referral question is important in all types of forensic mental health assessments (FMHAs), particularly in the context of risk assessments, because these evaluations require gathering extensive information, ideally through an interview, review of records, and third-party information. This information can be sensitive and include details of prior convictions for violent behavior and thus has the potential to be prejudicial for other aspects of the immigration case. MHPs should not comment on risk unless it is specifically part of the referral question and has been fully assessed.[78]

Evaluators in ICs are strongly discouraged from using unstructured clinical judgment when forming opinions about risk, since this approach is not scientifically supported. When selecting an instrument to be used in ICs, SPJ tools are recommended. Although all instruments have limitations when used cross-culturally, SPJ tools are more appropriate in this context because, unlike actuarial approaches, the risk factors are not derived from validation samples that have typically been culturally homogeneous. In fact, the application of actuarial tools to make predictions about future violence for individuals not studied in the derivation and validation samples is not scientifically supported. SPJ tools allow for more individualization and thus for consideration of cultural factors in the final risk judgment opinion. In addition, in ICs, sometimes IJs request a risk assessment based solely on the fact that the individual has a mental illness, even in the absence of any prior criminal convictions. In this situation, instruments such as the VRAG or the LSI would not be appropriate, as they have been developed and validated in justice-involved individuals. Furthermore, the IC context presents one important difference with the criminal justice system: Many immigrants in detention have never committed any crimes, and as a result they deviate significantly from the derivation and validation samples of the actuarial or RNR risk assessment instruments (e.g., criminal justice samples). An important limitation of risk assessment in IC is lack of information. Conducting a comprehensive risk assessment requires consideration of several sources of information and data covering different developmental stages. This information is often limited in ICs. Medical or education records from the country of origin are often difficult to obtain, and third-party information might not be available. Evaluators need to make a decision about whether there is enough information to rate the different risk factors and to form a final risk judgment. If not enough information is available, a final opinion might not be scientifically supported, or the evaluator must acknowledge the limitations of the final risk opinion. In addition, evaluators must be prepared to describe the instruments used, including their derivation and validation research and the limitations of their cross-cultural validity. As much as possible, the evaluator should be precise with respect to final opinions and indicate the level of risk, the seriousness, nature, or imminence of the potential behaviors, as well as any possible mitigation strategies. It is also recommended that final opinions be communicated using relative risk terms as opposed to specific percentages.[79] Before conducting risk assessments in ICs, MHPs need to obtain training on general principles of violence risk assessment and specific instruments. This training should include didactics and practice cases with feedback.[80]

Conclusion

The issue of dangerousness is an important consideration in the context of immigration law and IC proceedings. When immigrants seek discretionary release from immigration detention on bond, IJs have to consider flight risk and dangerousness when making decisions about some forms of release from immigration detention. Dangerousness is also relevant for some immigrants who have a mental illness and who might need to prove that their psychiatric disorder does not pose a threat to society. Even when dangerousness is not explicitly part of the application for relief, it is often a consideration for IJs. Before conducting a violence risk assessment with the purpose of aiding IJs in making decisions about dangerousness, it is important that the MHP and the lawyer have a prior discussion about the purpose of the evaluation, the approach to risk assessment being used, and the potential for prejudicial information to surface throughout the evaluation process. As in any other legal setting, MHPs need to be familiar with evidence-based approaches to risk assessment, and in the context of IC specifically they need to be knowledgeable about the different concerns with respect to cultural validity of the various risk assessment instruments and approach the process of risk assessment with cultural sensitivity.

Summary and Future Directions

More immigrants attempted to cross the southern border into the United States in March 2021 than in any other month since 2001.[1] This marks the peak of a trend in which more and more immigrants are undertaking dangerous migration journeys and risking their lives (approximately 7,000 people died on this journey from 1998 to 2016[2]) with the hope of escaping poverty, human rights abuses, violence, and persecution—all while dreaming of a better life for themselves and their families.

Some immigrants enter the country without proper documentation, while others do so with proper visas but stay longer than their documentation allows. Regardless of how they enter the country, all immigrants without proper documentation (and Legal Permanent Residents who commit certain crimes) can face deportation. Once they become "deportable," they are also at risk of being placed in immigration detention. Decisions about deportation and immigration detention are made by immigration adjudicators, mostly immigration judges (IJs) in immigration courts (ICs) managed by the Department of Justice.

Although noncitizens do not have the constitutional right to counsel, as immigration policies have become more restricted and increased numbers of immigrants are undergoing deportation proceedings and being detained, more immigration attorneys have begun to represent immigrants in removal proceedings, either through public defender agencies or as volunteers.[3] Similarly, an increased number of mental health professionals (MHPs) have become involved in this work, either as treatment providers to immigrants struggling with symptoms related to trauma and persecution, as volunteers through human rights organizations providing pro bono assessment to immigrants who have survived torture or persecution, or as experts retained by immigration attorneys to assess a range of other psycholegal issues (e.g., competency, hardship, dangerousness).

There are three important areas of knowledge at the intersection of immigration law and mental health that are essential for MHPs, immigration attorneys, and scholars interested in this area to acquire and that have served to organize this volume (*immigration law and the legal context of ICs, mental health issues* faced by undocumented immigrants, and *cultural and forensic considerations*). Most people have limited knowledge of immigration law, which changes rapidly and is heavily impacted by political decisions made by governmental bodies. MHPs need to have a foundational understanding of the legal context of immigration law and ICs. This includes being familiar with the different agencies and decision makers that might be involved in deportation proceedings, the different legal standards that immigrants need to meet in order to avoid deportation, the different situations under which immigrants might be detained, and how detention conditions might affect immigrants' psychological well-being. In addition, both mental health and legal professionals must become familiar with the different functions that a forensic mental health assessment (FMHA) can play based on the different courses of legal action and the psycholegal issues related to each type of legal standard (e.g., persecution-based, victimization-based, hardship-based, moral character–based, and bond).

Furthermore, both mental health and legal professionals need to understand the different roles that MHPs can play in the immigration law system (treatment provider/fact witness, forensic evaluator/expert witness, and consultant). This knowledge can help attorneys decide in which role they might want to involve a MHP and can help MHPs decide whether the role is within their scope of practice. In addition, to be able to do this work, MHPs should become familiar with the risk factors that place immigrants at increased risk for experiencing mental health difficulties, including having a history of sexual abuse and intimate partner violence and having been persecuted due to sexual orientation or gender identity. Children and adolescents, families who have been separated, and immigrants in detention are also groups that are particularly vulnerable to experiencing psychological distress.

Expertise in the assessment and documentation of cross-cultural trauma is one of the most important areas of specialized knowledge that MHPs must develop to undertake this type of work. Immigrants often leave their countries of origin after having experienced significant levels of trauma, which might be exacerbated by the dire migration conditions and the stressors associated with being undocumented and undergoing deportation proceedings. It is also important to consider that repeatedly being exposed to the suffering experienced by many immigrants can also take a toll on immigration lawyers and MHPs, in some cases resulting in what has been described as "vicarious trauma" (VT) or "secondary traumatic stress" (STS). They must be aware and alert to any signs of psychological distress that might result from working with this population.

Although FMHAs in ICs have not received as much attention as in other courts, such as criminal courts or family courts, expertise in this area is essential when conducting evaluations to assist ICs in making immigration legal decisions. MHPs who have not received this type of knowledge through their clinical education should seek out didactics and clinical training as well as supervision in this area. This training should include understanding the principles of FMHAs and the best-practice recommendations in the assessment of competency and risk, as these areas are not typically covered in nonspecialized clinical training. Similarly, immigration attorneys should have at least a rudimentary understanding of the principles underlying FMHAs to ensure that the MHPs they retain or work with are following the best standards of practice. Furthermore, it is advisable that mental health as well as legal professionals understand each other's ethical obligations and roles to minimize potential conflict and improve collaboration.

Finally, conducting evaluations in ICs means being exposed to a wide range of cultural backgrounds. Therefore, expertise in cross-cultural mental health is crucial. Cultural competency in this area requires understanding not only cross-cultural manifestations of trauma and mental illness but also the ways in which the MHPs' (and to a certain extent attorneys') own culture and biases can impact their interactions with immigrants, interpretation of the data, and clinical and forensic opinions.

FMHAs in ICs provide ample opportunities for the theoretical and empirical scholarship necessary to improve the practices of mental health and legal professionals in this area. In addition, policy changes at the intersection of mental health and immigration law are acutely needed to increase protections for noncitizens in removal proceedings. We offer the following research and policy suggestions, organized under four different areas: *FMHAs, cross-cultural assessment, mental health of noncitizens in immigration proceedings,* and *immigration policy.*

Forensic Mental Health Assessments in Immigration Courts: Future Directions

Extensive research has been devoted to defining forensic mental health concepts in criminal and other civil law (e.g., competency, mental state at the time of the offense, personal injury etc.). Conversely, most of the psycholegal issues involved in ICs are vague and lack specificity. As a result, more theoretical and empirical research is needed to better define the forensic mental health constructs and related functional abilities involved in ICs (e.g., hardship, persecution, substantial mental abuse). Survey research is needed to explore the current practices being employed by MHPs in ICs, as well as to identify the factors that go into the decision-making process of immigration adjudicators. Principles and guidelines for the practice of FMHAs in ICs are also required to improve consistency and quality.[4] The Executive Office of Immigration Review has provided such guidelines specifically in the area of competency, but these need to be extended to all other psycholegal issues.

It is imperative that more research be conducted on the cross-cultural validity of existing clinical assessment and forensically relevant instruments, specifically those developed for the assessment of trauma, response style in general, and malingering of trauma-related presentations. Additionally, FAIs need to be developed to evaluate legal constructs specific to ICs (e.g., competency).[5] Furthermore, given how much immigration adjudicators rely on complete consistency and accuracy when making decisions about credibility, research into memory recollections of persecution and trauma could significantly improve IJs' decision-making with respect to credibility.[6] Research is also needed on the cross-cultural validity of risk assessment instruments to be used specifically with immigrants involved in removal proceedings and in immigration detention. Finally, given how often MHPs conduct evaluations in ICs pro bono or as volunteers, additional research is required on the concept of forensic adversarial alliance (the tendency for some experts' opinions to drift toward the party retaining their services)[7] and how this applies to ICs.

Cross-Cultural Assessment in Immigration Court: Future Directions

One of the main challenges of conducting evaluations in ICs is the cultural variability among immigrants involved in the IC process. There are more than 276 languages spoken in immigration proceedings. Consequently, practicing in this context requires extensive knowledge, expertise, and sensitivity to cross-cultural issues. However, even with appropriate training, experience, and cultural sensitivity, MHPs encounter endless obstacles when conducting cross-cultural assessments in ICs, which makes research in this area essential. Specifically, practice guidelines are needed for the cross-cultural evaluation of trauma. Anecdotally, there seems to be tremendous variability across clinicians' approaches to assessing and documenting trauma and torture. The Istanbul Protocol for the documentation of torture was published in 1999, and to our knowledge no updates have been provided since then. Empirical scholarship is needed to explore the cross-cultural validity of posttraumatic stress disorder (PTSD), the newly described diagnosis of Complex PTSD, and any other trauma-related presentations. Additionally, the Cultural Formulation Interview (CFI) provides a promising procedure through which to conduct clinical interviews in a structured and culturally sensitive manner. However, further research is needed to explore CFIs' validity in forensic settings and the added contributions to standard clinical interviews. Of utmost importance is the exploration of the ways in which cultural factors and acculturation might impact the reliability and validity of existing psychological tests for use with individuals from diverse backgrounds, ass well as the development of assessment instruments that are property normed and validated with the types of immigrant groups involved in ICs.

Mental Health of Noncitizens in Immigration Proceedings: Future Directions

Immigrants experience a myriad of emotional stressors during and upon their arrival to the United States. Simply arriving in a "safe haven" does not guarantee security or safety. Immigrant populations—such as survivors of sexual violence, those fleeing homophobia and sexual identity discrimination, victims of intimate partner violence, those separated from their families, and those placed in detention—continue to face additional emotional distress once in this country. Professionals working with these populations must demonstrate sensitivity to immigrants' ongoing struggles. Surveys are needed to better understand the rates and types of mental illness among immigrants in deportation proceedings and those in detention. Furthermore, research needs to explore the ways in which the additional stressors faced by immigrants in deportation proceedings affect their presentation in court, their willingness to share their traumatic experiences, their competency for self-representation, and their credibility as perceived by immigration adjudicators.

Additionally, with the increased recognition of the detrimental impact of secondary traumatic VT and STS on the well-being of MHPs and attorneys who provide services to immigrant populations, it is critical that organizations (e.g., universities, medical centers, public defender organizations, or any other agencies that employ mental health and legal professionals) take proactive steps to acknowledge the reality of this ever-present problem. This needs to be done by addressing this issue at all levels (from leadership down) through interventions such as normalizing discussions of VT/STS, providing education and support, and teaching healthy coping skills. Although there is some research on the presence of STS/VT among mental health providers, there is a huge gap in the psychological literature with respect to the impact of this work on attorneys who work with traumatized populations. Further research with larger participants would provide greater insights into the experiences of service providers. In order for these professionals to provide competent services, they must also be cared for.

Immigration Policy Recommendations

Several specific policy recommendations could help alleviate some of the abuses inherent in the immigration system, especially for immigrants with mental illness and those who are victims of trauma. First, immigration detention should be severely curtailed or eliminated entirely, and counsel should be provided to all immigrants in removal proceedings. Detention inflicts needless cruelty on immigrants and refugees who have already suffered unimaginable hardship. Detention is also unnecessary:

alternatives to detention programs have proven themselves to be highly effective in ensuring that respondents will appear for their scheduled court dates. In the same vein, the detention of deportable immigrants—especially those with mental illness—does not serve the needs of public safety and is not necessary to ensure appearance at hearings. Aside from being cruel, detention and lack of counsel also lead to poorer decision-making by our ICs. Studies have shown that people who are detained and act pro se have only a 3% chance to prevail in immigration court, while those who are free and represented by counsel have a 75% chance of being granted relief.[8] This means that detention and lack of counsel are causing people with legitimate claims to be denied relief. This is bad for individual immigrants, but it is also not good for the integrity of the immigration system as a whole.

As a second recommendation, the harsh and often mandatory consequences of criminal convictions should be softened, especially given what we now know about the devastating effects of the drug war, the criminalization of mental illness, and the racial biases inherent in our criminal justice system. Although this book has discussed many forms of immigration relief, for many immigrants with a criminal record there is simply no relief available. There is no "safety valve" through which an IJ is allowed to consider mitigating circumstances (such as mental health issues or history of trauma), length of residence in the United States, community ties, family ties, successful treatment, work history, payment of taxes, business ownership, and so on. Many immigrants with mental illness fall into this category. And this should go without saying: no person who is incompetent to assist in their own defense should be deported.

Finally, given the serious and sometimes life-or-death nature of the issues that our ICs must adjudicate, they should become a truly independent court system. This would go a long way toward allowing a robust due process environment to flourish within the immigration court system.

ACKNOWLEDGMENTS

We are grateful to all the immigrants from diverse parts of the world whom we have treated, evaluated, or represented in immigration court; for all that we have learned from them; and for their willingness to share their stories. We also want to acknowledge Simge Huyal Genco for her contributions and Maria Aparcero-Suero for her contributions to chapter 9. The three of us have learned a tremendous amount from each other and are thankful for the friendship that developed while working on this project, over Zoom meetings, and in the middle of a global pandemic.

NOTES

INTRODUCTION

1 Abby Budiman, "Key Findings about U.S. Immigrants," Pew Research Center, Sept. 22, 2020, www.pewresearch.org.

2 Abby Budiman, Christine Tamir, Lauren Mora, and Luis Noe-Bustamante, "Immigrants in America: Key Charts and Facts," Pew Research Center's Hispanic Trends Project, Oct. 1, 2020, www.pewhispanic.org.

3 Shawn S. Sidhu and Ramnarine Boodoo, "US Case Law and Legal Precedent Affirming the Due Process Rights of Immigrants Fleeing Persecution," *Journal of the American Academy of Psychiatry and the Law* 45, no. 3 (2017): 365–373.

4 "Profile of the Unauthorized Population—US," migrationpolicy.org, Feb. 1, 2021, www.migrationpolicy.org.

5 "Seeking Safety at the Border," International Rescue Committee (IRC), www.rescue.org.

6 Ibid.

7 "By the Numbers: The United States of Refugees," *Smithsonian*, www.smithsonianmag.com.

8 "Immigration Detainers" American Civil Liberties Union, www.aclu.org.

9 Miriam Jordan and Caitlin Dickerson, "U.S. Continues to Separate Migrant Families Despite Rollback of Policy," *New York Times*, Mar. 9, 2019, www.nytimes.com.

10 "Southwest Border Deaths by Fiscal Year (Oct. 1st through Sept. 30th)," U.S. Border Patrol, www.cbp.gov.

11 Colin Atagi et al., "How Did it Happen? Why Were There 25 People in an SUV? A Visual Explanation," *USA Today*, Mar. 4, 2021, https://eu.usatoday.com.

12 Muzaffar Chrishti and Jessica Bolter, "Border Challenges Dominate, but Biden's First 100 Days Mark Notable Under-the-Radar Immigration Accomplishments," *MPI Migration Policy Institute*, Apr. 26, 2021, www.migrationpolicy.org.

13 "Statistics Yearbook. Fiscal Year 2018," U.S. Department of Justice, Executive Office for Immigration Review, 2018, www.justice.gov.

14 Kristen C. Ochia., Gregory L. Pleasants, Joseph V. Penn, and David C. Stone, "Disparities In Justice and Care: Persons with Severe Mental Illnesses in the US Immigration Detention System," *Journal of the American Academy of Psychiatry and the Law Online* 38, no. 3 (2010): 392–399.

15 Nina Bernstein, "New Scrutiny as Immigrants Die in Custody," *New York Times*, June 26, 2007, www.nytimes.com.

16 "ACLU Fact Sheet on Alternatives to Immigration Detention (ATD)," American Civil Liberties Union, www.aclu.org; "Immigration-Related Arrests by ICE Increase under President Trump," *ABC News*, https://abcnews.go.com.

17 "Working With Immigrant-Origin Clients an Update for Mental Health Professionals," American Psychological Association, 2013, www.apa.org.

18 "Deportation by Default," Human Rights Watch, 2010, www.hrw.org.

19 Jennifer Bronson and Marcus Berzofsky, "Indicators of Mental Health Problems Reported by Prisoners and Jail Inmates, 2011–12," *Bureau of Justice Statistics* (2017): 1–16.

20 Virginia Barber-Rioja and Alexandra Garcia-Mansilla, "Forensic Mental Health Assessment in Immigration Court," in *The Oxford Handbook of Psychology and Law*, ed. D. DeMatteo and K. C. Scherr (Oxford University Press, forthcoming).

21 Ibid.

22 Barton F. Evans III and Giselle A. Hass, *Forensic Psychological Assessment in Immigration Court: A Guidebook for Evidence-Based and Ethical Practice* (Routledge, 2018).

23 Erica Bryant, "Immigrants Facing Deportation Do Not Have the Right to a Publicly Funded Attorney. Here is How to Change That," Vera Institute of Justice, Feb. 9, 2021, www.vera.org.

24 "Joint Statement from NYIFUP Legal Providers on City Council Response Recommending $16.5 Million to Support Crucial Immigrant Legal Services," The Bronx Defenders, www.bronxdefenders.org.

25 "Answering the Call: Pro Bono Lawyers Respond to the Immigration Crisis," American Bar Association, www.americanbar.org.

26 Bruce I. Frumkin and Joan Friedland, "Forensic Evaluations in Immigration Cases: Evolving Issues," *Behavioral Sciences & the Law* 13, no. 4 (1995): 477–489.

27 James Neal Butcher, Giselle A. Hass, Roger L. Greene, and Linda D. Nelson. *Using the MMPI-2 in Forensic Assessment* (Washington, DC: American Psychological Association, 2015); Barton F. Evans III and Giselle A. Hass, *Forensic Psychological Assessment in Immigration Court: A Guidebook for Evidence-Based and Ethical Practice* (Routledge, 2018); David L. Shapiro and Lenore E. A. Walker, *Forensic Practice for the Mental Health Clinician* (TPI Press, 2019).

28 Barber-Rioja and Garcia-Mansilla, "Forensic Mental Health."

29 Rebecca A. Weiss and Barry Rosenfeld. "Navigating Cross-Cultural Issues in Forensic Assessment: Recommendations for Practice," *Professional Psychology: Research and Practice* 43, no. 3 (2012): 234.

30 Barber-Rioja and Garcia-Mansilla, "Forensic Mental Health."

1. A BRIEF OVERVIEW OF THE IMMIGRATION SYSTEM AND FORENSIC MENTAL HEALTH ASSESSMENT

1 "Who We Are," U.S. Immigration and Customs Enforcement, www.ice.gov.

2 "About CBP," U.S. Customs and Border Protection, www.cbp.gov.

3 "The Constitution in the 100-Mile Border Zone," ACLU, 2021, www.aclu.org.

4 "Executive Office for Immigration Review: An Agency Guide," U.S. Department of Justice, Dec. 2017, www.justice.gov.

5 "Immigration Court Listing," U.S. Department of Justice, www.justice.gov.

6 "U.S. Department of State," U.S. Department of State, www.state.gov.

7 "Diversity Visa Program," U.S. Department of State, https://travel.state.gov.

8 "Office of Refugee Resettlement (ORR)," U.S. Department of Health and Human Services, Administration for Children and Families, www.acf.hhs.gov.

9 "A Guide to the Rulemaking Process," Office of the Federal Register, 2011, www.federalregister.gov.

10 The Second Circuit recently ordered the BIA to make these unpublished opinions available to the public. These opinions "constitute the vast majority of the final decisions issued by the BIA each year, and are cited and relied upon by the BIA itself, by immigration judges, and by lawyers representing the government in immigration proceedings . . . [yet] are not readily available to lawyers representing clients in immigration proceedings." New York Legal Assistance Group v. Board of Immigration Appeals, 19-cv-3248 (2nd Cir. Feb 5, 2021).

11 Office of the Federal Register, "A Guide to the Rulemaking Process." USCIS policy memoranda can be found at www.uscis.gov.

12 Agency findings of fact, including credibility determinations, will be upheld as long as they are "supported by reasonable, substantial, and probative evidence on the record considered as a whole." INS v. Elias-Zacarias, 502 U.S. 478, 481 (1992). The agency's determination will not be overturned unless the facts compel the opposite conclusion—a very difficult standard to meet. The agency is also given deference with respect to its reasonable interpretations of the statutes and regulations that it administers. *See* Chevron v. Natural Res. Def. Council, 467 U.S. 837, 843–44 (1984). Additionally, specific to immigration law, there are many issues that the courts are not allowed to review. *See* Donald Dobkin, "Court Stripping and Limitations on Judicial Review of Immigration Cases," *Justice System Journal* 28, no. 1 (2007): 104, www.jstor.org.

13 Antiterrorism and Effective Death Penalty Act of 1996 (AEDPA), 110 Stat. 1214; Illegal Immigration Reform and Immigrant Responsibility Act of 1996 (IIRIRA), 110 Stat. 3009–546.

14 This is known as "expedited removal." 8 USC § 1225(b)(1)(A)(i) / INA § 235(b)(1)(A)(i); 8 CFR § 235.3.

15 Ibid.

16 8 USC § 1225(b)(1)(A)(ii).

17 8 USC § 1225(b)(1)(B)(v).

18 Being placed in removal proceedings sounds like an undesirable outcome for an asylum seeker, but the alternative is removal *without* the benefit of proceedings to adjudicate the validity of their claim.

19 *See* 8 USC §§ 1225(b)(1)(A)(ii), (B); 8 CFR § 235.3(b)(4) (for individuals subject to expedited removal).

20 Technically "are subject to removal" but, as explained in the introduction, the terms "deportation" and "deported" will be used instead of "removal" or "removed" in this book when referring to actions taken against human beings. "Removal proceedings" will still be used to refer to the type of court proceeding.

21 Anyone who is not a lawful permanent resident who has an aggravated felony conviction can subject to "administrative removal" without a hearing. INA § 238; 8 CFR § 238.1. People arriving at a port of entry can be subject to "expedited removal," again without a hearing. 8 USC § 1225(b)(1)(A)(i) / INA § 235(b)(1)(A)(i); 8 CFR § 235.3. Expedited removal can also be applied, however, should the Attorney General choose to do so, to anyone in the United States who was not admitted or paroled into the country and who cannot show that they have been physically present for more than two years. 8 U.S.C. §§ 1225(b)(1)(A)(i), (iii).

22 Yamataya v. Fisher, 189 U.S. 86 (1903).

23 It is not uncommon for an IJ to defer making a final decision on eligibility for relief until after the individual hearing, which means that a person might wait years and spend thousands of dollars in attorneys' fees to apply for a form of relief only to have the IJ deny them because they were not actually eligible in the first place.

24 8 USC § 1229a.

25 Matter of Wadud, 19 I&N 182 (BIA 1984).

26 See Matter of Ponce-Hernandez, 22 I&N Dec. 784 (BIA 1999); Matter of Toro, 17 I&N Dec. 340 (BIA 1980).

27 See, e.g., F. E. Marouf, "Incompetent but Deportable: The Case for a Right to Mental Competence in Removal Proceedings," 65 Hastings L.J. 929, 931 (2014) (making a case for immigration proceedings as "quasi-criminal").

28 "'Death Penalty Cases in a Traffic Court Setting': Lessons from the Front Lines of Today's Immigration Courts," ABA Practice Points, Jan. 15, 2019, www.americanbar.org.

29 "A Day in the Life of USCIS," U.S. Citizenship and Immigration Services, www.uscis.gov.

30 "Fee Schedule," U.S. Citizenship and Immigration Services, www.uscis.gov.

31 These include cancellation of removal for non–Lawful Permanent Residents, various inadmissibility waivers, and the T visa.

32 These include VAWA cancellation of removal, cancellation of removal for non–Lawful Permanent Residents, and naturalization.

33 These include cancellation of removal for Lawful Permanent Residents and relief under former INA § 212(c).

34 Matter of Fatahi, 26 I&N Dec. 791, 793–94 (BIA 2016); Matter of Adeniji, 22 I&N Dec. 1102, 1112–13 (BIA 1999); Matter of Garcia Arreola, 25 I&N Dec. 267 (BIA 2010).

35 Applicants for many types of relief will need to prove that their continued presence in the United States is justified on humanitarian grounds, to ensure family unity, or is in the public interest.

36 INA § 212(a)(1)(A)(iii) / 8 USC § 1182(a)(1)(A)(iii).

37 Matter of M-A-M-, 25 I&N Dec. 474 (BIA 2011).

38 *See* chapter 11.

2. DETENTION OF IMMIGRANTS

1 "Accessing Justice: The Availability and Adequacy of Counsel in Immigration Proceedings (New York Immigrant Representation Study)," Study Group on Immigrant Representation, Dec. 2011, https://justicecorps.org.

2 INA § 235(b) / 8 USC § 1225(b).

3 INA § 236(a) / 8 USC § 1226(a).

4 INA § 241(a) / 8 USC § 1231(a).

5 Immigrants arriving in the United States without the proper paperwork are subject to mandatory detention. This includes asylum seekers undergoing credible fear interviews. INA § 235(b)(1)(B)(iii)(IV) / 8 USC § 1225(b)(1)(B)(iii)(IV).

6 INA § 235(b)(1)(A)(ii) / 8 USC § 1225(b)(1)(A)(ii).

7 INA § 212(d)(5)(A) / 8 USC § 1182(d)(5)(A); *see also* 8 CFR §§ 212.5(b), 235.3. Under a long-standing interpretation of the Board of Immigration Appeals, asylum seekers who passed a credible fear hearing were eligible for a bond hearing. Then–Attorney General William Barr overruled that interpretation by issuing a precedent decision holding the opposite. Matter of X-K-, 23 I&N Dec. 731 (BIA 2005); Matter of M-S-, 27 I&N Dec. 509 (A.G. 2019). The Attorney General has the authority to issue precedent opinions that overrule the opinions of the BIA because the BIA is not actually a court but rather a part of the EOIR, which is itself a part of the DOJ, an administrative agency under the purview of the executive, rather than judicial, branch of the federal government.

8 INA § 236(a) / 8 USC § 1226(a).

9 "Average Time Pending Cases Have Been Waiting in Immigration Courts as of January 2021," TRAC Immigration, https://trac.syr.edu. According to ICE detention data from the first four months of FY 2021, the average (mean) stay in ICE custody after passing a credible fear interview was 293 days. For FY 2020 it was 133.7 days.

10 *See* "Adjudication Statistics: Median Times for Pending Detained Cases," Executive Office for Immigration Review, Oct. 23, 2019, www.justice.gov (median pending time for detained cases between 53 and 134 days). Meanwhile, BIA appeals take, on average, more than 3.5 months for detained cases and more than 16 months for nondetained cases. "Management of Immigration Cases and Appeals by the Executive Office for Immigration Review," U.S. Department of Justice Office of the Inspector General, 2012, https://oig.justice.gov.

11 EOIR uses median rather than mean. But many nonasylum cases resolve in only a few weeks, either because there is no relief available or because the immigrant cannot withstand detention and gives up their case. This tends to skew the median lower. Additionally, the use of median obscures cases at the other end of the spectrum that might have been pending for hundreds of days. For the BIA appeal data, the Office of Inspector General, which wrote the report, criticized the BIA's

numbers as inaccurate because they exclude certain time periods and therefore underreport actual processing times. Ibid. at iii. The processing time for asylum appeals is likely even longer than the typical appeal because asylum cases tend to be more complex.

12 "Detention Statistics," U.S. Immigration and Customs Enforcement, www.ice.gov. Information on length of stay after passing a credible fear interview is not available for earlier years.

13 A federal court that agrees to review a decision of the BIA can issue an order "staying" the removal of the affected individual while it makes its decision. Because removal orders are considered final after the BIA has ruled, if the federal court does not issue such a stay, there is nothing preventing DHS from deporting the person even while their case is under review by the federal court.

14 Appealing a removal order in federal court will normally take over a year. *See* "FAQ," Court of Appeals for the 9th Circuit, www.ca9.uscourts.gov (predicting a timeline of 12–20 months for a civil appeal). Success on appeal can result in a remand to the BIA for further consideration, after which the case might be sent back to the IJ or might require further appellate review. *See* "Prolonged Detention Fact Sheet," American Civil Liberties Union, www.aclu.org (providing examples of how someone fighting their immigration case can spend years in detention); *see also* "ICE's Compliance With Detention Limits for Aliens With a Final Order of Removal From the United States," DHS Office of Inspector General, OIG-07-28, 2007, www.oig.dhs.gov, 5 (a stay of removal pending judicial review will effectively "extend[] detention indefinitely").

15 *See* United Nations High Commissioner for Refugees, "Citizens of Nowhere: Solutions for the Stateless in the U.S.," 2012, www.refworld.org, 20–21, 26.

16 United Nations High Commissioner for Refugees, "Citizens of Nowhere" (describing how individuals who cannot be removed are commonly detained for at least 90 days, and sometimes much longer, even when there is no real expectation that they will actually be removed).

17 The "removal period" given to DHS to is 90 days, 8 USC § 1231(a)(2), but after that detention can continue for many individuals if the person is considered a danger to the community or unlikely to comply with the removal order. 8 USC § 1231(a)(6). The regulations implementing this statute shift the burden onto the individual, to prove that they are not a flight risk or a danger, and also as a practical matter extend the default time in custody from 90 days to six months. 8 CFR §§ 241.4, 241.13.

18 In the criminal justice system, the words "bail" and "bond" have slightly different meanings, with "bail" referring to an amount of money that must be paid to secure release from pretrial detention. The INA uses the term "bond" to mean basically the same thing. Following the INA's convention, the term "bond" is used by the people who work in and practice before the immigration courts and DHS. It therefore the word that readers of this book are most likely to encounter when interacting with the immigration system.

19 *See* Demore v. Kim, 538 U.S. 510, 528 (2003) (immigration detention "necessarily serves the purpose of preventing deportable criminal aliens from fleeing prior to or during their removal proceedings, thus increasing the chance that, if ordered removed, the aliens will be successfully removed"); Matter of Valdez-Valdez, 21 I&N Dec. 703, 709 (BIA 1997) (purpose of immigration detention is "ensuring community safety and the criminal alien's appearance at all deportation hearings."); Matter of Drysdale, 20 I&N Dec. 815, 817 (BIA 1994) ("[I]f the alien cannot demonstrate that he is not a danger to the community upon consideration of the relevant factors, he should be detained in the custody of the Service."); *see also* United States v. Salerno, 481 U.S. 739 (1987) (approving consideration of public safety as a justification for the decision to detain a criminal defendant without bail). Note that a few states do not permit judges to hold a pretrial defendant without bail for public safety reasons. *See* Mary T. Phillips, "A Decade of Bail Research in New York City," New York City Criminal Justice Agency (2012), www.prisonpolicy.org, 25–26.

20 This data comes from a study of the 75 largest urban counties in the United States. Brian A. Reaves, "Felony Defendants in Large Urban Counties, 2009—Statistical Tables," U.S. Department of Justice Bureau of Justice Statistics, NCJ 243777: 15, 2013, www.bjs.gov.

21 In the same study, 24% of pretrial defendants were released on nonfinancial conditions; bail was set for 72%. Ibid., 17, Table 12.

22 *See* Jenny Tsay, "After Arrest, How Long Until a Bond Hearing?," FindLaw, Apr. 9, 2014, https://blogs.findlaw.com.

23 *See* Matter of Fatahi, 26 I&N Dec. 791, 795 n.3 (BIA 2016) (the BIA has "consistently held that aliens have the burden to establish eligibility for bond while proceedings are pending"); Matter of Guerra, 24 I&N Dec. 37, 40 (BIA 2006).

24 A district court in New York held that due process requires DHS to conduct initial hearings within ten days of arrest. (While initial "master calendar" hearings are not bond hearings, they provide an opportunity for an immigrant who is eligible to request that a bond hearing be scheduled.) The ruling, which only applies to part of New York, was appealed by the Joseph Biden administration. Paul Moses and Tim Healy, "DOJ Appeals Ruling Limiting Immigrant Detentions Without a Court Hearing," *Documented*, Feb. 24, 2021, https://documentedny.com. In the geographic area covered by the court order, 84.2% of initial hearings were held within 10 days of an ICE arrest. Nationally, the opposite was true: 87% of the initial hearings were held after more than 10 days in detention. Ibid.

25 INA § 236(c) / 8 USC § 1226(c). The mandatory detention statute has been interpreted to strip discretion only from the immigration judge: DHS maintains its broad discretion over who to detain. In other words, "mandatory" detention is not really mandatory for DHS. DHS can decline to detain someone who is subject to the statute, but if they do choose to detain that person, an IJ has no power to set a bond or otherwise order their release.

26 People subject to mandatory detention include anyone who has ever been convicted (since 1998) of a broad list of crimes, regardless of how much time has passed since their conviction or their positive equities. INA § 236(c). The list of past crimes that subject an individual to mandatory detention includes drug possession (including marijuana), "crimes involving moral turpitude" (which can includes shoplifting and other minor property crimes), and prostitution. Mandatory detention applies even if the person was never sentenced to any jail time in the criminal case. Ibid.

27 8 CFR §§ 1003.19(i)(1), (2).

28 *See* Daniel Bush, "Under Trump Higher Immigration Bonds Mean Longer Family Separations," *PBS News Hour*, June 28, 2018, www.pbs.org (according to a DOJ spokesperson, EOIR does keep track of median bond amounts set, but it "does not keep data on the average [mean] bond amount for immigrants in detention, or the percentage of bond requests that are approved").

29 "Bond Hearings, 2001 to 2021," TRAC Immigration [query: "Bond Hearing Immigration Court State": All. "Nationality": All], https://trac.syr.edu.

30 Under the Barack Obama administration, immigration judges routinely set high bonds "often as high as $7,500[.]" Under the Donald Trump administration, according to immigration attorneys, DHS and IJs were more likely to deny bond altogether or set bonds noticeably higher, often in excess of $10,000. An anonymous immigration attorney reported that it was "not uncommon" to see bonds of $25,000 for asylum seekers. Bush, "Under Trump, Higher Immigration Bonds."

31 TRAC Immigration, "Bond Hearings, 2001 to 2021." Note that the change in the median bond amount over time does not appear to support the observations of immigration attorneys quoted in the PBS report that IJs and DHS set higher bonds under the Trump administration. The big jump in the median bond amount happened in FY 2016, which was during the Obama administration. The median bond statistic, however, takes into account only cases when bond is actually set and excludes cases when bond is denied. Additionally, it reflects only IJ bonds, not bonds set by DHS. Finally, if a significantly higher percentage of immigration cases were asylum cases because of the increase in asylum seekers at the border, we might expect that to have an impact on median bond amounts in some way—it might have led to lower bonds if asylum seekers were perceived as humanitarian migrants deserving of welcome and presenting little danger to the community. Conversely, it might have led to higher bonds if asylum seekers were considered a flight risk or if the larger numbers of people before them seeking asylum led to "compassion fatigue" among IJs.

32 Bernadette Rabuy and Daniel Kopf, "Detaining the Poor: How Money Bail Perpetuates an Endless Cycle of Poverty and Jail Time," Prison Policy Initiative, May 10, 2016, www.prisonpolicy.org. The article cites U.S. Department of Justice Bureau of Justice Statistics data from 2009 as the most recent available at time of publication. This appears to still be the case.

33 Phillips, "A Decade of Bail Research in New York City," 34.

34 The authors by no means intend to imply that having a criminal record should justify immigration detention. Approximately one-third of US citizens have criminal records, and no one argues that those individuals should be preventatively detained for public safety reasons.

35 Addington v. Texas, 441 U.S. 418 (1978). *See also* "Civil Commitment and the Mental Health Care Continuum: Historical Trends and Principles for Law and Practice," U.S. Dep't of Health and Human Services, Substance Abuse and Mental Health Services Administration, 2019, www.samhsa.gov.

36 Kansas v. Hendricks, 521 U.S. 346 (1997).

37 Immigrants in removal proceedings have the right to counsel "at no expense to the government." 8 USC § 1362. This means only that they have the right to hire a lawyer if they can afford one.

38 Demore v. Kim, 538 U.S. 510 (2003); Jennings v. Rodriguez, 138 S. Ct. 830, 841 (2018).

39 *See* Velasco Lopez v. Decker, 19-cv-2284 (2nd Cir. Oct. 27, 2020) (after fifteen months of detention with no end of proceedings in sight, due process required that the burden shift to government to justify the detained person's continued detention); *see also* Roman v. Decker, 20-cv-6752, 2020 WL 5743522 (S.D.N.Y. Sept. 25, 2020) (granting habeas on this theory and requiring the government to produce evidence to justify the continued detention of an immigrant held for 12 months).

40 Zadvydas v. Davis, 533 U.S. 678 (2001).

41 FY 2019 data. "Detention 101," Detention Watch Network, www.detentionwatch-network.org.

42 *See* Clyde Haberman, "For Private Prisons, Detaining Immigrants Is Big Business," *New York Times*, Oct. 1, 2018, www.nytimes.com.

43 For more detail on the different types of detention facilities and the number of detainees in each, *see* "ICE Does Not Fully Use Contracting Tools to Hold Detention Facility Contractors Accountable for Failing to Meet Performance Standards," DHS Office of the Inspector General, OIG 19–18: 3, Jan. 29, 2019, www.oig.dhs.gov.

44 "FY 2019 Detention Statistics," U.S. Immigration and Customs Enforcement, www.ice.gov. While data was available for FY 2020, FY 2019 was chosen to avoid any distortion of the data from the effects of the COVID-19 pandemic. Current data can be found on the ICE website, www.ice.gov.

45 Detention Watch Network, "Detention 101."

46 Public Law 114–4 (Mar. 4, 2015), www.congress.gov; *see also* "Detention Quotas," Detention Watch Network, www.detentionwatchnetwork.org.

47 Silky Shah, Mary Small, and Carol Wu, "Banking on Detention: Local Lockup Quotas and the Immigrant Dragnet," Detention Watch Network, 2015, www.detentionwatchnetwork.org.

48 U.S. Immigration and Customs Enforcement, "FY 2019 Detention Statistics."

49 *See* Eunice Hyunhye Cho, Tara Tidwell Cullen, and Clara Long, "Justice Free Zones: U.S. Immigration Detention under the Trump Administration,"

ACLU / Human Rights Watch / National Immigrant Justice Center, 2020, www. hrw.org; *see also* "Detention Facilities," U.S. Immigration and Customs Enforcement, www.ice.gov.

50 For example, the same conviction might be considered an "aggravated felony" in one circuit and not in another.

51 Grant rates vary tremendously for different immigration judges. This variation can be seen across different judges but also markedly across different immigration courts. "Asylum Decisions Vary Widely Across Judges and Courts—Latest Results (Jan. 13, 2020)," TRAC Immigration, 2020, https://trac.syr.edu.

52 *See* Alison Parker, "Locked Up Far Away: The Transfer of Immigrants to Remote Detention Centers in the United States," Human Rights Watch, Dec. 2, 2009, www.hrw.org.

53 While ICE has stated that they "prefer" not to transferring people who have representation away from where their attorney can reasonably visit them, there is nothing stopping them from doing so. *Id.*; *see also* "Briefing Paper: Access to Counsel and Due Process for Detained Immigrants," National Immigrant Justice Center, Apr. 16, 2007, https://immigrantjustice.org, 6–7. Such a transfer away from counsel might, however, violate due process.

54 "2011 Operations Manual ICE Performance-Based National Detention Standards," U.S. Immigration and Customs Enforcement, www.ice.gov.

55 "2019 National Detention Standards for Non-Dedicated Facilities," U.S. Immigration and Customs Enforcement, www.ice.gov.

56 *See* ibid. (Frequently Asked Questions -> How and when will NDS 2019 be implemented? -> "The new standards must be implemented through individual contract modifications with facilities. This can require detailed and lengthy negotiations with contractors, so the implementation process might last several months."); *see also* "Fact Sheet: ICE Detention Standards," U.S. Immigration and Customs Enforcement, Feb. 24, 2012, www.ice.gov ("Different versions of [the Performance-Based] national detention standards currently apply to ICE's various detention facilities. ICE has begun implementing PBNDS 2011 across its detention facilities, with priority initially given to facilities housing the largest populations of ICE detainees.").

57 "Family Residential Standards 2020," U.S. Immigration and Customs Enforcement, 2020, www.ice.gov.

58 *See* "Immigration Detention Oversight and Accountability Toolkit: A Guide for Members of Congress Visiting ICE Jails," National Immigrant Justice Center, May 22, 2019, immigrantjustice.org/research-items/toolkit-immigration-detention-oversight-and-accountability ("There are no formally binding regulations or statutory provisions governing the standards of care at ICE detention facilities. ICE has adopted three sets of detention standards that serve as guidance, but does not require contractors to adopt the most recent standards when it enters into new contracts or contract extensions. The result is a patchwork system in which

facilities are subject to differing standards and some are subject to no standards at all.").

59 Alice Speri, "Detained, Then Violated: 1,224 Complaints Reveal a Staggering Pattern of Sexual Abuse in Immigration Detention. Half of Those Accused Worked for ICE," *The Intercept*, Apr. 11, 2018, https://theintercept.com.

60 Victoria Bekiempis, "More Immigrant Women Say They Were Abused by ICE Gynecologist," *The Guardian*, Dec. 22, 2020, www.theguardian.com.

61 "Concerns about ICE Detainee Treatment and Care at Four Detention Facilities," DHS Office of Inspector General, OIG 19–74: 3–4, June 3, 2019, www.oig.dhs.gov.

62 Kristie Phillips, "Thousands of ICE Detainees Claim They Were Forced into Labor, a Violation of Anti-slavery Laws," *Washington Post*, Mar. 5, 2017, www.washingtonpost.com.

63 Nick Miroff, "Immigrant Detainees Get Poor Medical Care, Face Retaliation for Speaking Out, According to Democrat-Led Report," *Washington Post*, Sept. 21, 2020, www.washingtonpost.com.

64 *See* Michael Garcia Bochenek, "In the Freezer: Abusive Conditions for Women and Children in US Immigration Holding Cells," Human Rights Watch, Feb. 28, 2018, www.hrw.org.

65 Personal observation of author during volunteer trip to the border at Tijuana, Mexico, Feb. 2019.

66 (In Chambers) Order Re Plaintiffs' Motion to Enforce and Appoint a Special Monitor, Flores v. Sessions, 85-cv-04544 (C.D. Cal. June 27, 2017), www.aila.org.

67 *See* Patrick G. Lee, "Immigrants in Detention Centers Are Often Hundreds of Miles From Legal Help," *ProPublica*, May 16, 2016, www.propublica.org; *see also* Parker, "Locked Up Far Away."

68 *See* ProPublica, "Immigrants in Detention Centers Are Often Hundreds of Miles" (profiling a representative detention center in located in the small town of Lumpkin, Georgia, which has no hotel and is located over 100 miles from the nearest metropolitan area; finding only 6% of the detained immigrants have counsel as compared with the national average of 14%); *see also* Dora Schriro, "'Weeping in the Playtime of Others': The Obama Administration's Failed Reform of ICE Family Detention Practices," *JMHS* 5, no. 2 (2017): 452, 461–462 (describing the opening and closing of the Artesia detention facility for migrant families, in an area where "there were no immigration lawyers").

69 *See* "Treatment of Immigration Detainees Housed at Immigration and Customs Enforcement Facilities," DHS Office of Inspector General, 2006, www.dhs.gov (describing delays of at least 16 business days before detainees were allowed to call their lawyers, out-of-order phones, and detention staff present and able to overhear private legal calls).

70 *See* Eunice Hyunhye Cho and Joanna Naples-Mitchell, "Behind Closed Doors: Abuse and Retaliation Against Hunger Strikers in U.S. Immigration Detention," ACLU and Physicians for Human Rights, 2021, www.aclu.org.

71 U.N. Convention relating to the Status of Refugees (Geneva, Jul. 28, 1951) 189 U.N.T.S. 150, extended by the Protocol relating to the Status of Refugees (New York, Jan. 31, 1967) 19 U.S.T. 6223, 606 U.N.T.S. 267.

72 For example, President Trump's remarks at the final presidential debate when he falsely claimed that only 1% of asylum seekers return for their hearings. Tyler Sonnemaker, "Trump Falsely Claims That Only Migrants with 'the Lowest IQ' Return for Their Court Dates after Being Arrested by US Immigration Authorities," *Business Insider*, Oct. 23, 2020, www.businessinsider.com; *see also* Jane C. Timm, "Fact Check: Trump's Misleading Claims About 'Catch and Release,'" *NBC News*, May 2, 2018, www.nbcnews.com.

73 "Most Released Families Attend Immigration Court Hearings," TRAC Immigration, June 18, 2019, https://trac.syr.edu. Rates go up to 99% for asylum seekers with representation. Ibid.

74 Ibid.; *see also* Kristin Cooke and Mica Rosenberg, "No 'Day in Court': U.S. Deportation Orders Blindside Some Families," *Reuters*, July 26, 2019, www.reuters.com.

75 Stipulated Settlement Agreement, Flores v. Reno, No. 85-cv-4544 (C.D. Cal. 1997) (hereinafter "*Flores* Settlement Agreement"), *available at* American Immigration Lawyers Association, AILA InfoNet Doc. No. 14111359, www.aila.org; *see also* "Documents Relating to Flores v. Reno Settlement Agreement on Minors in Immigration Custody," American Immigration Lawyers Association, Sept. 27, 2019, www.aila.org.

76 *Flores* Settlement Agreement ¶ 11.

77 The *Flores* agreement provides that children should be released within 3–5 days, *Flores* Settlement Agreement ¶ 12, but the court expanded that to 20 days to account for emergency situations such as a dramatic increase in unaccompanied minors appearing at the border, so long as the government acts in good faith and with due diligence to screen children for release. Flores v. Lynch, 212 F. Supp. 3d 907, 914 (C.D. Cal. 2015), *aff'd in part, rev'd in part and remanded*, 828 F.3d 898 (9th Cir. 2016); *see also* "Fact Sheet: The Flores Settlement and Family Incarceration: Brief History and Next Steps," Human Rights First, Oct. 30, 2018, www.humanrightsfirst.org (hereinafter "HRF *Flores* Fact Sheet").

78 Pub. L. No. 110–457, 122 Stat. 5044; 8 USC § 1232; *see also* Flores, 828 F.3d at 904.

79 *See generally*, "Unaccompanied Alien Children: An Overview," Congressional Research Service, https://fas.org.

80 6 USC § 279(g)(2).

81 HRF *Flores* Fact Sheet; *see also* Schriro, "Weeping in the Playtime of Others," 455.

82 Flores Settlement Agreement ¶¶ 11, 14; *see also* 8 USC § 1232(c)(2)(A).

83 Camille Harper, "Care Provider Facilities Described Challenges Addressing Mental Health Needs of Children in HHS Custody," U.S. Department of Health and Human Services, Office of Inspector General, OEI-09-18-00431, 2019, 1–2, https://oig.hhs.gov. The report also mentions the two large "influx" facilities in Tornillo, Texas, and Homestead, Florida, which have since closed.

84 Ibid.

85 Ibid., 24–25.

86 *See* "Unaccompanied Children: Actions Needed to Improve Grant Application Reviews and Oversight of Care Facilities," U.S. Government Accountability Office, GAO-20-609, Sept. 2020, www.gao.gov (discussing ORR's FY 2018 and 2019 funding rounds).

87 Silvia Foster-Frau, "First Migrant Facility for Children Opens Under Biden," *Washington Post*, Feb. 22, 2021, www.washingtonpost.com.

88 "Facts and Data," Office of Refugee Resettlement, www.acf.hhs.gov.

89 *Flores* Settlement Agreement ¶¶ 12, 21; *see also* 8 USC § 1232 (c)(2)(A) ("[a] child shall not be placed in a secure facility absent a determination that the child poses a danger to self or others or has been charged with having committed a criminal offense."); *see also* "The Flores Settlement Agreement & Unaccompanied Children in Federal Custody," National Center for Youth Law (co-counsel in *Flores*) / Center for Human Rights and Constitutional Law / University of California Davis School of Law Immigration Clinic, Feb. 2019, https://youthlaw.org, 5 (hereinafter "Youth Law *Flores* Congressional Briefing").

90 *See* "Detention Management: Family Residential Centers" U.S. Immigration and Customs Enforcement, www.ice.gov; *see also* "Results of Office of Inspector General FY 2016 Spot Inspections of U.S. Immigration and Customs Enforcement Family Detention Facilities," DHS Office of Inspector General, OIG-17-65, June 2, 2017, www.oig.dhs.gov (hereinafter "2017 OIG Family Detention Inspection Report").

91 Schriro, "Weeping in the Playtime of Others," 462.

92 Ibid., 454 n.6.

93 Ibid., 460; *see also* "Statement by Secretary of Homeland Security Jeh Johnson Before the Senate Committee on Appropriations," July 10, 2014, www.dhs.gov (stating that detention would send a "message" to prospective migrants).

94 Schriro, "Weeping in the Playtime of Others," 463 n. 33, 35, 36.

95 *See* Schriro, "Weeping in the Playtime of Others," 464; *see also* Order, R.I.L-R v. Johnson, 15-cv-00011, 2015 U.S. Dist. LEXIS 20441 (D.D.C. Feb. 20, 2015) (because of the civil nature of immigration detention, it may not be used as a form of punishment; depriving a family of liberty to deter other potential migrants is therefore an impermissible use of detention); *see also* "RILR v. Johnson Practice Advisory," ACLU, Feb. 23, 2015, www.aclu.org (discussing the court's preliminary certification of a nationwide class and issuance of a preliminary injunction against the "no release" policy).

96 Flores v. Lynch, 828 F.3d 898 (9th Cir. 2016) (upholding the district court's ruling that the *Flores* agreement applies to children in family detention); *see also* HRF *Flores* Fact Sheet; *see also* Schriro, "Weeping in the Playtime of Others," at 464.

97 Schriro, "Weeping in the Playtime of Others," 464; *see also* Alexa Garcia-Ditta, "Judge Halts Child Care License for Dilley Detention Center," *Texas Observer*, June 2, 2016, www.texasobserver.org.

98 *See* Schriro, "Weeping in the Playtime of Others," 454, 461. The court battle over licensing is still ongoing. *See* Karen Shuey, "Detained Families Will Have a Voice in Berks County Residential Center's Licensing Case," *Reading Eagle*, Jan. 22, 2020, www.readingeagle.com. In February 2021, all detained families were released from Berks, but this does not mean that the facility is permanently closed. Mike Urban, "All Families Released from Berks Immigration Detention Center, Sen. Casey Announces," *Reading Eagle*, Mar. 1, 2021, www.readingeagle.com.

99 2017 OIG Family Detention Inspection Report, 3.

100 *See* Class Complaint for Injunctive and Declaratory Relief, Mons v. McAleenan, 19-cv-01593 (D.D.C. May 30, 2019) ¶¶ 52–55 (DHS's New Orleans field office granted 75.9% of release requests in 2016, 21.9% in 2017, and only 1.5% in 2018); *see also* Damus v. Nielsen, 313 F.Supp. 3d 317 (D.D.C. 2018) (considering allegations that DHS's El Paso field office denied parole in 100% of cases over an 8 month period, the court found that "asylum-seekers are able to demonstrate that individualized parole determinations are likely no longer par for the course"); *see also* Aracely R. v. Nielsen, 319 F.Supp. 3d 110 (D.D.C. 2018) ("Plaintiffs have shown that it is likely that they will succeed on the merits of their claims because they have supplied evidence tending to show that Defendants have considered immigration deterrence when making parole determinations, in contravention of binding agency policy.").

101 Roque Planas, "Texas Republicans Hope to Give Child Care Licenses to Family Detention Centers," *Huffington Post*, Mar. 30, 2017, www.huffpost.com.

102 Defendant's Memorandum of Points and Authorities in Support of Ex Parte Application for Relief from the Flores Settlement Agreement, Flores v. Sessions, 85-cv-04544 (C.D. Cal. June 21, 2018).

103 Apprehension, Processing, Care, and Custody of Alien Minors and Unaccompanied Alien Children, 83. Fed. Reg. 45486 (proposed Sept. 7, 2018) (to be codified at 45 CFR pt. 410).

104 Flores v. Barr, 407 F.Supp. 3d 909 (C.D. Cal. 2019) *aff'd in part rev'd in part* Flores v. Rosen, 984 F.3d 720 (9th Cir. 2020); Order Denying Defendants' Ex Parte Application for Limited Relief from Settlement Agreement, Flores v. Sessions, 85-cv-04544 (C.D. Cal. July 9, 2018); *see also* Jaclyn Kelley-Widmer, "A Federal Judge Blocked a Trump Administration Rule That Would Allow Children to be Detained Indefinitely. Here's What You Need to Know," *Washington Post*, Sept. 28, 2019, www.washingtonpost.com.

105 The government claimed that "[T]he Flores Agreement—as interpreted by this Court and the Ninth Circuit—put the government in the difficult position of having to separate families if it decides it should detain parents for immigration purposes." Defendant's Notice of Compliance, Flores v. Sessions, 85-cv-4544 (C.D. Cal. June 29, 2018), at 1. Government attorneys argued that in order to comply with an order to reunite separated families [in *Ms. L v. ICE*, discussed below] the government could no longer release the minors. The judge called this argument "tortured" and "cynical" because "absolutely nothing prevents the [govern-

ment] from reconsidering their current blanket policy of family detention and reinstating prosecutorial discretion." Victoria Kim and Kristina Davis, "Judge rejects Trump administration bid to indefinitely detain immigrant children with parents," *Los Angeles Times*, July 9, 2018, www.latimes.com.

106 *See* Linda Qiu, "Republicans Misplace Blame for Splitting Families at the Border," *New York Times*, June 14, 2018, www.nytimes.com.

107 Julia Ainsley and Jacob Soboroff, "Trump Cabinet Officials Voted in 2018 White House Meeting to Separate Migrant Children, Say Officials," *NBC News*, Aug. 20, 2020, www.nbcnews.com; *see also* Jonathan Blitzer, "How Stephen Miller Manipulates Donald Trump to Further His Immigration Obsession," *The New Yorker*, Feb. 21, 2020, www.newyorker.com (According to a top DHS official, Trump's senior policy adviser and architect of his immigration agenda, Stephen Miller, "was obsessed with the idea of consequences[.] . . . [He] made clear to us that, if you start to treat children badly enough, you'll be able to convince other parents to stop trying to come with theirs.").

108 William A. Kandel, "The Trump Administration's 'Zero Tolerance' Immigration Enforcement Policy," Congressional Research Service, R45266, https://fas.org. "Illegal entry" is technically a misdemeanor, but it was rarely prosecuted before Trump. Ibid. at 6.

109 These actions to curtail the right to seek asylum arguably violated both US and international law. *See* Complaint, Al Otro Lado v. Nielsen, 17-cv-02366 (S.D. Cal., July 12, 2017) https://ccrjustice.org; *see also* Robert Moore, "At the U.S. Border, Asylum Seekers Fleeing Violence Are Told to Come Back Later," *Washington Post*, June 13, 2018, www.washingtonpost.com (describing a father and son turned back nine times from seeking asylum at a port of entry).

110 *See* Russell Berman, "85 Immigrants Sentenced Together Before One Judge," The Atlantic, June 19, 2018, www.theatlantic.com.

111 Ibid.

112 *See* Dara Lind, "The Trump administration's separation of families at the border, explained," *Vox*, www.vox.com ("The Trump administration has stepped up detention of asylum seekers . . . [b]ut because there are such strict limits on keeping children in immigration detention, it's had to release most of the families it's caught. The government's solution has been to prosecute larger numbers of immigrants for illegal entry—including, in a break from previous administrations, large numbers of asylum seekers. That allows the Trump administration to ship children off to ORR, rather than keeping them in immigration detention.").

113 This was the case for the named plaintiff in one of the lawsuits that helped curtail family separation. The case was brought by a Congolese woman who presented herself at the border and asked for asylum; she was separated from her six-year-old daughter for five months. *See* Amended Complaint, Ms. L v. ICE, 18-cv-00428 (S.D. Cal. Mar. 9, 2018); *see also* Sarah Herman Peck and Ben Harrington, "The *Flores* Settlement and Alien Families Apprehended at the U.S. Border: Frequently

Asked Questions," Congressional Research Service, R-45297, https://fas.org, 9–10 (discussing the *Ms. L* case).

114 Kate Morrissey, "Executive Order to Reduce Family Separation at Border for Some, Not All," *San Diego Union-Tribune*, June 20, 2018, www.sandiegouniontribune.com; Richard Gonzales, "ACLU: Administration Is Still Separating Migrant Families Despite Court Order To Stop," *NPR*, July 30, 2019, www.npr.org.

115 Jessica Jones, Katharina Obser, and Jennifer Podkul, "Betraying Family Values: How Immigration Policy at the United States Border is Separating Families," Women's Refugee Commission / Lutheran Immigration and Refugee Services / Kids in Need of Defense, Jan. 10, 2017, https://supportkind.org.

116 Ms. L. v. ICE, 310 F.Supp. 3d 1133, 1144 (S.D. Cal. 2018) ("[T]he practice of separating these families was implemented without any effective system or procedure for (1) tracking the children after they were separated from their parents, (2) enabling communication between the parents and their children after separation, and (3) reuniting the parents and children after the parents are returned to immigration custody following completion of their criminal sentence. . . . The unfortunate reality is that under the present system migrant children are not accounted for with the same efficiency and accuracy as property. Certainly, that cannot satisfy the requirements of due process."); *see also* Jones et al., "Betraying Family Values," 7–8 (warning, in early 2017, about the lack of "consistent or comprehensive mechanisms to document family status or trace family members").

117 *See* Julia Ainsley and Annie Rose Ramos, "Inside Tornillo: The Expanded Tent City for Migrant Children," *NBC News*, Oct. 12, 2018, www.nbcnews.com; *see also* John Burnett, "Inside the Largest and Most Controversial Shelter for Migrant Children in the U.S.," *NPR*, Feb. 13, 2019, www.npr.org.

118 *See* previous note; *see also* Tom Hals and Kristina Cooke, "Hundreds of Migrant Children Held in U.S. Tent City for Months: Filings," Oct. 22, 2018, *Reuters*, www.reuters.com.

119 Youth Law *Flores* Congressional Briefing, 8–9; *see also* Miram Jordan, "Thousands of Migrant Children Could Be Released After Sponsor Policy Change," *New York Times*, Dec. 18, 2018, www.nytimes.com; *see also* Danielle Silva, "ICE Arrested 170 Immigrants Seeking to Sponsor Migrant Children," *NBC News*, Dec. 11, 2018, www.nbcnews.com.

120 Youth Law *Flores* Congressional Briefing, 8–12 (describing ORR demands on sponsors including move to a different neighborhood, move to a larger apartment or house, reduce the total number of children living in the home, get a second job to support the child, etc.).

121 Ibid. (discussing requirements that children take psychotropic medications before they would be released and further requiring the family to show that they could continue to pay for the medication; refusal to release children experiencing mental health issues until they are "stable" even though their distress was exacerbated by detention and separation from the families; institution of a new rule that required the director of ORR to personally approve release of any child who had

ever been in a heightened placement). The 2018 Office of the Inspector General's report touches briefly on use of psychotropic medicines at ORR facilities, discussing a few cases of potential misuse, but stops short of making any recommendations. *See* Harper, "Care Provider Facilities Described Challenges," 29.

122 Ibid., 3, 12 (Between Dec. 2017 and Dec. 2018 the population of children in ORR custody increased from appx. 7,000 to appx 14,000).

123 In FY 2018, the year the new rules went into effect, ICE referred 49,100 children to ORR and only 34,953 children were released to sponsors. The previous year, ICE referred 40,810 children to ORR and 42,497 children were released to sponsors. Facts and Data, Office of Refugee Resettlement, www.acf.hhs.gov.

124 Under pressure to stop separating children from their parents, President Trump directed that the children be detained *with* their parents during the pendency of the parents' criminal prosecutions. "Affording Congress an Opportunity to Address Family Separation," 83 Fed. Reg. 29435 (June 25, 2018). This "solution" was rejected by the court implementing *Flores*. Order Denying Defendant's' Ex Parte Application for Limited Relief from Settlement Agreement, Flores v. Sessions, 85-cv-04544 (C.D. Cal. July 9, 2018), at 5. At the same time, the court in *Ms. L* certified a nationwide class and issued a preliminary injunction ordering the administration to stop separating families unless the parent was found to be unfit and a danger to the child and further ordering the government to reunite the families already separated. Order Granting Plaintiffs' Motion for Classwide Preliminary Injunction, Ms. L v. ICE, 18-cv-0428 (S.D. Cal. June 26, 2018). These two rulings effectively forced the Trump administration to end the zero tolerance policy.

125 Congressional Research Service, "The Trump Administration's 'Zero Tolerance' Immigration Enforcement Policy," 2; *see also* Gonzales, "Administration Is Still Separating Migrant Families Despite Court Order."

126 Julia Ainsley and Jacob Soboroff, "Lawyers Have Found the Parents of 105 Separated Migrant Children in Past Month," *NBC News*, Feb. 24, 2021, www.nbcnews.com.

127 Jasmine Aguilera, "120 Children Remain in ICE Detention Despite Court Order for Them to Be Released Due to COVID-19 Concerns," *Time*, Aug. 14, 2020, https://time.com.

128 Ibid.

129 Patricia Sulbarán Lovera, "The Migrant Girl, 9, Detained by US for 531 Days and Counting," *BBC News*, Feb. 3, 2021, www.bbc.com. Parents can waive their children's right to release under *Flores*.

130 Sarah Mehta, "Deportation by Default: Mental Disability, Unfair Hearings, and Indefinite Detention in the U.S. Immigration System," ACLU / Human Rights Watch, July 2010, www.aclu.org, 16–17.

131 Sarah Filone and Christopher M. King, "The Emerging Standard of Competence in Immigration Removal Proceedings: A Review for Forensic Mental Health Professionals," *Psychology, Public Policy, and Law* 21, no. 1 (2015): 60 (estimating, in 2015, 1,000–1,700 detainees with serious mental illness on a given day).

132 Renuka Rayasam, "Migrant Mental Health Crisis Spirals in ICE Detention Facilities," Politico, July 21, 2019, www.politico.com (estimating that 3,000–6,000 detainees on a given day have a mental illness but citing practitioners who think the number is much larger, possibly as high as 30% of the total detainee population, which would be 15,000 per day or 125,000 per year at current detention rates).

133 Section 504 of the Rehabilitation Act of 1973, 29 USC § 794; Title II of the Americans with Disabilities Act, 42 USC § 1213; 6 CFR pt. 15.

134 "U.S. Immigration and Customs Enforcement Health Services Corps Fiscal Year 2020," U.S. Immigration and Customs Enforcement, www.ice.gov, 6.

135 Ibid., 10, 13, 23.

136 Performance Based National Detention Standards, U.S. Immigration and Customs Enforcement, 2011 (Rev. 2016), 4.3 Medical Care, www.ice.gov (hereinafter "ICE PBNDS").

137 Standards for mental health services in correctional facilities, National Commission on Correctional Health Care, 2015.

138 ICE PBNDS.

139 "Accreditation FAQs," National Commission on Correctional Health Care, 2021, www.ncchc.org.

140 "ICE Still Struggles to Hire and Retain Staff for Mental Health Cases in Immigration Detention," DHS Office of Inspector General, OIG-16–113-VR, July 21, 2016, www.oig.dhs.gov; see also Complaint, Fraihat v. U.S. Immigration and Customs Enforcement, 19-cv-01546 (C.D. Cal. Aug. 19, 2019) https://creeclaw.org, 111–113 (describing pervasive problems with understaffing in ICE facilities, including two facilities that only had a single social worker as the mental health provider despite each facility having over 50 detainees with mental health disabilities, and another facility with no full-time mental health provider at all).

141 See, e.g., "Complaint Filed with DHS Oversight Bodies Calls for Improvements to Medical and Mental Health Care of Immigrants in Aurora Detention Center," American Immigration Counsel, AILA Doc. No. 18060433, June 4, 2018, www.aila.org; see also "Concerns about ICE Detainee Treatment and Care at Four Detention Facilities," DHS Office of Inspector General, OIG-19–47, June 3, 2019, www.oig.dhs.gov; see also "Concerns about ICE Detainee Treatment and Care at Detention Facilities," DHS Office of Inspector General, OIG-18–32, Dec. 11, 2017, www.oig.dhs.gov.

142 See "ICE's Inspections and Monitoring of Detention Facilities Do Not Lead to Sustained Compliance or Systemic Improvements," DHS Office of Inspector General, OIG-18–67, June 26, 2018, www.oig.dhs.gov ("Neither type of inspection ICE uses to examine detention facilities ensures consistent compliance with detention standards or comprehensive correction of identified deficiencies. . . . Moreover, ICE does not adequately follow up on identified deficiencies or systematically hold facilities accountable for correcting deficiencies[.]"); see also "ICE Does Not Fully Use Contracting Tools to Hold Detention Facility Contractors Accountable for Failing to Meet Performance Standards," DHS Office of Inspector General,

OIG-19–18, Jan. 29, 2019, www.oig.dhs.gov ("Between . . . 2015, and . . . 2018, ICE imposed financial penalties on only two occasions, despite documenting thousands of instances of the facilities' failures to comply with detention standards. Instead of holding facilities accountable through financial penalties, ICE issued waivers to facilities with deficient conditions, seeking to exempt them from complying with certain standards.").

143 Harper, "Care Provider Facilities Described Challenges," 15–16.

144 "The Detention of Immigrant Children with Disabilities in California: A Snapshot," Disability Rights California, July 26, 2019, www.disabilityrightsca.org.

145 John Kelly, Secretary, DHS, "Enforcement of the Immigration Laws to Serve the National Interest," U.S. Department of Homeland Security, Feb. 20, 2017, www.dhs.gov.

146 Jeh Charles Johnson, Secretary, DHS, "Policies for the Apprehension, Detention and Removal of Undocumented Immigrants," U.S. Department of Homeland Security, Nov. 20, 2014, www.dhs.gov.

147 Author conversation with ICE officer, circa 2016; *see also* Rayasam, "Migrant Mental Health Crisis Spirals" (only 21 of the 230 ICE detention facilities offered any kind of in-person mental health services from the agency's medical staff in 2016; the detainee population has in the meantime grown more than 50%); *see also* "ICE Still Struggles to Hire and Retain Staff," 6 (recommending ICE place mentally ill detainees only at facilities that are equipped to care for them).

148 "Isolated: ICE Confines Some Detainees with Mental Illness in Solitary for Months," Project on Government Oversight, Aug. 14, 2019, www.pogo.org.

149 Spencer Woodman et al., "Solitary Voices: Thousands of Immigrants Suffer in Solitary Confinement in ICE Detention," *The Intercept*, May 21, 2019, https://theintercept.com.

150 INA § 212(d)(5)(A); 8 CFR § 212.5(b); 8 CFR § 235.3(c) (providing that asylum seekers who have established a credible fear of persecution and are referred to removal proceedings can be paroled under this standard).

151 8 CFR § 212.5(b).

152 "Parole of Arriving Aliens Found to Have a Credible Fear of Persecution or Torture," U.S. Immigration and Customs Enforcement, Dec. 8, 2009, www.ice.gov.

153 Ibid.

154 Ibid.; *see also* Damus v. Nielsen, 313 F.Supp. 3d 317 (D.D.C. 2018) (ordering DHS to follow the directive and provide individualized parole determinations to asylum seekers who have passed a credible fear interview).

155 Matter of Fatahi, 26 I&N Dec. 791, 795 n.3 (BIA 2016); Matter of Guerra, 24 I&N Dec. 37, 40 (BIA 2006).

156 *See* Mark Noferi and Robert Koulish, "The Immigration Detention Risk Assessment," 29 Georgetown Immigration Law Journal 45, 67–69 (2014) (describing how the 2013 RCA tool determines danger to the community and flight risk).

157 Ibid.

158 Mica Rosenberg and Reade Levinson, "Trump's Catch-and-Detain Policy Snares Many Who Have Long Called U.S. Home," *Reuters*, June 20, 2018, www.reuters.com.

159 Adi Robertson, "ICE Rigged Its Algorithms to Keep Immigrants in Jail, Claims Lawsuit," *The Verge*, Mar. 3, 2020, www.theverge.com.

160 "Seeking Release from Immigration Detention," American Immigration Council, Sept. 13, 2019, www.americanimmigrationcouncil.org; *see also* "Immigration: Alternatives to Detention (ATD) Programs," Congressional Research Service, R45804, July 8, 2019, https://fas.org.

161 "Immigration: Alternatives to Detention Programs."

162 Ibid; *see also* BI Incorporated website, https://bi.com.

163 Ibid., 7–8.

164 "The Family Case Management Program: Why Case Management Can and Must Be Part of the US Approach to Immigration," Women's Refugee Commission, June 13, 2019, www.womensrefugeecommission.org.

165 8 USC § 1231(a)(6); 8 CFR § 241.4; 8 CFR § 241.13; 8 CFR § 241.14.

166 Zadvydas v. Davis, 533 U.S. 678 (2001).

167 *Psychiatric Services in Jails and Prisons*, 3rd ed. (Arlington, VA: American Psychiatric Publishing, 2016).

168 Charles v. Orange County, 925 F.3d 73 (2nd Cir. 2019); *see also* Wakefield v. Thompson, 177 F.3d 1160 (9th Cir. 1999) (holding that the state has a duty to provide a supply of medication "sufficient to ensure that [the released prisoner] has that medication available during the period of time reasonably necessary to permit him to consult a doctor and obtain a new supply").

169 Experience of author. Most recently observed with a client released from ICE detention in January 2021.

170 Experience of authors; *see also* Charles, 925 F.3d 73 (describing manner of release of plaintiffs).

171 *See* "Sent 'Home' with Nothing: The Deportation of Jamaicans with Mental Disabilities," Georgetown University Law Center Human Rights Institute, 2011, http://scholarship.law.georgetown.edu, 24 (interview with Jamaican government minister who explains that the United States, unlike the United Kingdom, has no practice of informing Jamaican authorities of deportees' medical needs or providing them with medication).

3. FORMS OF REMOVAL RELIEF AND RELATED PSYCHOLEGAL ISSUES

1 Kirk Heilbrun, Thomas Grisso, Alan M. Goldstein, and Casey LaDuke, *Foundations of Forensic Mental Health Assessment* (Oxford University Press, 2013).

2 Thomas Grisso, *Evaluating Competencies: Forensic Assessments and Instruments*, vol. 16. (Springer Science & Business Media, 2006).

3 Heilbrun et al., *Foundations*.

4 This chapter is not meant to be a comprehensive guide for attorneys. Legal requirements and procedural contexts that present psycholegal issues are empha-

sized, while others that would not be relevant to the work of MHPs are deemphasized or elided.

5   Kirk Heilbrun, *Principles of Forensic Mental Health Assessment*, vol. 12. (Springer Science & Business Media, 2006).

6   INA § 208(b)(1)(B)(iii) / 8 U.S.C. § 1158(b)(1)(B)(iii) as amended by the REAL ID Act Pub.L. 109–13, 119 Stat. 302, enacted May 11, 2005; *see also* Matter of J-Y-C, 24 I&N Dec. 260 (BIA 2007) (finding respondent incredible for inconsistencies, some of which did not go to the heart of the claim); *see also* Lin v. Mukasey, 534 F.3d 162, 167 (2nd Cir. 2008) (IJ can rely on any inconsistency or omission in making an adverse credibility finding).

7   *See* Matter of Collado Reyes, 2018 WL 4692860 (BIA 2018) (unpublished) (IJ found respondent's testimony incredible based on inconsistencies that he alleged were due to memory issues); Matter of Acosta-Ponce, 2006 WL 1455324 (BIA 2006) (unpublished) ("while the respondent attempts to explain the contradictions by pointing to his testimony that he has memory problems . . . no medical evidence demonstrating that the respondent experiences memory difficulties has been submitted"); Matter of Ramirez, 2012 WL 3911867 (BIA 2012) (unpublished) (IJ found respondent not credible because he could not remember the name of the airport he flew into when he arrived in the United States; the BIA questioned this determination because respondent had difficulty remembering other things as well, such as the date of his marriage, that were not in doubt).

8   *See* Deborah Davis & William C. Follette, Foibles of Witness Memory for Traumatic/High Profile Events, 66 J. Air L. & Com. 1421 (2001); *see also* J. Douglas Bremner, "Traumatic Stress: Effects on the Brain," *Dialogues Clinical Neuroscience* 8 (2006): 445, 448–449; *see also* Juliet Cohen, "Questions of Credibility: Omissions, Discrepancies and Errors of Recall in the Testimony of Asylum Seekers," 13 *Int'l J. Refugee L.* 293 (2001).

9   In one case, the IJ found an asylum seeker incredible because "one normally doesn't forget" the date of such a "traumatic event" as rape. The BIA upheld the IJ's credibility determination. Longwe v. Keisler, 251 F. App'x 718, 720 (2nd Cir. 2007) (overturning the BIA). In another case, a rape survivor was found not credible because she forgot the number of times she was raped. The BIA and circuit court upheld the IJ's determination, relying in part on the failure of her experts to sufficiently connect the scientific literature to her particular case. One expert did not examine her, and the other stated generally that people with her diagnosis often experience amnesia for aspects of traumatic experiences but "did not say that [she] suffered those symptoms." Zeru v. Gonzales, 503 F.3d 59 (1st Cir. 2007).

10 Matter of A-S, 21 I&N Dec. 1106 (BIA 1998) ("Because an appellate body may not as easily review a demeanor finding from a paper record, a credibility finding which is supported by an adverse inference drawn from an alien's demeanor generally should be accorded a high degree of deference"), *citing* Sarvia-Quintanilla v. INS, 767 F.2d 1387, 1395 (9th Cir. 1985) (holding that an immigration judge is in the unique position to observe the alien's tone and demeanor, to explore inconsis-

tencies in the testimony, and to determine whether the testimony has "the ring of truth").

11 *See* Charles F. Bond Jr. and Bella M. DePaulo, "Accuracy of Deception Judgments," *Personality and Social Psychology Review* 10, no. 3 (Aug. 2006): 214–234 (stating people, including experienced judges, are not particularly good at identifying deception).

12 *See* Jia E. Loy, Hannah Rohde, and Martin Corley, "Cues to Lying May Be Deceptive: Speaker and Listener Behaviour in an Interactive Game of Deception," *Journal of Cognition* 1, no. 1 (2018): 42, http://doi.org/10.5334/joc.46.

13 *See, e.g.*, Matter of A-S, 21 I&N Dec. 1106 (BIA 1998) (upholding IJ's determination that respondent was not credible, in part because he testified in a "halting" and "hesitant" manner and left details vague); Matter of B-, 21 I&N Dec. 66 (BIA 1995) (the IJ below had found respondent not credible because he tended to look down at the desk rather than at the judge; the BIA overruled this determination, saying the respondent may have been looking down because he was concentrating on the question); *see also* Nicholas Narbutas, "The Ring of Truth: Demeanor and Due Process in U.S. Asylum Law," 50 *Colum. Hum. Rts. L. Rev.* 348 (2018) (arguing that demeanor, as currently employed within asylum adjudication, creates a drastic risk of erroneous denial of meritorious applications because judging based on demeanor invites personal bias into IJ decision-making, fosters and exacerbates institutional bias, is an inaccurate, widely discredited method of ascertaining truthfulness, and is unreviewable).

14 *See, e.g.*, Sanga v. Gonzalez, 121 F. App'x 841, 843 (10th Cir. 2005) (IJ found asylum applicant incredible when he testified that he remained hidden in the bathroom for an hour after soldiers broke into his home, shot his father, and raped his sister because it was not a "logical human response" to wait that long to emerge from hiding).

15 *See generally* Victoria Follette et al., "Cumulative Trauma," *Journal of Interpersonal Violence* 9, no. 25 (1996): 33; Judith Herman, *Trauma and Recovery: The Aftermath of Violence—From Domestic Abuse to Political Terrorism* (Hachette UK, 1992): 86–87; Naomi Breslau et al., "Previous Exposure to Trauma and PTSD Effects of Subsequent Trauma," *American Journal of Psychiatry* 156 (1999): 902, 906.

16 For a thorough discussion of the problems inherent in evaluating trauma survivors' credibility based on factors such as consistency, detail, inherent plausibility, and demeanor, *see* Stephen Paskey, "Telling Refugee Stories: Trauma, Credibility, and the Adversarial Adjudication of Claims for Asylum," 56 *Santa Clara L. Rev.* 457 (2016), https://digitalcommons.law.buffalo.edu.

17 *See, e.g.*, Huang v. Holder, 620 F.3d 33, 37 (1st Cir. 2010); Musollari v. Mukasey, 545 F.3d 505, 510 (7th Cir. 2008).

18 INA § 101(a)(42) / 8 USC § 1101(a)(42); *see also* INA § 208 / 8 USC § 1158; *see also* 8 CFR § 208.13. The mistreatment does not have to be based on an actual characteristic of the victim—it is sufficient that the persecutor perceives the victim as having particular characteristic and bases their persecution on that (for example,

an HIV+ individual may be persecuted because they are perceived as gay, regardless of their actual sexual orientation). *See* Matter of Kasinga, 21 I&N Dec. 357, 365 (BIA 1996); "RAIO Directorate Officer Training: Definition of Persecution and Eligibility based on Past Persecution," USCIS Refugee, Asylum, and International Operations Directorate, 2019, www.uscis.gov (hereinafter "USCIS RAIO Officer Training: Persecution")

19 *See* Matter of Laipenieks, 18 I&N Dec. 433, 457 (BIA 1983); Korablina v. INS, 158 F.3d 1038, 1043 (9th Cir. 1998); Miranda v. INS, 139 F.3d 624, 626 (8th Cir. 1998).

20 "It is important to take into account the individual circumstances of each case and to consider the feelings, opinions, age, and physical and psychological characteristics of the applicant in determining whether the harm suffered or feared rises to the level of persecution. For example, one may hold passionate political or religious convictions, the hindrance of which would cause great suffering; while another may not have such strong convictions." USCIS RAIO Officer Training: Persecution, 15–16.

21 *See* Ouk v. Gonzales, 464 F.3d 108, 111 (1st Cir. 2006) ("a finding of past persecution might rest on a showing of psychological harm"); Mashiri v. Ashcroft, 383 F.3d 1112, 1120 (9th Cir. 2004) ("Persecution may be emotional or psychological, as well as physical."); Fatin v. INS, 12 F.3d 1233, 1241–42 (3rd Cir. 1993); Matter of A-K-, 24 I&N Dec 275 (BIA 2007); Sumolang v. Holder, 723 F.3d 1080 (9th Cir. 2013).

22 USCIS RAIO Officer Training: Persecution, 31 ("Evidence of the applicant's psychological and emotional characteristics, such as the applicant's age or trauma suffered as a result of past harm, are relevant to determining whether psychological harm amounts to persecution.").

23 *See* Matter of Acosta, 19 I&N Dec. 211 (BIA 1985); INS v. Cardoza-Fonseca, 480 U.S. 421, 431 (1987); INS v. Stevic, 467 U.S. 407 (1984); Matter of Mogharrabi, 19 I&N Dec. 439, 445 (BIA 1987); *see also* "RAIO Directorate Officer Training: Well-Founded Fear," USCIS Refugee, Asylum, and International Operations Directorate, 2019, www.uscis.gov.

24 8 CFR §§ 208.13(b)(1)(ii); (iii).

25 Ibid.

26 As more people have sought refuge in the United States, the number of credible fear interviews has "skyrocketed." USCIS completed over 102,204 credible fear determinations in 2019 as compared with only 5,523 in 2009. Of these, 75,252 individuals passed the interview and were referred to removal proceedings. "Fact Sheet, Asylum in the United States," American Immigration Council, June 11, 2020, www.americanimmigrationcouncil.org.

27 INA §§ 208(b)(1)(B)(iii), 235(b)(1)(B)(v), 241(b)(3)(C).

28 INA § 208(b)(1)(B)(iii); *see also* "Policy Memorandum: Guidance for Processing Reasonable Fear, Credible Fear, Asylum, and Refugee Claims in Accordance with Matter of A-B," U.S. Citizenship and Immigration Services, PM 602–0162, July 11, 2018, www.uscis.gov.

29 *See* "Questions and Answers: Credible Fear Screening," U.S. Citizenship and Immigration Services, www.uscis.gov.

30 People who fail the credible fear interview can seek to appeal the asylum officer's determination to an immigration judge. The judge will make a de novo determination that includes a new assessment of the individual's credibility. 8 CFR § 1003.42.

31 *See* Matter of Frentescu, 18 I&N Dec. 244 (BIA1982); Matter of C-, 20 I&N Dec. 529 (BIA 1992); Matter of Gonzalez, 19 I&N Dec. 682 (BIA 1988).

32 Generally speaking, the BIA is immigration's highest "court" apart from the Supreme Court. But the circuit courts of appeals overrule the BIA for cases within their jurisdiction. As a result, the immigration law varies slightly throughout the country. *See* chapter 1 for more information.

33 Compare N-A-M-, 24 I&N Dec. 336, 343 (BIA 2007) ("offender characteristics" are irrelevant because they "may operate to reduce a sentence but do not diminish the gravity of a crime") *and* Matter of G-G-S, 26 I&N Dec. 339, 347 (BIA 2014) (mental health condition of the applicant should not be considered when determining whether the crime was "particularly serious") *with* Gomez-Sanchez v. Sessions, 887 F.3d 893 (9th Cir. 2018) (applicant's mental health condition at time of crime should be considered).

34 INA § 208(a)(2)(B); 8 CFR § 208.4.

35 Karen Musalo, Susan M. Meffert, and Akra Osman Abdo, "The Role of Mental Health Professionals in Political Asylum Processing," *Journal of the American Academy of Psychiatry and the Law* 38 (2010): 479.

36 INA §§ 208(b)(1), 240(c)(4)(A)(ii) / 8 USC §§ 1158(b)(1), 1229a(c)(4)(A)(ii); Matter of Pula, 19 I&N Dec. 467, 472–74 (BIA 1987); Matter of A-B-, 27 I&N Dec. 316 (A.G. 2018).

37 INA § 241(b)(3) / 8 USC § 1231(b)(3); 8 CFR § 208.16.

38 Ibid.

39 *See* Niang v. Gonzales, 492 F.3d 505, 512 (4th Cir. 2007) (psychological harm, by itself, cannot amount to persecution for the purposes of withholding). Note that this decision is binding only on immigration courts located in the Fourth Circuit.

40 8 CFR § 208.16(b)(1).

41 The regulations implementing the Convention can be found at 8 CFR §§ [1]208.16 to [1]208.18.

42 8 CFR § 1208.16(c)(2).

43 8 CFR § 1208.18(a)(1). To constitute torture under the Convention and implementing regulations, the act must also be committed by or at the acquiescence of the government, and it must be done for an improper purpose rather than as part of a lawful sanction. Id.

44 8 CFR § 1208.18(a)(2).

45 8 CFR § 1208.18(a)(3) (emphasis added).

46 Kone v. Holder, 620 F.3d 760 (7th Cir. 2010); *see also* Kone v. Holder, 596 F.3d 141 (2nd Cir. 2010) (no relation).

47 *See, e.g.*, Alexander v. Whittaker, 16-cv-4003 (2nd Cir. Jan. 8, 2019) (summary order), *available at* https://casetext.com.

48 8 CFR § 1208.16.

49 8 CFR § 1208.17(a).

50 8 C.F.R. § 208.17(d).

51 An "aggravated felony" includes any conviction (even if not a felony) for drug sale or possession with intent to sell, any conviction that involves violence or theft when the sentence is a year or more, even if that sentence is immediately suspended in favor of probation or rehabilitative treatment (as is common in many jurisdictions), and various other crimes, some of which are considered quite minor by the criminal justice system that imposed them. INA § 101(a)(43).

52 INA § 236(c) / 8 USC § 1226(c).

53 *See* E. F. Torrey et al., "More Mentally Ill Persons Are in Jails and Prisons Than Hospitals: A Survey of the States Treatment Advocacy Center," Treatment Advocacy Center, 2010, www.treatmentadvocacycenter.org.

54 Barton F. Evans III and Giselle A. Hass, *Forensic Psychological Assessment in Immigration Court: A Guidebook for Evidence-Based and Ethical Practice* (Routledge, 2018).

55 Gilberto De Jesús-Rentas, James Boehnlein, and Landy Sparr, "Central American Victims of Gang Violence as Asylum Seekers: The Role of the Forensic Expert," *Journal of the American Academy of Psychiatry and the Law Online* 38, no. 4 (2010): 490–498.

56 Stuart L. Lustig, Sarah Kureshi, Kevin L. Delucchi, Vincent Iacopino, and Samantha C. Morse. "Asylum Grant Rates Following Medical Evaluations of Maltreatment Among Political Asylum Applicants in the United States," *Journal of Immigrant and Minority Health* 10, no. 1 (2008): 7–15.

57 "Istanbul Protocol: Manual on the Effective Investigation and Documentation of Torture and Other Cruel, Inhuman or Degrading Treatment or Punishment," United Nations, 2004, www.ohchr.org.

58 Mitchell Bayne et al., "Assessing the Efficacy and Experience of In-Person Versus Telephonic Psychiatric Evaluations for Asylum Seekers in the US," *Psychiatry Research* 282 (2019): 112612.

59 Musalo et al., "The Role of Mental Health."

60 INA § 101(a)(15)(U) / 8 USC § 1101(a)(15)(U).

61 INA § 101(a)(15)(U)(iii) / 8 U.S.C. § 1101(a)(15)(U)(iii); 8 CFR § 214.14(b)(1).

62 8 CFR § 214.14(a)(8).

63 8 CFR § 214.14(b)(1).

64 Ibid.

65 8 CFR § 214.14(a)(14).

66 8 CFR § 214.14(a)(14)(i); *see also* "U Visa Law Enforcement Resource Guide," U.S. Citizenship and Immigration Services, 2019, www.uscis.gov, 8.

67 In re: Petitioner: [IDENTIFYING INFORMATION REDACTED BY AGENCY] (AAO, June 12, 2013), *available at* www.uscis.gov.

68 In re: Petitioner: [IDENTIFYING INFORMATION REDACTED BY AGENCY] (AAO, Nov. 27, 2013) 2013 WL 8118197.

69 INA § 204(a)(1)(A)(iii)(I)(bb); INA § 204(a)(1)(B)(ii)(I)(bb).

70 8 CFR § 204.2(c)(1)(vi).

71 INA § 204(a)(1)(A)(iii)(II)(bb); INA § 204(a)(1)(B)(ii)(bb).

72 INA § 204(a)(1)(C) / 8 USC § 1154(a)(1)(C). Only a very limited category of criminal convictions is eligible to be excused in this manner. *See* INA § 212(h) (list of pardonable convictions; does not include, *inter alia*, drug crimes beyond marijuana possession).

73 *See* Evan Stark, "Re-Presenting Woman Battering: From Battered Woman Syndrome to Coercive Control," 58 *Alb. L. Rev.* 973 (1994–95); *see also* Mary Ann Dutton and Lisa Goodman, "Coercion in Intimate Partner Violence: Towards a New Conceptualization," *Sex Roles* 52, nos. 11/12 (June 2005).

74 For example, PTSD caused by trauma might help explain why an individual committed a crime. *See* Susan Roth et al., "Complex PTSD in Victims Exposed to Sexual and Physical Abuse: Results from the DSM-IV Field Trial for Posttraumatic Stress Disorder," *Journal of Traumatic Stress*, 10 (1997): 539–555; Herman, *Trauma and Recovery*, 86–87 ("People subjected to prolonged repeated trauma develop an insidious, progressive form of post-traumatic stress disorder. . . . The intrusive symptoms [nightmares, flashbacks, extreme reactions to reminders of traumatic episodes] . . . may persist which little change for many years[.]").

75 "Coercion" is defined for the purpose of the T visa statute as "threats of serious harm to or physical restraint against any person; any scheme, plan, or pattern intended to cause a person to believe that failure to perform an act would result in serious harm to or physical restraint against any person; or the abuse or threatened abuse of the legal process." 8 CFR § 214.11(a).

76 8 CFR § 214.11(g)(1)(v).

77 8 CFR § 214.11(b)(3)(ii).

78 8 CFR § 214.11(b)(4).

79 *See* INA § 212(d)(13); INA § 212(d)(3).

80 Virginia Barber-Rioja and Alexandra Garcia-Mansilla, "Forensic Mental Health Assessment in Immigration Court," in *The Oxford Handbook of Psychology and Law*, ed. David DeMatteo & Kyle C. Scherr (New York, NY: Oxford University Press), in press.

81 Heilbrun, *Principles of Forensic*.

82 Randall D. Marshall, Mark Olfson, Fredric Hellman, Carlos Blanco, Mary Guardino, and Elmer L. Struening, "Comorbidity, Impairment, and Suicidality in Subthreshold PTSD," *American Journal of Psychiatry* 158, no. 9 (2001): 1467–1473.

83 Andrew W. Kane, Erin M. Nelson, Joel A. Dvoskin, and Steven E. Pitt, "Evaluation for Personal Injury Claims," in *Best Practices in Forensic Mental Health Assessment. Forensic Assessments in Criminal and Civil Law: A Handbook for Lawyers*, ed. R. Roesch and P. A. Zapf (Oxford University Press, 2013), 148–160.

84 Barber-Rioja and Garcia-Mansilla, "Forensic Mental Health."

85 William J. Koch, Rami Nader, and Michelle Haring, "The Science and Pseudoscience of Assessing Psychological Injuries," *in Psychological Science in the Courtroom: Consensus and Controversy*, ed. Kevin S. Douglas and Scott O. Lilienfeld (Guildford Press, 2009): 263–283.

86 Ibid.

87 INA § 240A(b)(1).

88 Matter of N-J-B-, Int. Dec. 3415 (BIA 1999); Matter of Monreal, 23 I&N Dec. 56 (BIA 2001).

89 The definition of "qualifying relative" varies based on the waiver, but usually includes a spouse or parent. Sometimes a child can be a qualifying relative as well.

90 INA § 212(h).

91 INA § 212(i).

92 INA § 212(a)(9)(B)(v) / 8 USC § 1182(a)(9)(B)(v); Provisional unlawful presence waiver. The provisional unlawful presence waiver is available to people who are married to a US citizen and are not eligible to get a green card because of the way they entered the country (without a visa, usually by crossing the border).

93 *See* Matter of Ngai, 19 I&N Dec. 245 (BIA 1984) ("Common results of the bar, such as separation, financial difficulties, etc. in themselves are insufficient to warrant approval of an application unless combined with much more extreme impacts"); *see also* USCIS Policy Manual Vol. 9 Part B Ch. 5 Extreme Hardship, U.S. Citizenship and Immigration Services, www.uscis.gov.

94 Ibid.; *see also* USCIS Policy Alert, Determining Extreme Hardship, U.S. Citizenship and Immigration Services, PA-2016–05, Oct. 21, 2016, www.uscis.gov (describing changes to the policy manual including the addition of the nonexhaustive list of factors).

95 Ibid.

96 Ibid.

97 INA § 212(i)(1).

98 8 § CFR 214.11(b)(4).

99 8 CFR § 214.11(i)(1) (stating that the hardship is a higher standard than "extreme hardship" as described in [former] 8 CFR § 240.58, which laid out the standard for suspension of deportation, a form of relief that has been removed from the INA but which remains echoed in current extreme hardship standards).

100 8 CFR § 214.11(i)(2).

101 INA § 245(l) / 8 USC § 1255 (l); 8 CFR § 245.23(e).

102 8 USC § 1101(a)(27)(J) / INA § 101(a)(27)(J); 8 USC § 1255(h) / INA § 245(h).

103 INA § 245(h)(2)(A).

104 INA § 245(h)(2)(B), as amended by the Miscellaneous and Technical Corrections Act of 1991 § 301(d)(2); *see also* "Memorandum, Trafficking Victims Protection Reauthorization Act of 2008: Special Immigrant Juvenile Status Provisions," U.S. Citizenship and Immigration Services, HQOPS 70, 8.5, Mar. 24, 2009, www.uscis.gov, 4–5.

105 INA § 209(c) / 8 USC § 1159(c).

106 INA § 245(m) / 8 USC § 1255(m); 8 CFR § 245.24(b)(6).

107 INA § 245(h)(2)(B) / 8 USC § 1255(h)(2)(B).

108 This language, or substantially similar language, is echoed in other parts if the immigration law as well. For example, being a member of the Communist Party is a ground of inadmissibility, but this ground is waivable for humanitarian purposes, to ensure family unity, or if it is otherwise in the public interest, so long as the immigrant does not pose a security risk. 8 USC § 1182(a)(3) (D)(4).

109 Bruce I. Frumkin and Joan Friedland, "Forensic Evaluations in Immigration Cases: Evolving Issues," *Behavioral Sciences & the Law* 13, no. 4 (1995): 477–489.

110 Randy Capps, Michael Fix, and Jie Zong, *A Profile of US Children with Unauthorized Immigrant Parents* (Washington, DC: Migration Policy Institute, 2016).

111 Evans and Hass, *Forensic.*

112 Cerola Suárez-Orozco, Irina LG Todorova, and Josephine Louie, "Making Up for Lost Time: The Experience of Separation and Reunification Among Immigrant Families," *Family Process* 41, no. 4 (2002): 625–643.

113 Wylonis and Billick, "Child and Adolescence."

114 Evans and Hass, *Forensic.*

115 B. A. Hake and D. L. Banks, "The Hake Hardship Scale: A Quantitative System for Assessment of Hardship in Immigration Cases Based on a Statistical Analysis of AAO Decisions," *Bender's Immigration Bulletin* 10 (2005): 403–420.

116 Requires good moral character for the past ten years. INA § 240A(b).

117 Requires good moral character for the past five years. INA § 240B / 8 USC § 1229c.

118 Requires good moral character for the past five years. INA § 316 / 8 USC § 1427.

119 INA §101(f) / 8 USC § 1101(f) (laying out the bars to good moral character).

120 Ibid.

121 Evans and Hass, *Forensic.*

122 Gary B. Melton, John Petrila, Norman G. Poythress, Christopher Slobogin, Randy K. Otto, Douglas Mossman, and Lois O. Condie, *Psychological Evaluations for the Courts: A Handbook for Mental Health Professionals and Lawyers* (Guildford Press, 2018).

123 Ibid, 287.

124 Ibid.

125 Ibid., 288.

126 Evans and Hass, *Forensic.*

127 Melton et al., *Psychological Evaluations*, 290.

128 USCIS Policy Manual Vol. 1 Part E Ch. 8 Discretionary Analysis, U.S. Citizenship and Immigration Services, www.uscis.gov, *citing* Matter of Marin, 16 I&N Dec. 581, 584 (BIA 1978); Matter of Buscemi, 19 I&N Dec. 628, 633 (BIA 1988); Matter of Edwards, 20 I&N Dec. 191, 195 (BIA 1990); Matter of Mendez-Morales, 21 I&N Dec. 296, 300 (BIA 1996).

129 Ibid., citing cases.

130 Ibid.

131 Being a "habitual drunkard" is a statutory bar to a finding of good moral character. INA § 101(f); 8 USC § 1101(f). Being a "drug abuser" or "addict" is a ground of inadmissibility. INA § 212(a)(1)(A)(iv); 8 USC § 1182(a)(1)(A)(iv).

132 Sharpless, Rebecca, "Addiction-Informed Immigration Reform," 94 *Wash. Law R.* 1891, 1910–11 (2019) https://digitalcommons.law.uw.edu.

133 Ibid.

134 8 CFR § 245.24 (b)(6). (Above this is discussed as a form of hardship-based relief because hardship is often considered when determining whether an immigrant's continued presence is in the public interest or is justified on humanitarian grounds. Hardship—to the applicant or others—is one potential equity that an adjudicator might consider when deciding whether a person deserves this or another discretionary form of relief.)

135 8 CFR §§ 245.24(d)(10–11); (f).

136 *See* USCIS Notice of Intent to Deny (Mar. 17, 2016) (applicant's arrests, which did not result in convictions, "appear to show you are a risk to the public safety and property of others") (on file with author).

137 INA § 240A(a).

138 *See* INS v. St. Cyr, 533 U.S. 289 (2001); Judulang v. Holder, 132 S. Ct. 476, 479 (2011); Matter of Abdelghany, 26 I&N Dec. 254 (BIA 2014).

139 "Fact Sheet: How the United States Immigration System Works," American Immigration Council, Oct. 2019, www.americanimmigrationcouncil.org (describing the major channels of legal immigration: family-based, employment-based, refugee/ asylee, and the diversity visa lottery).

140 To be immediately eligible for a green card the applicant must be an "immediate relative" of a US citizen. The only relationships that qualify are a spouse petitioning for a spouse, a parent petitioning for a child (the child must be under 21 and unmarried), and an adult over 21 petitioning for a parent. 8 USC § 1151(b)(2) (A)(i) / INA § 201(b)(2)(A)(i); INA § 101(b)(1) (definition of "child"). There is a backlog of many years for applicants who are petitioned by, for example, siblings or parents. *See* Visa Bulletin, U.S. Department of State, Feb. 2021, https://travel. state.gov. The longest waits are for married Mexican adult children of US citizens: people who applied on or before September 1, 1996, were finally eligible for their green cards in February 2021. Ibid.

141 This might happen because the criminal grounds of inadmissibility and deportability are not identical, and someone could be deportable for a conviction (i.e., gun possession) but still be admissible. *Compare* INA § 212(a)(2) / 8 USC § 1182(a) (2) *with* INA § 237(a)(2) / 8 USC § 1227(a)(2).

142 *See* USCIS Policy Manual Vol. 7 Part A Ch. 10 Legal Analysis and Use of Discretion, U.S. Citizenship and Immigration Services, www.uscis.gov.

143 *See* ibid. (current guidance as of February 2021); *see also* "Policy Alert: Use of Discretion for Adjustment of Status," U.S. Citizenship and Immigration Services, PA-2020–22, Nov. 17, 2020, www.uscis.gov (announcing the change); "Letter to

USCIS," Immigrant Legal Resource Center, Dec. 15, 2020, www.ilrc.org (objecting to the change).

144 Matter of Arai, 13 I&N Dec. 494 (BIA 1970), Matter of Lam, 16 I&N Dec. 432 (BIA 1978).

145 Final Rule: Inadmissibility on Public Charge Grounds, 84 FR 41292, effective Oct. 15, 2019, www.federalregister.gov. The rule was subsequently vacated by a court order, and the Biden administration has announced its intention to withdraw it. *See* "2019 Public Charge Rule Vacated and Removed; DHS Withdraws Proposed Rule Regarding the Affidavit of Support," DHS, Mar. 11, 2021.

146 Matter of D-A-C-, 27 I&N Dec. 575 (BIA 2019).

147 Ibid.

148 *See* "Consideration of Deferred Action for Childhood Arrivals (DACA)," U.S. Citizenship and Immigration Services, Jan. 21, 2021, www.uscis.gov.

149 *See* Demore v. Kim, 538 U.S. 510, 528 (2003); Matter of Valdez-Valdez, 21 I&N Dec. 703, 709 (BIA 1997); Matter of Drysdale, 20 I&N Dec. 815, 817 (BIA 1994).

150 *See generally* Aimee Mayer-Salins, "Practice Advisory, Mentally Incompetent But Deported Anyway: Strategies for Helping a Mentally Ill Client Return to the United States," Boston College Center for Human Rights and International Justice, Post-Deportation Human Rights Project, Sept. 2015, www.bc.edu; *see also* Aimee Mayer-Salins and Ann Garcia, "Practice Advisory Representing Noncitizens with Mental Illness," Catholic Legal Immigration Network, May 2020, https://clinicle-gal.org, 18–20.

4. ROLES OF MENTAL HEALTH PROFESSIONALS

1 Virginia Barber-Rioja and Alexandra Garcia-Mansilla, "Special considerations when conducting forensic psychological evaluations for IC," *Journal of Clinical Psychology* 75, no. 11 (2019): 2049–2059; Hope Ferdowsian, Katherine McKenzie, and Amy Zeidan, "Asylum medicine: Standard and best practices," *Health and Human Rights* 21, no. 1 (2019): 215–226.

2 Barber-Rioja and Garcia-Mansilla, "Special considerations;" Evert Bloemen, Erick Vloeberghs, and Celine Smits, "Psychological and psychiatric aspects of recounting traumatic events by asylum seekers," in R. Bruin, M. Reneman, and E. Bloemen, *Medico-legal reports and the istanbul protocol in asylum procedures* (Utrecht/Amsterdam: Pharos, Amnesty International, Dutch Council for Refugees, 2006); Barton F. Evans III and Giselle A. Hass, *Forensic psychological assessment in immigration court: A Guidebook for evidence-based and ethical practice* (Routledge, 2018); Bruce I. Frumkin, and Joan Friedland, "Forensic evaluations in immigration cases: Evolving issues," *Behavioral Sciences & the Law* 13, no. 4 (1995): 477–489.

3 "Immigration Officer Academy. Asylum officer basic training, lesson plan overview, interviewing. Part V: Interviewing survivors," USCIS, www.uscis.gov; "Immigration Officer Academy. Asylum officer basic training, interviewing. Part II: Eliciting testimony," USCIS, www.uscis.gov.

4 Adeyinka M. Akinsulure-Smith, and Maile O'Hara, "Working with forced migrants: Therapeutic issues and considerations for mental health counselors," *Journal of Mental Health Counseling* 34, no. 1 (2012): 38–55; Karen Musalo, Susan M. Meffert, and Akra O. Abdo, "The role of mental health professionals in political asylum processing," *Journal of the American Academy of Psychiatry and the Law* 38 (2010): 479–489; Maya Prabhu, and Madelon Baranoski, "Forensic mental health professionals in the immigration process," *Psychiatric Clinics* 35, no. 4 (2012): 929–946; Rachel Tribe, "Mental health of refugees and asylum-seekers," *Advances in Psychiatric Treatment* 8, no. 4 (2002): 240–247.

5 Frumkin and Friedland, "Forensic evaluations in immigration cases," 477–489; Stuart A. Greenberg, and Daniel W. Shuman, "Irreconcilable conflict between therapeutic and forensic roles," *Professional Psychology: Research and Practice* 28, no. 1 (1997): 50–57; Prabhu and Baranoski, "Forensic mental health professionals in the immigration process," 929–946.

6 Akinsulure-Smith and O'Hara, "Working with forced migrants," 38–55; Prabhu and Baranoski, "Forensic mental health professionals in the immigration process," 929–946; Kelcey Baker, Katherine Freeman, Gigi Warner, and Deborah M. Weissman, *Expert witnesses in US asylum cases: A handbook* (University of North Carolina at Chapel Hill, School of Law, 2018); Gilberto De Jesús-Rentas, James Boehnlein, and Landy Sparr, "Central American victims of gang violence as asylum seekers: The role of the forensic expert," *Journal of the American Academy of Psychiatry and the Law Online* 38, no. 4 (2010): 490–498; Evans and Hass, *Forensic*.

7 "National Consortium of Torture Treatment Programs," HealTorture.org, https://healtorture.org.

8 Ferdowsian, McKenzie, and Zeidan, "Asylum medicine," 215–226.

9 Baker et al., "Expert witnesses in US asylum cases."

10 Stuart A. Greenberg and Daniel W. Shuman, "When worlds collide: Therapeutic and forensic roles," *Professional Psychology: Research and Practice* 38, no. 2 (2007): 129–132.

11 Akinsulure-Smith and O'Hara, "Working with forced migrants," 38–55; Baker et al., "Expert witnesses in US asylum cases."

12 Tribe, "Mental health of refugees and asylum-seekers," 24.

13 Adeyinka M. Akinsulure-Smith, "Responding to the trauma of sexual violence in asylum seekers: A clinical case study," *Clinical Case Studies* 11, no. 4 (2012): 285–298.

14 Barber-Rioja and Garcia-Mansilla, "Special considerations," 2049–2059.

15 Luz M. Garcini, Melanie M. Domenech Rodríguez, Alfonso Mercado, and Manuel Paris, "A tale of two crises: The compounded effect of COVID-19 and anti-immigration policy in the United States," *Psychological Trauma: Theory, Research, Practice, and Policy* 12, no. S1 (2020): S230.

16 Kate Brumback, Deepthi Hajela, and Amy Taxin, "AP visits ICs across US, finds nonstop chaos," Associated Press, Jan. 19, 2020, https://apnews.com.

17 "Fact Sheet: U.S. Asylum Process," National Immigration Forum, Jan. 10, 2019, https://immigrationforum.org.

18 Akinsulure-Smith, "Responding to the trauma of sexual violence in asylum seekers," 285–298; Akinsulure-Smith and O'Hara, "Working with forced migrants," 38–55.

19 Bloemen, Vloeberghs, and Smits, "Psychological and psychiatric aspects of recounting traumatic events by asylum seekers"; Quentin Dignam, "The burden and the proof: Torture and testimony in the determination of refugee status in Australia," *International Journal of Refugee Law* 4, no. 3 (1992): 343–364; Jane Herlihy, and Stuart W. Turner. "The psychology of seeking protection," *International Journal of Refugee Law* 21, no. 2 (2009): 171–192.

20 Adeyinka M. Akinsulure-Smith, "Brief psychoeducational group treatment with re-traumatized refugees and asylum seekers," *Journal for Specialists in Group Work* 34, no. 2 (2009): 137–150.

21 Greenberg and Shuman, "Irreconcilable conflict between therapeutic and forensic roles," 50–57; Greenberg and Shuman, "When worlds collide," 129–132.

22 Gary B. Melton, John Petrila, Norman G. Poythress, Christopher Slobogin, Randy K. Otto, Douglas Mossman, and Lois O. Condie, *Psychological evaluations for the courts: A Handbook for mental health professionals and lawyers* (Guilford Publications, 2018), 43.

23 Barber-Rioja and Garcia-Mansilla, "Special considerations when conducting forensic psychological evaluations for IC," 2049–2059; Evans and Hass, *Forensic.*

24 Melton et al., *Psychological Evaluations*, viii.

25 Daniel C. Murrie, Marcus T. Boccaccini, Lucy A. Guarnera, and Katrina A. Rufino, "Are forensic experts biased by the side that retained them?" *Psychological Science* 24, no. 10 (2013): 1889–1897; Daniel C. Murrie, and Marcus T. Boccaccini, "Adversarial allegiance among expert witnesses," *Annual Review of Law and Social Science* 11 (2015): 37–55.

26 Greenberg and Shuman, "Irreconcilable conflict between therapeutic and forensic roles," 50–57; Greenberg and Shuman, "When worlds collide," 129–132.

27 Both affidavits (sworn and witnessed by an official such as a notary public) and declarations under penalty of perjury are acceptable forms of evidence in immigration court. *See* EOIR Immigration Court Practice Manual Ch. 5.2(e)(evidence) *available at* www.justice.gov; *see also* 28 U.S. Code § 1746.

28 Akinsulure-Smith, "Responding to the trauma of sexual violence in asylum seekers," 285–298; Akinsulure-Smith and O'Hara, "Working with forced migrants," 38–55; Hawthorne E. Smith, "Treatment techniques and priorities: A psychological approach to the patient," in *". . . Like a Refugee Camp on First Avenue": Insights and experiences from the Bellevue/NYU Program for Survivors of Torture*, ed. Hawthorne. E. Smith, Allen S. Keller and Dechen W. Lhewa (Bellevue/NYU Program for Survivors of Torture, 2007), 126–165.

29 Frumkin and Friedland, "Forensic evaluations in immigration cases," 477–489; Greenberg and Shuman, "Irreconcilable conflict between therapeutic and forensic

roles," 50–57; Greenberg and Shuman, "When worlds collide," 129–132; Terence Heltzel, "Compatibility of therapeutic and forensic roles," *Professional Psychology: Research and Practice* 38, no. 2 (2007): 122–128.

30 Garry Malphrus, "Expert witnesses in immigration proceedings," *Immigration Law Advisor* 4, no. 5 (2010): 1–14, www.justice.gov.

31 "Rule 702. Testimony by expert witnesses," Cornell Law School, www.law. cornell.edu.

32 Greenberg and Shuman, "When worlds collide," 129–132; Evans and Hass, *Forensic*.

33 Greenberg and Shuman, "When worlds collide," 129–132.

34 Melton et al., *Psychological Evaluations*, ix.

35 "Rule 702. Testimony by Expert Witnesses," Law.cornell.edu, www.law.cornell.edu.

36 Barber-Rioja and Garcia-Mansilla, "Special considerations when conducting forensic psychological evaluations for immigration court," 2049–2059; Bloemen, Vloeberghs, and Smits, "Psychological and psychiatric aspects of recounting traumatic events by asylum seekers"; Evans and Hass, *Forensic*.

37 Baker et al., "Expert witnesses in US asylum cases," 33.

38 Bloemen, Vloeberghs, and Smits, "Psychological and psychiatric aspects of recounting traumatic events by asylum seekers."

39 Musalo, Meffert, and Abdo, "The role of mental health professionals in political asylum processing," 479–489.

40 Adeyinka M. Akinsulure-Smith, Adriana Espinosa, Tracy Chu, and Ryan Hallock, "Secondary traumatic stress and burnout among refugee resettlement workers: The role of coping and emotional intelligence," *Journal of Traumatic Stress* 31, no. 2 (2018): 202–212.

41 Kate Aschenbrenner, "In pursuit of calmer waters: Managing the impact of trauma exposure on immigration adjudicators," *Kansas Journal of Law and Public Policy* 24 (2014): 401–461.

42 Andrew P. Levin, "Secondary trauma and burnout in attorneys: Effects of work with clients who are victims of domestic violence and abuse," *ABA Commission on Domestic Violence eNewsletter* 9, no. Winter (2008).

43 Yael Fischman, "Secondary trauma in the legal professions, a clinical perspective," *Torture* 18, no. 2 (2008): 107–115; Andrew P. Levin, Linda Albert, Avi Besser, Deborah Smith, Alex Zelenski, Stacey Rosenkranz, and Yuval Neria, "Secondary traumatic stress in attorneys and their administrative support staff working with trauma-exposed clients," *Journal of Nervous and Mental Disease* 199, no. 12 (2011): 946–955.

44 Stuart L. Lustig, "Symptoms of trauma among political asylum applicants: Don't be fooled," *Hastings Int'l & Comp. L. Rev.* 31 (2008): 725–734.

45 Musalo, Meffert, and Abdo, "The role of mental health professionals in political asylum processing," 479–489; Prabhu and Baranoski, "Forensic mental health professionals in the immigration process," 929–946.

46 De Jesús-Rentas, Boehnlein, and Sparr, "Central American victims of gang violence as asylum seekers: The role of the forensic expert," 490–498.

47 Barber-Rioja and Garcia-Mansilla, "Special considerations when conducting forensic psychological evaluations for IC," 2049–2059.

48 Evans and Hass, *Forensic*.

49 "Ethical Standards and Code of Conduct," National Association of Forensic Counselors, http://forensiccounselor.org.

50 Ivo Piskov, "Ethics Guidelines: AAPL—American Academy of Psychiatry and the Law," AAPL, www.aapl.org/ethics.htm.

51 American Psychological Association, "Specialty guidelines for forensic psychology," *The American Psychologist* 68, no. 1 (2013).

52 American Psychological Association, "Guidelines on multicultural education, training, research, practice, and organizational change for Psychologists," *American Psychologist 58*, no.5 (2003): 377–402.

53 American Psychological Association, "APA guidelines for providers of psychological services to ethnic, linguistic, and culturally diverse populations" (2008).

54 Rob P. Butters, and Viola Vaughan-Eden, "The ethics of practicing forensic social work," *Journal of Forensic Social Work* 1, no. 1 (2011): 61–72.

55 Akinsulure-Smith and O'Hara, "Working with forced migrants," 38–55; Ferdowsian, McKenzie, and Zeidan, "Asylum medicine," 215–226.

5. RISK FACTORS FOR MENTAL HEALTH DISTRESS IN IMMIGRANTS FACING REMOVAL PROCEEDINGS

1 Laurence J. Kirmayer et al., "Common mental health problems in immigrants and refugees: General approach in primary care," *Canadian Medical Association Journal* 183, no. 12 (2011): E959-E967; Andres J. Pumariega, Eugenio Rothe, and JoAnne B. Pumariega, "Mental health of immigrants and refugees," *Community Mental Health Journal* 41, no. 5 (2005): 581–597; Margaret M. Sullivan and Roberta Rehm, "Mental health of undocumented Mexican immigrants: A review of the literature," *Advances in Nursing Science* 28, no. 3 (2005): 240–251; David T. Takeuchi et al., "Immigration-related factors and mental disorders among Asian Americans," *American Journal of Public Health* 97, no. 1 (2007): 84–90; David R. Williams et al., "The mental health of Black Caribbean immigrants: Results from the National Survey of American Life," *American Journal of Public Health* 97, no. 1 (2007): 52–59.

2 Angela Nickerson et al., "Trauma and mental health in forcibly displaced populations: An international society for traumatic stress studies briefing paper" (2017); Yok-Fong Paat and Rachel Green, "Mental health of immigrants and refugees seeking legal services on the US-Mexico border," *Transcultural Psychiatry* 54, no. 5-6 (2017): 783–805; Dermot A. Ryan, Fiona E. Kelly, and Brendan D. Kelly, "Mental health among persons awaiting an asylum outcome in Western countries: A literature review," *International Journal of Mental Health* 38, no. 3 (2009): 88–111.

3 David Okech et al., "Social support, dysfunctional coping, and community reintegration as predictors of PTSD among human trafficking survivors," *Behavioral Medicine* 44, no. 3 (2018): 209–218; Siân Oram et al., "Human trafficking and

health: A survey of male and female survivors in England," *American Journal of Public Health* 106, no. 6 (2016): 1073–1078; Shireen Rajaram and Sriyani Tidball, "Survivors' voices—Complex needs of sex trafficking survivors in the Midwest," *Behavioral Medicine* 44, no. 3 (2018): 189–198; Sepali Guruge and Janice Humphreys, "Barriers affecting access to and use of formal social supports among abused immigrant women," *Canadian Journal of Nursing Research Archive* 41, no. 3 (2009): 64–85; Anita Raj and Jay Silverman, "Violence against immigrant women: The roles of culture, context, and legal immigrant status on intimate partner violence," *Violence Against Women* 8, no. 3 (2002): 367–398; Carolyn M. West, "African immigrant women and intimate partner violence: A systematic review," *Journal of Aggression, Maltreatment & Trauma* 25, no. 1 (2016): 4–17.

4 Quentin Dignam, "The burden and the proof: Torture and testimony in the determination of refugee status in Australia," *International Journal of Refugee Law* 4, no. 3 (1992): 343–364; Stuart L. Lustig, "Symptoms of trauma among political asylum applicants: Don't be fooled," *Hastings Int'l & Comp. L. Rev.* 31 (2008): 725–807.

5 Adeyinka M. Akinsulure-Smith and Maile O'Hara, "Working with forced migrants: Therapeutic issues and considerations for mental health counselors," *Journal of Mental Health Counseling* 34, no. 1 (2012): 38–55.

6 Dermot A. Ryan, Fiona E. Kelly, and Brendan D. Kelly, "Mental health among persons awaiting an asylum outcome in Western countries: A literature review," *International Journal of Mental Health* 38, no. 3 (2009): 88–111.

7 Nickerson et al., "Trauma and mental health in forcibly displaced populations"; Pumariega, Rothe and Pumariega, "Mental health of immigrants and refugees," 581–597; Ryan, Kelly, and Kelly, "Mental health among persons awaiting an asylum outcome in Western countries," 88–111; Samantha. L. Thomas and Stuart D. Thomas, "Displacement and health," *British Medical Bulletin* 69, no. 1 (2004): 115–127; Rachel Tribe, "Mental health of refugees and asylum-seekers," *Advances in Psychiatric Treatment* 8, no. 4 (2002): 240–247.

8 Akinsulure-Smith and O'Hara, "Working with forced migrants," 38–55; Cecilia Menjívar and Olivia Salcido, "Immigrant women and domestic violence: Common experiences in different countries," *Gender and Society* 16, no. 6 (2002): 898–920.

9 Diana Bögner, Chris Brewin, and Jane Herlihy, "Refugees' experiences of Home Office interviews: A qualitative study on the disclosure of sensitive personal information," *Journal of Ethnic and Migration Studies* 36, no. 3 (2010): 519–535; Cleo Van Velsen, Caroline Gorst-Unsworth, and Stuart Turner, "Survivors of torture and organized violence: Demography and diagnosis," *Journal of Traumatic Stress* 9, no. 2 (1996): 181–193.

10 Audrey Mumey, Srishti Sardana, Randall Richardson-Vejlgaard, and Adeyinka M. Akinsulure-Smith, "Mental health needs of sex trafficking survivors in New York City: Reflections on exploitation, coping, and recovery," *Psychological Trauma: Theory, Research, Practice, and Policy* 13, no. 2 (2021): 185–192.

11 Adeyinka M. Akinsulure-Smith and Evangeline I. Sicalides, "Female genital cutting in the United States: Implications for mental health professionals," *Professional Psychology: Research and Practice* 47, no. 5 (2016): 356–362, http://dx.doi.org/10.1037/pr0000079; Katherine Wikholm et al., "Female genital mutilation/cutting as grounds for asylum requests in the US: An analysis of more than 100 cases," *Journal of Immigrant and Minority Health* (2020): 1–7.

12 Wynne Russell, "Sexual violence against men and boys," *Forced Migration Review* 27 (2007): 22–23; Lynn Sorsoli, Maryam Kia-Keating, and Frances K. Grossman, "'I keep that hush-hush': Male survivors of sexual abuse and the challenges of disclosure," *Journal of Counseling Psychology* 55, no. 3 (2008): 333–345.

13 Wynne Russell et al., "Care and Support of Male Survivors of Conflict-Related Sexual Violence: Briefing Paper," *Sexual Violence Research Initiative* (2011).

14 Lucas R. Mendos, "State-sponsored homophobia," *ILGA, Geneva* (2019).

15 "Rainbow Welcome Initiative: An assessment and recommendations report on LGBT refugee resettlement in the United States," The Heartland Alliance, prepared for U.S. Department of Health and Human Services, Office of Refugee Resettlement, 2012, 1–46.

16 Ariel Shidlo and Joanne Ahola, "Mental health challenges of LGBT forced migrants," *Forced Migration Review* 42 (2013): 9.

17 Edward J. Alessi, Sarilee Kahn, and Sangeeta Chatterji, "'The darkest times of my life': Recollections of child abuse among forced migrants persecuted because of their sexual orientation and gender identity," *Child Abuse & Neglect* 51 (2016): 93–105; Mark Messih, "Mental health in LGBT refugee populations," *American Journal of Psychiatry Residents' Journal* 11, no. 07 (2016): 5–7; Shidlo and Ahola, "Mental health challenges of LGBT forced migrants."

18 Shidlo and Ahola, "Mental health challenges of LGBT forced migrants."

19 Sarilee Kahn et al., "Facilitating mental health support for LGBT forced migrants: A qualitative inquiry," *Journal of Counseling & Development* 96, no. 3 (2018): 316–326.

20 Kahn et al., "Facilitating mental health support for LGBT forced migrants," 316–326; Messih, "Mental health in LGBT refugee populations," 5–7; Shidlo and Ahola, "Mental health challenges of LGBT forced migrants."

21 Messih, "Mental health in LGBT refugee populations," 5–7; Shidlo and Ahola, "Mental health challenges of LGBT forced migrants"; Carol Pepper, "Gay men tortured on the basis of homosexuality: Psychodynamic psychotherapy and political asylum advocacy," *Contemporary Psychoanalysis* 41, no. 1 (2005): 35–54.

22 Nadine Nakamura and Carmen H. Logie, *LGBTQ mental health: International perspectives and experiences* (American Psychological Association, 2020).

23 Connor Cory, "The LGBTQ asylum seeker: Particular social groups and authentic queer identities," *Geo. J. Gender & L.* 20 (2018): 577–603.

24 David A. Murray, "Real queer: 'Authentic' LGBT refugee claimants and homonationalism in the Canadian Refugee System," *Anthropologica* (2014): 21–32.

25 Jenni Millbank, "From discretion to disbelief: Recent trends in refugee determinations on the basis of sexual orientation in Australia and the United King-

dom," *International Journal of Human Rights* 13, no. 2–3 (2009): 391–414; Murray, "Real queer," 21–32; Deniz Akin, "Queer asylum seekers: Translating sexuality in Norway," *Journal of Ethnic and Migration Studies* 43, no. 3 (2017): 458–474; Deniz Akin, "Discursive construction of genuine LGBT refugees," *Lambda Nordica* 23, no.3–4 (2019): 21–46.

26 Akin, "Queer asylum seekers," 458–474; Cory, "The LGBTQ asylum seeker," 577–603.

27 Murray, "Real queer," 29.

28 Jamila K. Stockman, Hitomi Hayashi, and Jacquelyn C. Campbell, "Intimate partner violence and its health impact on ethnic minority women," *Journal of Women's Health* 24, no. 1 (2015): 62–79.

29 Raj and Silverman, "Violence against immigrant women," 367–398.

30 Menjívar and Salcido, "Immigrant women and domestic violence," 898–920.

31 Ilze Earner, "Double risk: Immigrant mothers, domestic violence and public child welfare services in New York City," *Evaluation and Program Planning* 33, no. 3 (2010): 288–293.

32 Margaret E. Adams and Jacquelyn Campbell, "Being undocumented & intimate partner violence (IPV): Multiple vulnerabilities through the lens of feminist intersectionality," *Women's Health & Urban Life* 11, no. 1 (2012): 15–34; Sepali Guruge and Janice Humphreys, "Barriers affecting access to and use of formal social supports among abused immigrant women," *Canadian Journal of Nursing Research Archive* 41, no. 3 (2009): 64–85; West, "African immigrant women and intimate partner violence," 4–17.

33 Adams and Campbell, "Being undocumented & intimate partner violence (IPV): Multiple vulnerabilities through the lens of feminist intersectionality," 15–34.

34 Adeyinka M. Akinsulure-Smith, Tracy Chu, Eva Keatley, and Andrew Rasmussen, "Intimate partner violence among West African immigrants," *Journal of Aggression, Maltreatment & Trauma* 22, no. 2 (2013): 109–126; Menjívar and Salcido, "Immigrant women and domestic violence," 898–920.

35 "Global Trends: Forced Displacement 2019," United Nations High Commissioner for Refugees, 2020, www.unhcr.org.

36 Zachary Steel et al., "Impact of immigration detention and temporary protection on the mental health of refugees," *British Journal of Psychiatry* 188, no. 1 (2006): 58–64; Janet Cleveland, and Cécile Rousseau, "Psychiatric symptoms associated with brief detention of adult asylum seekers in Canada," *Canadian Journal of Psychiatry* 58, no. 7 (2013): 409–416; A. Keller et al., "From persecution to prison: The health consequences of detention for asylum seekers," *Boston and New York City: Physicians for human rights and the Bellevue/NYU Program for Survivors of Torture* (2003).

37 Katy Robjant, Rita Hassan, and Cornelius Katona, "Mental health implications of detaining asylum seekers: Systematic review," *British Journal of Psychiatry* 194, no. 4 (2009): 306–312; Martha von Werthern et al., "The impact of immigration detention on mental health: A systematic review," *BMC Psychiatry* 18, no. 1 (2018): 1–19.

38 "Locking up Family Values: The Detention of Immigrant Families," Lutheran Immigration and Refugee Services / Women's Commission for Refugee Women and Children, 2007.

39 "Detention 101," Detention Watch Network, www.detentionwatchnetwork.org.

40 Silove, Derrick, Zachary Steel, and Charles Watters, "Policies of deterrence and the mental health of asylum seekers," *Journal of the American Medical Association* 284, no. 5 (2000): 604–611.

41 Peter L. Markowitz, "Barriers to representation for detained immigrants facing deportation: Varick Street Detention Facility, a case study," *Fordham L. Rev.* 78 (2009): 541–575.

42 Ian Urbina and Catherine Rentz, "Immigrants held in solitary cells, often for weeks," *New York Times*, Mar. 13, 2013.

43 Shana Tabak and Rachel Levitan, "LGBTI migrants in immigration detention," *Forced Migration Review* 42 (2013): 48.

44 United Nations High Commission for Refugees, "Global Trends in Forced Displacement 2019"

45 Jeanne-Marie R. Stacciarini et al., "I didn't ask to come to this country . . . I was a child: The mental health implications of growing up undocumented," *Journal of Immigrant and Minority Health* 17, no. 4 (2015): 1225–1230.

46 Lisa R. Fortuna and Michelle V. Porche, "Clinical issues and challenges in treating undocumented immigrants," *Psychiatric Times* 31, no. 1 (2014): 24G.

47 United Nations High Commission for Refugees, "Global Trends in Forced Displacement 2019."

48 Sarah Mares, "Mental health consequences of detaining children and families who seek asylum: A scoping review," *European Child & Adolescent Psychiatry* (2020): 1–25, https://doi.org/10.1007/s00787-020-01629-x; Sarah A. MacLean, "Mental health of children held at a United States immigration detention center," *Social Science & Medicine* 230 (2019): 303–308; Louise K. Newman and Zachary Steel, "The child asylum seeker: Psychological and developmental impact of immigration detention," *Child and Adolescent Psychiatric Clinics of North America* 17, no. 3 (2008): 665–683.

49 Lisseth Rojas-Flores, Mari L. Clements, J. Hwang Koo, and Judy London, "Trauma and psychological distress in Latino citizen children following parental detention and deportation," *Psychological Trauma: Theory, Research, Practice, and Policy* 9, no. 3 (2017): 35.

50 C. Andrew Conway et al., "Family separation and parent–child relationships among Latinx immigrant youth," *Journal of Latinx Psychology* 8, no. 4 (2020): 300.

51 Obianujunwa Anakwenze and Andrew Rasmussen, "The impact of parental trauma, parenting difficulty, and planned family separation on the behavioral health of West African immigrant children in New York City," *Psychological trauma: Theory, research, practice, and policy* (2021).

52 Nina Tove Wylonis and Stephen Bates Billick, "Child and adolescent forensic psychiatry examination and analysis of US citizen children with illegal immigrant parents facing deportation," *Psychiatric Quarterly* (2020): 1–10.

53 Vincent J. Felitti et al., "Relationship of childhood abuse and household dysfunc-
    tion to many of the leading causes of death in adults: The Adverse Childhood Ex-
    periences (ACE) Study," *American Journal of Preventive Medicine* 14, no. 4 (1998):
    245–258.

54 Randy Capps, Michael Fix, and Jie Zog, "A profile of US children with unauthor-
    ized immigrant parents," *Migration Policy Institute*, Jan. 2016, www.migrationpol-
    icy.org.

55 Johayra Bouza et al., "The science is clear: Separating families has long-term
    damaging psychological and health consequences for children, families, and com-
    munities," *Society for Research in Child Development* 20 (2018).

56 Michael D. Shear and Zolan Kanno-Youngs, "Trump slashes refugee cap to
    18,000, curtailing US role as haven," *New York Times*, Sept. 26, 2019, www.ny-
    times.com.

57 Marissa Esthimer, "Crisis in the courts: Is the backlogged US immigration court
    system at its breaking point?" *Migration Policy Institute*, Oct. 3, 2019, www.migra-
    tionpolicy.org.

58 Peter L. Markowitz, "Barriers to representation for detained immigrants facing
    deportation: Varick Street Detention Facility, a case study," *Fordham L. Rev.* 78
    (2009), 545.

59 "U.S. Citizenship and Immigration Services fee schedule and changes to certain
    other immigration benefit request requirements," 85 Federal Register, Aug. 3,
    2020: 46788–46929, www.federalregister.gov.

60 Daniel E. Chand, M. Apolonia Calderon, Daniel P. Hawes, and Lauren O'Keeffe,
    "Serving immigrant communities: Effectiveness of nonprofit legal aid organiza-
    tions in an age of heightened enforcement," *VOLUNTAS: International Journal of
    Voluntary and Nonprofit Organizations* (2020): 1–13.

61 "U.S. Asylum aystem: Significant variation existed in asylum outcomes across im-
    migration courts and judges," U.S. General Accounting Office, Sept. 2008, www.
    gao.gov; Ruth Ellen Wasem, "Asylum and 'credible fear' issues in US immigration
    policy," Congressional Research Service, 2011.

6. ASSESSMENT OF TRAUMA IN IMMIGRANTS FACING REMOVAL PROCEEDINGS

1 Barton F. Evans III and Giselle A. Hass, *Forensic psychological assessment in immigration court: A guidebook for evidence-based and ethical practice* (Routledge,
   2018), 13.

2 Bayne, Mitchell, Sokoloff Lara, Rinehart Rebecca, Axel Epie, Leeza Hirt, and
   Craig Katz, "Assessing the efficacy and experience of in-person versus telephonic
   psychiatric evaluations for asylum seekers in the US," *Psychiatry Research* 282
   (2019): 112612.

3 Emile Whaibeh, Hossam Mahmoud, and Hady Naal, "Telemental health in the
   context of a pandemic: The COVID-19 experience," *Current Treatment Options in
   Psychiatry* 7, no. 2 (2020): 198–202.

4 Donald M. Hilty, Daphne C. Ferrer, Michelle B. Parish, Barb Johnston, Edward J. Callahan, and Peter M. Yellowlees, "The effectiveness of telemental health: A 2013 review," *Telemedicine and e-Health* 19, no. 6 (2013), 444.

5 Judith L. Herman, *Trauma and recovery: The aftermath of violence—from domestic abuse to political terror* (UK: Hachette, 2015).

6 American Psychiatric Association, *Diagnostic and statistical manual of mental disorders (DSM-5)*, American Psychiatric Pub, 2013.

7 John Briere and Catherine Scott, "Complex trauma in adolescents and adults: Effects and treatment," *Psychiatric Clinics* 38, no. 3 (2015): 515–527; Herman, *Trauma and recovery*.

8 David Pelcovitz, Bessel Van der Kolk, Susan Roth, Francine Mandel, Sandra Kaplan, and Patricia Resick, "Development of a criteria set and a structured interview for disorders of extreme stress (SIDES)," *Journal of Traumatic Stress* 10, no. 1 (1997): 3–16.

9 Briere and Scott, "Complex trauma in adolescents and adults," 515–527; Herman, *Trauma and recovery*.

10 "ICD-11 International Classification of Diseases," WHO, https://icd.who.int; Thanos Karatzias, Marylene Cloitre, Andreas Maercker, Evaldas Kazlauskas, Mark Shevlin, Philip Hyland, Jonathan I. Bisson, Neil P. Roberts, and Chris R. Brewin, "PTSD and Complex PTSD: ICD-11 updates on concept and measurement in the UK, USA, Germany and Lithuania," *European Journal of Psychotraumatology* 8, no. sup7 (2017): 1418103.

11 Edward J. Alessi, Sarilee Kahn, and Sangeeta Chatterji, "'The darkest times of my life': Recollections of child abuse among forced migrants persecuted because of their sexual orientation and gender identity," *Child Abuse & Neglect* 51 (2016): 93–105.

12 Madeleine Kissane, Lawrence Szymanski, Rachel Upthegrove, and Cornelius Katona, "Complex posttraumatic stress disorder in traumatised asylum seekers: A pilot study," *European Journal of Psychiatry* 28, no. 3 (2014): 137–144.

13 Frédérique Vallières, Ruth Ceannt, F. Daccache, R. Abou Daher, J. Sleiman, B. Gilmore, S. Byrne, Mark Shevlin, Jamie Murphy, and Philip Hyland, "ICD-11 PTSD and complex PTSD amongst Syrian refugees in Lebanon: The factor structure and the clinical utility of the International Trauma Questionnaire," *Acta Psychiatrica Scandinavica* 138, no. 6 (2018): 547–557.

14 Virginia Barber-Rioja and Alexandra Garcia-Mansilla, "Forensic Mental Health Assessment In Immigration Court," in *The Oxford handbook of psychology and law*, ed. David DeMatteo and Kyle C. Scherr (Oxford University Press, forthcoming)

15 Randall D. Marshall, Mark Olfson, Fredric Hellman, Carlos Blanco, Mary Guardino, and Elmer L. Struening, "Comorbidity, impairment, and suicidality in subthreshold PTSD," *American Journal of Psychiatry* 158, no. 9 (2001): 1467–1473.

16 Boris Drozdek, "If you want to go fast go alone, if you want to go far go together: On context-sensitive group treatment of asylum seekers and refugees traumatized

by war and terror" (PhD diss., Utrecht University, 2014); Ruth Wells, David Wells, and Catalina Lawsin, "Understanding psychological responses to trauma among refugees: The importance of measurement validity in cross-cultural settings," in *Journal and Proceedings of the Royal Society of New South Wales* 148, no. 455/456 (2015): 60–69.

17 Briere and Scott, "Complex trauma in adolescents and adults," 515–527.

18 Rebecca A. Weiss and Barry Rosenfeld, "Navigating cross-cultural issues in forensic assessment: Recommendations for practice," *Professional Psychology: Research and Practice* 43, no. 3 (2012): 234–240.

19 American Psychiatric Association, *Diagnostic and statistical manual of mental isorders (DSM-5)*, American Psychiatric Pub, 2013, https://doi.org/10.1176/appi. books.9780890425596.

20 Daniel J. Lee, Sarah E. Kleiman and Frank W. Weathers, "Assessment of trauma- and stressor-related disorders," in *The Cambridge handbook of clinical assessment and diagnosis*, ed. Martin Sellbom and Julie A. Suhr (UK: Cambridge University Press, 2019), 347–370.

21 Lee et al., "Assessment of Trauma," 353.

22 Devon E. Hinton and Roberto Lewis-Fernández, "The cross-cultural validity of posttraumatic stress disorder: Implications for *DSM-5*," *Depression and Anxiety* 28, no. 9 (2011): 783–801.

23 Hinton and Lewis-Fernández. "The cross-cultural validity," 783–801.

24 Ibid., 793.

25 Ibid., 791.

26 Ibid., 793.

27 Ibid., 793.

28 Lillian Comas-Díaz, Gordon Nagayama Hall, and Helen A. Neville, "Racial trauma: Theory, research, and healing: Introduction to the special issue," *American Psychologist* 74, no. 1 (2019): 1.

29 Diana Bögner, Chris Brewin, and Jane Herlihy, "Refugees' experiences of Home Office interviews: A qualitative study on the disclosure of sensitive personal information," *Journal of Ethnic and Migration Studies* 36, no. 3 (2010): 519–535; Cleo Van Velsen, Caroline Gorst-Unsworth, and Stuart Turner, "Survivors of torture and organized violence: Demography and diagnosis," *Journal of Traumatic Stress* 9, no. 2 (1996): 181–193.

30 Wynne Russell, "Sexual violence against men and boys," *Forced Migration Review*, 27 (2007): 22–23; Wynne Russell, Alastair Hilton, Michael Peel, Lizle Loots, and Liz Dartnall, "Care and support of male survivors of conflict-related sexual violence: Briefing paper," *Sexual violence research initiative* (2011).

31 Allen S. Keller, Barry Rosenfeld, Chau Trinh-Shevrin, Chris Meserve, Emily Sachs, Jonathan A. Leviss, and Elizabeth Singer et al. "Mental health of detained asylum seekers," *The Lancet* 362, no. 9397 (2003): 1721–1723; Katy Robjant, Rita Hassan, and Cornelius Katona, "Mental health implications of detaining asylum seekers: Systematic review," *British Journal of Psychiatry* 194, no. 4 (2009): 306–

312; Martha von Werthern, Katy Robjant, Zoe Chui, Rachel Schon, Livia Ottisova, Claire Mason, and Cornelius Katona, "The impact of immigration detention on mental health: A systematic review," *BMC Psychiatry* 18, no. 1 (2018): 1–19.

32 Briere and Scott, "Complex trauma in adolescents and adults," 517.

7. VICARIOUS TRAUMA AND SECONDARY TRAUMATIC STRESS IN LAWYERS AND MENTAL HEALTH PROFESSIONALS

1 Charles R. Figley and Marné Ludick, "Secondary traumatization and compassion fatigue," in *APA handbook of trauma psychology: Foundations in knowledge*, ed. S. N. Gold (American Psychological Association, 2017): 574.

2 Sean Collins and Ann Long, "Working with the psychological effects of trauma: Consequences for mental health-care workers–a literature review," *Journal of Psychiatric and Mental Health Nursing* 10, no. 4 (2003): 417–424; Figley and Ludick, "Secondary traumatization and compassion fatigue"; Christian Pross, "Burnout, vicarious traumatization and its prevention," *Torture* 16, no. 1 (2006): 1–9; Robyn L. Trippany, Victoria E. White Kress, and S. Allen Wilcoxon, "Preventing vicarious trauma: What counselors should know when working with trauma survivors," *Journal of Counseling & Development* 82, no. 1 (2004): 31–37.

3 Lisa I. McCann and Laurie A. Pearlman, "Vicarious traumatization: A framework for understanding the psychological effects of working with victims," *Journal of Traumatic Stress* 3, no. 1 (1990): 131–149.

4 Trippany et al., "Preventing vicarious trauma," 31–37.

5 Ying Yang and Jeffrey A. Hayes, "Causes and consequences of burnout among mental health professionals: A practice-oriented review of recent empirical literature," *Psychotherapy* 57, no. 3 (2020): 426–436.

6 Charles R. Figley, "Compassion fatigue: Toward a new understanding of the costs of caring" (1995).

7 Collins and Long, "Working with the psychological effects of trauma," 417–424; Yael Fischman, "Secondary trauma in the legal professions: A clinical perspective," *Torture* 18, no. 2 (2008): 107–115; Turgoose, David, and Lucy Maddox, "Predictors of compassion fatigue in mental health professionals: A narrative review," *Traumatology* 23, no. 2 (2017): 172–185.

8 Collins and Long, "Working with the psychological effects of trauma," 417–424; Carlton D. Craig and Ginny Sprang, "Compassion satisfaction, compassion fatigue, and burnout in a national sample of trauma treatment therapists," *Anxiety, Stress, & Coping* 23, no. 3 (2010): 319–339; Richard L. Harrison and Marvin J. Westwood, "Preventing vicarious traumatization of mental health therapists: Identifying protective practices," *Psychotherapy: Theory, Research, Practice, Training* 46, no. 2 (2009): 203–219; Amy R. Hesse, "Secondary trauma: How working with trauma survivors affects therapists," *Clinical Social Work Journal* 30, no. 3 (2002): 293–309; Kyle D. Killian, "Helping till it hurts? A multimethod study of compassion fatigue, burnout, and self-care in clinicians working with trauma survivors," *Traumatology* 14, no. 2 (2008): 32–44; Rachel Sabin-Farrell and Graham

Turpin, "Vicarious traumatization: Implications for the mental health of health workers?," *Clinical Psychology Review* 23, no. 3 (2003): 449–480; Leo Sexton, "Vicarious traumatisation of counsellors and effects on their workplaces," *British Journal of Guidance and Counselling* 27, no. 3 (1999): 393–403; Beth Hudnall Stamm, "Work-related secondary traumatic stress," *PTSD Research Quarterly* 8 (1997): 1–7; Lyndall G. Steed and Robyn Downing, "A phenomenological study of vicarious traumatisation amongst psychologists and professional counsellors working in the field of sexual abuse/assault," *Australasian Journal of Disaster and Trauma Studies* (1998); Turgoose and Maddox, "Predictors of compassion fatigue in mental health professionals," 172–185.

9 Miriam Potocky and Kristen L. Guskovict, "Addressing Secondary Traumatic Stress: Models and Promising Practices—Grantmakers Concerned with Immigrants and Refugees," 2020.

10 Monica K. Miller and Brian H. Bornstein, eds., *Stress, trauma, and wellbeing in the legal system* (Oxford University Press, 2013).

11 Fischman, "Secondary trauma in the legal professions," 107–115; Andrew P. Levin and Scott Greisberg, "Vicarious trauma in attorneys," *Pace L. Rev.* 24 (2003): 245–847.

12 Lisa Morgillo, "Do not make their trauma your trauma: Coping with burnout as a family law attorney," *Family Court Review* 53, no. 3 (2015): 456–473.

13 Andrew P. Levin, "Secondary trauma and burnout in attorneys: Effects of work with clients who are victims of domestic violence and abuse," *ABA Commission on Domestic Violence eNewsletter* 9, Winter 2008.

14 Peter G. Jaffe, Claire V. Crooks, and David A. Wolfe, "Legal and policy responses to children exposed to domestic violence: The need to evaluate intended and unintended consequences," *Clinical Child and Family Psychology Review* 6, no. 3 (2003): 205–213.

15 Kate Aschenbrenner, "Ripples against the other shore: The impact of trauma exposure on the immigration process through adjudicators," *Mich. J. Race & L.* 19 (2013): 53–111.

16 Lin S. Piwowarczyk et al., "Secondary trauma in asylum lawyers," *Bender's Immigration Bulletin* 14, no. 5 (2009): 263–269; Line Rønning, Jocelyn Blumberg, and Jesper Dammeyer, "Vicarious traumatisation in lawyers working with traumatised asylum seekers: A pilot study," *Psychiatry, Psychology, and Law* (2020): 1–13.

17 Stuart L. Lustig et al., "Burnout and stress among United States immigration judges," *Annual Reviews* 12 (2008): 22–35.

18 Aschenbrenner, "Ripples against the other shore," 53; Collins and Long, "Working with the psychological effects of trauma," 417–424; Kathleen M. Palm, Melissa A. Polusny, and Victoria M. Follette, "Vicarious traumatization: Potential hazards and interventions for disaster and trauma worker," *Prehospital and Disaster Medicine* 19, no. 1 (2004): 73–78; Pross, "Burnout, vicarious traumatization and its prevention," 1–9; Trippany et al., "Preventing vicarious trauma," 31–37.

19 "Crushing immigration judge caseloads and lengthening hearing wait times," TRAC Immigration, 2019, https://trac.syr.edu; "COVID-19 pandemic drives up

immigration court backlog and delays: TRAC," Lexis Nexis Legal Newsroom, Sept. 18, 2020, www.lexisnexis.com.

20 Collins and Long, "Working with the psychological effects of trauma," 417–424; Doukessa Lerias and Mitchell K. Byrne, "Vicarious traumatization: Symptoms and predictors," *Stress and Health: Journal of the International Society for the Investigation of Stress* 19, no. 3 (2003): 129–138.

21 Diane L. Bridgeman and Daniel I. Galper, "Listening to our colleagues: 2009 practice survey—Worries, wellness, & wisdom," in *118th Annual Convention of the American Psychological Association, San Diego, CA* (2010).

22 Charles R. Figley, "Compassion fatigue: Psychotherapists' chronic lack of self care," *Journal of Clinical Psychology* 58, no. 11 (2002): 1433.

23 Aschenbrenner, "Ripples against the other shore," 53; Fischman, "Secondary trauma in the legal professions," 107–115; Levin and Greisberg, "Vicarious trauma in attorneys," 245; Lustig et al., "Burnout and stress among United States immigration judges," 22–35.

24 Figley, "Compassion fatigue," 1433–1441; Figley and Ludick, "Secondary traumatization and compassion fatigue"; Levin, "Secondary trauma and burnout in attorneys," Pross, "Burnout, vicarious traumatization and its prevention," 1–9; Trippany et al., "Preventing vicarious trauma," 31–37.

25 Stephanie Baird and Sharon R. Jenkins, "Vicarious traumatization, secondary traumatic stress, and burnout in sexual assault and domestic violence agency staff," *Violence and Victims* 18, no. 1 (2003): 71–86; Cheryl Tatano Beck, "Secondary traumatic stress in nurses: A systematic review," *Archives of Psychiatric Nursing* 25, no. 1 (2011): 1–10.

26 Aschenbrenner, "Ripples against the other shore," 53; Trippany et al., "Preventing vicarious trauma," 31–37.

27 Angela Li et al., "Group cohesion and organizational commitment: Protective factors for nurse residents' job satisfaction, compassion fatigue, compassion satisfaction, and burnout," *Journal of Professional Nursing* 30, no. 1 (2014): 89–99; Peter J. O'brien, "Creating compassion and connection in the work place," *Journal of Systemic Therapies* 25, no. 1 (2006): 16–36; Palm, Polusny, and Follette, "Vicarious Traumatization," 73–78; Trippany et al., "Preventing vicarious trauma," 31–37.

28 Mary Ann Dutto et al., "A holistic healing arts model for counselors, advocates, and lawyers serving trauma survivors: Joyful Heart Foundation retreat," *Traumatology* 23, no. 2 (2017): 143–152.

29 Morgillo, "Do not make their trauma your trauma," 456–473; Trippany et al., "Preventing vicarious trauma," 31–37.

30 Brian Miller and Ginny Sprang, "A components-based practice and supervision model for reducing compassion fatigue by affecting clinician experience," *Traumatology* 23, no. 2 (2017): 153–164; Trippany et al., "Preventing vicarious trauma," 31–37.

31 Levin, "Secondary trauma and burnout in attorneys."

32 O'brien, "Creating compassion and connection in the work place," 16–36.

33 Levin, "Secondary trauma and burnout in attorneys"; Lise Anne Slatten, Kerry David Carson, and Paula Phillips Carson, "Compassion fatigue and burnout: What managers should know," *The Health Care Manager* 30, no. 4 (2011): 325–333.

34 Li et al., "Group cohesion and organizational commitment," 89–99.

35 Fischman, "Secondary trauma in the legal professions," 107–115.

36 Li at al., "Group cohesion and organizational commitment," 89–99; O'brien, "Creating compassion and connection in the work place," 16–36.

37 Levin, "Secondary trauma and burnout in attorneys."

38 Adeyinka M. Akinsulure-Smith, Adriana Espinosa, Tracy Chu, and Ryan Hallock, "Secondary traumatic stress and burnout among refugee resettlement workers: The role of coping and emotional intelligence," *Journal of Traumatic Stress* 31, no. 2 (2018): 202–212; Adeyinka M. Akinsulure-Smith, Eva Keatley, and Andrew Rasmussen, "Responding to secondary traumatic stress: A pilot study of torture treatment programs in the United States," *Journal of Traumatic Stress* 25, no. 2 (2012): 232–235; Angelika Birck, "Secondary traumatization and burnout in professionals working with torture survivors," *Traumatology* 7, no. 2 (2001): 85–90; Russell McKenzie Deighton, Norbert Gurris, and Harald Traue, "Factors affecting burnout and compassion fatigue in psychotherapists treating torture survivors: Is the therapist's attitude to working through trauma relevant?," *Journal of Traumatic Stress* 20, no. 1 (2007): 63–75; Adriana Espinosa, Adeyinka M. Akinsulure-Smith, and Tracy Chu, "Trait emotional intelligence, coping, and occupational distress among resettlement workers," *Psychological Trauma: Theory, Research, Practice, and Policy* 11, no. 1 (2019): 28–34; Rolf Holmqvist and Kjell Andersen, "Therapists' reactions to treatment of survivors of political torture," *Professional Psychology: Research and Practice* 34, no. 3 (2003): 294–300; Elin Kjellenberg, Frida Nilsson, Daiva Daukantaité, and Etzel Cardeña, "Transformative narratives: The impact of working with war and torture survivors," *Psychological Trauma: Theory, Research, Practice, and Policy* 6, no. 2 (2014): 120–128.

39 Lustig et al., "Burnout and stress among United States immigration judges," 22–35; Piwowarczyk et al., "Secondary trauma in asylum lawyers," 263–269; Rønning, Blumberg, and Dammeyer, "Vicarious traumatisation in lawyers working with traumatised asylum seekers," 1–13.

8. SPECIAL CONSIDERATIONS FOR COLLABORATION BETWEEN LAWYERS AND MENTAL HEALTH PROFESSIONALS

1 Model Rules of Professional Conduct, American Bar Association, 2020, www.americanbar.org, *hereinafter* "ABA Rules."

2 "Alphabetical List of Jurisdictions Adopting Model Rules," American Bar Association, www.americanbar.org.

3 8 CFR § 1003.102; 8 CFR § 1003.2.

4 8 CFR § 292.3 (laying out procedures for disciplining attorneys who violate the rules in 8 CFR § 1003.102).

5 ABA Rule 1.7(a)(2); ABA Rule 1.3 Comment 1 ("A lawyer should pursue a matter on behalf of a client despite opposition, obstruction or personal inconvenience to the lawyer, and take whatever lawful and ethical measures are required to vindicate a client's cause or endeavor. A lawyer must also act with commitment and dedication to the interests of the client and with zeal in advocacy upon the client's behalf. A lawyer is not bound, however, to press for every advantage that might be realized for a client. For example, a lawyer may have authority to exercise professional discretion in determining the means by which a matter should be pursued."); *see also* 8 CFR § 1003.102 (nothing in ethical rules should be read to denigrate "practitioner's duty to represent zealously his or her client within the bounds of the law"); *see also* ABA Rule 3.3 Comment 2.

6 *See* Daniel Markovits, *A Modern Legal Ethics: Adversary Advocacy in a Democratic Age*, Princeton University Press (2011): 27–28 (the duty of loyalty has "made a constant presence in all major codes of legal ethics adopted over the past century").

7 ABA Rule 1.6: Confidentiality of Information.

8 ABA Rule 1.6 Comment 3.

9 ABA Rule 1.6(b)(1). The official commentary on the ABA rules gives, by way of example, a scenario in which a client discloses that he has released toxic waste into the city water supply. ABA Comment on Rule 1.6 [6].

10 ABA Rule 1.6(b)(2), (3).

11 ABA Rule 1.6 Comment 17.

12 ABA Rule 3.3.

13 *Id.* Rule 3.3 provides in part: "A lawyer shall not knowingly: (1) make a false statement of fact or law to a tribunal or fail to correct a false statement of material fact or law previously made to the tribunal by the lawyer; (2) fail to disclose to the tribunal legal authority in the controlling jurisdiction known to the lawyer to be directly adverse to the position of the client and not disclosed by opposing counsel; or (3) offer evidence that the lawyer knows to be false. If a lawyer, the lawyer's client, or a witness called by the lawyer, has offered material evidence and the lawyer comes to know of its falsity, the lawyer shall take reasonable remedial measures, including, if necessary, disclosure to the tribunal. A lawyer may refuse to offer evidence, other than the testimony of a defendant in a criminal matter, that the lawyer reasonably believes is false."

14 ABA Rule 3.3(c); *see also* ABA Rule 3.3 Comment 2 ("A lawyer acting as an advocate in an adjudicative proceeding has an obligation to present the client's case with persuasive force. Performance of that duty while maintaining confidences of the client, however, is qualified by the advocate's duty of candor to the tribunal. Consequently, although a lawyer in an adversary proceeding is not required to present an impartial exposition of the law or to vouch for the evidence submitted in a cause, the lawyer must not allow the tribunal to be misled by false statements of law or fact or evidence that the lawyer knows to be false.").

15 *See* ABA rule 1.0(m) (definition of "tribunal"); *but see* New York State Bar Association Committee on Professional Ethics, Opinion 1011 (Jul. 29, 2014) *available at*

https://nysba.org (finding that USCIS is not a tribunal triggering the obligations of Rule 3.3 but noting that ethics opinions from several other states do consider it to be a tribunal).

16 ABA Rule 3.3 (a)(3).

17 ABA Rule 3.3 Comment 10.

18 ABA Rule 3.3 Comment 8.

19 8 C.F.R. § 1003.02(c).

20 ABA Rule 4.1.

21 ABA Rule 4.1 Comment 1; *see also* ABA Rule 3.3 Comment 3 ("There are circumstances where failure to make a disclosure is the equivalent of an affirmative misrepresentation."); *see also* "When is it OK for a Lawyer to Lie?," American Bar Association, Dec. 2018, www.americanbar.org.

22 ABA Rule 1.6(b) (1–3).

23 Ibid.

24 ABA Rule 1.2(d) ("A lawyer shall not counsel a client to engage, or assist a client, in conduct that the lawyer knows is criminal or fraudulent, but a lawyer may discuss the legal consequences of any proposed course of conduct with a client and may counsel or assist a client to make a good faith effort to determine the validity, scope, meaning or application of the law.").

25 ABA Rule 1.2; ABA Rule 1.2 comment 2 ("Clients normally defer to the special knowledge and skill of their lawyer with respect to the means to be used to accomplish their objectives, particularly with respect to technical, legal and tactical matters.").

26 ABA Rule 1.2 comment 2 (If a lawyer has a fundamental disagreement with the client the lawyer may withdraw from representation; conversely, the client may resolve the disagreement by discharging the lawyer.).

27 ABA Rule 1.14.

28 Ibid.; *see also* "Practice Advisory: Representing Detained Immigration Respondents of Diminished Capacity: Ethical Challenges and Best Practices," American Bar Association Commission on Immigration, July 2015, www.americanbar.org (hereinafter "ABA Practice Advisory on Diminished Capacity"), 7.

29 ABA Rule 1.14(b). Importantly, several states, including California and Texas, have not adopted, or not fully adopted, Rule 1.14(b). Readers are encouraged to research the most up to date information about the local rules in their jurisdiction.

30 *See* Matter of M-J-K-, 26 I&N Dec. 773 (BIA 2016); *see also* "Practice Advisory: Representing Noncitizens with Mental Illness," Catholic Legal Immigration Network, May, 2020.

31 Ibid. at 7 n. 24.

32 *See* ABA Practice Advisory on Diminished Capacity for a discussion of attorneys' options in such a situation, including possibly the appointment of a guardian ad litem or next friend.

33 "Ethical Principles of Psychologists and Code of Conduct," American Psychological Association, American Psychological Association, 2017, www.apa.org.

34 David DeMatteo, Sarah Fishel, Kellie Wiltsie, and Aislinn Tansey, "Legal and Ethical Issues in Mental Health Assessment and Treatment," in *The Oxford Handbook of Mental Health Assessment and Treatment in Jails*, ed. Virginia Barber-Rioja, Alexandra Garcia-Mansilla, Bipin Subedi, and Ashley Battastini (Oxford University Press, forthcoming).

35 "American Psychological Association, Specialty guidelines for forensic psychology," *The American Psychologist* 68, no. 1 (2013): 7–19.

36 Gary B. Melton et al., *Psychological Evaluations for the Courts: A Handbook for Mental Health Professionals and Lawyers* (Guilford Publications, 2017); Lawrence Wrightsman and Solomon N. Fulero, *Forensic Psychology* (Thomson Learning, 2005).

37 Wrightsman, *Forensic*, 11.

38 Ibid., 11.

39 "Summary Guide for Mandated Reporters in New York State," Office of Children and Family Services, Jan. 2019, https://ocfs.ny.gov.

40 *See* ABA Rule 1.2 Comment 9 on the "critical distinction" between recommending a course of action and advising a client of the actual consequences that appear likely to result for the client's conduct.

41 *See, e.g.,* "LSAT Sample Questions (Analytical Reasoning)," Law School Admission Council, www.lsac.org.

42 As an example, an attorney representing a mentally disabled client will likely be looking for a simple analogy to explain the client's functioning to the court (e.g., "He has the I.Q. of a six-year-old") when, from the MHP's perspective, this might be a gross oversimplification that does not provide a complete picture of the client's capabilities. A MHP must, of course, write their report consistent with the highest professional and clinical standards. But this does not preclude them from working with the attorney to brainstorm concrete examples or a compelling analogy that will help the court understand the client's ability to comprehend or process information in various situations.

43 American Psychological Association, "Specialty Guidelines," 8.

44 Randy K. Otto, Richart DeMier, and Marcus Boccaccini, *Forensic Reports and Testimony: A Guide to Effective Communication for Psychologists and Psychiatrists* (John Wiley & Sons, 2014).

45 Ibid., 52.

46 Ibid., 52.

47 *See* 8 CFR § 1003.102 (an attorney may not knowingly, or with reckless disregard, make a false statement of material fact or law or offer false evidence). If, when asked by the attorney, the client denies the truth of a detail in the MHP's report, the attorney must decide whether they can ethically continue to rely on the client's story or whether they would be acting with "reckless disregard" for the truth to do so in light of contrary information. The attorney will need to consider all the factors, including the potential for error in the report, and proceed with caution.

48 Kelcey Baker, Katherine Freeman, Gigi Warner, and Deborah M. Weissman, "Expert Witnesses in U.S. Asylum Cases: A Handbook," University of North Carolina, 2018, https://law.unc.edu.

49 Aimee Mayer-Salina and Ann Garcia, "Practice Advisory Representing Noncitizens with Mental Illness," Catholic Legal Immigration Network, May 2020, https://cliniclegal.org.

50 Ibid., 27–28.

9. CULTURAL CONSIDERATIONS

1 "FY 2012 Statistical Yearbook," Justice.gov, 2012, www.justice.gov.

2 American Psychological Association, "Guidelines on multicultural education, training, research, practice, and organizational change for psychologists," *American Psychologist* 58, no. 5 (2003): 377–402; Ivo Piskov, "Ethics Guidelines: AAPL—American Academy of Psychiatry and the Law," AAPL, www.aapl.org.

3 Janet E. Helms and Donelda Ann Cook, *Using race and culture in counseling and psychotherapy: Theory and process* (Allyn & Bacon, 1999).

4 American Psychological Association, "Guidelines," 380.

5 Ibid.

6 Ibid.

7 José M. Causadias, Joseph A. Vitriol, and Annabelle L. Atkin, "Do we overemphasize the role of culture in the behavior of racial/ethnic minorities? Evidence of a cultural (mis) attribution bias in American psychology," *American Psychologist* 73, no. 3 (2018): 243.

8 Barton F. Evans III and Giselle A. Hass, *Forensic psychological assessment in immigration court: A guidebook for evidence-based and ethical practice* (Routledge, 2018).

9 Causadias, "Do we overemphasize," 244.

10 American Psychological Association, "Guidelines," 377.

11 Richard H. Dana, "Assessment of acculturation in Hispanic populations," *Hispanic Journal of Behavioral Sciences* 18, no. 3 (1996): 317–328.

12 American Psychological Association. "Guidelines," 377; American Psychological Association, *Multicultural guidelines: An ecological approach to context, identity, and intersectionality* (American Psychological Association, 2017), www.apa.org.

13 Urie Bronfenbrenner, *Ecological systems theory* (Jessica Kingsley Publishers, 1992); American Psychological Association, *Multicultural guidelines*, 10.

14 Joseph R. Betancourt, Alexander R. Green, J. Emilio Carrillo, and I. I. Owusu Ananeh-Firempong, "Defining cultural competence: A practical framework for addressing racial/ethnic disparities in health and health care," *Public Health Reports* (2016).

15 Lillian Comas-Díaz, *Multicultural care: A clinician's guide to cultural competence*, American Psychological Association (2012).

16 Barber-Rioja, Virginia, and Alexandra Garcia-Mansilla. "Special considerations when conducting forensic psychological evaluations for immigration court," *Journal of Clinical Psychology* 75, no. 11 (2019): 2049–2059.

17 Evans, *Forensic*, 23.

18 American Psychological Association, *Ethical principles of psychologists and code of conduct* (American Psychological Association, 2017), www.apa.org.

19 Causadias, "Do we overemphasize," 244.

20 Ibid.

21 Some guidelines to consider: *Guidelines on multicultural education, training, research, practice and organizational change for psychologists* (American Psychological Association, 2003); *Multicultural guidelines: An ecological approach to context, identity, and intersectionality* (American Psychological Association, 2017); *Multicultural and social justice counseling competencies: Guidelines for the counseling profession* (American Counseling Association 2016); and *Standards and indicators for cultural competence in social work practice* (National Association of Social Workers, 2015).

22 Fabricio E. Balcazar, Yolanda Suarez-Balcazar, and Tina Taylor-Ritzler. "Cultural competence: Development of a conceptual framework," *Disability and Rehabilitation* 31, no. 14 (2009): 1153–1160.

23 Patricia A. Zapf, Amanda Beltrani, and Amanda L. Reed, "Psychological assessment in forensic settings," in *The Cambridge handbook of clinical assessment and diagnosis*, ed. Martin Selbom and Julie A. Suhr (Cambridge University Press, 2020), 462–471.

24 María del Rosario Basterra, Elise Trumbull, and Guillermo Solano-Flores, eds., *Cultural validity in assessment: Addressing linguistic and cultural diversity* (Routledge, 2011).

25 Virginia Barber-Rioja and Barry Rosenfeld, "Addressing linguistic and cultural differences in the forensic interview," *International Journal of Forensic Mental Health* 17, no. 4 (2018): 377–386.

26 WAC 182-538D-0200, https://apps.leg.wa.gov.

27 American Psychiatric Association, *Diagnostic and statistical manual of mental disorders (DSM-5)* (American Psychiatric Association, 2013), 758.

28 Ibid.

29 Ibid.

30 Ibid.

31 Derald Wing Sue, David Sue, Helen A. Neville, and Laura Smith, *Counseling the culturally diverse: Theory and practice* (John Wiley & Sons, 2019).

32 Barber-Rioja and Rosenfeld, "Addressing linguistic," 380.

33 Arthur L. Whaley, "Ethnicity/race, paranoia, and psychiatric diagnoses: Clinician bias versus sociocultural differences," *Journal of Psychopathology and Behavioral Assessment* 19, no. 1 (1997): 1–20.

34 T. A Snyder, and J. E. Barnett, "Informed consent and the process of psychotherapy," *Psychotherapy Bulletin* 41, no. 2 (2006): 37–42; R. M. Yousuf, A. R. M. Fauzi, S. H. How, A. G. Rasool, and K. Rehana, "Awareness, knowledge and attitude towards informed consent among doctors in two different cultures in Asia:

A cross-sectional comparative study in Malaysia and Kashmir, India," *Singapore Medical Journal* 48, no. 6 (2007): 559.

35 Lawrence O. Gostin, "Informed consent, cultural sensitivity, and respect for persons," *JAMA* 274, no. 10 (1995): 844–845.

36 Barber-Rioja and Rosenfeld, "Addressing linguistic."

37 American Psychological Association, *Ethical*, 7.

38 Linda K. Knauss, "Ethical and professional issues in assessment," in *Clinical Assessment and Diagnosis*, ed. Martin Selbom and Julie A. Suhr (Cambridge University Press, 2020), 113.

39 John Sommers-Flanagan, Veronica J. Johnson and Maegan Rides At The Door, "Clinical interviewing," in *Clinical Assessment and Diagnosis*, ed. Martin Selbom and Julie A. Suhr (Cambridge University Press, 2020), 113–122.

40 Zapf, "Psychological," 462.

41 Joshua N. Hook, Don E. Davis, Jesse Owen, Everett L. Worthington Jr, and Shawn O. Utsey, "Cultural humility: Measuring openness to culturally diverse clients," *Journal of Counseling Psychology* 60, no. 3 (2013): 353.

42 Barber-Rioja and Rosenfeld, "Addressing linguistic."

43 Pamela A. Hays, *Addressing cultural complexities in practice: Assessment, diagnosis, and therapy* (American Psychological Association, 2008).

44 American Psychiatric Association, *Diagnostic*.

45 Roberto Lewis-Fernandez, Neil Krishan Aggarwal, and Laurence Kirmayer, "Introduction," in *DSM-5* handbook on the cultural formulation interview*, ed. by Roberto Lewis-Fernández (Arlington, VA: American Psychiatric Association, 2015).

46 James Boehnlein, Joseph Westermeyer, and Monica Scalto, "Supplemental module 11: Immigrants and refugees," in *DSM-5* handbook on the cultural formulation interview*, ed by Roberto Lewis-Fernández (Arlington, VA: American Psychiatric Association, 2015).

47 Frederick T. L. Leong, P. Priscilla Lui, and Zornitsa Kalibatseva, "Multicultural issues in clinical psychological assessment," in *The Cambridge handbook of clinical assessment and diagnosis*, ed. Martin Selbom and Julie A. Suhr (Cambridge University Press, 2020), 25–37.

48 American Psychiatric Association, *Diagnostic*, 749.

49 Ibid.

50 Ibid.

51 Ibid.

52 Ravi DeSilva, Neil Krishan Aggarwal, and Roberto Lewis-Fernández, "The *DSM-5* Cultural Formulation Interview: Bridging barriers toward a clinically integrated cultural assessment in psychiatry," *Psychiatric Annals* 48, no. 3 (2018): 154–159.

53 Charles J. Golden, and Philinda Smith Hutchings, "The Mental Status Examination," in *Basic interviewing: A practical guide for counselors and clinicians*, ed. Hersen Michel, and Vincent B. Van Hasselt (Psychology Press, 1998), 107–128.

54 Stephane M. Shepherd, and Roberto Lewis-Fernandez, "Forensic risk assessment and cultural diversity: Contemporary challenges and future directions," *Psychology, Public Policy, and Law* 22, no. 4 (2016): 427.

55 Barber-Rioja and Rosenfeld, "Addressing linguistic."

56 Sue, *Counseling.*

57 Whaley, "Ethnicity/race."

58 Sue, *Counseling.*

59 Barber-Rioja and Rosenfeld, "Addressing Linguistic."

60 Ibid.

61 Randy K. Otto, Richart DeMier, and Marcus Boccaccini, *Forensic reports and testimony: A guide to effective communication for psychologists and psychiatrists* (John Wiley & Sons, 2014).

62 Steven Regeser Lopez, and Peter J. Guarnaccia, "Cultural psychopathology: Uncovering the social world of mental illness," *Annual Review of Psychology* 51, no. 1 (2000): 571–598.

63 Anna Bredström, "Culture and context in mental health diagnosing: Scrutinizing the *DSM-5* revision," *Journal of Medical Humanities* 40, no. 3 (2019): 347–363.

64 Ibid.

65 American Psychiatric Association, *Diagnostic,* 166.

66 American Psychiatric Association, *Diagnostic,* 661.

67 Joseph Westermeyer, "Psychiatric diagnosis across cultural boundaries," *American Journal of Psychiatry* (1985); Leong T. L. Frederick, Priscilla Lui, and Zornitsa Kalibatseva. "Multicultural issues in psychological assessment," in *The Cambridge handbook of clinical assessment and diagnosis,* ed. Martin Selbom and Julie A. Suhr (Cambridge University Press, 2020), 25–37.

68 Ibid.

69 Anu, J. Asnaani, Anthony Richey, Ruta Dimaite, Devon E. Hinton, and Stefan G. Hofmann, "A cross-ethnic comparison of lifetime prevalence rates of anxiety disorders," *Journal of Nervous and Mental Disease* 198, no. 8 (2010): 551.

70 American Psychiatric Association, *Diagnostic,* 833.

71 Leong, *The Cambridge handbook,* 27.

72 Otto et al., *Forensic reports.*

73 Maile O'Hara, and Adeyinka M. Akinsulure-Smith, "Working with interpreters: Tools for clinicians conducting psychotherapy with forced immigrants," *International Journal of Migration, Health and Social Care,* 7, no. 1 (2011).

74 Ibid.

75 Ibid.

76 O'Hara et al., "Working with interpreters."

77 Barber-Rioja and Rosenfeld, "Addressing linguistic."

78 Evans and Hass, *Forensic.*

79 O'Hara et al, "Working with interpreters."

80 Barber-Rioja and Rosenfeld, "Addressing linguistic."

81 O'Hara et al., "Working with interpreters."

82 Joseph Henrich, Steven J. Heine, and Ara Norenzayan, "The weirdest people in the world?" *Behavioral and Brain Sciences* 33, no. 2–3 (2010): 61–83.

83 Cecil. R. Reynolds, and Lisa A. Suzuki, "Bias in psychological assessment: An empirical review and recommendations," in *Handbook of psychology: Assessment psychology*, ed. John R. Graham, Jack A. Naglieri, and Irving B. Weiner (John Wiley & Sons, 2013), 82–113.

84 Hede Helfrich, "Beyond the dilemma of cross-cultural psychology: Resolving the tension between etic and emic approaches," *Culture and Psychology* 5, no. 2 (1999): 131–153.

85 Richard Rogers, John W. Donnelly, and Amor A. Correa, "Translated measures in forensic evaluations with specific applications to feigned mental disorders," *Psychological Injury and Law* 12, no. 3–4 (2019): 191–203.

86 Üstün Öngel, and Peter B. Smith, "Who are we and where are we going? JCCP approaches its 100th issue," *Journal of Cross-Cultural Psychology* 25, no. 1 (1994): 25–53.

87 Fons J. R. Van de Vijver and Jia He, "Bias and equivalence in cross-cultural personality research," in *Handbook of personality across cultures: Trait psychology across cultures*, vol. 1, ed. A. Timothy Church (Praeger/ABC CLIO, 2017), 251–277.

88 Margarita Alegria, Doryliz Vila, Meghan Woo, Glorisa Canino, David Takeuchi, Mildred Vera, Vivian Febo, Peter Guarnaccia, Sergio Aguilar-Gaxiola, and Patrick Shrout, "Cultural relevance and equivalence in the NLAAS instrument: Integrating etic and emic in the development of cross-cultural measures for a psychiatric epidemiology and services study of Latinos," *International Journal of Methods in Psychiatric Research* 13, no. 4 (2004): 270–288; Helfrich, "Beyond the dilemma"; Harry. C. Triandis, "Cross-cultural research in social psychology," in *Social judgment and intergroup relations: Essays in honor of Muzafer Sherif*, ed. Donald Granberg and Gian Sarup (Springer, 1992), 229–243.

89 Fanny M. Cheung, Kwok Leung, Ruth M. Fan, Wei-Zheng Song, Jian-Xin Zhang, and Jian-Ping Zhang, "Development of the Chinese Personality Assessment Inventory (CPAI)," *Journal of Cross-cultural Psychology* 27 (1996): 181–199.

90 American Educational Research Association, American Psychological Association, and National Council on Measurement in Education, *Standards for educational and psychological testing*, 4th ed. (Authors, 2014); Kurt. F Geisinger, "Cross-cultural normative assessment translation and adaptation issues influencing the normative interpretation of assessment instruments," *Psychological Assessment* 6, no. 4 (1994): 304–312; International Test Commission, "ITC guidelines for translating and adapting tests (2nd ed.)," www.intestcom.org.

91 American Psychological Association. *Ethical principles of psychologists and code of conduct* (American Psychological Association, 2017).

92 Rebecca Weiss and Barry Rosenfeld, "Navigating cross-cultural issues in forensic assessment: Recommendations for practice," *Professional Psychology: Research and Practice* 43, no. 3 (2012): 234–240.

93 American Psychological Association, "Specialty guidelines for forensic psychology," *American Psychologist* 68, no. 1 (2013): 7–19.

94 International Test Commission, "ITC guidelines for translating and adapting tests."

95 Yossef S. Ben-Porath and Auke Tellegen, *MMPI-2-RF manual for administration, scoring, and interpretation* (University of Minnesota Press, 2008); Yossef. S Ben-Porath., and Auke Tellegen, *MMPI-3 technical manual* (University of Minnesota Press, 2020); James N. Butcher, W. Grant Dahlstrom, John R. Graham, Auke Tellegen, and Beverly Kaemmer, *MMPI-2 Manual* (University of Minnesota Press, 1989).

96 Leslie C. Morey, *Personality assessment inventory professional manual*, 2nd ed. (Psychological Assessment Resources, 2007).

97 David Wechsler, *Wechsler Adult Intelligence Scale—Fourth Edition (WAIS-IV)* (Pearson, 2008).

98 Richard. W. Woodcock, Criselda G. Alvarado, Fredrick A. Schrank, Kevin S. McGrew, Nancy Mather, and Ana F. Muñoz-Sandoval, *Batería IV Woodcock-Muñoz* (Riverside Insights, 2019).

99 Butcher et al., "MMPI-2 manual."

100 Ben-Porat and Tellegen, "MMPI-2-RF manual."

101 James. N Butcher, Carolyn Williams, John R. Graham, Auke Tellegen, Yossef S. Ben-Porath, Robert P. Archer, and Beverly Kaemmer, *Manual for the administration, scoring, and interpretation of the adolescent version of the MMPI* (University of Minnesota Press, 1992).

102 University of Minnesota Press Test Division (n.d.), "Available translations," University of Minnesota Press, www.upress.umn.edu.

103 Lillian L. Bopp, "Detecting malingering and defensiveness in the translated versions of the MMPI-2 and MMPI-2-RF: A systematic review" (master's thesis, Fordham University, 2020); Rogers et al., "Translated measures in forensic evaluations."

104 Bopp, "Detecting malingering and defensiveness in the translated versions."

105 For a review of the strengths and challenges of feigning research with the translated versions of the MMPI-2 and MMPI-2-RF, *see* Rogers et al., "Translated measures in forensic evaluations."

106 Roger L. Greene, *The MMPI-2: An interpretive manual*, 2nd ed. (Allyn & Bacon, 2000); Gordon C. N. Hall, Anita Bansal, and Irene R. Lopez, "Ethnicity and psychopathology: A meta-analytic review of 31 years of comparative MMPI/ MMPI-2 research," *Psychological Assessment* 11, no. 2 (1999): 186–197; Robert W. Robin, Roger L. Greene, Bernard Albaugh, Alex Caldwell, and David Goldman, "Use of the MMPI-2 in American Indians: Comparability of the MMPI-2 between two tribes and with the MMPI-2 normative group," *Psychological Assessment* 15, no. 3 (2003): 351–359; Rodney E. Timbrook and John R. Graham, "Ethnic differences on the MMPI-2?" *Psychological Assessment* 6, no. 3 (1994): 212–217.

107 James N. Butcher, Jose Cabiya, Emilia Lucio, and Maria Garrido, *Assessing Hispanic clients using the MMPI-2 and MMPI-A* (American Psychological Association Press, 2007); Antonio Zapata-Sola, Tony Kreuch, Richard N. Landers, Tim Hoyt, and James N. Butcher, "Personality assessment in personnel selection using the MMPI-2: A cross-cultural comparison," *International Journal of Clinical and Health Psychology* 9, no. 2 (2009): 287–298.

108 Ben-Porath and Tellegen, "MMPI-3 technical manual."

109 David C. Tsai and Patricia L. Pike, "Effects of acculturation on the MMPI-2 Scores of Asian American Students," *Journal of Personality Assessment* 74, no. 2 (2000): 216–230.

110 Fanny M. Cheung, Jessica Y. Y. Kwong, and Jianxin Zhang, "Clinical validation of the Chinese Personality Assessment Inventory," *Psychological Assessment* 15, no. 1 (2003): 89–100.

111 Leslie M. Morey, *Tasa de Inventario de la Personalidad, Versión en español de Carlos J. Cano, Asesoramiento técnico de Pedro M. Ferreira [The Personality Assessment Inventory, Spanish version by Carlos J. Cano, Technical advice by Pedro M. Ferreira]* (Psychological Assessment Resources, 1992).

112 Leslie M. Morey (adaptación española: Ortiz-Tallo, Margarita, Pablo Santamaria, Violeta Cardenal, and Sanchez). *PAI. Inventario de Evaluación de la Personalidad* (Personality Assessment Inventory: European Spanish With Norms) (TEA Ediciones, 2011).

113 Juliana B. Stover, Alejandro Castro-Solano, and Mercedes Fernández-Liporace, "Personality Assessment Inventory: Psychometric analyses of its Argentinean version," *Psychological Reports*, 117, no. 3 (2015): 799–823.

114 Samuel Jurado-Cardenas, Sergio Santamaría-Súarez, Leticia Salazar-Garza, Victor Colotla, Patricia Campos-Coy, Adolfo Lizárraga-Patrón, Cosby Yazbeck, Quintana Sarmiento, María Guadalupe, Vargas Alvarado, and Luis E. Ocampo-Banda, "Propiedades psicométricas del Inventario de Personalidad (PAI) en México," *UCV-Scientia* 7, no. 2 (2015): 143–150.

115 Richard Rogers, Johnny Flores, Karen Ustad, and Kenneth Sewell, "Initial validation of the Personality Assessment Inventory–Spanish version with clients from Mexican American communities," *Journal of Personality Assessment* 64, no. 2 (1995): 340–348.

116 Amor A. Correa, Richard Rogers, and Margot M. Williams, "Malingering and defensiveness on the Spanish Personality Assessment Inventory: An initial investigation with mostly Spanish-speaking outpatients," *Assessment* 27, no. 6 (2020): 1163–1175; Krissie Fernandez, Marcus T. Boccaccini, and Ramona M. Noland, "Detecting over- and underreporting of psychopathology with the Spanish-language Personality Assessment Inventory: Findings from a simulation study with bilingual speakers," *Psychological Assessment* 20, no. 2 (2208): 189–194; Christopher J. Hopwood, Claudia G. Flato, Suman Ambwani, Beth H. Garland, and Leslie C. Morey, "A comparison of Latino and Anglo socially desirable responding," *Journal of Clinical Psychology* 65, no. 7 (2009): 769–780.

117 Jurado-Cardenas et al., "Propiedades psicométricas del Inventario de Personalidad (PAI) en México"; Margarita Ortiz-Tallo, Violeta Cardenal, Marta Ferragut,
and Pablo Santamaría, "Spanish and Chilean standardizations of the Personality
Assessment Inventory: The influence of sex," *Spanish Journal of Psychology* 18, no.
E48 (2015): 1–12.

118 Robert J. Sternberg and Elena L. Grigorenko, "Ability testing across cultures," in
*Handbook of multicultural assessment: Clinical, psychological, and education appli-
cation*, ed. Lisa A. Suzuki and Joseph G. Ponterottto (San Francisco, CA: Jossey-
Bass/Wiley, 2008), 449–470; Eka Roivainen, "European and American WAIS IV
norms: Cross-national differences in perceptual reasoning, processing speed and
working memory subtest scores," *Scandinavian Journal of Psychology* 60, no.6
(2019): 513–519.

119 Patricia M. Greenfield, "You can't take it with you: Why abilities assessments don't
cross cultures," *American Psychologist* 52, no. 10 (1997): 1115–1124.

120 Richard E. Nisbett,. *The geography of thought: Why we think the way we do* (Free
Press, 2003).

121 José Pons, Leída Matías-Carrelo, Mary Rodríguez, Juana M. Rodríguez, Laura L.
Herrans, María E. Jimenez, . . . James Yang, "Estudios de validez de la Escala de
Inteligencia Wechsler para Adultos versión III, Puerto Rico (EIWA-III)," *Revista
Puertorriqueña de Psicología* 19 (2008): 75–111.

122 Emily C. Duggan, Lina M. Awakon, Cilia C. Loaiza, and Mauricio A. Garcia-
Barrera, "Contributing towards a cultural neuropsychology assessment decision-
making framework: Comparison of WAIS-IV norms from Colombia, Chile,
Mexico, Spain, United States, and Canada," *Archives of Clinical Neuropsychology*
34, no. 5 (2019): 657–681; Cynthia M. Funes, Juventino Hernandez-Rodriguez, and
Steven Regeser-Lopez, "Norm comparisons of the Spanish-language and English-
language WAIS-III: Implications for clinical assessment and test adaptation,"
Psychological Assessment 28, no. 12 (2016): 1709–1715.

123 Woodcock et al., "Batería IV Woodcock-Muñoz."

124 Linda Brown, Rita Jean Sherbenou, and Susan K. Johnsen. *Test of Nonverbal Intelligence: TONI-4* (Austin, TX: Pro-ed, 2010).

125 Richard Rogers, Kenneth W. Sewell, and Nathan D. Gillard, *SIR-2: Structured
Interview of Reported Symptoms: Professional manual*, 2nd ed. (Psychological Assessment Resources, 2010).

126 Michelle R. Widows, and Glenn P. Smith. *SIMS: Structured Inventory of Malingered Symptomatology: Professional manual* (Psychological Assessment Resources,
2005).

127 Holly A. Miller, *M-FAST: Miller Forensic Assessment of Symptoms Test professional
manual* (Psychological Assessment Resources, 2001).

128 Tom N. Tombaugh, *Test of Memory Malingering: TOMM* (Multi-Health Systems,
1996).

129 Kyle B. Boone, Po Lu, and D. Herzberg, *The Dot Counting Test manual* (Western
Psychological Services, 2002).

130 Paul Green, *The Word Memory Test* (Green's Publishing, 2003).
131 Muriel D. Lezak, *Neuropsychological assessment* (Oxford University Press, 1983); André Rey, *L'examen clinique en psychologie* (Presses universitaires de France, 1964).
132 Amor A. Correa, Richard Rogers, and Raquel Hoersting, "Validation of the Spanish SIRS with monolingual Hispanic outpatients," *Journal of Personality Assessment* 92, no. 5 (2010): 458–464.
133 Chang Liu, Zhening Liu, Helen F. K. Chiu, Tam W-C. Carl, Huiran Zhang, Peng Wang, Guowei Wu, Tumbewene E. Mwansisya, Longlong Cao, Aimin Hu, Yu Wang, and Zhimin Xue, "Detection of malingering: Psychometric evaluation of the Chinese version of the structured interview of reported symptoms—2," *BMC Psychiatry*, 13, no. 254 (2013): 1–7.
134 Liu et al., "Detection of malingering: Psychometric evaluation of the Chinese version."
135 Alfons van Impelen, Harald Merckelbach, Marko Jelicic, and Thomas Merten, "The Structured Inventory of Malingered Symptomatology (SIMS): A systematic review and meta-analysis," *Clinical Neuropsychologist* 28, no. 8 (2014): 1336–1365.
136 Alicia Nijdam-Jones, and Barry Rosenfeld, "Cross-cultural feigning assessment: A systematic review of feigning instruments used with linguistically, ethnically, and culturally diverse samples," *Psychological Assessment* 29, no. 11 (2017): 1321–1936.
137 Glenn Smith, "Brief measures for the detection of feigning and impression management," in *Clinical assessment of malingering and deception*, ed. Richard Rogers and Scott D. Bender (Guilford Press, 2018), 449–472.
138 Laura S. Guy and Holly A. Miller, "Screening for malingered psychopathology in a correctional setting: Utility of the Miller-Forensic Assessment of Symptoms Test (M-FAST)," *Criminal Justice and Behavior* 31, no. 6 (2004): 695–716.
139 Orbelin Montes and Michelle R. Guyton, "Performance of Hispanic inmates on the Spanish Miller Forensic Assessment of Symptoms Test (M-FAST)," *Law and Human Behavior* 38, no. 5 (2014): 428–438.
140 Rebecca Weiss, "Differentiating genuine versus feigned posttraumatic stress disorder in a sample of torture survivors" (PhD diss., Fordham University, 2014).
141 Myriam J. Sollman and David T. R. Berry, "Detection of inadequate effort on neuropsychological testing: A meta-analytic update and extension," *Archives of Clinical Neuropsychology* 26, no. 8 (2011): 774–789.
142 Raquel Vilar López, Miguel Pérez-García, and Antonio E. Puente, *Adaptación española del TOMM, Test de simulación de problemas de memoria, [Spanish adaptation of the TOMM, Test of Memory Malingering]* (TEA Ediciones, 2011).
143 Weiss, "Differentiating genuine versus feigned posttraumatic stress disorder."
144 Alicia Nijdam-Jones, Diego Rivera, Barry Rosenfeld, and Juan C. Arango-Lasprilla, "A cross-cultural analysis of the Test of Memory Malingering among Latin American Spanish-speaking adults," *Law and Human Behavior* 41, no. 5 (2017): 422—428.

145 Nijdam-Jones et al., "A cross-cultural analysis of the Test of Memory Malingering"; Maria J. Prieto De Estebecorena, "Evaluating the role of education and acculturation in the performance of Hispanics on a non-verbal test" (PhD diss., Fielding Graduate University, 2007); Adriana M. Strutt, Bonnie M. Scott, Veronica J. Lozano, Phoebe G. Tieu, and Shelley Peery, "Assessing sub-optimal performance with the Test of Memory Malingering in Spanish speaking patients with TBI," *Brain Injury* 26, no. 6 (2012): 853–863.

146 Lawrie Reznek, "The Rey 15-item memory test for malingering: A meta-analysis," *Brain Injury* 19, no. 7 (2005): 539–543; Sollman and Berry, "Detection of inadequate effort;" Chad D. Vickery, David T. R. Berry, Tina H. Inman, Monica J. Harris, and Stephen A. Orey, "Detection of inadequate effort on neuropsychological testing: A meta-analytic review of selected procedures," *Archives of Clinical Neuropsychology* 16, no. 1 (2001): 45–73.

147 Nijdam-Jones and Rosenfeld, "Cross-cultural feigning assessment."

148 Luz Robles, Enrique López, Xavier Salazar, Kyle B. Boone, and Debra F. Glaser, "Specificity data for the b Test, Dot Counting Test, Rey-15 Item Plus Recognition, and Rey Word Recognition Test in monolingual Spanish speakers," *Journal of Clinical and Experimental Neuropsychology* 37, no. 6 (2015): 614–621; Rebecca Weiss, and Barry Rosenfeld, B, "Cross-cultural validity in malingering assessment: The Dot Counting Test in a rural Indian sample," *International Journal of Forensic Mental Health* 9, no. 4 (2010): 300–307.

149 Nijdam-Jones and Rosenfeld, "Cross-cultural feigning assessment."

10. FORENSIC ASSESSMENT CONSIDERATIONS

1 Kirk Heilbrun, Thomas Grisso, and Alan Goldstein, *Foundations of forensic mental health assessment* (Oxford University Press, 2009).

2 Heilbrun et al., *Foundations*.

3 Heilbrun et al.

4 Heilbrun et al.

5 Gary B. Melton, John Petrila, Norman G. Poythress, Christopher Slobogin, Randy K. Otto, Douglas Mossman, and Lois O. Condie, *Psychological evaluations for the courts: A handbook for mental health professionals and lawyers* (Guilford Publications, 2018).

6 Thomas Grisso, *Evaluating competencies: Forensic assessments and instruments*, 2nd ed. (Kluwer Academic/Plenum Press, 2003); Heilbrun et al., 2009.

7 Hawthorne E. Smith, Stuart Lustig, and David Gangsei, "Incredible until proven credible: Mental health expert testimony and the systemic and cultural challenges facing asylum applicants," *Adjudicating refugee and asylum status: The role of witness, expertise, and testimony* (2015): 180–201.

8 Heilbrun et al., *Foundations*.

9 Ronald Roesch and Patricia A. Zapf, ed, *Forensic assessments in criminal and civil law: A handbook for lawyers* (Oxford University Press, 2013).

10 Heilbrun et al., *Foundations*, 99. (Heilbrun et al. provide a full list and explanation.)

11 Heilbrun et al., 100.

12 Heilbrun et al., 101.

13 *See* Heilbrun et al., 102.

14 Smith et al., "Incredible until proven."

15 Smith et al.

16 Daniel C. Murrie, Marcus T. Boccaccini, Lucy A. Guarnera, and Katrina A. Rufino, "Are forensic experts biased by the side that retained them?," *Psychological Science* 24, no. 10 (2013): 1889–1897; Daniel C. Murrie and Marcus T. Boccaccini, "Adversarial allegiance among expert witnesses," *Annual Review of Law and Social Science* 11 (2015): 37–55.

17 Heilbrun et al., *Foundations*, 103.

18 Heilbrun et al., 103.

19 Barton F. Evans III and Giselle A. Hass, *Forensic psychological assessment in immigration court: A guidebook for evidence-based and ethical practice* (Routledge, 2018).

20 Heilbrun et al., *Foundations*, 107.

21 Zapf et al., "Psychological assessment."

22 Heilbrun et al., *Foundations*, 108.

23 Heilbrun et al.

24 Heilbrun et al., 110.

25 Donald N. Bersoff, David De Matteo, D. and Elizabeth Foster, "Assessment and testing," in *APA Handbook of Ethics in Psychology, vol. 2*, ed. S. J. Knapp (Washington DC; American Psychological Association, 2012), 45–74.

26 Evans and Hass, *Forensic*.

27 Randy K. Otto, Richart DeMier, and Marcus Boccaccini, *Forensic reports and testimony: A guide to effective communication for psychologists and psychiatrists* (John Wiley & Sons, 2014).

28 Heilbrun et al., *Foundations*; Otto et al., *Forensic reports*.

29 Heilbrun et al., *Foundations*, 112.

30 Heilbrun et al.

31 Heilbrun et al., 113.

32 Heilbrun et al.

33 Heilbrun et al.

34 Heilbrun et al.

35 "Phase I of plan to provide enhanced procedural protections to unrepresented detained respondents with mental disorders," wordpress.com, Dec. 31, 2013, http://immigrationreports.files.wordpress.com.

36 Heilbrun et al., *Foundations*, 114.

37 Ibid.

38 *See* EOIR Immigration Court Practice Manual Ch. 5.2(e)(evidence) *available at* www.justice.gov; *see also* 28 U.S. Code § 1746.

39 Heilbrun et al., *Foundations*, 114.
40 American Psychological Association, "Specialty guidelines for forensic psychology," *American Psychologist* 68, no. 1 (2013): 7–19.
41 Heilbrun et al., *Foundations*, 115.
42 Ibid.
43 Federal Rule of Civil Procedure 26.2(a).
44 Otto et al., *Forensic Reports*.
45 Otto et al., 59.
46 Otto et al., *Forensic Reports*, 76.
47 Otto et al., 16.
48 American Psychological Association, "Specialty guidelines," 16.
49 Thomas Grisso, "Forensic report writing," American Academy of Forensic Psychology Workshops, Las Vegas: Nevada. 2012. As cited in Otto et al., *Forensic Reports*, 37.
50 Otto et al., *Forensic Reports*, 38.
51 Heilbrun et al., *Foundations*, 116.
52 Heilbrun et al.
53 Heilbrun et al.
54 Stanley L. Brodsky, *Coping with cross-examination and other pathways to effective testimony*, American Psychological Association, 2004.
55 Marcus T. Boccaccini., Phylissa P. Kwartner, and Paige B. Haris, "Testifying in court: Evidenced-based recommendations for expert-witness testimony," in *Learning forensic assessment: Research and practice*, ed. Jackson, Rebecca, and Ronald Roesch, Routledge (2015), 506.
56 Otto et al., *Forensic reports*, 38.
57 Smith et al., "Incredible Until Proven."
58 Virginia Barber-Rioja and Alexandra Garcia-Mansilla, "Forensic mental health assessment in immigration Court," in *The Oxford handbook of psychology and law*, ed. D. DeMatteo and K. Scherr (Oxford University Press), in press.
59 "Questions and answers: Credible fear," USCIS, July 15, 2015, www.uscis.gov.
60 Evans and Hass, *Forensic*.
61 Smith et al., "Incredible until proven."
62 8 U.S.C § 1158(b)(1)(B)(iii).
63 Karen Musalo, Susan M. Meffert, and Akra Osman Abdo, "The role of mental health professionals in political asylum processing," *Journal of the American Academy of Psychiatry and the Law* 38 (2010): 479.
64 Deborah E. Anker, "Determining asylum claims in the United States: A case study on the implementation of legal norms in an unstructured adjudicatory environment," *Immigr. & Nat'lity L. Rev.* 14 (1992): 227; Michael Kagan, "Is truth in the eye of the beholder-objective credibility assessment in refugee status determination," *Geo. Immigr. L.J.* 17 (2002): 367; Sara L. McKinnon, "Citizenship and the performance of credibility: Audiencing gender-based asylum seekers in US immigration courts," *Text and Performance Quarterly* 29, no. 3 (2009): 205–221.

65 Smith et al., "Incredible until proven."
66 Jane Herlihy, Peter Scragg, and Stuart Turner, "Discrepancies in autobiographical memories—implications for the assessment of asylum seekers: Repeated interviews study," *Bmj* 324, no. 7333 (2002): 324–327.
67 Sven-Ake Christianson, and Martin A. Safer, "Emotional events and emotions in autobiographical memories," in *Remembering our past: Studies in autobiographical memory*, ed. D. C. Rubin (Cambridge University Press, 1996), 218–241.
68 Juliet Cohen, "Errors of recall and credibility: Can omissions and discrepancies in successive statements reasonably be said to undermine credibility of testimony?," *Medico-Legal Journal* 69, no. 1 (2001): 25–34.
69 Herlihy et al, "Discrepancies."
70 Sarah Filone, and David DeMatteo, "Testimonial inconsistencies, adverse credibility determinations, and asylum adjudication in the United States," *Educational Publishing Foundation* 3, no. 2 (2017).
71 Chris R. Brewin, "Autobiographical memory for trauma: Update on four controversies," *Memory* 15, no. 3 (2007): 227–248.
72 Smith et al., "Incredible Until Proven," 252.
73 Smith et al., 258.
74 Smith et al., 259.
75 American Psychiatric Association, *Diagnostic and statistical manual of mental disorders: DSM-5* (American Psychiatric Association, 2013), 726.
76 American Psychiatric Association, *Diagnostic and statistical manual*, 727.
77 Richard Rogers and Scott D. Bender, "Evaluation of malingering and related response styles," in *Handbook of psychology*, 2nd ed., vol. 11., ed. R. Otto and I. Weiner (Hoboken, NJ: John Wiley & Sons, 2013), 517–540.
78 Steven B. Taylor, Christopher Frueh, and Gordon JG Asmundson, "Detection and management of malingering in people presenting for treatment of posttraumatic stress disorder: Methods, obstacles, and recommendations," *Journal of Anxiety Disorders* 21, no. 1 (2007): 22–41.
79 Maya Prabhu and Madelon Baranoski, "Forensic mental health professionals in the immigration process," *Psychiatric Clinics* 35, no. 4 (2012): 929–946.
80 Philip Resnick, Sarah West, and Joshua W. Payne, J, "Malingering of posttraumatic disorders," in *Clinical assessment of malingering and deception*, ed. R. Rogers (Guilford Press, 2008), 109–127.
81 Isaac R. Galatzer-Levy and Richard A. Bryant, "636,120 ways to have posttraumatic stress disorder," *Perspectives on Psychological Science* 8, no. 6 (2013): 651–662.
82 *See* Mikel Matto, Dale E. McNiel, and Renée L. Binder, "A systematic approach to the detection of false PTSD," *Journal of the American Academy of Psychiatry and the Law* 47, no. 3 (2019): 325–334.
83 Jill M. Flitter, Klotz, Jon D. Elhai, and Steven N. Gold, "MMPI-2 F scale elevations in adult victims of child sexual abuse," *Journal of Traumatic Stress: Official Publication of The International Society for Traumatic Stress Studies* 16, no. 3 (2003):

269–274; Jon D. Elhai, Kenneth J. Ruggiero, B. Christopher Frueh, Jean C. Beckham, Paul B. Gold, and Michelle E. Feldman, "The Infrequency-Posttraumatic Stress Disorder Scale (Fptsd) for the MMPI-2: Development and initial validation with veterans presenting with combat-related PTSD," *Journal of Personality Assessment* 79, no. 3 (2002): 531–549.

84 World Health Organization, *International statistical classification of diseases and related health problems*, 11th ed., tabular list, vol. 1 (World Health Organization, 2018).

85 Musalo et al., "The role of mental health professionals."

86 Matto et al., "A systematic approach."

87 Matto et al.

88 Matto et al.

89 Matto et al.

90 Rogers and Bender, "Evaluation of malingering," in *Clinical assessment of malingering and deception*, ed. Richard Rogers (Guilford Press, 2003), 109–127.

91 Rogers and Bender, "Evaluation of malingering."

92 John Briere, *The Trauma Symptom Inventory-2 professional manual* (Psychological Assessment Resources, 1995), 2011.

93 Rebecca A. Weiss and Barry Rosenfeld, "Identifying feigning in trauma-exposed African immigrants," *Psychological Assessment* 29, no. 7 (2017): 881.

94 Sarah Filone and David DeMatteo, "Assessing 'credible fear': A psychometric examination of the Trauma Symptom Inventory-2 in the context of immigration court evaluations," *Psychological Assessment* 29, no. 6 (2017): 701.

95 Melton et al., *Psychological*, vii.

96 Melton et al.

11. COMPETENCY TO PARTICIPATE IN IMMIGRATION PROCEEDINGS

1 Patricia A. Zapf and Ronald Roesch, *Evaluation of Competence to Stand Trial* (Oxford University Press, 2009).

2 A. J. Robertson, "The Laws of the Kings of England from Edmund to Henry I, Cambridge" (1925).

3 Gary B. Melton, John Petrila, Norman G. Poythress, Christopher Slobogin, Randy K. Otto, Douglas Mossman, and Lois O. Condie, *Psychological Evaluations for the Courts: A Handbook for Mental Health Professionals and Lawyers* (Guilford Publications, 2018).

4 Richard J. Bonnie, "The Competence of Criminal Defendants: Beyond Dusky and Drope," *U. Miami L. Rev.* 47 (1992): 539.

5 Fatma E. Marouf, "Incompetent but Deportable: The Case for a Right to Mental Competence in Removal Proceedings," *Hastings L.J.* 65 (2013): 929.

6 Allison H. Schwartz, "Fundamentally Unfair: A Call for the Creation of Competency Standards," *Immigr. & Nat'lity L. Rev.* 29 (2008): 917.

7 Padilla v. Kentucky, 559 U.S. 365, 374 (2010).

8   *See, e.g.,* Daniel Kanstroom, "The Right to Deportation Counsel in *Padilla v. Kentucky*: The Challenging Construction of the Fifth-and-a-Half Amendment," *UCLA Law Review,* no. 58 (2011): 1461–1514.

9   Schwartz, "Fundamentally Unfair," 917.

10 Sarah Filone, and Christopher M. King, "The Emerging Standard of Competence in Immigration Removal Proceedings: A Review for Forensic Mental Health Professionals," *Psychology, Public Policy, and Law* 21, no. 1 (2015): 60.

11 David L. Shapiro and Lenore E. A. Walker, *Forensic Practice for the Mental Health Clinician* (The Practice Institute/TPI Press, 2019).

12 Dusky v. United States, 362 U.S. 402, 402 (1960).

13 Drope v. Missouri, 420 U.S. 162, 171 (1975).

14 Patricia A. Zapf and Ronald Roesch, "Evaluation of Competence to Stand Trial in Adults," in *Forensic Assessments in Criminal and Civil Law: A Handbook for Lawyers,* ed. Ronald Roesch and Patricia Zapf (Oxford University Press, 2013), 17.

15 Zapf and Roesch, "Evaluation," 6.

16 Patricia A. Zapf, Karen L. Hubbard, Virginia G. Cooper, Melissa C. Wheeles, and Kathleen A. Ronan, "Have the Courts Abdicated Their Responsibility for Determination of Competency to Stand Trial to Clinicians?," *Journal of Forensic Psychology Practice* 4, no. 1 (2004): 27–44.

17 Zapf and Roesch, "Evaluation," 19.

18 Matter of M-A-M-, 25 I&N Dec. 474 (BIA 2011).

19 Filone and King, "Emerging," 63.

20 *M-A-M-,* at 475.

21 *M-A-M-,* 476; *see also* Robert A. Leark, 2015, "International Symposium on Competency," in *International Association of Forensic Mental Health Conference,* Manchester, England.

22 *M-A-M-,* at 479 (emphasis added).

23 *M-A-M-,* at 481.

24 Even if the respondent is not found incompetent, safeguards may still be appropriate. *See* Matter of J-R-R-A-, 26 I&N Dec. 609 (BIA 2015) (applying safeguards for a mentally-ill but not incompetent respondent).

25 *M-A-M-,* at 483.

26 Matter of E-S-I-, 26 I&N Dec. 136, 144 (BIA 2013).

27 Matter of J-R-R-A-, 26 I&N Dec. 609, 612 (BIA 2015).

28 Note that administrative closure would not necessarily result in the release of a detained respondent as ICE has fought to hold people in this situation in custody as long as possible, including beyond the six months that are considered presumptively unreasonable by courts.

29 Matter of Castro-Tum, 27 I&N Dec. 271 (A.G. 2018); *see also* EOIR Final Rule: "Appellate Procedures and Decisional Finality in Immigration Proceedings; Administrative Closure," Federal Register, Vol. 85, No. 242, Dec. 16, 2020, www.justice.gov. There are currently various lawsuits alleging that, because EOIR failed to

follow established rulemaking procedures, this regulation is invalid. *See* CLINIC v. EOIR, No. 21-cv-094 (D.D.C.); *see also* Centro Legal de la Raza v. EOIR, No. 21-cv-463 (N.D. Cal.).

30 *See* Sarah Sherman-Stokes, "Sufficiently Safeguarded?: Competency Evaluations of Mentally Ill Respondents in Removal Proceedings," 67 *Hastings L.J.* 1023, 1051–52 n. 163–68 (May 2016), www.hastingslawjournal.org. The author relates a number of interviews with IJs and immigration practitioners. One IJ is quoted as saying "I feel like I can sort this out. . . . [T]hey don't need to be devoid of paranoia, they just need to know what's going on in [the courtroom]." Another explains "if they tell you I could be deported—then they know [the nature of the proceeding]." Meanwhile, practitioners related experiences in which IJs didn't understand the difference between a "rational" and "factual" understanding of the proceedings; another believed a client to be competent when "he could answer [questions about the] dates he came here and siblings' names" and only realized upon cross examination by counsel that the respondent exhibited "disoriented thinking and delusions." (Of course, not all respondents will have counsel to advocate for them in this manner.) Practitioners also expressed the opinion that, "if someone really struggles, [IJs will] keep asking questions, [until it] becomes more and more leading, until they elicit the 'right' answers," and that judges tend to find respondents competent, even if they struggle, as long as they "basically feel like they're oriented to place and time and that they've demonstrated a basic understanding that [the Immigration] Judge could either deport them or grant them relief or release."

31 *M-A-M-*, at 478–480; *see also* Dalia N. Balsamo and Reena Kapoor, "Competency in Immigration Proceedings," *Journal of the American Academy of Psychiatry and the Law Online* 44, no. 1 (2016): 132–134.

32 *M-A-M-* does not explain who will pay for these evaluations or how they might be arranged. In the authors' experience, when a respondent is represented it has been considered the responsibility of counsel, even pro bono counsel, to arrange and pay for the examination.

33 Amelia Wilson, Natalie H. Prokop, and Stephanie Robins, "Addressing All Heads of the Hydra: Reframing Safeguards for Mentally Impaired Detainees in Immigration Removal Proceedings," *NYU Rev. L. & Soc. Change* 39 (2015): 313a.

34 *M-A-M-*, at 481–482.

35 *M-A-M-*, at 484.

36 Matter of J-S-S-, 26 I. & N. Dec. 679, 679 (BIA 2015).

37 Franco-Gonzalez v. Holder, 10-cv-2211 (C.D. Cal.); *see also* "*Franco-Gonzalez v. Holder*," American Civil Liberties Union, www.aclu.org.

38 Ibid.

39 Partial Judgment and Permanent Injunction, Franco-Gonzalez v. Holder, 10-cv-2211 (C.D. Cal. Apr. 23, 2013), *also available at* www.aclu.org.

40 Department of Justice, Executive Office for Immigration Review, "Department of Justice and the Department of Homeland Security Announce Safeguards for Unrepresented Immigration Detainees with Serious Mental Disorders or Condi-

tions," Apr. 22, 2013, www.justice.gov; *see also* "EOIR Publishes 'Phase I Guidance' Regarding Protections for Detained, Unrepresented Aliens Who May Be Mentally Incompetent," American Immigration Lawyers' Association, AILA Doc. No. 13123160, Dec. 31, 2013, www.aila.org (hereinafter "Phase I Guidelines").

41 Phase I Guidelines.

42 *See* "Recognition and Accreditation Program," EOIR, www.justice.gov (describing the requirements to become a BIA-accredited representative).

43 Phase I Guidelines.

44 Department of Justice, "National Qualified Representative Program (NQRP)" www.justice.gov; National Qualified Representative Program, Vera Institute of Justice, www.vera.org.

45 Interview with NQRP staff, Mar. 9, 2021; *see also* Vera Institute, "A Federal Defender Service for Immigrants: Why We Need a Universal, Zealous, and Person-Centered Model," Feb. 2021, www.vera.org.

46 Interview with NQRP staff, Mar. 9, 2021.

47 Wilson et al., "Addressing," 317.

48 Interview with NQRP staff, Mar. 9, 2021; *see also* "EOIR Immigration Court Listing," www.justice.gov.

49 Jorge Loweree and Gregory Chen, "The Biden Administration and Congress Must Guarantee Legal Representation for People Facing Removal," Jan. 15, 2021, www.americanimmigrationcouncil.org.

50 Interview with NQRP staff, Mar. 9, 2021; *see also* Thompson, "One Bit of Good News" ("It is up to an immigration judge—and not a licensed psychologist—to determine whether someone is competent. A judge can choose to order an evaluation, but many judges rarely do. The monitor [following up on compliance with the court order in the *Franco* litigation] also found that the screening forms used in detention centers failed to flag every case. And it sometimes took months to identify a detainee as mentally ill. 'We're concerned people are being missed at the screening stage in detention centers. The forms at the facilities are extremely lacking,' said [] a senior staff attorney at pro bono law firm Public Counsel and co-counsel on the Franco case. 'And immigration judges who are not psychologists are making competency determinations without a medical expert.'").

51 Interview with NQPR Staff, Mar. 9, 2021; *see also* Department of Justice, "National Qualified Representative Program (NQRP)," www.justice.gov; Vera Institute of Justice, National Qualified Representative Program, www.vera.org.

52 *See* chapter 2.

53 *See* Loweree and Chen, "The Biden Administration and Congress Must Guarantee"; *see also* "A Federal Defender Service for Immigrants."

54 *See* Sherman-Stokes, "Sufficiently Safeguarded," discussing weaknesses in the nationwide policy.

55 Order Further Implementing This Court's Permanent Injunction, Franco-Gonzalez v. Holder, No. 10–cv-0221, 2014 WL 5475097, at *7–8 (C.D. Cal. Oct. 29, 2014).

56 Order Further Implementing This Court's Permanent Injunction, Franco-Gonzalez v. Holder, 1–6. This includes the requirement that an "appropriately licensed psychiatrist, physician, physician assistant, psychologist, clinical social worker, licensed nurse practitioner, or registered nurse" give a screening that utilizes a written screening questionnaire designed to identify mental disorders and conditions and also asks the screener to "interpret behavior" and "ask the individual questions to gauge his or her understanding of his or her current situation."

57 Order Further Implementing This Court's Permanent Injunction, *Franco-Gonzalez v. Holder*, 4.

58 Phase I Guidelines; *see also* John Morton, Director, "Civil Immigration Detention: Guidance for New Identification and Information-Sharing Procedures Related to Unrepresented Detainees with Serious Mental Disorders or Conditions," ICE Policy No. 11063.1, Apr. 22, 2013, www.ice.gov; *see also* Thomas Horman, Executive Associate Director, "Identification of Detainees with Serious Mental Disorders or Conditions," ICE Policy No. 11067.1, May 7, 2014 (directing facilities staffed by the ICE Health Service Corps to develop procedures "to ensure that . . . all immigration detainees will be initially screened when they enter the facility and will receive a more thorough medical and mental health assessment within 14 days of their admission" and, for all other facilities, for ERO and IHSC personnel to work with the facility's medical staff to "develop procedures to identify detainees with serious mental disorders or conditions that may impact their ability to participate in their removal proceedings[.]"). These ICE policy guidelines were not incorporated into the Performance Based National Detention Standards until 2017. *See* ICE, FY 2017 Report to Congress, "Progress in Implementing 2011 PBNDS Standards and DHS PREA Requirements at Detention Facilities," Mar. 19, 2018, www.dhs.gov, 10. As explained more thoroughly in chapter 2, the version of the detention standards that applies to a given facility depends on the contract ICE entered into with that facility, the detention standards are not legally enforceable, and ICE has been lax about ensuring compliance.

59 Order Appointing Monitor, Franco-Gonzalez v. Holder, No. 10–cv-0221 (C.D. Cal. Mar. 2, 2015).

60 "Phase I of Plan to Provide Enhanced Procedural Protections to Unrepresented Detained Respondents with Mental Disorders," wordpress.com, Dec. 31, 2013, http://immigrationreports.files.wordpress.com.

61 "Phase I of Plan," 2.

62 "Phase I of Plan."

63 "Phase I of Plan."

64 "Phase I of Plan."

65 "Phase I of Plan."

66 "Phase I of Plan," 12.

67 "Phase I of Plan."

68 Zapf and Roesch, *Evaluation*, 37.

69 Zapf and Roesch, *Evaluation*, 38.
70 Filone and King, "Emerging," 65.
71 Filone and King, "Emerging," 66.
72 Zapf, and Roesch, *Evaluation*, 40.
73 "Phase I of Plan," 12.
74 Filone and King, "Emerging," 66.
75 Gianni Pirelli, Patricia A. Zapf, and William H. Gottdiener, "Competency to Stand Trial Research: Guidelines and Future Directions," *Journal of Forensic Psychiatry & Psychology* 22, no. 3 (2011): 340–370.
76 Jorge G. Varela, Marcus T. Boccaccini, Ernie Gonzalez Jr, Laadan Gharagozloo, and Shara M. Johnson, "Do Defense Attorney Referrals for Competence to Stand Trial Evaluations Depend on Whether the Client Speaks English or Spanish?," *Law and Human Behavior* 35, no. 6 (2011): 501.
77 "Phase I of Plan," 2.
78 Filone and King, "Emerging," 67.
79 Godinez v. Moran, 113 S. Ct. 2680 (1993).
80 Indiana v. Edwards, 554 U.S. 164 (2008).
81 Wilson, "Addressing," 351.
82 Maraouf, "Incompetent," 962.
83 Norman G. Poythress, Robert A. Nicholson, Randy K. Otto, John F. Edens, Richard J. Bonnie, John Monahan, Steven K. Hoge, *MACCAT-CA: The MacArthur Competence Assessment Tool-Criminal Adjudication; Professional Manual* (Professional Resource Press, 1999).
84 Ronald Roesch, Patricia A. Zapf, and Derek Eaves, *FIT-R: Fitness Interview Test-Revised, A structured interview for assessing competency to stand trial* (Professional Resource Press/Professional Resource Exchange, 2006).
85 Richard Rogers, Chad E. Tillbrook, and Kenneth W. Sewell, *Evaluation of Competency to Stand Trial—Revised (ECST-R)* (Psychological Assessment Resources, 2004).
86 Shapiro and Walker, *Forensic practice*, 229.
87 David L. Shapiro, "Development of a Competency Assessment Instrument for Deportation proceedings," paper presented in American Psychology-Law Society Annual Meeting, New Orleans, Louisiana (2014).
88 Filone and King, "Emerging," 69.
89 Maraouf, "Incompetent," 981.
90 Jackson v. Indiana, 406 U.S. 715 (1972), 738.
91 Zapf and Roesch, "Evaluation," 19.
92 Filone and King, "Emerging," 69.
93 "Phase I of Plan," 10.
94 "Phase I of Plan," 10.
95 "Phase I of Plan," 10.
96 "Phase I of Plan," 13. The items have been reformatted as a list for clarity.
97 Maraouf, "Incompetent," 998.

12. VIOLENCE RISK ASSESSMENT

1 Kirk Heilbrun, *Evaluation for risk of violence in adults* (Oxford University Press, 2009).

2 *See* Matter of Fatahi, 26 I&N Dec. 791, 793–94 (BIA 2016).

3 INA § 212(a)(1)(A)(iii); 8 USC § 1182(a)(1)(A)(iii).

4 Laura S. Guy, Kevin S. Douglas, and Stephen D. Hart, "Risk assessment and communication," in *APA handbook of forensic psychology, vol. 1: Individual and situational influences in criminal and civil contexts* (American Psychological Association, 2015), 35–86.

5 Guy et al., "Risk assessment and communication."

6 Lessard v. Smith, 349 F. Supp. 1078 (1972)

7 O'Connor v. Donaldson, 422 U.S. 563 (1975); Ibid.

8 Baxtrom v. Herold, 383 U.S. 107 (1966)

9 Guy et al., "Risk assessment."

10 Heilbrun, *Evaluation*.

11 Barefoot v. Estelle. 463 U.S. 880 (1983).

12 Guy et al., "Risk assessment."

13 Kansas v. Hendricks, 521 U. S. 346 (1997)

14 Kirk Heilbrun, Stephanie Brooks Holliday, and Christopher King, "Evaluation of violence risk in adults," in *Best practices in forensic mental health assessment. Forensic assessments in criminal and civil law: A handbook for lawyers* (Oxford University Press, 2013), 148–160.

15 John Monahan and Henry J. Steadman, eds, "Violence and mental disorder: Developments in risk assessment" (University of Chicago Press, 1996).

16 Heilbrun, *Evaluation*.

17 Heilbrun, *Evaluation*.

18 Don A. Andrews, James Bonta, and Robert D. Hoge, "Classification for effective rehabilitation: Rediscovering psychology," *Criminal Justice and Behavior* 17, no. 1 (1990): 19–52; Gary B. Melton, John Petrila, Norman G. Poythress, Christopher Slobogin, Randy K. Otto, Douglas Mossman, and Lois O. Condie, *Psychological evaluations for the courts: A handbook for mental health professionals and lawyers* (Guilford Press, 2018).

19 Guy et al., "Risk assessment."

20 Kevin. S. Douglas, Stephen D. Hart, and Christopher D. Webster, "HCR-20 V3 Assessing risk for violence" (Mental Health, Law, and Policy Institute, Simon Fraser University, 2013), 6.

21 Kirk Heilbrun, "Prediction versus management models relevant to risk assessment: The importance of legal decision-making context," *Law and Human Behavior* 21, no. 4 (1997): 347.

22 Kevin S. Douglas and Jennifer L. Skeem, "Violence risk assessment: Getting specific about being dynamic," *Psychology, Public Policy, and Law* 11, no. 3 (2005), 347–383.

23 Merrill Rotter, Virginia Barber-Rioja, and Faith Schombs, "Recovery and recidivism reduction for offenders with mental illness," in *Care of the mentally disordered offender in the community*, ed. Alec Buchanan, and Lisa Wootton (Oxford University Press, 2017).

24 Heilbrun, *Evaluation*; Stephen D. Hart, Christopher D. Webster, and Kevin S. Douglas, "Risk management using the HCR-20: A general overview focusing on historical factors," *HCR-20 violence risk management companion Guide* (2001): 27.

25 Guy et al., "Risk assessment."

26 Kevin S. Douglas and Jennifer L. Skeem, "Violence risk assessment: Getting specific about being dynamic," *Psychology, Public Policy, and Law* 11, no. 3 (2005): 347.

27 Douglas and Skeem, "Violence risk assessment."

28 Heilbrun, *Evaluation*.

29 Edward P. Mulvey and Charles W. Lidz, "Conditional prediction: A model for research on dangerousness to others in a new era," *International Journal of Law and Psychiatry* 18, no. 2 (1995): 129–143.

30 John Monahan, Henry J. Steadman, Eric Silver, Paul S. Appelbaum, Pamela Clark Robbins, Edward P. Mulvey, Loren H. Roth, Thomas Grisso, and Steven Banks, *Rethinking risk assessment: The MacArthur study of mental disorder and violence* (Oxford University Press, 2001).

31 Henry J. Steadman, John Monahan, Paul. S. Appelbaum, Thomas. Grisso, Edward P. Mulvey, Loren H. Roth, Pamela C. Robbins, and Deidre Klassen, "Designing a new generation of risk assessment research," in *Violence and mental disorder: Developments in risk assessment* (University of Chicago Press, 1994), 297–318.

32 Steadman et al., "Designing a new generation."

33 Heilbrun, *Evaluation*; Douglas et al., "HCR-20 V3."

34 William M. Grove and Paul E. Meehl, "Comparative efficiency of informal (subjective, impressionistic) and formal (mechanical, algorithmic) prediction procedures: The clinical–statistical controversy," *Psychology, Public Policy, and Law* 2, no. 2 (1996): 293.

35 Heilbrun, *Evaluation*.

36 Guy et al., "Risk assessment."

37 Melodie Foellmi, Barry Rosenfeld, Merrill Rotter, Michael Greenspan, and Ai Khadivi, "Decisions, decisions . . . Violence risk triage practices in community psychiatric settings," paper presented at the American Psychology-Law Society Annual Conference, Portland, OR, 2013.

38 Guy et al., "Risk assessment."

39 Heilbrun, *Evaluation*.

40 Melton et al., *Psychological Evaluations*.

41 Guy et al., "Risk assessment."

42 Douglas et al., "HCR-20 V3."

43 Pamela R. Blair, David K. Marcus, and Marcus T. Boccaccini, "Is there an allegiance effect for assessment instruments? Actuarial risk assessment as an exemplar," *Clinical Psychology: Science and Practice* 15, no. 4 (2008): 346–360.

44 Stephen D. Hart, Christine Michie, and David J. Cooke, "Precision of actuarial risk assessment instruments: Evaluating the 'margins of error'of group v. individual predictions of violence," *British Journal of Psychiatry* 190, no. S49 (2007): s60–s65.

45 Jean-Pierre Guay and Geneviève Parent. "Broken legs, clinical overrides, and recidivism risk: An analysis of decisions to adjust risk levels with the LS/CM," *Criminal Justice and Behavior* 45, no. 1 (2018): 82–100.

46 Douglas et al., "HCR-20 V3."

47 Beth Schwartzapfel, "Can racist algorithms be fixed?" themarshallproject.org, July 1, 2019, www.scribbr.com.

48 Heilbrun, *Evaluation.*

49 Douglas et al., "HCR-20 V3."

50 Guy et al., "Risk assessment"; Guay and Parent, "Broken legs;" Min Yang, Stephen C. P. Wong, and Jeremy Coid, "The efficacy of violence prediction: A meta-analytic comparison of nine risk assessment tools," *Psychological Bulletin* 136, no. 5 (2010), 740; Jay P. Singh, Martin Grann, and Seena Fazel, "A comparative study of violence risk assessment tools: A systematic review and metaregression analysis of 68 studies involving 25,980 participants," *Clinical Psychology Review* 31, no. 3 (2011): 499–513; Karl R. Hanson, Andrew J. R. Harris, Terri-Lynne Scott, and Leslie Helmus, *Assessing the risk of sexual offenders on community supervision: The dynamic supervision project,* vol. 5, no. 6 (Public Safety Canada, 2007).

51 Grant T. Harris, Marnie E. Rice, and Vernon L. Quinsey, "Violent recidivism of mentally disordered offenders: The development of a statistical prediction instrument," *Criminal Justice and Behavior* 20, no. 4 (1993): 315–335.

52 Grant T. Harris, Christopher T. Lowenkamp, and N. Zoe Hilton, "Evidence for risk estimate precision: Implications for individual risk communication," *Behavioral Sciences & the Law* 33, no. 1 (2015): 111–127; Marnie E. Rice, Grant T. Harris, and Carol Lang, "Validation of and revision to the VRAG and SORAG: The Violence Risk Appraisal Guide—Revised (VRAG-R)," *Psychological Assessment* 25, no. 3 (2013): 951.

53 Douglas et al., "HCR-20 V3."

54 Douglas et al.

55 Jay P. Singh, "The international risk survey (IRiS) project: Perspectives on the practical application of violence risk assessment tools," in annual conference of the American Psychology-Law Society, Portland, OR. 2013.

56 Douglas et al., "HCR-20 V3."

57 Douglas et al., 62.

58 Michiel de Vries Robbé, Vivienne de Vogel, and Eva de Spa, "Protective factors for violence risk in forensic psychiatric patients: A retrospective validation study of the SAPROF," *International Journal of Forensic Mental Health* 10, no. 3 (2011): 178–186.

59 Donald A. Andrews, James Bonta, and S. J. Wormith, *Level of service/case management inventory: LS/CMI* (Multi-Health Systems, Canada, 2004).

60 Andrews Bonta, and Wormith, *Level of service.*

61 Andrews Bonta, and Wormith, *Level of service.*

62 Robert D. Hare, *The psychopathy checklist–revised*, Toronto, ON 412 (2003).

63 Kevin S. Douglas, Natalia L. Nikolova, Shannon E. Kelley, and John F. Edens, "Psychopathy," in *APA handbook of forensic psychology*, vol.1, ed. Brian L. Cutler and Patricia A. Zapf (APA Handbooks in Psychology, 2015), 257–323; Jennifer L. Skeem, Devon L. L. Polaschek, Christopher J. Patrick, and Scott O. Lilienfeld, "Psychopathic personality: Bridging the gap between scientific evidence and public policy," *Psychological Science in the Public Interest* 12, no. 3 (2011): 95–162.

64 Paul S. Appelbaum, "Public safety, mental disorders, and guns," *JAMA Psychiatry* 70, no. 6 (2013): 565–566.

65 Appelbaum, "Public safety"; Jeffrey W. Swanson, Sue Estroff, Marvin Swartz, Randy Borum, William Lachicotte, Catherine Zimmer, and Ryan Wagner, "Violence and severe mental disorder in clinical and community populations: The effects of psychotic symptoms, comorbidity, and lack of treatment," *Psychiatry* 60, no. 1 (1997): 1–22; Marvin S. Swartz, Jeffrey W. Swanson, Virginia A. Hiday, Randy Borum, H. Ryan Wagner, and Barbara J. Burns, "Violence and severe mental illness: The effects of substance abuse and nonadherence to medication," *American Journal of Psychiatry* 155, no. 2 (1998): 226–231; Jeffrey W. Swanson, Marvin S. Swartz, Susan M. Essock, Fred C. Osher, H. Ryan Wagner, Lisa A. Goodman, Stanley D. Rosenberg, and Keith G. Meador, "The social–environmental context of violent behavior in persons treated for severe mental illness," *American Journal of Public Health* 92, no. 9 (2002): 1523–1531.

66 Eve K. Mościcki, "Epidemiology of completed and attempted suicide: Toward a framework for prevention," *Clinical Neuroscience Research* 1, no. 5 (2001): 310–323.

67 Roberto Maniglio, "Severe mental illness and criminal victimization: A systematic review," *Acta Psychiatrica Scandinavica* 119, no. 3 (2009): 180–191.

68 Guy et al., "Risk assessment."

69 Kevin S. Douglas, Laura S. Guy, and Stephen D. Hart, "Psychosis as a risk factor for violence to others: A meta-analysis," *Psychological Bulletin* 135, no. 5 (2009): 679.

70 John Monahan et al., "An actuarial model of violence risk assessment for persons with mental disorders," *Psychiatric Services* 56, no. 7 (2005): 810–815.

71 Stephane M. Shepherd and Roberto Lewis-Fernandez, "Forensic risk assessment and cultural diversity: Contemporary challenges and future directions," *Psychology, Public Policy, and Law* 22, no. 4 (2016): 427.

72 Joselyne L. Chenane, Pauline K. Brennan, Benjamin Steiner, and Jared M. Ellison, "Racial and ethnic differences in the predictive validity of the Level of Service Inventory–Revised among prison inmates," *Criminal Justice and Behavior* 42, no. 3 (2015): 286–303; Stephane M. Shepherd, Yolonda Adams, Elizabeth McEntyre, and Roz Walker, "Violence risk assessment in Australian Aboriginal offender populations: A review of the literature," *Psychology, Public Policy, and Law* 20, no. 3 (2014): 281; Bronwen Perley-Robertson, L. Maaike Helmus, and Adelle Forth,

"Predictive accuracy of static risk factors for Canadian Indigenous offenders compared to non-Indigenous offenders: Implications for risk assessment scales," *Psychology, Crime & Law* 25, no. 3 (2019): 248–278.

73 Ewert v. Canada, FC 1093 (2015).

74 Shepherd and Lewis-Fernandez, "Forensic risk assessment."

75 Shepherd and Lewis-Fernandez.

76 Shepherd and Lewis-Fernandez.

77 Samantha Venner, Diane Sivasubramaniam, Stefan Luebbers, and Stephane M. Shepherd, "Cross-cultural reliability and rater bias in forensic risk assessment: A review of the literature," *Psychology, Crime & Law* (2020): 1–17.

78 Heilbrun, *Evaluation.*

79 Guy et al., "Risk assessment."

80 Guy et al.

SUMMARY AND FUTURE DIRECTIONS

1 Muzaffar Chrishti and Jessica Bolter, "Border Challenges Dominate, but Biden's First 100 Days Mark Notable Under-the-Radar Immigration Accomplishments," MPI Migration Policy Institute, Apr. 26, 2021, www.migrationpolicy.org.

2 "Southwest Border Deaths by Fiscal Year (Oct. 1st through Sept. 30th)," U.S. Border Patrol, www.cbp.gov.

3 "Answering the Call: Pro Bono Lawyers Respond to the Immigration Crisis," American Bar Association, www.americanbar.org.

4 Sarah Filone and Christopher M. King, "The Emerging Standard of Competence in Immigration Removal Proceedings: A Review for Forensic Mental Health Professionals," *Psychology, Public Policy, and Law* 21, no. 1 (2015): 60.

5 Virginia Barber-Rioja and Alexandra Garcia-Mansilla, "Forensic Mental Health Assessment in Immigration Court," in *The Oxford Handbook of Psychology and Law*, ed. David. DeMatteo and Kyle C. Scherr (Oxford University Press, forthcoming).

6 Barber-Rioja and Garcia-Mansilla, "Forensic Mental Health Assessment."

7 Daniel C. Murrie and Marcus T. Boccaccini, "Adversarial Allegiance Among Expert Witnesses," *Annual Review of Law and Social Science* 11 (2015): 37–55.

8 "Accessing Justice: The Availability and Adequacy of Counsel in Immigration Proceedings (New York Immigrant Representation Study)," Immigrant Justice Corps, Dec. 2011, https://justicecorps.org.

INDEX

Page numbers in *italics* indicate Tables

ABOUT THE AUTHORS

VIRGINIA BARBER-RIOJA obtained her PhD in clinical forensic psychology from John Jay College of Criminal Justice of the City University of New York. Since 2016, she has worked as the Clinical Director and Co-chief of Mental Health with NYC Health + Hospitals/Correctional Health Services, which oversees mental health treatment in the New York City jail system and court-ordered forensic evaluations (competency to stand trial and presentencing evaluations) in the city's court system. She is also an adjunct professor in the Psychology Department of New York University, where she teaches in the graduate program. She has over 15 years of experience working in correctional and forensic contexts. Dr. Barber-Rioja worked as an attending psychologist in the forensic inpatient unit of Bellevue Hospital Center, as the clinical director of several mental health courts, diversion, and reentry programs in New York City, and as a consultant for the juvenile correctional system in Puerto Rico. With the goal of bringing knowledge of forensic psychology to applied audiences and policy makers, Dr. Barber-Rioja has provided a great deal of teaching to probation and parole officers, police officers, defense attorneys, prosecutors, and judges. She has published and presented workshops on the topics of criminal justice diversion, mental health courts, forensic mental health assessment, implementation of risk assessment instruments in special jurisdiction courts, and psychological evaluations in the context of immigration proceedings. Dr. Barber-Rioja maintains an independent forensic practice in which she conducts forensic evaluations in immigration court (with a special focus on Spanish-speaking immigrants), as well as criminal, federal, and civil courts. She is a board member of the Iberoamerican Association of Therapeutic Jurisprudence and a former member of the American Psychological Association's Committee on Legal Issues (COLI).

ADEYINKA M. AKINSULURE-SMITH, PhD, ABPP, is a licensed psychologist who is originally from Sierra Leone. She is Board Certified in Group Psychology by the American Board of Professional Psychology (ABPP). Dr. Akinsulure-Smith is a tenured Professor in the Department of Psychology at the City College of New York, the City University of New York (CUNY), and at the Graduate Center, CUNY. She has cared for forced migrants, as well as survivors of torture, armed conflict, and human rights abuses from around the world at the Bellevue Program for Survivors of Torture since 1999. Dr. Akinsulure-Smith served on the American Psychological Association's Task Force on the Psychological Effect of War on Children and Families who are refugees from armed conflicts residing in the United States (PEWCF). Dr. Akinsulure-Smith has participated in human rights investigations in Sierra Leone with Physicians for Human Rights and the United Nations Mission in Sierra Leone, Human Rights Division, and served as a Joint Expert on Gender Crimes and Post Traumatic Stress Disorder for the International Criminal Court. She provides forensic evaluations and human rights consultations and frequently works with attorneys handling cases involving torture, trauma, and maltreatment. Through the years, her work has taught her about the impact of Secondary Traumatic Stress, Vicarious Trauma, and Compassion Fatigue, highlighting the importance of self-care. Drawing on her experiences and research in this area, Dr. Akinsulure-Smith has conducted workshops addressing the importance of self-care for mental health service providers nationally and internationally. In addition to her teaching and clinical work, Dr. Akinsulure-Smith is the recipient of several grants, including a 2014–2015 Fulbright Africa Regional Research Program award and a CUNY Distinguished Fellowship. Dr. Akinsulure-Smith's work has included developing and examining mental health interventions in Sierra Leone and Nigeria. She has written extensively about service provision to and mental health challenges facing forced migrants, including recent scholarly publications in *Journal of Traumatic Stress, Psychological Trauma: Theory, Research, Practice, and Policy, Journal of Immigrant and Refugee Studies, Professional Psychology: Research and Practice, Journal of Child and Family Studies, Human Development, PLOS, Journal of Immigrant & Minority Health, American Journal of Community Psychology, and Journal of Aggression,* and *Maltreatment & Trauma.*

SARAH VENDZULES graduated from New York University School of Law in 2008. She clerked for the Honorable James Orenstein, United States Magistrate Judge, in the Eastern District of New York. After her clerkship, Vendzules founded the Immigration Practice at Brooklyn Defender Services (BDS). She helped supervise the *Padilla* team in its core mission of advising clients and defenders on the immigration consequences of their criminal and family court cases and working to mitigate those consequences. As part of this work, Vendzules also represented clients in removal proceedings before the immigration court, in habeas corpus petitions in federal and state courts, in appeals before the Board of Immigration Appeals, and in affirmative applications before United States Citizenship and Immigration Services. She also trained lawyers, court personnel, and community members on immigration issues, ran community clinics to help people apply for TPS and DACA, and engaged in other forms of advocacy on behalf of immigrant communities. After leaving BDS, Vendzules taught at New York University School of Law in the Lawyering Department for two years. While there, she also supervised students in the Immigrant Rights Clinic and participated in efforts to respond to enhanced immigration enforcement and the curtailing of lawful avenues for immigration. Vendzules also taught a class on the "crim-imm" intersection as an Adjunct Professor at Brooklyn Law School. She is currently a Staff Attorney at Appellate Advocates, where she represents clients on direct appeals and applications for post-conviction relief and consults on immigration-related matters.

About the Contributor

MARIA APARCERO is a doctoral candidate in Clinical Psychology with a Forensic Psychology concentration at Fordham University, New York. She received her Master's degree in Criminal Justice and Criminology from East Tennessee State University and her Bachelor's degree in Psychology from Universidad of Huelva, Spain. Her areas of interest include forensic psychological assessment, violence risk assessment, feigning assessment, and cross-cultural adaptation and validation of FAIs. Aparcero is the current past-president of the International Association of Forensic Mental Health Services (IAFMHS) student board. Aparcero made significant contributions to chapter 9 ("Cultural Considerations").